A Global History of Relocation in Counterinsurgency Warfare

A Global History of Relocation in Counterinsurgency Warfare

Edited by
Edward J. Erickson

BLOOMSBURY ACADEMIC
LONDON • NEW YORK • OXFORD • NEW DELHI • SYDNEY

BLOOMSBURY ACADEMIC
Bloomsbury Publishing Plc
50 Bedford Square, London, WC1B 3DP, UK
1385 Broadway, New York, NY 10018, USA

BLOOMSBURY, BLOOMSBURY ACADEMIC and the Diana logo are trademarks
of Bloomsbury Publishing Plc

First published in Great Britain 2020

Copyright © Edward J. Erickson, 2020

Edward J. Erickson has asserted his right under the Copyright, Designs and Patents Act,
1988, to be identified as Editor of this work.

Cover Image: Map of the island of Cuba : compiled from the most reliable Spanish
authorities. 1855 (© Everett Collection Historical / Alamy Stock Photo) Portrait: General
Valeriano Weyler y Nicolau, Marques de Tenerife (© Library of Congress / Getty Images)

All rights reserved. No part of this publication may be reproduced or transmitted
in any form or by any means, electronic or mechanical, including photocopying,
recording, or any information storage or retrieval system, without prior permission
in writing from the publishers.

Bloomsbury Publishing Plc does not have any control over, or responsibility for, any
third-party websites referred to or in this book. All internet addresses given in this
book were correct at the time of going to press. The author and publisher regret any
inconvenience caused if addresses have changed or sites have ceased to exist, but
can accept no responsibility for any such changes.

A catalogue record for this book is available from the British Library.

A catalog record for this book is available from the Library of Congress.

ISBN: HB: 978-1-3500-6258-0
PB: 978-1-3500-6259-7
ePDF: 978-1-3500-6260-3
eBook: 978-1-3500-6261-0

Typeset by Deanta Global Publishing Services, Chennai, India

To find out more about our authors and books visit www.bloomsbury.com
and sign up for our newsletters.

THE COVER IMAGE

General Valeriano Weyler y Nicolau and the evolution of a Template for Destruction

It is unlikely that any reader will recognize the stern image of Spanish General Valeriano Weyler y Nicolau (17 September 1838 – 20 October 1930) which appears on the cover of this book. Weyler served as a governor general in the Spanish Philippines and in Cuba. In an otherwise distinguished career, General Weyler's brutal suppression of the Cuban rebellion in the mid-1890s led to the Yellow Press bestowing the nickname 'Butcher Weyler' on him. Although the removal of rebellious populations in modern history had occurred before General Weyler (see Chapters 1 and 2), it was his policy of what he called *reconcentración* that established relocation as a formal military approach to counterinsurgency. We might call Weyler and his counterinsurgency campaign in Cuba as the point of origin of relocation as a formal strategy in counterinsurgency.

How did General Weyler's *reconcentración* work? In Chapter 3, Major Mark Askew explains its major components. But, to summarize, Weyler faced a mounting rebellion and did not have enough soldiers to defeat it. He built fortified lines of blockhouses and barbed wire called *trocha* across Cuba thereby cutting the island into sectors. Within these sectors Weyler then forcibly relocated the civilian population into temporary camps and then proceeded to hunt down the rebels (who were weakened by the loss of logistical and moral support from the people). General Weyler's *reconcentración* then became what I call a 'template for destruction' for the forcible relocation of people in the twentieth century. I used the phrase 'A Template for Destruction' as a chapter heading in my book *Ottomans and Armenians, A Study in Counterinsurgency* (2013) to describe the impact of Spanish, American, and British campaigns of relocation in counterinsurgency in Cuba, the Philippines, and South Africa. Sadly, the very words 'concentration camp', coined by the British in South Africa, mirrored Weyler's *reconcentración* and, as the reader will observe, an approach to counterinsurgency based on forcibly relocating people continued into the 1970s.

Edward J. Erickson
Norwich, New York

CONTENTS

List of maps ix
List of contributors x

Introduction *Dr Edward J. Erickson* 1

1 Exile without end: The Acadian expulsion
   Major Christine Keating 17

2 The Long Walk of the Navajo: Relocation in the
   American Southwest *Dr Jonathan F. Phillips* 39

3 War answered with war: The Spanish in Cuba
   Major Mark Askew 59

4 A howling wilderness: America in the Philippines
   Dr Ethan H. Harding 83

5 Methods of barbarism: The Boer War *Dr John Sheehan* 95

6 Uneven repression: The Ottoman state and its
   Armenians *Maxime Gauin* 115

7 From the Pale: The Russians and the Jews
   LtCol Kevin D. Glathar 141

8 They are our enemies: The Japanese-American
   internment *Dr Edward J. Erickson* 157

9 A collective measure: Population resettlement in
   the Malayan Emergency *LtCol Gregory J. Reck* 185

10 *Centres de Regroupement*: The French in Algeria
   Dr James N. Tallon 209

11 Counterinsurgency at the 'rice roots' level:
   South Vietnam's Strategic Hamlet Campaign
   Dr Nathan R. Packard 225

12 Resettlement in the Portuguese Colonial Wars:
   Africa, 1961–75 *Dr Kalev I. Sepp* 255

Conclusions: Relocation in counterinsurgency warfare
   Dr Edward J. Erickson 267

Appendix: Relocation statistics 277
Index 279

MAPS

Map 1   A Global History of Relocation in Counterinsurgency Warfare 2

Map 2   French Acadia 18

Map 3   The Long Walk of the Navajo 40

Map 4   The Cuban Insurrection 60

Map 5   The Boer War 96

Map 6   Ottoman-Armenian Relocations 116

Map 7   The Pale 142

Map 8   Japanese-American Internment 158

Map 9   British Malaya 186

Map 10   French Algeria 210

CONTRIBUTORS

Major Mark Askew is a strategist with US Army Central Command. He holds a Bachelor of Science degree in Military History from the US Military Academy at West Point and a Master's Degree in History from Texas A&M. He has taught Military History and Military Theory at the US Military Academy at West Point and is currently ABD at Texas A&M. His research interests include the US Army, strategy, war and society, and military occupations.

Dr Edward J. Erickson is a Professor of International Relations at Antalya Bilim University in Antalya, Turkey. Dr Erickson is retired regular US Army officer and a retired professor of Military History from the Marine Corps University. He has a PhD in history from the University of Leeds and has published numerous books and articles about counterinsurgency in the early twentieth century.

LtCol Kevin D. Glathar is a retired regular US Marine Corps officer who deployed around the globe and participated in joint and coalition humanitarian relief and contingency operations in Albania, Bosnia, the Democratic Republic of the Congo, Croatia, Iraq, Japan and the Philippines. He is a graduate of the US Naval Academy, US Marine Corps Amphibious Warfare School, US Army Command & General Staff College and the Joint Forces Staff College. He has a Masters in Military Arts and Science and taught at the Marine Corps University. His research areas of interest are in religious history, cognitive warfare and counterinsurgency.

Maxime Gauin is a French historian, and he is a PhD candidate (ABD) from Middle East Technical University in Ankara, Turkey. He is well-published in academic journals, and his research focuses on contemporary aspects of the Armenian question and Franco-Turkish relations.

Dr Ethan H. Harding, lieutenant colonel (US Marine Corps, Retired), served as an armour officer and a Middle East and North Africa regional affairs officer. He served in Afghanistan and Iraq and also served as Deputy Director of Warfighting at the USMC's Command and Staff College. Dr Harding earned his doctoral degree from Kings College London in the UK. He has authored numerous articles and a book, *Identifying the Pillars of*

Stability Operations: Using Social Science To Bridge A Gap In Operational Doctrine. His research interests include military history, asymmetric warfare and international relations.

Dr Lisa Johnson-DiMarco is a biologist and illustrator. She has a Bachelor of Science degree from SUNY Cortland and a doctoral degree from New York Chiropractic College. Lisa is currently teaching earth science, physical science, life science and biology to middle and high schoolers. She has taught biology courses at SUNY Cortland and New York Chiropractic College. Lisa began using various digital media to create illustrations and animations for use in her classrooms which later transitioned her to creating illustrations for publication.

Major Christine Keating is a brigade executive officer in the US Army Military Police Corps. Major Keating served in Iraq and Afghanistan. She holds a Bachelor of Science degree in International and Strategic History from the US Military Academy at West Point and a Master's Degree in Brazilian History from Brown University. She lives in Olympia, Washington, with her husband Daniel and their four children.

Dr Nathan R. Packard is an Assistant Professor of Military History at the US Marine Corps Command and Staff College in Quantico, Virginia. Dr Packard received his PhD (2015) in History from Georgetown University. He also holds an MA (2014) in National Security and Strategic Studies from the US Naval War College. Dr Packard is a lieutenant colonel in the US Marine Corps Reserve and a veteran of *Operation Iraqi Freedom* having served as an adviser to an Iraqi infantry battalion in Al Anbar Province in 2007.

Dr Jonathan F. Phillips is Dean of Academics at the US Marine Corps Command and Staff College (MCCSC) in Quantico, Virginia. Before joining the faculty at MCCSC, Dr Phillips held positions at the University of South Carolina, Texas A&M University and Old Dominion University. He earned his doctorate in history at the University of North Carolina at Chapel Hill. His scholarly interests include US military, war and society, and civil-military relations.

LtCol Gregory J. Reck is the Special Operations Forces Chair, Marine Corps University, Quantico, VA. In this capacity, he is USSOCOM's representative to the USMC's Professional Military Education institution and is responsible for the integration of Special Operations theory and knowledge into the curriculum of the individual colleges. He has three master's degrees ranging from literature to defence analysis with a concentration in Terrorism and Terrorist Financing from the Naval Postgraduate School. He has publications pertaining to psychological operations and special operations.

Dr John Sheehan teaches history and cultural anthropology for SUNY Cortland and LeMoyne College. He has published several books and refereed articles since receiving his doctorate in 2000 from St. John's University in Queens, NY. His publications and presentations reflect his training in interdisciplinary and multicultural history.

Dr Kalev I. Sepp has taught history at the US Military Academy at West Point, NY, and the US Naval Postgraduate School at Monterey, Calif. A former US Army Special Forces officer, after earning his PhD from Harvard University, he served as a Assistant Deputy Secretary of Defense, and as a policy adviser in Iraq and Afghanistan. His research interests include irregular warfare, influence operations and strategy in undeclared wars

Dr James N. Tallon is Associate Professor at Lewis University in Romeoville, Illinois. He has a PhD in Near Eastern Languages and Civilization from the University of Chicago and has published several articles about the Middle East, the Balkans and the Islamic World in the twentieth century.

Introduction

Dr Edward J. Erickson

*This is the forest primeval; but where are the hearts that beneath it
Leaped like the roe, when he hears in the woodland the voice
of the huntsman?
Where is the thatch-roofed village, the home of Acadian farmers—
Men whose lives glided on like rivers that water the woodlands,
Darkened by shadows of earth, but reflecting an image of heaven?
Waste are those pleasant farms, and the farmers forever departed!
Scattered like dust and leaves, when the mighty blasts of October
Seize them, and whirl them aloft, and sprinkle them far o'er
the ocean.*

HENRY WADSWORTH LONGFELLOW, 1847
Evangeline, A Tale of Acadie

Prologue

American poet Henry Wadsworth Longfellow's epic poem *Evangeline* begins with the dramatic opening phrase '*This is the forest primeval*' (emphasis mine) and the rest of first stanza frames a question 'What happened to the people who lived here?'. Some readers today might recognize Longfellow's epic poem for its contribution to American literature but few will note its roots in historical fact. In truth, the story of the Acadian expulsion or 'exile without end' was an early and pragmatic variant of a campaign of counterinsurgency by relocation. Even fewer readers will note that the Acadians, who were the French inhabitants of the colony, exiled to Louisiana would become known as 'Cajuns' (Map 1). This study begins with the case of the British exile of the Acadians as the proximate start of deliberate removal of populations as a military policy in modern war.

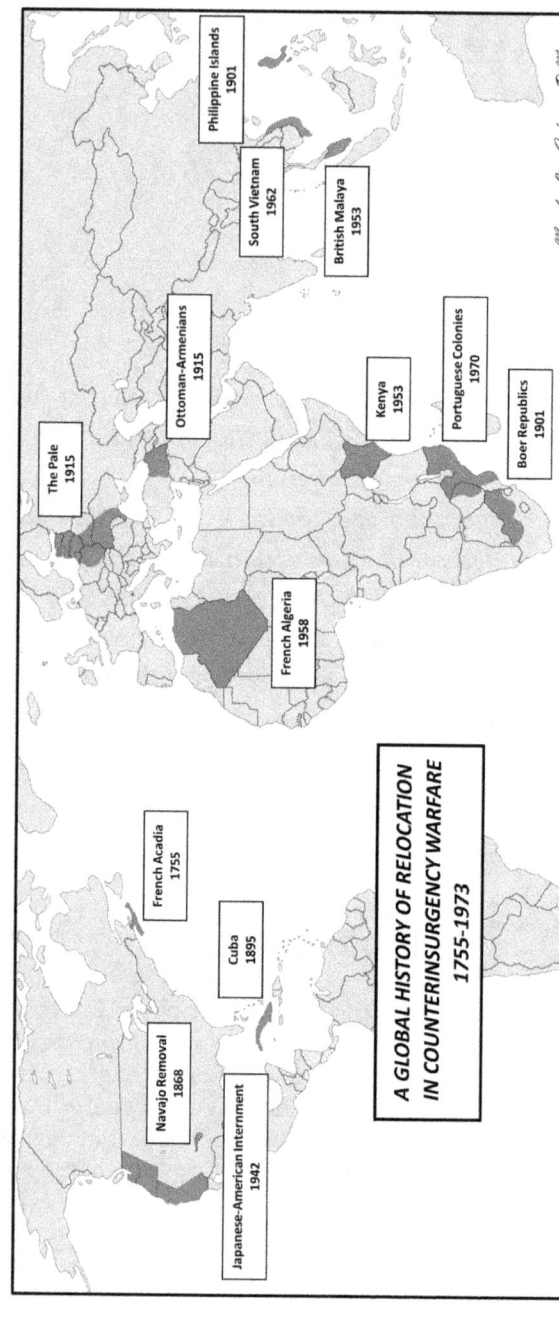

MAP 1 A Global History of Relocation in Counterinsurgency Warfare. The global scope of relocation in counterinsurgency; counter-guerrilla, counter-indigenous and counter-fifth column campaigns is evident on this map. Campaigns of relocation have occurred in four of six continents inhabited by humans.

After the British conquest of French Acadia (composed mostly of the modern Canadian province of readers Nova Scotia), the restive French inhabitants resisted British occupation. Together with local Indian tribes, the French Acadians periodically waged guerrilla war against the British and helped supply the French fortress at Louisbourg. In addition to irregular warfare, some Acadians formed military units and even bested the British in small conventional battles. As a military solution to what had turned into a persistent rebellion, the British chose a counterinsurgency strategy of what was then called 'expulsion' and, in 1755, began the first of a series of permanent relocations.

The Sepp thesis

This book is an outcome of research that I conducted while working on *Ottomans and Armenians, A Study in Counterinsurgency* (New York: Palgrave Macmillan, 2013) and, as that book evolved, I became aware that relocation as an operational approach in counterinsurgency had been a not uncommon form of counterinsurgency warfare. As late as 2016, when I presented this book proposal to the acquisition editors at Bloomsbury Academic, I believed I had an original topic that had not been academically theorized into a coherent thesis statement. Much to my surprise and after contracting this book with our publisher, one of my contributors (Lieutenant Colonel Ethan Harding, USMC) made me aware of the earlier work of a now well-known scholar. I would be remiss if I did not now identify him and acknowledge his groundbreaking thesis.

In 1992, US Army Major Kalev I. Sepp presented an MA thesis to the faculty of the US Army Command and General Staff College. Major Sepp titled his thesis *Resettlement, Regroupment, Reconcentration: Deliberate Government Directed Population Relocation in Support of Counter-Insurgency Operations*.[1] The thesis was released for unlimited public distribution by the Defense Technical Intelligence Center (DTIC) on 1 June 1992. As a federal government DTIC publication, Major Sepp's thesis is in the public domain and easily accessible online. Readers who are interested in the subject of relocation in counterinsurgency warfare are invited to read the thesis in full.

Major Kalev Sepp's thesis is, to my knowledge, the first unified examination of the problem of relocation in counterinsurgency operations. His research question was straightforward and intellectually elegant: 'Does government-directed population relocation help win counter-insurgencies?' Major Sepp was the first scholar to study holistically the issue of relocation in counterinsurgency warfare, and he examined a number of case studies which appear in this book; these are the Second Anglo-Boer War, the Philippine Insurrection, the Malayan Emergency, the Kenyan Emergency, the

Algerian Insurrection, the Vietnam War and Portuguese Colonial Wars. He also included a number of smaller non-operational level relocation efforts, which include the Greek Civil War (1944–9) and the Hukbalahap Rebellion (1946–54). Retiring from the US Army as a colonel, Dr Sepp is now a senior lecturer in the Department of Defense Analysis, Naval Postgraduate School, Monterey, California, and he is a recognized expert in the fields of strategy, counterinsurgency and intelligence. I am pleased to note that Dr Sepp is a contributor to this book.

The answer provided by Major Sepp in 1992 to his problem statement was: 'Historical evidence strongly suggests that forced resettlements at the direction of a government threatened by insurgency, when carefully planned, adequately resourced, and efficiently administered have contributed to defeat of the insurgents by physically and morally isolating them from the population they required for support.'[2] As will be demonstrated in this book, Major Sepp was largely correct but sometimes this was a short-term operational and tactical gain achieved against a longer-term strategic dilemma. In many cases there were negative strategic effects which had to be dealt with by successor administrations and governments. *A Global History of Relocation in Counterinsurgency Warfare* continues the inquiry that Major Sepp began in 1992. It has no single stand-alone thesis – rather our book is designed as a broad survey examining the military decision making which led to the major forcible relocations of a defined group of people thought to a threat to security in wartime.

Relocation in modern counterinsurgency warfare[3]

Eight of the cases examined in this study are what we would today call campaigns of counterinsurgency, but our book's title belies the inclusion of four additional cases involving what might be termed a counter-indigenous campaign (the Native Americans in the United States), a counter-guerrilla campaigns (the Second Anglo-Boer War), and two counter-fifth column campaigns (the Jews from the Pale in 1915 and the Japanese-Americans in 1942). In all twelve cases, though, a unifying theme emerges – people were forcibly relocated in wartime as an operational approach to the problem of an actively or potentially hostile population either in revolt or in league with the enemy. The distinctions between the twelve cases in this book, as well as the similarities, are an important part of the narrative and are explained more fully below. We hope that through comparison and contrast more nuanced understandings will emerge for the reader.

At the dawn of the twentieth century, counterinsurgency policies based on the deliberate removal and forced relocation of civilian populations by governments emerged as viable and acceptable practices in Western warfare.

Three wars, in particular, set important precedents for the Western world in the way in which militaries dealt with guerrillas and irregular insurgents. These wars involved Spain in Cuba (1895–8), the United States in the Philippines (1899–1902), and Britain in South Africa (1899–1902), and all three saw the evolution of similar strategic, operational and tactical practices by the Western powers. At the strategic level, the powers sought the destruction of insurgent and guerrilla forces in order to end insurgencies and, in the case of the Boers, end a conventional war that had entered a guerrilla warfare phase. Operationally, the powers employed campaign designs that focused on separating the guerrillas from their principal sources of support, which were the friendly civilian populations, thereby enabling the military defeat of the weakened irregular forces. At lower tactical levels, military commanders isolated the irregulars by establishing fortified lines that cut their operational areas into manageable sectors and then removed the civilian populations. Simultaneously, they swept the sectors clean of enemy forces by driving the insurgents and guerrillas to destruction against fixed barriers. To varying degrees these campaigns were successful.

Relocation as a strategy and operational approach in war would reappear in various forms over the next seventy years. In the First World War, the Ottomans relocated some 400,000 Armenians to camps in the Euphrates valley while the Russians relocated well over a million Jews from the Pale (their western provinces and Poland). In the 1950s, the British in Malaya relocated over a quarter million ethnic Chinese into New Villages under the auspices of the Briggs Plan. At about the same time during the Kenyan Emergency, the British relocated over a million Africans to detainee camps. The French relocated over three million Algerians in the late 1950s to *Regroupement Centres* under the infamous *Quadrillage* system. The South Vietnamese employed the same principle in Vietnam, in the 1960s, by relocating hundreds of thousands of villagers into what they called Strategic Hamlets. In the last cases of the twentieth century the Portuguese would use this approaching in attempting to hold on to three of their African colonies. The number of people relocated in these campaigns is truly staggering (see Appendix).

In a somewhat different context, in 1942, the United States removed Japanese-American citizens from California to internment camps in the Nevada deserts in order to deal with a perceived fifth column threat to national security. Like the experiences of Jews from the Pale, this was campaign of fear-based pre-emption rather than an actual armed threat. Nevertheless, whether the process was called exile, relocation, deportation, detention or internment – and whether the destinations defined as concentration camps, zones of protection, *Regroupement Centres*, relocation camps, internment centres, new villages, strategic hamlets or reservations[4] – the basic strategy of relocation employed to weaken or pre-empt a threat, either kinetically or non-kinetically, remained the same.

Terminology, language and historical neutrality

A Global History of Relocation in Counterinsurgency Warfare presents a chronological survey of the major forced relocations of people which were conducted as a deliberate operational approach to the problem of internal threats in modern wars and conflicts. The intent of the editor and the contributors is to tell the story, to the greatest extent possible, in an objective and historically neutral narrative. Our aim is not to justify decisions but to explain why these events unfolded as they did. However, to some readers, this study may appear to be sanitized or skewed by the use of euphemistic language. To others it may appear as an apologia for heavy-handed tactics against harmless civilian populations, and some may even categorize this book as a study in genocide denial. Our book may also be criticized by some readers for the selection of cases which are either included or not included. Importantly the twelve cases of relocation comprising this book were the direct result of war and conflict and, while there were certainly pre-existing prejudices in all cases, it was war that created the conditions and enabled the decisions leading to the forced relocation of people.

We believe that it is critical to understand the terminology used in this book as well as why certain words are used and why other words are not. Some readers may find the term 'relocation' to be far too mild for these events. In truth, inflammatory vocabulary and verbiage is often the enemy of balanced historical interpretation. In the context of this study 'relocation' is used to convey the deliberate and forcible mass movement of a population to somewhere within their own country (or in the case of the Acadians to another colony). This is different than deportation, which means being sent somewhere without the government's intent to return them to their homes (in the relocations of the Acadians and the Navajo, this was the case). Other similar terms include, but are not limited to, resettlement, transfers, evacuations, expulsion and displacement. Readers interested in this topic and its definitions may wish to read the Convention Relative to the Protection of Civilian Persons in Time of War (commonly known as the Fourth Geneva Convention, 12 August 1949)[5] with the caution that this treaty pertains to occupying powers and not to internationally recognized states operating within their own territory. The term 'relocation' in this study is chosen for its neutrality and for its general applicability to all the cases presented in this book. The focus of the book is to explain why a defined group of people were moved deliberately and forcibly in wartime rather than to examine their grievances or whether or not they were an actual threat.

Readers must also keep in mind that, in most cases, the ruling power was not an 'occupying power' in the modern sense. For example, Cuba in 1895 was a Spanish colony, Malaya in 1951 was a British colony, Algeria in 1955 was an actual province of the French Republic, and the government of the Republic of Vietnam was an internationally recognized legitimate government. In such circumstances the affected people were considered legal inhabitants or citizens of the lands in which they lived (although we recognize that the people themselves may not have considered themselves as such). However, it may be argued, persuasively I believe, that in the cases of the Acadians, the Native American Navajo, and the Boers, the affected people may be accurately considered as the population of an occupied area.

Likewise, we recognize that the term 'counterinsurgency' itself is a modern term which was not in general use until the mid-1950s. Certainly no person in the time of the French and Indian Wars, or even as late as the First World War, or any historian of these events before the case of the Malayan Emergency would use this term. With that said, this study uses the overarching term 'counterinsurgency' as a unifying approach to describe the reactions of a state to forms of unrest that include insurgency, rebellion, irregular warfare, Fifth Column activities, and coordination by revolutionary groups with the enemy. There are also many definitions for the term 'insurgency', but the purposes of this book, insurgency is defined as an organized movement aimed at the weakening or overthrow of a constituted government through use of subversion and armed conflict.[6] However, in many of the cases in this book, the insurgent objective was as varied as self-determination, autonomy or independence.

A word associated with some of these cases is the term 'genocide' which is, by United Nations convention, defined as 'acts committed with intent to destroy, in whole or in part, a national, ethnical, racial or religious group'.[7] The convention, signed in 1948, was an outcome of collective global revulsion and anger over the Holocaust. It is important to keep in mind that the UN treaty was specifically written to implicate and punish individual perpetrators rather than to assign responsibility to nation states or to specific governments. Some of the cases in this study, to a greater or lesser extent, have genocidal outcomes which are repugnant to twenty-first-century readers. However, none of the cases examined in this study began with a plan designed to exterminate a group (either in whole or in part), although this outcome occurs in several of the cases.

We must also define certain military terminology used in this study. 'Strategy' is an overarching term, and according to Professor Lawrence Freedman, an established specialist on security studies and strategic thought, 'There is no agreed-upon definition of *strategy* that describes the field and limits its boundaries.'[8] Freedman continues with his own definition which we shall use in this study, 'One common contemporary definition describes it as being about *maintaining* a balance between ends, ways, and means; about *identifying* objectives; and about *resources and methods available* for meeting such objectives.'[9] The term itself may be used at any level and in any field; for example, there are strategies for investments, strategies for winning the Super Bowl, and strategies for passing the motor vehicle driving test. In the context of this book, we will limit the term to the strategic level (or national level) of war. For example, the failure of negotiations between Britain and the Boer Republics resulted in the Second Anglo-Boer War (1899–1902).

In the initial phase of the war, British strategy balanced the objective of forcing mining concessions by forcing the Boers to surrender (the ends) using a conventional offensive military campaign (the ways) employing about 27,500 men under the command of second rate commanders (the means).[10] This strategy failed because of insufficient resources necessary to subdue the Boers, who were far more effective than the British thought them to be. In the second phase, the British brought down another 180,000 men and their best commanders, handily defeating the Boer regular army and occupying the Boer Republics. However, the Boers did not surrender and reverted to a guerrilla warfare strategy. In turn, the British strategy for the war's third phase further revised the means by increasing its forces to over 200,000 men and adjusting the ways to a draconian counter-guerrilla campaign. There are, therefore, three distinct strategies for the British direction of the Second Anglo-Boer War.

Another term which is applicable to this study is 'campaign' as well as the 'operational level of war'. A campaign is a series of battles or engagements designed to achieve a strategic purpose or objective. The operational level of war (like the word strategy) is poorly defined, but in this study, we define it as the level of war at which major forces are employed in campaigns. The operational commander is almost always a theatre or field army commander and his mission is to arrange the sequence of actions which will produce the military conditions necessary to achieve the strategic goals.[11] This study addresses operational decisions which result in military campaign plans designed to forcibly relocate entire populations in order to change the ends, ways, and means equation.

The cases in this study

A Global History of Relocation in Counterinsurgency Warfare presents a chronological survey of the major forcible relocations of people which were conducted as a deliberate operational approach in modern conflicts of counterinsurgency. It is a military history rather than a cultural, social or humanitarian history, and, as such, the study will not render judgements on the morality or ethics of decisions or actions; nor will we render judgements on humanitarian concerns. Each chapter is a campaign analysis and is written to inform the reader of the military decisions, the military plans and their execution, and the military outcome. Each contributing author will address the question, 'From a military point of view, was the campaign successful or unsuccessful?' In effect, each chapter seeks to analyze the operational and tactical effects of the campaign (i.e. did it do what the commanders thought it would do?) and assess the strategic effect (i.e. did the campaign achieve or contribute to its intended strategic outcome?). Because the scope of the study is narrowly defined (as well as because of the word count limitations) the human and social consequences of the campaigns, and our memory of these events today, will be presented only in very brief form.

In our opening chapter, 'Exile without End, The Acadian Expulsion', Major Christine Keating informs us of the first use of forcible relocation as a counterinsurgency approach in modern warfare. By 1713, the British had occupied most of the French colony known as Acadia (modern Nova Scotia and the Maritime provinces of Canada). Over the next forty years the French inhabitants waged a quasi-guerrilla war against the occupation. Frustrated at their inability to deal with the Acadians with military means, the British decided to exile the French population. This secured the colony and access to the fortress of Louisburg. Starting in 1755, over 7,000 French Acadians were sent into Permanent Exile.

Dr Jonathan Phillips's chapter 'The Long Walk of the Najavo, Relocation in the American Southwest' moves us forward to 1846–68 for the US Army's removal of the Native American Navajo and Apache nations to the Bosque Redondo reservation, in the famously mischaracterized 'Long Walk of the Navajo'. More accurately the 'Long Walk' was a 'forced march' resulting in the deaths of hundreds of Native Americans. Dr Phillips's chapter pays particular attention to the evolution of a vocabulary and its effects on the development of policy. In addition to ending a Native American uprising, the United States also saw the Navajo relocation as a way of civilizing and Christianizing the tribes through a legal framework of treaties. This chapter highlights the importance of an evolving meme-like vocabulary in identifying the population in question as hostile. While there were other instances of the US government relocating Native Americans, Dr Phillips has selected this case as representative of the whole.

In 'War Answered with War, The Spanish in Cuba', Major Mark Askew presents the first professionally planned campaign of forcible relocation in Spanish-controlled Cuba. Faced with a mounting insurgency in Cuba that the Spanish were unable to suppress, General Valeranio Wyler implemented what he called *la Reconcentratión*. Wyler deliberately sought to separate the population from the rebel guerrillas. Over 500,000 Cubans were forcibly removed from their homes into camps while the weakened guerrillas were destroyed. In the process perhaps over 150,000 Cubans died in captivity. Wyler is notable for establishing something of a template for dealing with insurgencies and guerrillas through the tactics of forcible relocation.

Lieutenant Colonel Ethan Harding's chapter 'A Howling Wilderness, America in the Philippines' complements Major Askew's work in nearly contemporaneous terms. Unable to quell a gathering rebellion on the islands of Luzon and Samar, and hit hard by the massacre of American soldiers at Balangiga, American commanders launched a population removal campaign. Over 600,000 Filipinos were removed from their homes to Zones of Concentration after which the American commanders conducted search and destroy tactics to eliminate the guerrillas. Thousands of civilians died in the process while the rebellion on Samar and Luzon was crushed.

Dr John Sheehan's chapter 'Methods of Barbarism, The Boer War' presents insights into the historical and cultural background of the most well-known population removal of the age when British commanders removed the entire Boer civilian population from their homes into concentration camps. Dr Sheehan details why and how Generals Roberts and Kitchener designed an approach which separated the people from the guerrillas. After doing this they divided the Boer Republics into sectors with blockhouses and barbed wire and they hunted the Boer commandos to surrender. About 115,000 Boer civilians were forcibly relocated and many thousands died in camps from diseases caused by overcrowding, unsanitary conditions, and malnutrition.

In 'Uneven Repression, The Ottoman State and Its Armenians', Maxime Gauin addresses the forcible relocation of Ottoman-Armenians in 1915. In May 1915, the Ottoman government reacted to an emerging Armenian rebellion in its six eastern Anatolian provinces by removing some 400,000 Ottoman-Armenian citizens in order to separate what was thought to be a supporting popular base from Armenian revolutionaries. In the process of doing this thousands of Ottoman-Armenians were killed or died en route in what has come to be known as the Armenian Genocide. Thousands more died in the camps while the nascent rebellion was crushed. Dr Gauin demonstrates that the relocations were a military campaign against small, but determined, groups of rebels who were encouraged and supported by the Allied powers.

Lieutenant Colonel Kevin Glather's chapter 'From the Pale, The Russians and the Jews' reveals the little-known relocations of Russians Jews during the First World War. When Russia went to war with Germany and Austria-Hungary in 1914, there were over a million Russian citizens, who were Jewish, in the area known as the Pale (today eastern Poland and Belarus). The Czarist government and its military commanders believed that many Russian Jews were sympathetic to the enemy and were, therefore, a direct threat to the war effort. Over the course of the first year of the war the Russian government removed them east into the interior in order to eliminate the possibility that they might assist and support the advancing German army. Many were treated very brutally and the relocations resembled lethal pogroms in some locations. Making this case singularly unique, rather than being detained in camps, the relocated Russian Jews were distributed in towns and cities well behind the war zone.

In 'They Are Our Enemies, The Japanese-American Internment', Dr Ed Erickson examines the military rationale for the well-known removal of over 100,000 Japanese-Americans to Internment Camps in 1942. Regarded as a potential fifth column after Pearl Harbor the US government presumed the Japanese-Americans were a threat to the war effort and, as such, their removal was deemed necessary in the purported interests of national security. The evidence justifying removal at the time was specious and nothing has surfaced since to change that fact. Indeed, the intelligence was deliberately packaged in such a way as to condemn the entire West Coast Japanese-

American population as a dangerous enemy fifth column. Unquestionably racism fed the relocation decision but that should not obscure the fact that, in a military sense, the removal was a carefully planned theatre-level counter fifth column campaign.

Lieutenant Colonel Gregory Reck introduces us to the post-war world of decolonization with the British experience in 'A Collective Measure, Population Resettlement in the Malayan Emergency'. Faced with a failing counterinsurgency campaign in Malaya, the British turned to General Gerald Templer to implement the Briggs Plan, which was based on the removal and relocation of 225,000 ethnic Chinese from their homes to New Villages. Colonel Reck demonstrates that the resettlement program under the Briggs Plan facilitated the successful conclusion of the counterinsurgency efforts by means of isolating the insurgents from the population, legitimizing the government, and creating a more inclusive Malaya.

Dr James Tallon's chapter '*Centres de Regroupement*, The French in Algeria' introduces us to the largest relocation of peoples in this study. In one of the bitterest and most violent counterinsurgency campaigns of the twentieth century, the French instituted a strategy called *Quadrillage*, which quartered insurgent areas of Algeria into manageable sectors. Integral to this was the forcible relocation of over 3,000,000 Algerians into camps called Regroupement Centres where they could not assist or support the insurgents. Arguably, in combination with harsh tactics the insurgency was largely contained by 1958.

Dr Nathan Packard's detailed examination of 'Counterinsurgency at the "Rice Roots" Level, South Vietnam's Strategic Hamlet Campaign' extends many of Britain's counterinsurgency approaches into a different context. The program was not a stand-alone relocation campaign per se, and it had a number of objectives including separating guerrillas from the people, establishing security and safety for rural villagers, and increasing opportunity for participating in government to be achieved by relocating them involuntarily to secure villages. By design the program isolated and weakened the Viet Cong, who were in many areas reliant on the local villages for support but, at the same time, its heavy-handed implementation alienated much of the rural population. Some 400,000 Vietnamese were relocated forcibly over the life of the program (1961–3), but in the end, the program proved counterproductive to building support for the government.

In 'Resettlement in the Portuguese Colonial Wars, Africa, 1961–75', Dr Kalev Sepp concludes this study with the final cases of mass relocation used as a counterinsurgency approach in three Portuguese African colonies. This exposition of the little-known Portuguese experiences in Angola, Mozambique, and Portuguese Guinea focuses us on the lack of connectivity between the act of relocation and achieving a durable strategic purpose. Moreover, according to Dr Sepp, the most important outcome of the Portuguese relocations was the 'generation of time' which allowed Lisbon enough time to find a political solution.

The cases not in this study

Some readers may question why certain cases have been excluded from this study. In particular, the infamous Imperial German campaigns against the Herero and Namaqua in German South West Africa may strike readers as worthy of inclusion. While these were bloody in the extreme, resulting in what many term as genocide, the Germans relocated the surviving tribesmen and their families to concentration camps *after* the rebellion was crushed.[12] These peoples were not moved in a way designed to change the operational equations in a counterinsurgency campaign. Similarly, the infamous American relocation of the Cherokees known as the 'Trail of Tears', conducted by the Jackson administration in the 1830s, was not the result of war or military activity. There is also the singularly unique case of the Holocaust and the deportation of 6,000,000 European Jews to extermination camps. In this case the Nazi state did not relocate Europe's Jews for military reasons nor were they moved because they were considered to be a wartime threat. The fact that Germany was at war had nothing to do with the decisions to relocate and exterminate people. The Nazis did what they did for political reasons based on an ideological position of racial superiority but not for reasons of operational imperatives.

The largest and thematically most important campaign of forcible relocation that is excluded from this study is the case of the Kenyan Emergency (1952–63) which is also called the Mau Mau Rebellion. Our book's word limits have forced the editor to exclude the Kenyan Emergency – not because it is unimportant – but because the relocations mirrored the British experience in Malaya. While the context, people, terrain, and politics of Kenya were different than Malaya, the Briggs-Templer New Villages/'hearts and minds' approach to the Malayan Emergency were mirrored by General Sir George Erskine's (the British commander in chief of East Africa) campaign in Kenya. To a certain extent, if the reader understands relocation in the Malayan Emergency, he or she will understand relocation in the subsequent Kenyan Emergency.

The rebellion began in 1952 mostly among the Kikuyu tribe, who had been economically disenfranchised through losing their small plots of land to large plantations owned by white Europeans.[13] In late 1953, General Erskine, with the concurrence of the governor of Kenya, forcibly relocated Kikuyu tribal members out of the Aberdares highlands into brand new settlements, using techniques of the Malayan 'Briggs Plan'. This process became known as 'Villagization', and after a difficult start, it yielded positive results. Erskine's new villages were built according to a common plan under close government supervision. The displaced natives had to construct their new homes with locally available materials and prepare village defences, which was an acceptable approach in the resettlement areas chosen by the government. They also provided their own security by joining the Tribal

Police and Kikuyu Home Guard volunteers. Eventually, the incorporation of schools, clinics, churches and government welfare projects into the villages helped speed the program along. When Villagization was considered complete in late 1954, about 1,000,000 Kikuyu (some 80 per cent of the entire tribe) had been resettled. In the end British suppressed the Mau Mau uprisings and restored economic normalcy and the rule of law. In most ways the British secured a similar end state in Kenya as they had secured in Malaya.

There are also the cases of the Greek Civil War and the Hukbalahap Rebellion, but those operations were essentially conducted at tactical-level involving smaller numbers of people and smaller percentages of the population.[14] In the case of the recent Sri Lankan Civil War, the absence of a mature literature makes the reasons for the relocation of Internally Displaced Persons (IDPs) unclear today.[15] In separating which cases 'made the cut' the editor weighed the scope of the relocations relative to the extant population, the variances in the particular approaches, as well as the consideration of the operational versus the tactical levels of war. In arriving at the number of cases presented in this study, we have achieved a broad, but thorough, survey of the problem of forcible relocation used as an approach in counterinsurgency warfare (as well as examining the closely related categories of counter-indigenous irregular, counter-guerrilla, and counter-fifth column warfare).

Conclusion

Historically and militarily speaking, campaigns of forcible relocation have been designed to weaken the strength of insurgent, indigenous, guerrilla and ethnic populations thought to pose a danger or a threat to the power controlling the territory. In almost every case the levels of brutality, both intentional and unintentional, led to large numbers of civilian casualties from the relocated population. The world has not seen a counterinsurgency campaign based on forcible relocation since the 1970s, and the reader might reasonably ask why. We might speculate that the operational and tactical 'return on investment' today makes such an approach uneconomical or unpopular politically. We certainly have better understandings today of potentially unfavourable strategic consequences. We might also speculate that our contemporary world is something of 'a kinder and gentler place' (in part a result of post-1945 international accords) or that an absence of total war (as seen in the First and Second World Wars) makes a relocation-based approach less useful in guarding humanitarian concerns. We might also speculate that the post-colonial world has removed many of the imperatives leading to campaigns of counterinsurgency. And, finally, we might note that the character of insurgency itself has evolved into a newer form in the twenty-first century. While all or some of these might make decision making leading to a counterinsurgency approach based on forcible relocation more difficult – none of these situations automatically preclude a relocation-based approach. In the end, all we can state with surety is that the continuing absence of population removal as an acceptable or useful method of warfare in the future is not a certainty.

Notes

1. Kalev I. Sepp, *Resettlement, Regroupment, Reconcentration: Deliberate Government Directed Population Relocation in Support of Counter-Insurgency Operations*, MA Thesis, US Army Command and General Staff College, Fort Leavenworth, Kansas, 1992. In this book the editor uses the proper French spelling 'Regroupement' however the Sepp thesis is cited correctly.
2. Ibid., 114–15.
3. The use of the term 'modern warfare' is malleable and is defined here as the period after the rise of nation states (or about 1648).
4. For recent work on the subject of concentration camps by journalist Andrea Pitzer, see Andrea Pitzer, *One Long Night: A Global History of Concentration Camps* (New York: Little, Brown, and Company, 2017).
5. See the International Committee of the Red Cross website (Treaties, States Parties and Commentaries), Article 49. Convention Relative to the Protection of Civilian Persons in Time of War, 1949, Available online: https://ihldatabases.icrc.org/applic/ihl/ihl.nsf/Treaty.xsp?documentId=AE2D398352C5B028C12563CD002D6B5C&action=openDocument (accessed 24 January 2018).
6. U.S. Army, *FM 100-20, Military Operations in Low-Intensity Conflict* (Washington, DC: Department of the Army, 5 December 1990), Glossary-4. This particular publication defines insurgency as 'an organized movement aimed at the overthrow of a constituted government through use of subversion and armed conflict'. However, in many of the cases in this book, the insurgent objective was as varied as self-determination, autonomy or independence.
7. Office of the High Commissioner (UNHCR), Convention on the Prevention and Punishment for the Crime of Genocide, 9 December 1948, Available online: https://treaties.un.org/doc/publication/unts/volume%2078-i-1021-english.pdf (accessed 24 January 2018).
8. Lawrence Freedman, *Strategy: A History* (Oxford: Oxford University Press, 2013), xi; emphasis in original.
9. Ibid.
10. Field Marshal Lord Michael Carver, *The National Army Museum Book of the Boer War* (London: Sidgwick & Jackson, 1999), 10–11.
11. David Jablonsky, 'Strategy and the Operational Level of War: Part I', *Parameters*, Spring 1987: 65–76.
12. Pitzer, *One Long Night*, 78–81.

13 The following paragraphs have been extracted from Sepp, *Resettlement, Regroupment, Reconcentration: Deliberate Government Directed Population Relocation in Support of Counter-Insurgency Operations*, 58–60.
14 See Sepp, *Resettlement, Regroupment, Reconcentration: Deliberate Government Directed Population Relocation in Support of Counter-Insurgency Operations*, 33–41 and 42–7 for an excellent short summary of these campaigns.
15 Estimates regarding the total number of IDPs range from 350,000 to 800,000.

1

Exile without end:

The Acadian expulsion

Major Christine Keating

> *But Contrary to their expectation the Gate was shut and they confined as Prisoners.*[1]
> LIEUTENANT-COLONEL JOHN WINSLOW
> Grand Pré, 16 September 1755

Introduction

The small church in the village of Grand Pré sat nestled at the heart of the community. For its Catholic, French Acadian congregants, the church represented the heart and soul of their efforts to make their land productive, to live peacefully with their Mi'kmaq neighbours and to remain free of earthly obligation to foreign rule. But on 5 September 1755, the church would become something else entirely: that symbol of salvation would become the prison in which 418 Acadian men and boys were held captive by British colonial troops. Lured there by the orders of Colonel John Winslow for a proclamation, it was there that the Acadian men would discover that they and their families were to be ripped from their land and deported, dispersed throughout the more southern British colonies in North America. Taking only what they could carry, their homes would be burned, their cattle commandeered, their farms settled by white families from New England.

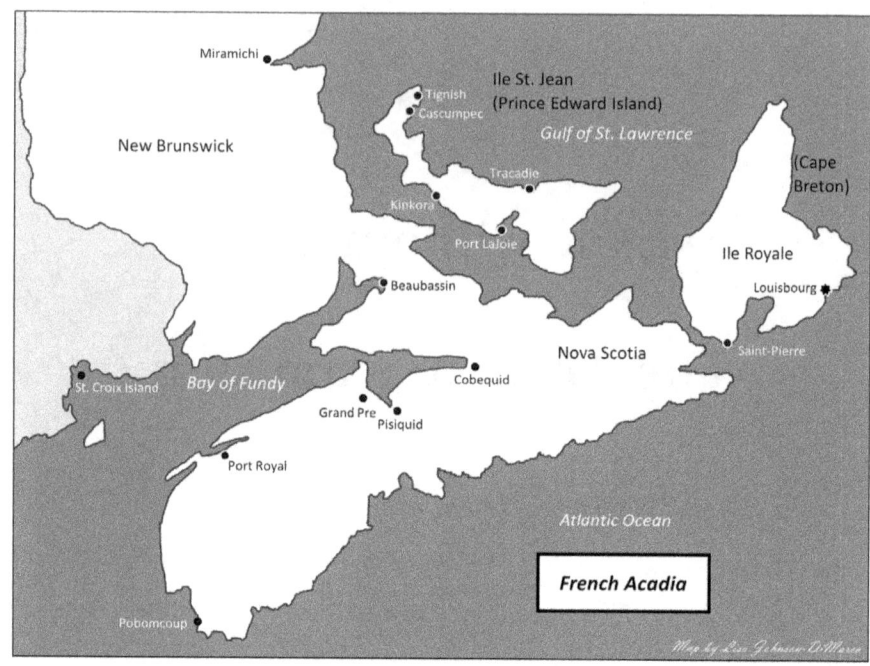

MAP 2 *French Acadia 1755. Acadia was colonized by France in 1604 but was conquered by Britain in 1713. The permanent expulsions in 1755 forcibly emptied Acadia of nearly all of its French inhabitants. The modern Canadian provinces of New Brunswick, Nova Scotia and Prince Edward Island comprise what was Acadia. Many of the exiled Acadians moved to Louisiana where they are today known as Cajuns.*

In the surrounding weeks and months, similar scenes would play out across Acadia. Ultimately, nearly 7,000 Acadians would be relocated, scattered throughout the British North American colonies.[2] Many wound up forming a new cultural epicentre in what is now Cajun country in Louisiana, and many more lost their community altogether, struggling to find a place in an English-speaking northern colony. Peaceful inhabitants of land that had transferred from French to British control in 1713 as a condition of the Peace of Utrecht that ended the War of Spanish Succession, the Acadians were Catholic and spoke French, anathema to the Protestant British. Although the War of Spanish Succession ended with British victory, the two mother countries continued to fight in Europe and in the Colonies, directly or through proxies, for decades to come. Within the context of this continued strife, the 'French neutrals', as the Acadians were known in the colonial press, became an increasing threat to the security of an ill-defined border zone between the French and British colonies. This threat was enhanced by the Acadians' blunt refusal to swear an oath of allegiance to King George II, preferring to maintain their neutrality. Colonial authorities in Nova Scotia and New England worried that disgruntled Acadians and neighbouring Mi'kmaq indigenous people were passing information and supplies to French troops garrisoned nearby. When British troops discovered Acadians within the captured Fort Beauséjour (later rechristened Fort Cumberland) in 1755, this proved their worst fears of collusion. Lieutenant Governor and Colonel Charles Lawrence decided the only way forward was to rid Nova Scotia of the Acadians entirely.

Throughout June and July 1755, Lawrence and New England Governor William Shirley devised a plan to expunge Nova Scotia of its formerly French inhabitants. This was a political decision, carried out by local colonial regiments and militia purpose-built for the operation. To say that the British expelled the Acadians is inaccurate; it was local colonial governments, charged with their own protection by a distant and disinvested mother country thousands of miles away, that devised and carried out a solution to the perceived Acadian threat. The Acadian expulsion was a military solution to a political problem, with financial and social benefits for Nova Scotia and New England. Decades of careful drainage and cultivation by farmers determined to make the coastal marshlands fruitful, made Acadian farmland particularly desirous. Acquiring that land for Protestant New England settlers became a priority, creating rich, religiously homogenous settlements and simultaneously securing a buffer zone against French attack by sea in the North Atlantic.

Although the political rhetoric surrounding the decision to expel the Acadians focused on the supposed security threat posed by the 'neutrals', the concept of military necessity is demonstrated here in a less developed, less distinct way than in later conflicts described in this book. Where later we will see military commanders executing relocations for strategic ends, sometimes predicated on political imperatives, in the case of Acadia, government and military decision making were one and the same. It was not the royal British standing army that marched on Grand Pré; it was local colonial regiments and militias called exclusively for that purpose by colonial governors William Shirley of Massachusetts and Charles Lawrence of Nova Scotia. Colonies were responsible for their own defence, and it was common practice at that time to muster militias for particular threats or campaigns (often against native populations). Thus the political exigencies of the day *were* the military exigencies of the day, and often vice versa. This was not a case of a military sent to occupy land and subdue a population, where the commander decided that the only way to achieve that end was through relocation; this was a military mission conceived of by political leaders who appointed commanders explicitly for the purpose of expelling the 'neutral French'.

That distinction would be of little comfort to the scores of Acadians who died offshore in holding ships, or to the thousands who never saw loved ones again following the confusion and haste of the 'Great Upheaval'. But using the military to achieve political ends in Nova Scotia was also not a new proposal; forcefully ridding the province of its Acadian inhabitants had been suggested as early as 1713, when the Peace of Utrecht offered newly minted Nova Scotians the choice between fealty or flight. Every time a new governor came on board, the question of how to deal with incorrigible Acadian independence, often interpreted as loyalty to France, arose anew. By the time Lawrence actually carried out the relocation in the 1750s, more than two generations of Acadians had lived with the threat of expulsion haunting and defining their relationship with the ruling British colonial leadership. The decision to expel the Acadians was a deliberate colonial project aimed at securing Nova Scotia and New England for British interests and Protestant British settlers. It was a long time in coming and was carried out by colonial militias raised specifically for that endeavour. Unlike other examples in this collection that demonstrate military exigency or a failure to grasp larger political objectives, the Acadian expulsion was the end result of decades of political pressure building up and finally releasing under military execution.

How to measure the success of this British imperial project is another thing altogether. Although Acadian collective identity in Nova Scotia was effectively shattered by Lawrence's efforts, less than half of the Acadian population was actually removed from the region. Some peripheral communities remained intact; entire families fled into the deep woods surrounding their former homelands and managed to survive; many sought refuge with their Mi'kmaq neighbours or crossed into Canada, where they were welcomed by the French colonial government. Many of those who stayed went on to stage violent resistance to British rule and settlement. What's more, many of the expelled Acadians eventually found their way back to Nova Scotia, much to Lawrence's personal chagrin. Furthermore, the continued presence of the Mi'kmaq, whose right to live in Nova Scotia was not contested, nevertheless perpetuated the narrative of violent 'French and Indian' resistance that the British had hoped to break by expelling the Acadians, the perceived agitators or enablers. Indeed, the French and Indian War would rage on for another eight years following the initial expulsion. Finally, the southern colonies wanted no part of Lawrence's project, turning a blind eye to Acadian efforts to return or rejecting them outright. Rather than disabling French lines of communication, intelligence and logistical support, the Acadian eviction seems to have simply compounded Nova Scotian security woes, for now they had to deal with damaged political relationships with fellow colonies, a return flow of displaced persons and an internal guerrilla resistance from an armed refugee population in addition to the French threat across the border.

Acadia

On 15 July 1604, the French ship *Jonas* pulled into port at Canso, on Cape Breton, carrying forty French settlers.[3] These men (for they were all men), battered by eight weeks at sea, were the forefathers of those who would come to be known as Acadians. Historian John Mack Faragher suggests two possible origins of the name 'Acadia'. The first credits Tuscan explorer Giovanni da Verrazano with coining the name after observing the beauty of the northern Atlantic coast in 1524. Verrazano's 'Arcadia' derived its name from a popular 1502 pastoral of the same title, and *l'Arcadie* became the French cartographic standard name for the region in the sixteenth century. Coincidentally, the local Mi'kmaq suffix – *akadie* describes places of abundance, which Acadia certainly became for the *Jonas*'s descendants.[4] Whichever story – or combination of the two – is true, the name came to refer to a huge swath of land south of the Gulf of Saint Lawrence. Much of the modern Canadian provinces of Prince Edward Island, Nova Scotia, and New Brunswick, and the American state of Maine, was 'Acadia' to these early French settlers. The vastness of *l'Acadie*, and the absence of defined borders as French settlement expanded, would have repercussions when the land passed into British hands a century later. Defined only by its 'ancient borders', Acadia was difficult to pinpoint on a map, and the Acadian descendants of the *Jonas*'s sailors would suffer in the ensuing contests over the border.

Acadian heritage can still be seen today in the borderland areas of South-eastern Canada and the North-eastern United States. Despite the best efforts of colonial armies conducting the expulsion, the Acadian name and culture survive to this day, calling into question the fullness and effectiveness of the British campaign to eradicate French influence. Local residents on both sides of the border actively claim and celebrate Acadian heritage; 'Acadia' and '*Acadie*' feature prominently on signage throughout the region. The beautiful drive up the north-eastern seaboard of the United States takes travellers through Acadia National Park, and once across the border into Canada, extant French speakers remain a living reminder of former French colonial aspirations and of Acadian presence.[5] Similarly, Mi'kmaq native culture still thrives in the region, forming part of the fabric of Nova Scotian daily life in a way that would be unimaginable in Puritan New England, long since stripped of its native inhabitants. Many of the heritage sites and museums that mark the Acadian story in Nova Scotia have trilingual signage, explaining the historical significance of the site in English, French and Mi'kmaq. This is not to downplay in any way the betrayals and brutality endured by the Mi'kmaq at the hands of the British. It simply emphasizes the incompleteness of any colonial project to fully Anglicize Acadia.

To those first French settlers, the lands that would one day be the site of so much bitter suffering by their descendants might have seemed an ill match for a permanent settlement, were it not for happy chance of their points of origin in France. The tides along the Bay of Fundy, then known as *la Baie Francoise*, are the highest in the world, peaking at nearly fifty feet in some places. Twice a day, at low tide, towering columns of red sandstone rise out of the water, imposing monolithic records of millions of years of geological history. Observers can 'walk the ocean floor', hunting fistfuls of amethyst, agates and other semiprecious gemstones that comprise the Fundy beaches. While starkly and surreally beautiful, the landscape does not immediately suggest prime farmland. Yet the early French came primarily from Rochelle, Saintonge and Puitou, marshy coastal regions in France where the practice of dyke-building kept the sea at bay.[6] Those early French settlers saw potential; with the drastic tides came miles of broad tidal plains saturated with nutrients. If the water could be kept out, or only allowed in according to a rigorous irrigation plan, the area could yield an incredible return on the settlers' labour. As daunting as this task was, dyking the coastal region was preferable to clearing inland forests of old growth trees (Evangeline's 'forest primeval') and glacial boulders. Past experience with the methods and maintenance of dykes allowed the settlers to envision fruitful plains where none existed; within a generation, the Acadian heartland yielded enough wheat and other crops to support multiple large permanent settlements.[7] By the time of the expulsion, an estimated 4,100 acres had been dyked and drained in the Grand Pré and Canard regions alone.[8] Thus the Acadians literally created their homelands from nothing, raising their towns and fields out of the sea. It was these rich farmlands the British would come to covet, yet over which they could claim no right of discovery.

The indigenous Mi'kmaq had a cordial relationship with the Acadians, and had done for generations. Converted to Catholicism by French Catholic missionaries in the early seventeenth century, at the dawn of French imperial ambitions on the North American continent, the Mi'kmaq shared a religion, territory and trade with their French neighbours. This relationship with Mi'kmaq people would also be additional facet of perceived threat during French/Indian Wars.

By the time British-French animosity reached a head in the colonies in the early eighteenth century, more than one hundred years of alliance and friendship cemented the Mi'kmaq-Acadian community. This friendly relationship became yet another reason for the British to doubt the sincerity of Acadian neutrality. Repeated Mi'kmaq raids on British settlements, ships and fortifications throughout the 1720s prompted repeated assumptions that the French – and by extension, the Acadians – were assisting in the planning, resourcing and execution of these attacks.[9] At the same time, lack of funding for British frontier fortifications frustrated attempts by colonial and military leadership to interdict French trade or to drive a wedge between French-Mi'kmaq-Acadian trade. Nova Scotian governor Richard Philipps had to pay out of his own pocket to outfit a schooner to patrol the Bay of Fundy off Annapolis Royal in 1724; though he petitioned the Treasury for reimbursement, it never arrived.[10]

Meanwhile, violent encounters between natives and settlers were escalating elsewhere in the North American borderlands. Clashes between Massachusetts militias and the Abenaki Native Americans in what is now Maine reached a bloody peak during 'Lovewell's War'. A deliberate campaign waged by Captain John Lovewell against the Abenaki, the war escalated into a cross-border conflict involving not only the Abenaki but their Maliseet and Mi'kmaq allies as well, united against the British. Known on the Nova Scotian side as the Maliseet-Mi'kmaq War, the years 1722–6 saw British colonial forces embroiled against retaliatory Native attacks on multiple fronts. Rumours swirled among British forces that Acadians were aiding the Mi'kmaq, in the form of transportation, shelter, intelligence and supplies of powder, musket balls and muskets. Two Acadians in particular – Guillaume Godet and Paul Petitpas – were singled out in Nova Scotian intelligence, and their alleged crimes became blanket accusations against the entire population.[11] The slow case against the Acadians continued to accrue. Neutral though they claimed to be, their continued presence threatened British colonial success. Overt or covert alliances with the French and the Mi'kmaq condemned them in British eyes.

The Acadians and the British

To understand the origins of the Acadian suffering, we must begin generations earlier and thousands of miles away across the Atlantic, where the chronically ill king of Spain is dying young, at the age of thirty-eight. In 1700, Spanish and Hapsburg King Charles II, of fragile health since birth, died without a biological heir, leaving his Catholic kingdom up for grabs. Charles's legal heir was a distant nephew, the French Bourbon Philip, Duke of Anjou, appointed mere weeks before the king's death after a series of family squabbles involving the interrelated thrones of England, France, Spain, Austria, Bavaria and the Spanish Netherlands. However, Philip's ascendancy was far from assured: a complex network of marriages, alliances, deaths, broken diplomatic promises and compromises led England and France to war in 1702 over ownership of the Spanish crown – and its rich worldwide colonial holdings. What followed was the War of Spanish Succession.

The war concluded with a set of eleven treaties that together have come to be known as the Treaty of Utrecht, or the Peace of Utrecht, after the Dutch province where the war's belligerents signed the treaties. Of these, the main peace agreement between Britain and France redefined colonial boundaries in North America and would, in time, indirectly define the fate of the Acadian people. Specifically, the treaty granted 'all Nova Scotia or Acadie, with its ancient boundaries' to Great Britain, and made allowances for residents of those formerly French lands to either leave (with all of their property) or stay and become British subjects, with the notable allowance that those who stayed could continue to practice Catholicism.[12] These clauses set three important conditions for future Acadian-British relations: first, the default assumption established in the treaty was that Acadian land – now Nova Scotian land – was *British* and that Acadians were invited to stay and bend the knee to Queen Anne. It was most clearly *not* defined the other way around – a British government falling in on an existing settled population. In this way, Utrecht attempted to reset the clock, ignoring the previous generations of Acadian culture and starting fresh with British territory inhabited by British subjects. Second, the treaty allowed the continued practice of Catholicism insofar as Catholicism was allowed anywhere else in the British Empire. While seemingly a positive concession for the Acadians, this provoked the continued 'othering' of the Acadian population by Protestant Nova Scotia and New England colonists in the coming decades, stoking mistrust between colonial leadership and Acadian subjects. Third, the treaty failed to define the geographical limits of Acadia, beyond simply citing 'its ancient boundaries'. Where exactly those boundaries lay would be a point of violent contention between Britain and France, and the loyalties of Acadians during the ensuing border skirmishes would be the source of much speculation and worry on the part of colonial governors.

The treaty allowed Acadians to decide for themselves whether they would willingly remain and become sworn subjects of the British crown, or whether they would retain loyalty to France and move away from the province. Article XIV of the treaty

> expressly provided that in all the said places and colonies to be yielded and restored by the most Christian King (Louis XIV) ... the subjects of the said King may have liberty to remove themselves, within a year, to any other place, as they shall think fit, together with all their moveable effects. But those who are willing to remain there, *and to be subject to the Kingdom of Great Britain*, are to enjoy the free exercise of their religion, according to the usage of the church of Rome, as far as the laws of Great Britain do allow the same.[13]

Thus, a precedent was established: those who had remained on the land now known as Nova Scotia had consciously chosen to become subjects of Great Britain; to stay and yet assert loyalty to France or even political neutrality carried risk of expulsion. When the Great Upheaval finally occurred nearly forty years later, that decision was built upon inherited assumptions by generations of British colonial rulers that refusal to swear an oath to the Crown of England was tantamount to a decision to leave Acadia.

The failure to clearly define borders had, arguably, an even more severe lasting impact on the Acadians than their continued practice of Catholicism or their refusal to swear an oath of allegiance in 1755. It certainly had a greater impact from a military standpoint, for the campaign to expel the Acadians was born in large part from an assumption that the Acadians were aiding colonial French in cross-border or extraterritorial raids. This, in turn, was built upon conflicting British and French understandings of where that border lay. Following the establishment of peace at Utrecht, Acadia existed in a 'state of outward peace and of covert war' between the French and native inhabitants on the one side, and the newly ruling British colonial government on the other.[14] Porous borders, distant seats of governments and ill-defined boundaries enabled the French to continue to assert claims over disputed territories, or in some cases, over territories claimed outright by the British. The uncertainty on what was French and what was British put the Acadians in the centre of an ugly tug-of-war, in which their greatest crime was to attempt neutrality.

In the decades immediately following the Peace of Utrecht, the French continued to build fortifications at Niagara and Lake Champlain.[15] When the War of Austrian Succession again pitted the French and British against one another in 1740, the conflict again spilled into the colonies, sparking borderland skirmishes across New England, New York and Nova Scotia. In 1745, after a siege lasting six weeks, the New England colonial militia raised by Governor William Shirley of Massachusetts and led by William Pepperell of Maine captured the French fort at Louisburg. This would be the beginning of a long partnership between Shirley and Pepperell for the security of New England, culminating in the disastrous campaign against French border fortifications during the French and Indian War a decade later, the winter after the Acadian deportation began. The 1745 victory, however, was bittersweet; instead of underwriting the sacrifices of Pepperell's militia and exploiting the strategic foothold in the North Atlantic, Great Britain ceded the fort back to French in the Peace of Aix-la-Chapelle at the close of this latest war. It would be another thirteen years before the British would win back Louisburg and dismantle the French fortifications.

Shirley himself contributed to the debate over whether French forts were actually within British territory, having served as one of the British commissioners in charge of surveying and defining Acadia in a series of 'Memorials' published in the first half of the 1750s. Shirley and his French counterparts cited hundreds of years of letters, treaties and claims, drawing and redrawing maps, testifying and rebutting the opposing country's claims, spewing polite diplomatic insults at each other but never reaching an agreement on the exact positioning of the elusive 'ancient boundaries'. In these memorials, hothead politicians on both sides published pamphlets accusing the opposite side of intrigue, villainy and outright theft. A 1756 retort to French claims outlined two types of government: one 'founded on the strictest rules of honesty, justice, equity, integrity, benevolence and humanity; in short, conformable to the invariable laws of reason and nature', and that which 'derives its principles from the sources of fraud, deceit, double-dealing, artifice, finesse, chicanery, dissimulation, partiality, oppression, perfidy, force, and tyranny'.[16] Invoking the deceit and plotting of Cardinal Richelieu more than a century earlier, the pamphleteer made sweeping character assessments and accused France of deliberately undermining the 'most *express* terms' of the Treaty of Utrecht.[17] Multiple maps accompanied the pamphlet, outlining the British understanding of Acadia's 'ancient boundaries' and showing France's allegedly spurious interpretation of the same. While certainly inflaming tensions between Britain and France, these memorials did little to settle the debate, leaving the Acadians stranded between culture and crown.

The undefined borders became a particular source of agitation for Lieutenant Governor Lawrence, as he sought to secure his province and eliminate the threat of French invasion. By 1754, when Lawrence and Shirley began developing war plans to push back against nearby French fortifications, Lawrence's decision to raise a force 'with the greatest privacy and despatch [sic]' was specifically aimed at the 'reduction of the Fort the French have contrary to Treaty set up in his Majesty's undoubted Territory's [sic] at a place on the Basin of Chignecto by them called Beauséjour as well as to remove them from any Encroachments they have made on his Majesty's dominions in the Province'.[18] The lieutenant governor justified his attack on French fortifications by claiming them to be within British territory – within those ill-defined 'ancient borders' of Acadia.

Antecedents and Acadian rebellion

In the early days following the Treaty of Utrecht, while the Acadians still had leeway to pick up and leave if they wanted to, the neighbouring French actively courted Acadian defectors. Struggling to successfully encourage emigration from Europe, the French were all too glad to find a source of new settlers right next door. To that end, they set their sights on the island of Ile Royal. Separated from the rest of Acadia only by a narrow channel, the Treaty of Utrecht classified Ile Royal as an island. It therefore remained French, despite its proximity to Acadia.[19] In 1714, the French founded Louisbourg and began fortifying the town and naval base. It soon became a hub of regional trade, such as fishing and shipping, and an attractive alternative to British rule for local French speakers. However, although Newfoundlanders would move in mass numbers to Ile Royal after the start of British rule, the French colonial city never developed the same allure for rural Acadians.[20] That notwithstanding, Louisbourg became a stronghold of French defence and power projection in North America. A generation later, Lawrence warned that Louisbourg posed a threat to British counter-fortifications at Chignecto and that it was 'high time to make some effort to drive (the French) from the north side of the Bay of Fundy'.[21]

Meanwhile, the British, too, were working to expand and cement regional control. As British colonial control of Nova Scotia gradually solidified throughout the early decades of the eighteenth century, the proposal to uproot the Acadian population and replace it with Anglican settlers popped up over and over again. Although repeatedly dismissed or denied by the ruling party, more than one colonial governor wrote back to the crown suggesting that the easiest way to assert royal authority was to simply eliminate any resistant population. Before the dust had even settled on the War of Spanish Succession, Scottish imperialist, adventurer and one-time smuggler Samuel Vetch petitioned for Acadian deportation. A mastermind behind the initial British conquest of Acadia as an extension of the War of Spanish Succession, Vetch opposed initial offers to allow French inhabitants to remain with all their property and actively petitioned London to allow him to deport the Acadians.[22] Ruling Tories denied his request, on the grounds that existing (and vanquished) settlers would make valuable labourers and taxpayers.[23] Yet in 1721, the newest governor, Richard Philipps, again proposed deportation.[24] By then the Whigs were in power. However, while they might usually have been enthusiastic about such colonial projects, the collapse of the publicly traded South Sea Company the previous summer had left a devastating mark upon the British economy, and overseas expansionist endeavours held less attraction than before. Like Vetch before him, Philips received no support for his proposal.

As the 1720s crept on, conditions for the British in Nova Scotia did not reach a steady state. War was escalating with the Mi'kmaq, and some Acadians provided food, intelligence or safe harbour for their Mi'kmaq neighbours. Acadian unhappiness with British rule escalated, and in 1745 'some took arms against the English, and many others aided the enemy with information and supplies'.[25] By 1749, reports from Halifax to London routinely used the word 'rebellion'.

A detailed report in December 1749 identified individual Acadians by name, who had taken up arms with the Mi'kmaqs, and had attacked a fort held by British Captain Handfield.[26] The attack brought British Governor General of Nova Scotia, Captain-General Edward Cornwallis to order that his forces 'seize the rebellious inhabitants' and bring them to Halifax for trial.[27] While some of the named men were apprehended, others fled over the border into the adjacent French Canadian interior. Unable to fully quell the rebellious Acadians, Cornwallis brought schooners to Halifax and offered to bring anyone who desired free passage to French Canada or to Europe. By the end of 1751 some 2,000 Acadians had left the peninsula.[28] At the same time Cornwallis launched a military expedition to subdue the Mi'kmaq at Chidnecto. Cornwallis's efforts towards the Mi'kmaq were accelerated by his horror at the atrocities committed by the Mi'kmaq when ambushing isolated British columns.

Cornwallis was also convinced that French Catholic priests and clergy were doing their best to stir up opposition to British rule. He was especially critical of the anti-British activities of Louis Joseph Le Loutre, the vicar-general of Acadia. According to the famous nineteenth-century American historian Francis Parkman, the French colonial government in Quebec actively supported and aided the Acadians and Mi'kmaqs by 'supplying merchandise, guns, and munitions ... under the pretext of trading in furs with the savages'.[29]

In April 1750, Cornwallis decided to isolate Acadia by occupying the town of Beaubassin which sat astride the isthmus joining the Acadian peninsula to the mainland (see Map 2). The expedition, led by a Major Lawrence, was composed of 400 soldiers. Le Loutre burned the town and then led a mixed Acadian and Mi'kmaq force which occupied the high ground at Beauséjour overlooking the town. This forced Lawrence to withdraw into a newly built palisade called Fort Lawrence. One morning, under a white flag, British Captain Edward Howe met with some French officers, when they were fired upon by Mi'kmaq's hidden along a stream. Howe was mortally wounded and Cornwallis blamed Le Loutre for inflaming the Mi'kmaqs. The French reinforced the Beauséjour position turning it into a fort, continued to encourage the Mi'kmaqs, and the opposing forces settled into to watch each other. In August 1752, Peregine Thomas Hopson succeeded Cornwallis who returned to England.

Contrary to his predecessor and later successor, Governor Colonel Peregrine Hopson saw wisdom in befriending and integrating both the Mi'kmaq and Acadian populations. He made great strides in mending the British relationship with the Mi'kmaq, outlawing the previous bounty for native scalps and even signing a peace treaty with local leader Jean-Baptiste Cope. Unfortunately, this progress was undone in short order, when a party of shipwrecked English sailors murdered and scalped their Mi'kmaq rescuers, prompting the local chief to burn the treaty.[30] Hopson's alliance with the Acadians, however, was a bit more lasting. He took steps to normalize the relationship: he repealed a requirement for priests to swear an oath of allegiance, and recognized that imposing an unconditional oath on the larger Acadian population might prove 'difficult, if not impossible' and could have 'ill consequences'.[31] He also instructed the officers, non-commissioned officers and soldiers of the colonial regiments to treat Acadians with respect, to avoid insult, and to only engage in commerce or labour at fair market prices. These instructions were published in French on every fort throughout Nova Scotia, ensuring that Acadians knew their rights and the intent of the new governor.[32] Perhaps most notably, Hopson decided to keep Protestant and Catholic settlements separated, rather than pursing Cornwallis's policy of infiltrating, diluting and eventually replacing Acadian settlements with Protestant. He worried that mixed settlements would cause Acadians to 'immediately quit the Province' – a loss that Hopson considered detrimental to the growth of a flourishing colony. To that end, in the summer of 1753, Hopson settled 2,000 German Protestant immigrants (recruited by Britain to import their faith and work ethic) at a new town some sixty-five miles southwest of Halifax.[33]

The man chosen for the job was Charles Lawrence. Within months, Lawrence would replace Hopson completely. By autumn of 1753, Hopson was incapacitated with an infection and returned to London to seek treatment, leaving Lawrence in charge.

At the heart of British agitation was the Acadians' refusal to pledge an unqualified oath of allegiance to King George III. The Acadians adamantly clung to original British promises that they could practice their faith and retain their property, with the added clause that they could not be compelled to bear arms against anyone. That is, they could not be conscripted to fight the French or Mi'kmaq. But the Acadians *had* sworn such an oath, or rather their fathers had, to King George III's father, King George II, in 1727. That oath was the culmination of a decade of careful negotiation between the British colonial government and the 'French neutrals', who adamantly maintained their political independence, despite the conditions of the Treaty of Utrecht. That oath bound the Acadians as subjects of the British crown while respecting their rights to practice Catholicism, to retain private property and to leave the province at any time, and exempting them from any requirement to take up arms against anyone.[34] Importantly, the 1727 oath dictated that its adherents *and their descendants* enjoyed these rights. But by mid-century, neutrality had come to be seen as disloyalty and adamance as defiance.

Ironically, it was the Acadians' very insistence on neutrality that damned them in the eyes of the British crown and made their loyalty suspect. The Acadians refused to swear an oath that might oblige them to take up arms against the French or, more probably, against the Mi'kmaq. But as the years wore on, this stance came to be seen as a veneer, beneath which lingered loyalty to France. By 1750, Lawrence insisted on an unconditional oath – full loyalty to the King of Great Britain, no strings attached.

Eventually, even universal acceptance of an unconditional oath would not have been enough to satisfy the increasingly wary Nova Scotian and New England leadership. The discovery of 'Inhabitants' (the Acadian refugees from Beaubassin) at Fort Beauséjour had confirmed the worst assumptions that the Acadians were in league with the French and had strengthened a growing resolve to eliminate that threat altogether. As the momentum towards deportation picked up, Massachusetts Lieutenant Governor Spencer Phips asked Charles Lawrence 'whether the danger with which his Majesty's Interest is now threatened will not remove any scruples which may heretofore have subsisted with regard to the French Neutrals'.[35] He posited that it had become 'both just and necessary that they should be removed unless some more effectual security can be given for their fidelity than the common obligation of an oath, for by the principles of their Religion this may easily be dispensed with'.[36] The Treaty of Utrecht had secured for the Acadians their right to practice their religion; yet when their loyalty continued to be called into question, their Catholicism became tautological evidence of their untrustworthiness. Never mind their refusal to take the oath, Phips said – how could we even trust them if they did? 'What confidence can ever be placed in Subjects who are inclined to revolt whenever they can?'

The relocation decision

The eventual decision to relocate the Acadian population lay with Lawrence, with Shirley's aid and consent. In May 1754, Shirley reported to colonial minister Sir Thomas Robinson that Acadians and Mi'kmaq working in concert had violated the border with Maine, effectively invading Shirley's New England. Where Shirley derived this intelligence from is unknown, but it proved unfounded. Nevertheless, Robinson, who was unaware of the faulty nature of the report, wrote dispatches in November of that same year to both Shirley and Lawrence urging them to 'frustrate the designs of the French' through joint action.[37] The two governors interpreted this nebulous response to their advantage, translating Robinson's missive as broadly as possible. Writing to Lawrence, the New England governor opined that Robinson's guidance equalled 'orders to us to act in concert for taking any advantages to drive the French of Canada out of Nova Scotia'.[38] Lawrence concurred.

Within days of receiving Robinson's vague instructions, Lawrence charged Lieutenant Colonel Robert Monckton – then commander of the vital fort at Annapolis Royal – with the duty of raising an army of 2,000 men specifically for a campaign against the French. He sent Monckton to Boston with two things: correspondence for Shirley and with a writ for unlimited credit to draft and outfit the new regiment. His intention was clear – together, Nova Scotia and New England would spare no expense to rid the colony of French incursion. Perceived Acadian collusion with French troops put them in the crosshairs of Lawrence's plan.

On 1 June 1755, Monckton landed his force at Fort Lawrence, where his colonial forces were joined by the British regulars of the Nova Scotia garrison. He laid siege to the French Fort Beauséjour, and there followed several skirmishes between the forces. Blockaded and then isolated by the Royal Navy, the French and Acadians surrendered on 16 June after a four-day artillery bombardment. Throughout the siege the Acadians and the Mi'kmaqs constantly attacked the English, but were beaten off.[39] However, this added to the British belief that an active rebellion was in progress. The rogue cleric Le Loutre escaped to Quebec to cause further discomfort to the British.

The expulsion

If the British had imagined an insurgency among the Acadians *before* the deportation, and indeed used this as a justification *for* the deportation, their actions certainly summoned violent rebellion into being once the expulsion had begun. Acadians desperate to maintain family integrity and to avoid imprisonment fled into the surrounding woods or sought refuge with their

Mi'kmaq neighbours, and from there planned and executed a handful of 'last stand' battles against the British. Exactly how much violence in Nova Scotia during this time period was committed by renegade Acadians, versus by Mi'kmaq or combinations of the two, is difficult to discern from correspondence; in his reports back to the British Board of Trade, Governor Lawrence routinely yet unsurprisingly conflated the actions of natives and refugee Acadians. In the months and years after the expulsion began, he frequently referred to 'French Inhabitants and Indians' in one breath, accusing them of committing hostile acts such as 'lying in wait in the roads where our parties pass and repass, (awaiting) opportunities of killing and scalping some of our people'.[40] Seldom is one group of belligerents mentioned independently of the other.

To some extent this reflects the reality of Acadian displacement and Mi'kmaq hospitality; many Acadians found refuge with their native neighbours. But the Mi'kmaq suffered because of the deportation as well. The expulsion had disrupted more than just Acadian life; it had also disrupted long-standing trade networks and mutually supporting French, Mi'kmaq and Acadian communities. Forced closer together than ever before for survival, it is little wonder that Lawrence saw the threat posed by Mi'kmaq and Acadian as one and the same.

Other Acadians attempted to thwart British decree without resorting to violence, sheltering in nearby woods or making their way to Ile Royal or other nearby French settlements. 'Notwithstanding the vigilance of the Officers commanding at the different outposts and the with which they executed their orders for embarking the French Inhabitants on board the Transports', recorded a British report in the early spring of 1756, 'several of them made their escape into the Woods and have found means of subsistence during the Winter'.[41] Some families fled into French territory, and there hoped to wait out the British and to one day return to their homeland. Years later, the grandson of one such couple recalled that

> when the Acadians were summoned by Winslow to Grand Pré, the people of (his grandparents') village did not go, but taking from their houses what they could, went south into the woods. ... There for eleven months they lived in huts. ... Always hoping the French would recover Acadia, they used often to ... look eagerly across the Basin to see whether the French colours were visible there.[42]

When finally they lost hope of regaining their homeland, the family migrated further west into French territory with the rest of their neighbours. While this story is told third hand and years after the fact, it demonstrates simultaneously the completeness and incompleteness of the British undertaking. While not all Acadians responded to Winslow's call, choosing instead to try their luck on the frontier or to stage resistance to British rule, still those persons were pushed out of their homes and villages. These refugees and rebels hid in the thick surrounding woodlands or sought asylum with their Mi'kmaq or French neighbours – surviving, yes, but no longer occupying coveted farmland or posing the threat of a unified political body. Conditions for the refugees were dire. Dysentery, malnutrition, cold and starvation plagued Acadian encampments through the winter of 1755–6.[43]

Cui Bono?

Recall again that in this case, the line between citizen and soldier was quite blurred; those who enacted the expulsion would be those who would benefit from the wealth left behind. Generations of Acadian farmers had painstakingly dyked the swampy lowlands one block of sod at a time, until the marshes were drained and the area yielded some of the richest farmland on the Eastern seaboard. Herds of cattle could not be taken on ships and were appropriated by colonial authorities. Soldiers and government officials involved with the expulsion would be the beneficiaries of these involuntarily abandoned assets.

The colonies to the south of Nova Scotia made no secret of these aspirations. In September 1755, shortly after efforts to remove the Acadians had begun, the *Pennsylvania Gazette* boasted that should the expulsion be successful, it would prove to 'be one of the greatest Things that ever the English did in America; for by all Accounts, that part of the Country [the Acadians] possess, is as good Land as any in the World: In case therefore we could get some good English Farmers in their Room, this Province would abound with all Kinds of Provisions'.[44] But who would settle the land? By February 1756, Shirley was pessimistic that 'good Protestant Subjects' could be enticed to settle the more remote northern colony, accustomed as New Englanders were to 'being governed by general assemblies, consisting of a Governor, Council, and House of Representatives, (and) likewise of Charters'.[45] This not-so-subtle dig at the underdeveloped Nova Scotian government was compounded by Lawrence's inability to guarantee the safety of any would-be settlers. The threat of French or Native attack was still very real and discouraged settlement. Alternatively, the idea that the New England militia might stay, and transition from occupying force to pioneering settlers, seemed an obvious choice. But although Lawrence pressured Governor Shirley to let his battalions remain, by early summer of 1756, Shirley had ordered his militiamen back to Massachusetts.[46] The British Board of Trade began to lose what patience remained with Lawrence's apparent short-sightedness. Since the 'recall of the two thousand New England troops (put) an end to any view which might have been entertained of converting them into Settlers upon the land left vacant by the transportation of the French inhabitants', the Lords of Trade warned Lawrence that they would 'remain extremely anxious until we hear What occurs to you' as an alternate plan to settle the vacated Acadian farms.[47] (Distribution of Acadian property, burning of homes, allocation of cattle to British settlers.)

Unexpected outcomes

Lawrence and Shirley's bilateral and irreversible action received mixed reviews from the mother country. Back in London, neither Parliament nor King George was aware of the plan prior to its execution. In turn there were unexpected outcomes as well as unexpected criticism.

Prolific orator and author Edmund Burke, a Member of Parliament during the expulsion, decried the act, fuming that Britain 'had more skill and ability in destroying than in settling a colony'. He lamented that the colonial government had 'most inhumanely, and upon pretences that in the eye of an honest man are not worth a farthing, root(ed) out this poor innocent deserving people, whom our utter inability to govern, or to reconcile, gave us no sort of right to extirpate'.[48] Burke, a renowned conservative, laid the blame for the colony's political and military strife squarely at the feet of the government, rather than making allowances for bad behaviour on the part of the Acadians.

Nor did the governors on the receiving end of the expulsion provide a warm welcome to their newest residents. Lawrence intended that the debarred Acadians be dispersed throughout the more southern British colonies, injecting new blood into those of His Majesty's colonies as could use new settlers and simultaneously breaking up any remaining collective Acadian identity. His fellow governors were not as enthusiastic. The refugees were expensive, often unannounced and frankly unwelcome. Even Massachusetts, with its long shared history of struggle against northeastern Native tribes and neighbouring French aggression, complained that its share of the now-homeless Acadians had arrived 'when the Winter Season was so far advanced' that the Massachusetts government could 'do but little for their Support'.[49] Rather than sympathizing with Lawrence's massive undertaking, Shirley left it to his lieutenant governor, Spencer Phips, to present the Nova Scotian governing council with a letter laying out his expectations that Massachusetts would be 'indemnified from all charges that might arise upon their [the Acadians'] Account'.[50] (Recall that it was Phips who had egged Lawrence on during the summer of 1755 to remove the Acadians in the first place.) Furthermore, Shirley apologized to the Massachusetts legislature that taking in a portion of the Acadians was 'likely to prove so burthensome [sic]', offering his personal assurances that Lawrence had meant no harm by it and that he (Shirley) would personally petition the king for reimbursement.[51]

Although the Acadians were no longer in Nova Scotia, colonial governments down the eastern seaboard and across the Atlantic did not hesitate to make it known that disposition of the Acadians – and the expenses incurred for their care – was still very much a Nova Scotian problem. Governors in Virginia, South Carolina and Georgia turned the migrant population right around and put them back on ships, or allowed them to slip away in boats of their own. In July of 1756, an irate Board of Trade alerted Lawrence that despite his assurances that the Acadians had successfully landed in their new southern colonial homes, 'several hundred of them have since been sent over here (England) from Virginia, and several from South Carolina'.[52] When ninety Acadians bearing passports from Georgia, South Carolina and New York harboured in Massachusetts after making their way back north, Phips again wrote to Lawrence, asking him to decide their fates for a second time. Massachusetts, Phips contended, had already 'received and supported here, a number much beyond our proportion' and could not afford to take in any more.[53] Yet neither would Phips 'suffer them to proceed any further' north towards Nova Scotia; and so the drifting Acadians were held, continuing to rack up charges that Lawrence's accountants in Boston refused to pay.[54] Exasperated, Lawrence finally agreed to pay Massachusetts's demand, but wrote an angry circular to the rest of the continental governors beseeching them to stop granting the Acadians safe passage north. He encouraged the other governors to destroy any boats, wagons or other means of transport the Acadians might have scraped together to attempt the return journey. Not only had Nova Scotia already expended a considerable sum in expelling them in the first place, but an Acadian return, Lawrence warned, would prove 'fatal ... to His Majesty's interest in this part of the world'.[55]

In Maryland, on the other hand, the government appealed to private goodwill to look after the Acadian refugees, with tragic results. When Christian charity unsurprisingly failed to provide for the needs of these 'bare and destitute ... objects of compassion', as the *Maryland Gazette* described the Acadians, many were forced to overwinter outdoors, begging for food.[56] By spring, the Maryland Assembly legalized the imprisonment of indigent wayfarers and encouraged the placement of their children with 'some person upon the best terms they can make'.[57] New York took the same route. The majority of Acadian children who made it to Maryland and New York were forcibly removed by those colonies' governments and conscripted to work, for the 'crime' of their parents' state-imposed destitution.[58] If expulsion from their homeland and loss of all possessions were not enough, these supposed British subjects continued to find themselves impoverished, despised, criminalized and forcibly separated from loved ones.

Money was often front and centre when it came to deciding how to proceed with the Acadian 'threat'. By 1757, nearly two years after the dislocation had begun, the British Board of Trade again censured Lawrence for the continued pockets of resistance in Nova Scotia, furious that 'notwithstanding the great expence [sic] which the public has been at in removing the French inhabitants, there should yet be enough of them remaining to molest and disturb the Settlements'.[59] Rather than eliminating a threat and preserving prime farmland for British profit, Lawrence's best efforts seemed to have made the problem worse. Fields lay fallow while forests harboured outlaw groups of Acadians desperate to return home. This volatility discouraged Protestant Anglo settlement; Lawrence and the Board of Trade agreed that 'vexed and harassed as the Province is by the Hostilities of the French and Indians, it will be in vain to attempt to induce hardy and industrious People to leave Possessions ... to come and settle'.[60]

Conclusion

The quotation from Longfellow's *Evangeline* that opened this book hints at the ultimate fate of the Acadians. The 'pleasant farms' of the rich Acadian lowlands lay waste, 'and the farmers forever departed!' The poet mourns that 'naught but tradition remains of the beautiful village of Grand-Pré', its inhabitants 'scattered like dust and leaves ... far o'er the ocean'. The fictional Evangeline and her beloved Gabriel, separated on the turbulent shores of Acadie, (spoiler alert!) only find each other again decades later when the latter is on his deathbed. Finally reunited, he dies in her arms.[61] Personal tragedies such as these – family separation, homeless wandering, poverty and death – played out on a massive scale. Thousands of Acadians died as a result of the expulsion, whether through direct action by the British, such as drowning on the ships, or through the secondary effects of disease, starvation and circumstances brought on by deprivation and hardship.

But what about the British? Did Nova Scotia truly become more secure and stable, once the supposedly insurgent Acadians were gone? In short, no. It would be inaccurate to declare that the Acadians were ever truly 'gone' from Nova Scotia in the first place, notwithstanding the hardships endured and the best efforts of Lawrence and his successors. The 1755 campaign deported fewer than half of the total Acadian population of the region.[62] As has been shown, small groups found ways to stay, and even more found ways to return. Almost a decade later, the governor of Nova Scotia, then Montague Wilmot (who had served at Fort Cumberland as a lieutenant colonel during the initial expulsion), was still wrestling with the same security concerns that had worried British leadership after the Treaty of Utrecht. Wilmot reported back to London that the Acadian population remaining in Nova Scotia were 'most inflexibly devoted to France and the Romish Religion, and being much connected with the Indians by intermarriages, their power and disposition to be mischievous is more to be dreaded'.[63] Furthermore, Wilmot reported that the Acadians were lazy, expensive and 'inconsistent with the safety of (the Province)' – the same complaints that Nova Scotian leadership had been registering against the Acadians for more than half a century.[64] One historian characterized the Acadians as a 'fifth-column'.[65] The frustrated governor lamented that the Acadians could not be relocated for a second time, but recognized the futility of such a measure, given the Acadians' demonstrated tenacity in returning 'after their expulsion in the year 1755 ... from so considerable a distance as South Carolina' and their subsequent 'audacity to attack the King's Troops more than once'.[66]

Notes

1. John Mack Faragher, *A Great and Noble Scheme: The Tragic Story of the Expulsion of the French Acadians from their American Homeland* (New York: W. W. Norton and Company, 2005), 394.
2. Geoffrey Plank, *An Unsettled Conquest: The British Campaign against the Peoples of Acadia* (Philadelphia: University of Pennsylvania Press, 2001), 149. See also Carl A. Brasseaux, *The Founding of New Acadia: The Beginnings of Acadian Life in Louisiana, 1763–1803* (Baton Rouge: Louisiana State University Press, 1987) and M. A. MacDonald, *Fortune & La Tour: The Civil War in Acadia* (Toronto: Methuen, 1983).
3. Faragher, *A Great and Noble Scheme*, 4–5.
4. Ibid., 6.
5. These echoes of colonial influence reminded me forcibly of the American Southwest, where a vibrant Hispanic community serves as a reminder of Spanish colonial power followed by Mexican rule that did not diminish until well into the mid-nineteenth century.
6. Arthur Wentworth Hamilton Eaton, *The History of Kings County Nova Scotia, Heart of the Acadian Land* (Salem: The Salem Press Company, 1910), 26.
7. For some idea of size: at the time of the expulsion, the colonial militia burned 225 houses, 276 barns, 11 mills and multiple outbuildings in the district of Grand Pré alone. See Ibid., 28.
8. Eaton, *The History of Kings County Nova Scotia*, 32.
9. Ibid., 21.
10. John Grenier, *The Far Reaches of Empire: War in Nova Scotia, 1710–1760* (Norman: University of Oklahoma Press, 2008), 63.
11. Ibid., 65–6.
12. Treaty of Utrecht, Article XII, The text of the treaty may be found at https://en.wikisource.org/wiki/Peace_and_Friendship_Treaty_of_Utrecht_between_Spain_and_Great_Britain (accessed 4 December 2018).
13. Treaty of Utrecht, Article XIV; emphasis added by author.
14. J. W. Fortescue, *A History of the British Army, Volume II* (London: MacMillan and Co., Limited, 1899), 257.
15. Ibid., 257.
16. Commissioners for Adjusting the Boundaries for the British and French Possessions in America, *The Memorials of the English and French Commissaries Concerning the limits of Nova Scotia or Acadia* (London, 1755), French Memorials, 1.

17 Commissioners for Adjusting the Boundaries for the British and French Possessions in America, *The Memorials of the English and French Commissaries Concerning the limits of Nova Scotia or Acadia* (London, 1755), French Memorials, 4.
18 Thomas B. Akins (ed.), *Selections from the Public Documents of the Province of Nova Scotia* (Halifax, NS: C. Annand, 1869), 391.
19 Plank, *An Unsettled Conquest*, 62.
20 Ibid., 42, 62–5.
21 Akins, *Selections from the Public Documents of the Province of Nova Scotia*, 377.
22 Plank, *An Unsettled Conquest*, 55.
23 Ibid., 59.
24 Ibid., 87.
25 Francis Parkman, *Montcalm and Wolfe* (Barnes and Noble reprint of the 1884 edition), 49. American historian Parkman presents an exceptionally pro-British version of these events.
26 Statement of Davidson, 13 December 1749 and Statement of Captain-General Edward Cornwallis, 23 December 1749, Akins, *Selections from the Public Documents of the Province of Nova Scotia*, 177.
27 Ibid.
28 Parkman, *Montcalm and Wolfe*, 58.
29 Ibid., 55.
30 Faragher, *A Great and Noble Scheme*, 272–3.
31 Ibid., 273.
32 Ibid., 274.
33 Ibid., 274–5.
34 Ibid., 275.
35 Akins, *Selections from the Public Documents of the Province of Nova Scotia*, 410.
36 Ibid.
37 Faragher, *A Great and Noble Scheme*, 296, Akins, *Selections from the Public Documents of the Province of Nova Scotia*, 384.
38 Akins, *Selections from the Public Documents of the Province of Nova Scotia*, 380.
39 Parkman, *Montcalm and Wolfe*, 134–6.
40 Ibid., 302.
41 Ibid., 298.
42 Eaton, *The History of Kings County Nova Scotia*, 31.
43 Faragher, *A Great and Noble Scheme*, 349.
44 As quoted in Faragher, *A Great and Noble Scheme*, Front Matter.
45 Akins, *Selections from the Public Documents of the Province of Nova Scotia*, 421. Emphasis in original.

46 Ibid., 297–8, 301.
47 Ibid., 301.
48 Edmund Burke, 'Speech on Presenting to the House of Commons, February 11, 1780, A Plan for the Better Security of the Independence of Parliament, and the Economical Reform of the Civil and Other Establishments', in *The Works of Edmund Burke, Vol. 2* (Boston, MA: Freeman and Bolles, Printers, 1839), 216.
49 Akins, *Selections from the Public Documents of the Province of Nova Scotia*, 294.
50 Ibid., 294.
51 Ibid., 296.
52 Ibid., 300.
53 Ibid., 301.
54 Ibid., 301–2.
55 Ibid., 303.
56 Faragher, *A Great and Noble Scheme*, 375.
57 Ibid.
58 Ibid., 375–6.
59 Akins, *Selections from the Public Documents of the Province of Nova Scotia*, 304.
60 Ibid., 304.
61 See also Manning Hawthorne and Henry Wadsworth Longfellow Dana, 'The Origin of Longfellow's "Evangeline"', *The Papers of the Bibliographical Society of America*, Vol. 41, No. 3 (Third Quarter, 1947), 165–203.
62 Faragher, *A Great and Noble Scheme*, 393.
63 Akins, *Selections from the Public Documents of the Province of Nova Scotia*, 344.
64 Ibid., 344–5.
65 Allen E. Begnaud, 'Acadian Exile', *The Journal of the Louisiana Historical Association*, Vol. 5, No. 1(Winter, 1964), 87–91.
66 Akins, *Selections from the Public Documents of the Province of Nova Scotia*, 345.

2

The Long Walk of the Navajo:

Relocation in the American Southwest

Dr Jonathan F. Phillips

Introduction

When considering examples of 'relocation' in Native American history, one naturally thinks of the removal of Eastern tribes from their ancestral homes to lands west of white settlement, and with the passage of the Indian Removal Act of 1830, to government parcels west of the Mississippi River. The Cherokee 'Trail of Tears' of the 1830s is the best known example of 'relocation' of an Eastern tribe although the Florida Seminoles, beginning in the 1820s, endured a decade's long relocation effort by federal authorities. Yet, these types of relocation differ from those typically undertaken during a counterinsurgency operation. The removal of the Cherokees was not conducted by a government in an attempt to weaken or end an insurgency as the tribe had already assimilated, willingly so, into the greater American society and had accepted, even embraced, federal government authority.[1] In the case of the Florida Seminoles, in what is called the Second Seminole War, the removal actions by federal authorities actually caused the insurgency.[2] Thus, the Cherokees and Seminole episodes are not examples of counterinsurgency relocation; there was no intent to decouple insurgents from their means of support or separate insurgents from other, more peaceful members of the same group (Map 3).

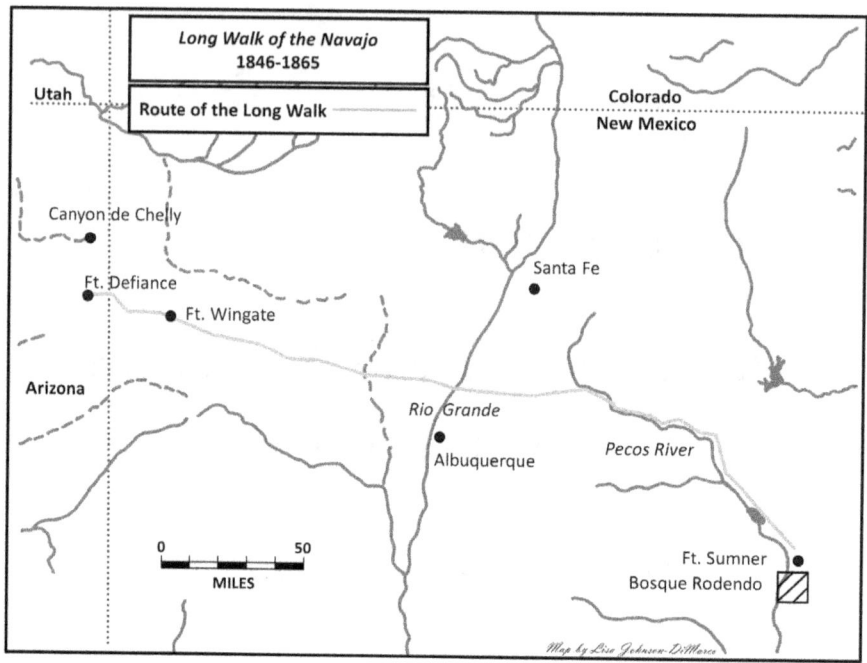

MAP 3 *The Long Walk of the Navajo. The forcible relocation of the Navajos to the Bosque Rodendo Reservation was the result of nineteen-year period of nearly constant wars and quasi-wars between the United States and Native Americans in the American Southwest. In the end, the surviving Navajo lost their homelands and much of their cultural identity.*

Relocation as an actual component of a counterinsurgency operation would more clearly manifest itself west of the Mississippi, especially in the subjugation campaigns in areas taken as a result of the Mexican War. In addition to gaining vast tracts of land, the victorious United States also acquired long running insurgencies in what would become the American Southwest. Indigenous peoples, most prominently and persistently the Navajo and Apache, had challenged Spanish and then Mexican rule for over three centuries. This collision of peoples and cultures, and the resulting interaction, impacted Native American societies in different ways. The Apache continued their nomadic, hunter gatherer means of sustenance while the Navajo became horse and sheep raisers, as well as agriculturalists, adopting and embracing Spanish customs, and trading and intermarrying extensively with those of European heritage. In addition, with their mastery of horses, the Navajo expanded their reach and increased their interaction with other indigenous peoples. The arrival of the horse impacted Navajo society almost as much as it did the peoples of the Great Plains; raiding became a means of livelihood and status gain. Overall, the complex, interactive relationship of the Navajo and Spanish New Mexicans, sometimes warring adversaries, sometimes trading partners, often at the same time, would make conflict resolution especially complicated.[3]

The legacies of conquest

By 1600, the patterns of conflict in what is now the American Southwest had been well established. Indigenous peoples fought each other even within the tribal unit, joined forces to push back against colonial overlords, and occasionally allied with colonial overlords to protect themselves from attacks perpetrated by other tribes. Warfare could be best described as episodic. Land encroachment, typically the most serious cause for conflict between colonial occupiers and indigenous peoples elsewhere in the Americas, did not play a prominent role in New Mexico until the mid-1800s with the arrival of the Americans. Instead, the acquisition of slaves drove conflict.[4]

Beginning in the 1500s, and contrary to the laws of Spain, indigenous peoples were captured and enslaved on a regular basis, sometimes as part of the *encomienda* or *repartimiento* system but more likely not. The Spanish and later Mexican lust for human chattel, and not land, was the primary cause of conflict with the Navajo. Of course, to be fair, the Navajo rarely missed an opportunity to steal livestock from their indigenous neighbours or from the Spanish, and captured slaves on occasion as well. Beginning in the early 1800s, the Navajo enjoyed a few decades of relative peace with the Spaniards and used this opportunity to dominate the weaker and less numerous indigenous peoples of the region; the Navajo were considered bullies by lesser tribes. From this point forward, the Navajo would face almost continuous warfare against the Spanish, the Mexicans (after 1822) and finally the Americans. And with the arrival of the Americans, land encroachment finally did figure prominently in the cause of conflict.[5]

On 15 August 1846, American General Stephen Watts Kearny announced to the people of Santa Fe, in eastern New Mexico, that their province now belonged to the United States. He emphasized that they would be well treated by their new rulers and, most important, would now receive the protection that they had never enjoyed under Spanish and then Mexican rule. 'The Apaches and Navajos come down from the mountains and carry off your sheep, and even your women, whenever they please. My government will correct all of this. It will keep off the Indians, protect you in your persons and property.'[6] He said nothing of the Mexican practice of kidnapping and enslaving Navajo children, sometimes with the assistance of other Navajos. In the decades to follow, Kearny and his successors would learn that correcting all of this would be far more easily said than done.[7]

The evolution of a vocabulary and policy

The US government never grasped the complexity of the conflict and, as a result, would fail to adopt a coherent, effective and humane policy for the indigenous peoples now under its care. In the end, the Navajo (and some of their Apache brethren) would be forced on their own 'trail of tears' in 1864, dubbed the 'Long Walk', as General James F. Carleton and his troops, in a series of *forced marches*, not 'walks', drove the majority of Navajos to Bosque Redondo some 400 miles to the east of their homeland in an attempt to turn Indian herders into white farmers and to separate the 'good' Navajo from the 'bad' Navajo. One of the leading authorities on US Army pacification campaigns would go so far as to say that Carleton, in forcing the Navajos eastward, sought to protect them from their white neighbours.[8] Perhaps, but he couldn't have selected a less hospitable venue than Bosque Redondo if he had tried to do so. As historian Lynn Bailey noted, 'The once "Lords of New Mexico" grubbed out a meagre existence from alkali impregnated soil, or died of dysentery from saline water, and syphilis contracted from the garrison. ... Navajos would reckon all future events from that day.' The government would eventually recognize the error of its ways, and in 1868 the Navajo were allowed to return to their ancestral homelands. Carleton considered the campaign a stunning success – a justification of the Indian Bureau's reservation policy as well as a demonstration of the effectiveness of the scorched earth, 'hard hand' of war tactics that eventually brought the Navajo to heel. And, Carleton had a point; the Navajo were deeply impacted by the tragedy along the Pecos River and never challenged the authority of the government again.[9]

Just as the Cherokees are remembered for their forcible removal, the Apache are remembered as the dominant warrior people in the Southwest. Their distant cousins, the Navajo, are typically presented as peaceful nineteenth-century herder-farmers or remembered for their contributions during the Second World War as 'code talkers'. While the Navajo were certainly farmers, hence Navajo, a Tewa-Pueblan word meaning those that have farmland or large cultivated areas, they were hardly peaceful. Thus, there are those who argue that the Pueblos actually had a more derogatory term for the people typically called the Navajo or 'Navahu', Apachu Navajo, literally, 'Apaches who farm', which some interpret as 'thieves who farm'.[10] Yet it is these 'thieves who farm', and not the Apache, who would prove to be the greatest threat to the governance and stability of New Mexico in the 1850s and 1860s. Only with the eventual pacification of the Navajo, who refer to themselves as the Dine, could the Apache claim mantel of the Southwest's most determined and effective warriors.

General Kearny's 1846 Santa Fe speech was particularly ill timed as the Navajo were approaching the peak of their power. With a population of approximately 13,000 including some 2,500 warriors, these farming, herding and hunting people proved to be far more prosperous, organized and numerous than either the Utes, of northern New Mexico and Colorado, or the Apaches, and far more militarily capable than the Utes. As historian Robert Utley has noted, 'The Navajos acknowledged no masters and accommodated themselves to no aliens.'[11] It would remain to be seen how the small and largely scattered US occupation forces would back up General Kearny's claims.

By the early fall of 1846, General Kearny concluded that his assertive posture had little impact on the behaviour of the Utes and Navajos, both of whom continued their depredations in western New Mexico. Kearny decided to return to the oft attempted carrot and stick approach, or in this case, more precisely treaty or war. He instructed his commanders to meet with Navajo leaders and enact a peace treaty that included all warring parties: the Navajo, the New Mexicans and the Anglo-Americans. If the carrot did not work, then the stick would be applied forcefully. Of course, what he failed to mention is that his policy to this point had been all stick and no carrot – and it had failed miserably.[12]

In the attempt to reach out to the Navajo, Kearny's negotiating team enlisted the support of a band of 'enemy Navajos', members of the tribe who not only had broken away from the greater Navajo community of clans but had also allied themselves with the New Mexicans and regularly captured and enslaved other Navajo for the purposes of selling them to the New Mexicans. Needless to say, the other Navajo leaders were reluctant to meet with Kearny's soldiers, knowing that they were being advised and guided by the 'enemy Navajo' band. The American negotiators told the Navajo that the United States had taken possession of New Mexico from the Mexican government. The Americans wanted to live peacefully with the Navajo, protect the Navajo from the New Mexicans, but also protect New Mexicans from the Navajo. The Navajos were confused by the entreaties of the American soldiers. After all, were not the Navajo fighting New Mexicans, just like the Americans?[13]

Ultimately, the Navajo were persuaded by the economic argument, that is, the American soldiers guaranteed mutual trade among all of the parties as long as the parties agreed to return all of the stolen property. The Navajos, at least the heads of the clans present, agreed to the treaty – and then promptly ignored the terms and continued their predations. As historians have noted, it would have taken a little more than a 'treaty' to change 250 years of behaviour. Also, the Navajo had no real sense of the power of the US government. The military, for its part, failed to understand that the Navajo did not have a central political authority with whom one could negotiate a treaty; the Navajo tribe was, in essence, a loose collection of bands.[14]

Within a year, the American army would be dispatched westward to give the Indians a thorough 'chastising'. Military leadership initially concluded that this follow-on expedition in the spring of 1847, one that included New Mexican irregulars, brought the Navajo to heel, but ultimately it had the opposite effect as the Navajo increased their depredations.[15] During the following four years of military governance, the situation remained largely unchanged as the American government struggled to develop a coherent policy or devote sufficient resources to the Navajo insurgency.[16]

As a result of continuing aggression in the late 1840s, the New Mexican civilian government pushed for more stick and less carrot. Legislators advocated for a range of 'total war' options, from annihilation to enslavement, and urged the outmanned military to move aggressively against the Navajo menace.[17] Far to the east in Washington, DC, US government officials also struggled with what to do although they certainly recognized that the outcome of the Mexican War required a change in Native American policy.[18]

The 'Jeffersonian' solution to the so-called Indian problem had been the policy of removal, so aggressively pursued by Presidents James Monroe and Andrew Jackson against the Cherokees and Seminoles. Simply put, remove the Native Americans from eastern lands and put them out west in lands not inhabited by whites. Little thought was given to the impact of this policy on either the Eastern tribes removed or the Western tribes who suddenly found themselves crowded by recent arrivals.[19]

Throughout the 1830s and 1840s, eastern Native Americans ceded 100 million acres of their lands and were forced to live on 32 million acres west of the 95th meridian. Some groups experienced multiple episodes of migration as they were forced off land initially granted when said land became desirable by whites for agriculture, grazing, transportation corridors, or mineral extraction.[20]

Prior to the outbreak of hostilities with Mexico, the United States had established military posts from Minnesota to Louisiana, in theory delineating eastern white lands from what was called the 'permanent Indian frontier'. One prominent historian of the era dubbed this frontier a 'tantalizing abstraction', one that never actually existed, but even in theory 'crumbled' with the arrival of American troops during the Mexican War and eventually 'collapsed altogether' in the 1850s with the flood of whites seeking opportunity in the vast American West.[21] Just as American whites had forced their government to 'remove' Native Americans in the 1830s and 1840s; whites now demanded action from their government to solve the new 'Indian Problem', caused by the Western movement of these very whites themselves into the Trans-Mississippi West.[22]

'Indian policy' in the wake of the Mexican War focused on three primary objectives in the Trans-Mississippi West: protection of white settlers, nullification or rejection of titles held by Native Americans for land now possessed or desired by whites, and the redistribution of Native Americans within what could no longer be called the 'Permanent Indian Frontier'.[23] In 1846 in support of this policy, Congress authorized funding for a series of forts along the Oregon Trail as well as for a small force to occupy them. With this action, President James Knox Polk claimed in 1848 that the army was sufficiently robust for 'all contingencies' but no official stationed in the West agreed with him. This small Western force 'confronted a new geography and a new enemy'.[24] As the soldiers soon learned, life in the West was hard enough with the extreme climactic conditions and inhospitable terrain, which, when combined with the vast size of the region, made logistics especially challenging; the effectiveness of the enemy made this difficult situation just that much more challenging. The peoples of the 'West' proved to be very adept at guerrilla warfare. Most were mounted and masters of their particular environment, and many, especially those in the Southwest, were experienced in confronting conventional military units thanks to centuries of practice against the Spanish and later the Mexicans.[25]

As was seen in New Mexico in the late 1840s, and was all too often the case, the US military units did what they could do against these very capable insurgents, not necessarily what needed to be done. And, the majority of the forts were located where the white settlers wanted them, not where they needed to be most effective militarily. Typically, the military would send out patrols, too small and too few to have much impact on Native American behaviour. Occasionally, the army would send viable offensive units into the hinterlands but they met with limited success, typically bested by climate, vast distances and a wily foe that fought by its own rules and not those of a European-type military. Most policy makers, to be fair, recognized that a string of small outposts did not represent a viable solution to the challenges in the Trans-Mississippi West.[26] Some even had the foresight to recognize, in current-day parlance, that the long-term problem would not have a military solution.

Indicative of the 'civilianization' of the thinking at the time, the Bureau of Indian Affairs, created in 1824, was moved to the Department of the Interior when the latter was established in 1849. Its senior official, the Commissioner of Indian Affairs, oversaw a network of superintendents and agents in the field. At its most basic level, this organization made sense because it provided civilian 'boots on the ground' who could develop expertise and perspective over time, even if they did not begin their duties with the requisite knowledge. Unfortunately, in a time before the formalization of the civil servant, the system was vulnerable to the evils of the spoils system, often resulting in the appointment of incompetent and corrupt agents. To make matters worse, in the West, the superintendent was typically 'dual hatted' as the territorial governor, thus almost guaranteeing partisan political influence.[27]

The Indian Bureau focused on nullifying Native American land titles and figuring out what to do with those people dispossessed of their land; both actions directly impacted the Navajo in New Mexico and Arizona. The bureau's leadership felt confident that it could artfully employ deceptive treaty language that would guarantee nullification. What to do about the dispossessed people now that the Permanent Indian Frontier no longer existed proved to be far more problematic. The eventual solution originated from James Knox Polk's Commissioner of Indian Affairs, William Medell, who recommended that the bureau create 'colonies' for Native Americans in the Trans-Mississippi West. This would allow whites to settle on the remaining and generally far more desirable land. Informal reservations had existed east of the Mississippi for decades, but the concept did not harden into official policy until the 1850s.[28]

In the simplest terms, reservations were intended to 'concentrate' Native Americans on tracts of land in order to keep them away from whites. Those who saw reservations as a moral good argued that the policy would keep Native Americans from being contaminated by whites while also providing opportunities for the resettled to learn how to farm and embrace the ways of Christian civilization. Of course, the policy also removed Native Americans from the most desirable lands and kept them away from travel routes. Thus, those who saw the Native American as noble savages and those who saw them as just plain savages found much to like in the policy of reservations. As one historian has noted, politicians 'often disagreed on which lands to set aside and how much to pay for them, but the policy itself attracted broad and consistent support'.[29]

Ultimately, the shift from a policy of removal to one of the reservations was more continuation than departure. After all, movement to a reservation policy still meant removal to a less than desirable location for Native Americans and to an area not wanted by whites. On occasion, it resulted in indigenous peoples staying on ancestral homelands, just the smaller and typically less desirable portion of it. This shift in policy did, however, enable later relocation efforts because it brought the process of forcible movements of people down from the strategic to the operational level. Strategic-level removal and the establishment of reservations could be war aims with the intention of subjugation; they were ends in themselves. Alternatively, operational-level relocation as was eventually practised in the Southwest was part of a strategy to reach the desired end of pacification and subjugation.

Developing a treaty-based approach

The treaty remained the primary vehicle employed by the Indian Bureau to carry out nullification of land deeds and eventual movement to reservations. And, as was seen repeatedly, American policy makers rarely felt obligated to adhere to the agreement, or at least did not feel as obligated as they would with a European nation.[30] As historian Robert Utley noted, 'Whatever a group's experience, sooner or later it involved a treaty council. Government emissaries appeared, treaty in hand, and the bargaining began over the transfer of title to a larger share of the group's traditional range and the definition of a small tract, increasingly called a reservation, within which people were now to live.'[31]

Such was the case with the Laguna Negra Treaty of 1855. Pursued by David Meriwether, the governor of the Territory of New Mexico *and* the superintendent of Indian Affairs, the Laguna Negra Treaty sought to reach an agreement with all of the New Mexico indigenous peoples, especially with Navajo, considered by whites to be the biggest troublemakers. The behaviour of the Navajo had been monitored since 1853 by a small contingent of soldiers at a post of relative insignificance, ambitiously named Fort Defiance, located to the east of the Navajo homeland.[32] For the past few years, a precarious peace had existed between the Navajo and the military, in part due to the balanced leadership of the local military commander, Major Henry L. Kendrick, and the presence of Fort Defiance. Considering that the military had its hands full with other tribes in the region, the relative quiet from the Navajos was a welcome relief. But most of the credit was due in large part to the presence and actions of a remarkably capable local agent, Henry Dodge, assigned to the Navajo in 1853, a member of the famous Iowa political family. Dodge married a Native American and was known for his almost constant engagement with the Navajo as he travelled from one end of the homeland to the other. He managed to keep the most aggressive Navajo in check although banditry continued on a smaller scale.[33]

Even with the presence of the conscientious Dodge, the treaty negotiations of 1855 took on a familiar form. The US officials tried to make a very bad deal for the Navajo look like a generous offer, complete with annuity payments and the retention of a large portion of Navajo ancestral lands. The Navajo representatives listened intently but probably never understood that the treaty would take away most of their ancestral lands and force them to live in an area half the size of their existing territory.[34] And, as was all too often the case in negotiations with Native Americans, the government assumed that the Navajo leadership actually had the power to control all of the respective clans. Whites correctly assessed that many indigenous groups were at least somewhat democratic; they incorrectly concluded that someone was in charge overall. The Navajo's political system of the 1850s could be best described as anarchic, with no single entity actually in charge.[35]

Regardless, once the treaty was signed, the Navajo made no effort to live by it. No one moved to the correct side of the 'dividing line', the first attempt made to create a boundary between the Navajo and the New Mexicans. The treaty also required the Navajo to 'surrender tribesmen' guilty of crimes to the whites so that they could be punished according to the laws of New Mexico.[36] And, even though the Navajo ignored the treaty as they had so many others, at least in this case they ignored a document that turned out to be illegitimate as the US Senate refused to consent to ratification due to the high cost of the annuities. Irrespective of its illegitimacy, the failure of the Navajo to abide by the treaty provided the justification for more aggressive actions by whites in the near future.[37]

From the Navajo perspective, the white authorities responded to Indian depredations with what could best be described as a timorous response, especially in the aftermath of a vicious Navajo raid in the spring of 1856 on a group of New Mexicans at an outpost called Peralta.[38] As one historian has noted, the army 'could not put a command in the field capable of doing more than advertising ... [its] weakness'.[39] With the death of Henry Dodge, killed by Mogollon Apaches in 1857, the sole remaining voice of moderation was gone. In some respects, New Mexico was experiencing its own political crisis of the 1850s, and much like the crisis to the east, each side continued to take escalatory steps that only worsened the situation.[40]

The late 1850s saw a return to the internecine warfare that had dominated the conflict since Kearny's strong words of 1846. In August 1858, the army dispatched a force of some 300 into Canyon de Chelly, the heart of Navajo country, in a raid of retribution. This, followed by a latter raid, persuaded the Navajo leaders that it was time, once again, for 'peace talks' at Fort Defiance. The stipulations of the agreement, dubbed the Christmas Accord, lasted for little more than a year, but by early 1860, the 'war' party Navajos were once again in the ascendancy as the Navajos became tired of the restrictions placed upon them by the Christmas Accord. By late April 1860, the troops at Fort Defiance found themselves under assault from a force approaching a thousand warriors. The army and its Native American auxiliaries would respond in kind with a multi-pronged attack led by names known well to Civil War historians: Canby, McLaws and Sibley. This operation eventually failed due as much to a drought as to enemy opposition.

Secretary of War Floyd ordered a follow-on expedition in which infantry and not cavalry would be used. In a departure from the 'total war' methods typically employed by the army, Floyd urged a more humanitarian approach, thus avoiding 'wantonly destroying their flocks and herds'.[41] The army under Colonel Edward Canby's command largely ignored Floyd's directive, at least the humanitarian aspect, but it did use infantry, and did so effectively, so much so that by January 1861, the 'peace' faction of the Navajos seriously considered how they could cooperate with the army against the 'war' faction. Further complicating the situation, in the fall of 1860, New Mexican Volunteer irregular units engaged in predatory acts that strengthened the hand of the 'war' Navajos. By April 1861, the army had good reason to think that it might finally have the Navajos under control, but within a few months a much more dangerous threat from the south, Confederate raiders from Texas, would shift the balance of power in western New Mexico.[42]

With the coming of the Civil War, the already complicated situation for the Navajos became more so. Some Navajos continued to engage in legitimate trade with New Mexicans while both groups continued to raid one another. The army found itself acting as a mediator as much as anything else. But in 1861, the regular army troops departed for the conflict in the east and New Mexico irregulars, typically more bandits than soldiers, donned the blue uniforms of the national army. Further complicating the situation, the Navajos were still divided into two groups, the aforementioned war and peace factions. The war faction, or *ladrones* (thieves), were more likely to be poor, as compared to the peace faction, known as the *ricos* (wealthy), who were, as their name suggests, more prosperous. The *ladrones* tended to live in the hinterlands while the *ricos* lived closer to New Mexican settlements.

The *ladrones* were far more likely to raid New Mexican settlements while the New Mexicans were far more likely to retaliate against the *ricos* who were both more accessible to the New Mexicans and had more to offer in terms of the spoils of raiding. As one historian has noted, 'As the tempo of military activity quickened in the late 1850s, *rico* and *ladrone* became synonymous with peace party and war party. Progressive impoverishment by Hispanic raiders transformed *ricos* into *ladrones*, proportionately swelling the war party and weakening the peace party.'[43]

In the second half of 1861 and early 1862, Navajo raiders took full advantage of the distractions of the greater Civil War and struck hard at New Mexican settlements; this time the spark was, surprisingly, a disagreement over the outcome of a series of horse races at an army post in which Navajo and New Mexican entrees competed against one another. What started as a protest over race results ended in a pitched battle including the employment of field artillery.[44] By the summer, the strategic situation had also changed with the defeat of local Confederate forces; the army could now refocus its attention on the Navajo, as well as the far less numerous but very troublesome Mescalero Apache. In addition, new bluecoats from the west joined with the New Mexicans in order to defeat the Navajo, Apaches and Utes. In this binary and interactive world of *ladrones* and *ricos*, regulars and irregulars, Hispanic and Anglo-Americans, Confederates and Unionists, entered another significant pairing, two army officers with very different backgrounds, who would ultimately shake the Navajo nation to the core.[45]

The relocation decisions

In the second half of 1862, Brigadier General James F. Carleton arrived from California, took command of the Department of New Mexico and renewed his friendship with the famous mountain man turned soldier, Kit Carson, now a colonel of volunteers.[46] Carleton embraced much of Colonel Edward Canby's military and diplomatic 'hard war' approach (focus on means of sustenance not direct combat against Native Americans) of 1860 and 1861 in an aggressive attempt to break the 'deadly pattern of raid and retaliation in which the Navajo and the New Mexican had become locked by generations of practice'.[47] But more important, Canby had concluded by December 1861 that, at least regarding the Navajo, 'there is no choice between their absolute extermination or their removal and colonization at points so remote from the settlements as to isolate them entirely from the inhabitants of the territory'.[48] The army would begin the removal or relocation process with the smaller and less formidable Mescalero Apache. In short order, Union forces and New Mexico volunteers under the command of the Carson, now Colonel of the 1st New Mexico Volunteers, defeated the Mescalero Apaches. Once defeated, Carleton removed the Mescalero from their mountain homeland and dispatched them to the barren landscape of far south-eastern New Mexico. By March 1863, the Mescalero, 400 of a tribe of 500, were forcibly settled in Bosque Redondo (literally 'round grove of trees') along an unusually dry part of the already dry Pecos River. It was here that the Apaches would learn how to be civilized, learn how to farm, learn how to act like white people, all under the watchful eye of federal troops stationed at the recently built Fort Sumner.[49] For Carleton, Bosque Redondo served as both a test and a vindication of the Indian Bureau's reservation policy. Here, Native Americans would learn how to read and write, and embrace Christianity. He noted that as older Native Americans died off, so too would their 'murdering and robbing ways'. The next generation would act just like white Americans. The Navajos knew that they were next.[50]

In the spring of 1863, two peace party Navajo leaders, Barboncito and Delgadito, met with Carleton. Carleton made it very clear to them that he was determined to separate 'good' Navajos from 'bad' Navajos; a good Navajo must agree to relocate to Bosque Redondo, just like the Mescalero, and would have until 20 July to submit to federal authority and move to the Pecos River reservation. After July, any Navajo found in western New Mexico and Arizona would be considered 'hostile and treated accordingly'.[51]

The Navajos would learn quickly that Carleton was a man of his word. Carson and the New Mexican volunteers were dispatched into the ancestral Navajo homeland, sweeping around Canyon de Chelly and the Little Colorado, in a series of 'total war' raids designed to kill people, but more importantly to destroy crops, and wherever possible, 'seize' livestock. Other native peoples joined in, sensing an opportunity to profit from the Carson raids and enjoy a bit of 'payback' against the notoriously bullying Navajo.[52] By the end of 1863, the Navajo were on their knees and could do little in January of 1864 when Carson and his men struck directly through Canyon de Chelly, the citadel that represented the heart of Navajo country. Dozens of Navajo surrendered as they watched their herds seized and fruit trees destroyed. By March, 6,000 Navajo camped around army posts awaiting deportation to Bosque Redondo. The 'Long Walk', the Navajo's 'Trail of Tears' started henceforth – a 400 hundred mile journey to the barren Pecos River bottom. By the end of 1864, some 8,000 Navajo, the great majority of the tribe, had arrived at Bosque Redondo, and now shared their suffering with their cousins, the Mescalero, an enemy for the past century.[53]

But not all Navajos surrendered in 1864. Several groups remained at large and refused to submit to federal authority. The most prominent holdout was Manuelito, the 'first among equals' in Navajo leadership. Manuelito had been considered a *rico* until continuing depredations by Carson's men forced him into the 'war' party camp.[54] His band retreated far to the north along the Little Colorado River, temporarily out of reach of the bluecoats. After surviving the harsh winter, Manuelito's people moved south to the outpost now known as Fort Canby.[55] He let the army know that he intended to settle there, grow crops and let his band's sheep graze. The army answered with a resounding no. 'There is but one place for you', the commander replied, 'and that is to go to the Bosque'. Manuelito feared that the people would be attacked as soon as they congregated for the move, much like the experience at the horse races a few years before. By the fall, Manuelito was the last of the *rico* holdouts.[56]

The few Navajos that had managed to escape Bosque Redondo returned to the homelands with stories of the horrible treatment and wretched conditions experienced along the Pecos. Soldiers treated the Navajo like prisoners of war the army considered them to be. Food and replacement clothing was scarce, firewood even scarcer and shelter unavailable – but crop-killing insects were in abundance as were other native peoples ready and willing to steal what sheep remained. Malnutrition and exposure weakened immune systems and hundreds perished. The soldiers contributed little but venereal disease and poor management; the troops suffered from the extreme conditions and poor supply as well. The Navajo, even in their depleted state, still found ways to bully the Mescaleros.[57]

Measuring the outcomes

General Carleton, of course, saw the experiment at Bosque Redondo as an unalloyed success. 'There is no reason why they will not be the most happy and prosperous and well-provided-for Indians in the United States.' He recognized that the Pecos River settlement was costly, but 'we can feed them cheaper than we can fight them'.[58] His follow-on comments were very telling regarding his true motivation for Bosque Redondo and demonstrate the great variety of motives and rationalizations for the establishment of reservations. In 1861, Colonel Canby had concluded that the Navajo must be either exterminated or sent far away, to separate them from the inhabitants of the territory, and by inhabitants of the territory he meant non-Native American inhabitants.[59] Carleton had previously stated that he saw Bosque Redondo as an opportunity to separate good Indians (*rico* or peace party) from bad Indians (*ladrone* or war party) in order to weaken the bad Indians, somewhat in line with classic counterinsurgency relocation strategy. Carleton had overlooked the fact that the army's operations to date had actually accomplished to opposite and had driven many Navajo, most of them reluctantly, into the war faction. But, like many others who supported the greater reservation efforts writ large, Carleton *also* saw the reservation as a vehicle for Christianizing and 'American-izing' the Navajo with the hope that future generations would forsake their 'murdering and robbing ways', as previously mentioned.[60]

But now that the great majority of Mescalero and Navajo had been removed from their homelands and firmly if unfortunately settled along the Pecos, General Carleton revealed a less noble reason for relocation. 'When it is considered what a magnificent pastoral and mineral country they have surrendered to us—a country whose value can hardly be estimated—the mere pittance, in comparison, which must at once be given to support them, sinks into insignificance as a price for their natural heritage.'[61] Carleton sought to 'spin' this rationale and emphasize the importance of generously providing for the Navajo because they have given up so much or, as he put it, 'Feeling that having sacrificed to us their beautiful country, their homes, the associations of their lives, the scenes rendered classic in their traditions, we will not dole out to them a miser's pittance in return for what they know to be and what we know to be a princely realm.'[62]

But one prominent Navajo chief, Manuelito, arguably the most important of all, had not surrendered. As long as Manuelito and his band remained free from captivity, Carleton could not claim complete success. Manuelito served as a beacon, a lodestar, and a rallying point for those Navajo who managed to escape the clutches of the army at Fort Sumner and Bosque Redondo and made their way north and west to the ancestral homeland or had managed to avoid subjugation by hiding.[63]

In February of 1865, Carleton sent Manuelito a message stating that his people, now numbering about a hundred, must surrender before spring or face extermination. Manuelito wavered on whether or not to surrender, especially after meeting with other Navajo leaders sent up from Bosque Redondo, but finally decided to stand firm. Carleton tried to work a deal with the neighbouring Zunis to trick and capture Manuelito, as he occasionally met with them to resupply, but he was too wily to be captured in that manner. The army had enough trouble dealing with the near constant Bosque Redondo escapes to devote complete energy to capturing Manuelito. Another senior Navajo leader, Barboncito, slipped away to freedom in the late summer of 1865.[64]

Crop failures in the fall only increased the death rate along the Pecos and also resulted in greater numbers of escapees. Much to Carleton's surprise, New Mexicans were now criticizing the poor conditions at Bosque Redondo, less from a sense of decency and more from the fact that a poorly run reservation resulted in larger numbers of escapees, and these free Navajos and Mescaleros would likely want their homelands back. Finally, almost a year later, in September 1866, Manuelito and his small, hungry, sickly and exhausted band capitulated to government forces. 'His surrender', noted historian Robert Utley, 'marked the final triumph of the military campaign, and in route to Bosque Redondo, Carleton had him paraded as a prisoner through the streets of Santa Fe'.[65] With the capitulation of Barboncito a few weeks later, his second time doing so, the Navajo Wars effectively came to an end.[66]

General Carleton's reign in the Department of New Mexico came to an end as well just eighteen days after Manuelito's surrender. The region's civilian leadership had tired of his haughtiness and abrasiveness.[67] The Navajo would remain at Bosque Redondo for another two years while the reservation and its governance came under constant criticism. Some officials had humanitarian concerns while others were more interested in financial mismanagement and reducing expenditures. In June 1868, after signing a treaty swearing that they would never again take up arms against Americans, the Navajo were permitted to leave Bosque Redondo by none other than General William Tecumseh Sherman. They returned to their ancestral homelands although the eventual borders of the reservation left much of the most desirable land, especially grazing areas, in the hands of white settlers.[68] In October of 1870, Fort Sumner, the Bosque Redondo post, was sold for the princely sum of $5,000.[69]

Conclusions

The experiment at Bosque Redondo had failed. The notion that the Navajo nation could be transported and transformed proved both illusory and misguided. The army either never understood or chose not to understand the complexity and character of Navajo organization, and consistently pursued policies that ended up driving 'good' Navajo into the 'bad' Navajo camp. Reacting to *ladrone* raids by attacking *rico* Navajos made little sense, and the inability to control the behaviour of New Mexican volunteers led to continual escalation from both sides. Little thought was given to practical applications, instead of unenforceable treaties, that would contribute to de-escalation. While it certainly made sense to 'isolate' actual insurgents from the greater population, the army never figured out how to do so without removal or relocation, actions that would likely lead to the destruction of the Navajo as a people.[70] All that being said, certain Navajo groups proved to be chameleons and played each situation to their best advantage. Historian Robert Wooster noted that, in the context of army operations against Native Americans, 'the department commander who perceived his region as one that welcomed white settlement or offered lucrative natural resources tended to take an aggressive posture against Indians' in contrast to those who saw their region as less fit for whites and, therefore, took a more tolerant approach. This statement certainly applies to Carleton and may explain why the Navajo received so much of his attention while many Apache bands, with the exception of the Mescalero, were largely ignored, at least in the 1860s.[71]

Yet, as ruthless and mistaken as the Canby-Carleton plan may have been, it did achieve the ultimate goal of pacifying the Navajo. Never again would the Dine take up arms against the national government. In fact, substantial numbers of Navajo went on the serve as irregulars *with* the army in campaigns against other Native Americans.[72] Perhaps historian Dee Brown, in his path breaking work, *Bury My Heart at Wounded Knee* (1970), summed up the plight of the Navajo as well as anyone. 'Bad as it was, the Navajos would come to know that they were the least unfortunate of all of the western Indians. For the others, the ordeal had hardly begun.'[73]

While the Navajo were subdued by Carleton's aggressive campaign, the Apaches responded with truculence. Warfare would continue in the Southwest for decades and Carleton's methods continued to be the government's default position. The Apaches who refused to accept reservation life used their remarkable skill and determination to hold the army at bay. When the army got too close, the Apaches would slip across the border into Mexico.[74] In 1875 in an attempt to 'consolidate' reservations, two Apache groups numbering almost 1,500 would be forced off of the Rio Verde Indian Reserve established in their homeland and sent 180 miles to the far less hospitable San Carlos Indian Agency. The Apache were held there for twenty-five years. Very few ever returned to their native land. Certainly by the end of the Indian Wars in the 1880s, the Navajo had come to understand that they were indeed the 'least unfortunate'.[75]

Notes

1 Theda Perdue and Michael D. Green, *The Cherokee Removal: A Brief History with Documents* (Boston, MA: Bedford, St. Martin's Press, 2005), 19–24.

2 John Missall and Mary Lou Missall, *The Seminole Wars: America's Longest Indian Conflict* (Gainesville: University Press of Florida, 2004), 82–92.

3 Peter Iverson, *Dine: A History of the Navajos* (Albuquerque: University of New Mexico Press, 2002), 21–4, 32; Lynn R. Bailey, *The Long Walk: A History of the Navajo Wars, 1846–1868* (Pasadena, CA: Westernlore Publications, 1978), 2–3. The Navajo also adopted agricultural practices from the Pueblo.

4 Frank McNitt, *Navajo Wars: Military Campaigns, Slave Raids, and Reprisals* (Albuquerque: University of New Mexico Press, 1972), 12–15.

5 McNitt, *Navajo Wars*, 3–91, for a review of the Navajo experience before US conquest; Robert M. Utley, *Frontiersmen in Blue: The United States Army and the Indian, 1848–1865* (Lincoln: University of Nebraska Press, 1967), 78–84.

6 Bailey, *The Long Walk*, 1.

7 Ibid., 2; Utley, *Frontiersmen in Blue*, 80–7.

8 Andrew J. Birtle, *US Army Counterinsurgency and Contingency Operations Doctrine, 18601941* (Washington, DC: Center of Military History, US Army, 2003), 82; Iverson, *Dine*, 48–52.

9 Bailey, *The Long Walk*, 1; Robert M. Utley, *The Indian Frontier of the American West, 1846–1890* (Albuquerque: University of New Mexico Press, 1984), 82–4; Utley, *Frontiersmen in Blue*, 243–7.

10 Iverson, *Dine*, 26; Michael Haederle, 'Thief or Fields, It Still Offends', *Los Angeles Times*, 29 October 1992.

11 Utley, *Frontiersmen in Blue*, 80–4, quote on 81.

12 Bailey, *The Long Walk*, 2–4.

13 Iverson, *Dine*, 29; Bailey, *The Long Walk*, 5–14.

14 Bailey, *The Long Walk*, 2–14.
15 Ibid., 2–14.
16 Utley, *Frontiersmen in Blue*, 80–1, 84–5.
17 Bailey, *The Long Walk*, 13.
18 Utley, *Indian Frontier*, 39.
19 Ibid, 37.
20 Ibid.
21 Ibid., 37.
22 Ibid., 39.
23 Ibid., 39–41.
24 Ibid., 40–1, quote on 41.
25 Ibid., 41.
26 Ibid.
27 Ibid., 42.
28 Ibid., 42–6.
29 Ibid., 46.
30 Ibid., 43–4.
31 Ibid., 47.
32 Robert W. Frazer, *Forts of the West: Military Forts and Presidios and Posts Commonly Called Forts West of the Mississippi River to 1898* (Norman: University of Oklahoma Press, 1977, originally published in 1965), 8; Iverson, *Dine*, 41.
33 Utley, *Frontiersmen in Blue*, 165–6.
34 Utley, *Indian Frontier*, 48–51.
35 Utley, *Frontiersmen in Blue*, 166.
36 Ibid., 166.
37 Utley, *Indian Frontier*, 48–51.
38 Utley, *Frontiersmen in Blue*, 167.
39 Ibid., 167.
40 Ibid., 167–8, quote on 167.
41 Ibid., 169–72, quote on 172; Iverson, *Dine*, 47–8.
42 Utley, *Frontiersmen in Blue*, 172–3.
43 Utley, *Indian Frontier*, 81.
44 Utley, *Frontiersmen in Blue*, 238.
45 Utley, *Indian Frontier*, 81–3.
46 Ibid., 82; Utley, *Frontiersmen in Blue*, 234.
47 Utley, *Frontiersmen in Blue*, 237.
48 Ibid., 238.
49 Frazer, *Forts of the West*, 104.

50 Utley, *Indian Frontier*, 82–4; Utley, *Frontiersmen in Blue*, 234–7. See also, Iverson, *Dine*, 48–51.
51 Utley, *Indian Frontier*, 83; Utley, *Frontiersmen in Blue*, 239.
52 Utley, *Indian Frontier*, 84–5; Utley, *Frontiersmen in Blue*, 240.
53 Utley, *Indian Frontier*, 84–5; Utley, *Frontiersmen in Blue*, 243–6.
54 Utley, *Indian Frontier*, 86.
55 Frazer, *Forts of the West*, 8.
56 Dee Brown, *Bury My Heart at Wounded Knee: An Indian History of the American West* (New York: Picador, Henry Holt and Company, 1970), 29–30.
57 Ibid., 30; Utley, *Indian Frontier*, 85; Utley, *Frontiersmen in Blue*, 246; Robert M. Utley and Malcolm Washburn, *Indian Wars* (Boston, MA: Houghton Mifflin Company, 1987, originally published by American Heritage, 1977), 201; Robert M. Utley, *Frontier Regulars, The United States Army and the Indian, 1866–1890* (New York: MacMillan Publishing Co., 1973), 169; Iverson, *Dine*, 59; Bailey, *The Long Walk*, 177–218, for a detailed analysis of the experience at Bosque Redondo.
58 Brown, *Bury My Heart at Wounded Knee*, 30.
59 Utley, *Frontiersmen in Blue*, 238.
60 Utley, *Indian Frontier*, 82–4; Utley, *Frontier Regulars*, 234–7; Iverson, *Dine*, 48–51.
61 Brown, *Bury My Heart at Wounded Knee*, 30–1.
62 Ibid.
63 Ibid., 31.
64 Ibid., 32–3.
65 Utley, *Indian Frontier*, 86; Iverson, *Dine*, 56.
66 Brown, *Bury My Heart at Wounded Knee*, 32–3.
67 For a brief review of Carleton's engagement with local civilian authorities and politics, see Richard N. Ellis, 'The Political Role of the Military on the Frontier', in James B. Tate, editor, *The American Military on the Frontier, Proceedings of the 7th Military History Symposium, United States Air Force Academy, 30 September–1 October 1976* (Washington, DC: Office of Air Force History, Headquarters USAF, and US Air Force Academy, 1978), 76–8. See also, Iverson, *Dine*, 62.
68 Brown, *Bury My Heart at Wounded Knee*, 33–6; Utley, *Frontier Regulars*, 169; Iverson, *Dine*, 62–4, 68. It is worth noting that substantial numbers of Navajo were never caught and forced to move to Bosque Redondo. Some of those who resided in the far western and northwestern sections of Navajo land remained out of reach. See Iverson, *Dine*, 57.
69 Bailey, *The Long Walk*, 1; Frazer, *Forts of the West*, 104.
70 Robert Wooster, *The Military and United States Indian Policy, 1865–1903* (New Haven, CT: Yale University Press, 1988), 198.
71 Ibid., 208.
72 Ibid., 34.

73 Brown, *Bury My Heart at Wounded Knee*, 36; Utley, *Frontier Regulars*, 169.
74 Wooster, *The Military and United States Indian Policy*, 95–6.
75 Utley, *Frontier Regulars*, 169; Wooster, *The Military and United States Indian Policy*, 186–91; Frazer, *Forts of the West*, 9, 11; Utley and Washburn, *Indian Wars*, 193–201, for a brief review of the Apache experience in the 1870s and 1880s.

3

War answered with war:

The Spanish in Cuba

Major Mark Askew

> *By 1900, the Spanish term* reconcentración *had already been translated into English and was used to describe British 'concentration camps'.*
> ROBERT GERWARTH AND STEPHAN MALINOWSKI
> Hannah Arendt's Ghosts, 2009[1]

Introduction

From 1895 to 1898, revolution against Spanish rule swept Cuba, and as a result the island lost more than 10 per cent of its pre-war population.[2] Most of these deaths can be attributed to the implementation of a combination of insurgent and Spanish strategies of 'reconcentration', or relocation, of the Cuban populace (Map 4). Like many rebellions, neither side had much patience or sympathy for people who wanted to remain politically neutral. Thus, when the rebellion in Cuba became island-wide in late 1895, both sides tried to protect areas that were sympathetic to their political goals and to blockade areas that were hostile to them. This chapter will examine whether or not, from a military perspective, population relocation achieved what it was designed to achieve: namely, the pacification of a rebellious colony. Although Spain did make major headway in breaking up the

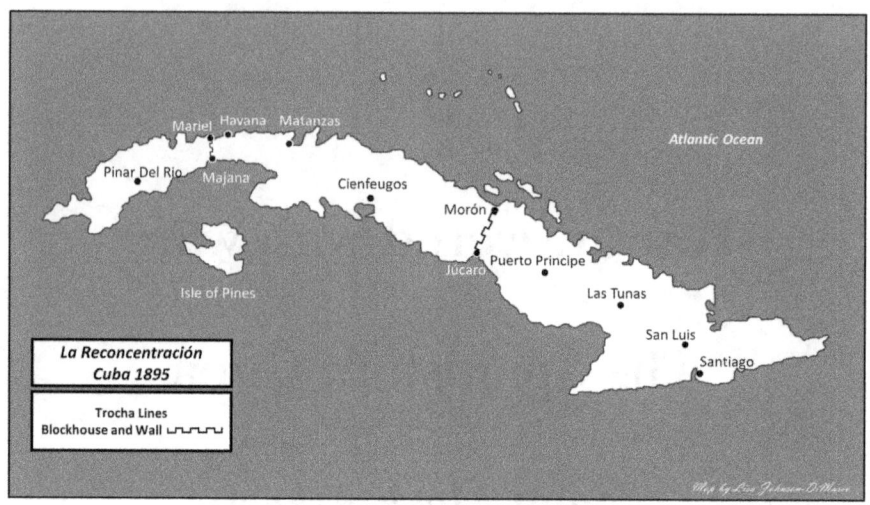

MAP 4 *The Cuban Insurrection. Under an approach called* Reconcentración *Spanish General Valeriano Weyler y Nicolau built fortified lines called* trocha *that divided Cuba into tactically manageable sectors. Within these sectors Weyler forcibly relocated the civilian population so that they could not resupply and assist the Cuban rebels. Weyler's tactics became a template for subsequent forcible relocations in the twentieth century.*

largest concentrations of Cuban insurgents, for the most part, the Cuban Revolution survived in each province. Relocation did not achieve Spain's goals for two reasons: the logistical efforts required by reconcentration were beyond Spain's means and Cuba's insurgent movement exploited the mismanagement of population relocation to build support for independence both in Cuba and abroad. Spain achieved significant positive tactical effects but their shortcomings at the operational level of war limited their strategic options and put Spain on the road to defeat by a combination of US and Cuban forces in 1898.

Strategic overview

Until 1868, Spain ruled Cuba as an overseas dependency with little serious opposition. After 1868, people both in Cuba and in Spain began to challenge the nature of this political relationship. Two uprisings cemented the island's growing involvement in politics: the Ten Years War (1868–78) and 'La Guerra Chequita' (1879–80). During this timeframe and immediately following three major political factions developed on the island: independence-minded activists, the Autonomist Party and the Constitutional Unionists. Most of the island's independence-minded activists had been driven into exile as a result of the previous failed insurrections. Thus by 1880 only the Autonomist Party and the Constitutional Unionists remained.[3]

The Autonomists were native Cubans that believed that the island's best long-term interests were best served by maintaining Spanish rule on the island, albeit with local control of purely island-related affairs and modest economic reforms. In the aftermath of the Ten Years War, the Autonomists had tried, largely in vain, to get Spain to honour many of its promises that had led to the end of the Ten Years War. Spain dismissed out of hand most efforts at even unexceptional administrative reforms in Cuba. Further compounding the Autonomists' problems, Spanish authorities and local Peninsular elites viewed the Autonomist Party as a stalking horse for the independence movement. Spanish officialdom often toyed with the idea of banning the party altogether.[4] Needless to say, the party possessed significant challenges going into 1895.

The main domestic political rivals of the Autonomist Party were the island's Constitutional Unionists. The Constitutional Unionists wanted to retain Peninsular control over the island and continuously lobbied Madrid to defeat any attempts at administrative or economic reform, even those recommended by royal officials in Havana. The local Peninsular Spanish – who made up the rank and file of the Constitutional Unionist Party – viewed the patronage positions within Cuba's government as important symbols that both preserved their wealth and the mechanisms of Spain's colonial rule on the island. Reform, they felt, would place the island on the slippery slope to popular suffrage and the loss of their monopoly on political and economic power.[5]

After the Ten Years War, Spanish officials authorized the introduction of limited popular voting but had rigged the electoral qualifications in such a way that virtually only Peninsular Spaniards possessed any ability to vote. As a result, the Constitutional Unionists dominated these proceedings.[6] As a consequence, neither political party was well situated to deal with mass discontent. The Constitutional Unionists, who possessed the authority, did not have the desire to modify or reform any of the island's institutions. The Autonomists lacked the political power to effect change. Critically, however, both parties agreed that they preferred continued Spanish rule to any other alternative. Thus, the island's politics remained frozen as shifts in the sugar market brought on an island-wide recession in 1894.

The political situation in Spain was little better. Spain remained divided among various social, political, regional and economic interests which occasionally fuelled outbreaks of violence. Violence came from both the political left and the right.[7] Domestically this led to a revolving door of various Spanish governments (both liberal and conservative). Given the political weakness of the Bourbon regency, the army intervened early and often in domestic Spanish politics to maintain order but underlying tensions remained.[8] While there was little unity on questions of domestic policy, there was at least superficial unity on colonial questions. Both the Liberal and Conservative parties believed that Spain's colonies remained integral to Spanish power and remained opposed to any political reforms that might threaten Spanish control. The rapid industrialization of the Basque region and Catalonia (also the most separatist-minded areas in Spain) meant that domestic order in these regions hinged at least in part on the Spanish government's ability to find and protect markets for these provinces' finished goods.[9] Colonies were an important component of fulfilling those goals. Thus, even modest attempts at administrative reform that threatened Peninsular Spanish economic standing (in Spain or Cuba) were decisively defeated in Spain's Cortes.[10]

By late 1894, the political and economic situation in Cuba was ripe for rebellion. Neither the metropole nor the colony had found an adequate balance between the island's interests and those of the mother country. Cuba's economy and society remained volatile. The transition from slave to wage labour had led to new and unfamiliar social problems. Spain had emancipated the island's slaves but had followed through on few other promised reforms. To make matters worse, a Spanish-American trade dispute resulted in the American imposition of sugar tariffs, the island's most important cash crop, and Spain's government refused to make any changes to its colonial trade policy. Sugar production, and by proxy the demand for wage labourers, plummeted. This left many of the colony's agricultural workers angry and idle at just the moment the latest revolt was about to begin.[11]

The rebellion erupts

Revolutionaries outside the island noticed these vulnerabilities and took action too. Jose Martí, a self-starting firebrand and veteran of the Ten Years War, had been clandestinely working for two years to create a united movement composed of civilian and military revolutionary leadership from the Ten Years War behind the banner of his Cuban Revolutionary Party (PRC). Martí believed if Cuba was ever going to realize its independence, the island's military and political leaders would need to improve their organization. The previous failed revolutions had demonstrated the limitations of situational cooperation between insurgent bands. Although an optimist, Martí was also practical and had focused the PRC's efforts on developing a revolutionary movement with political, military and organizational cohesion. Equally important, Martí had garnered the support of the two most important *insurrecto* commanders of the previous war, Máximo Gómez and Antonio Maceo, who agreed that a new revolution would need tighter integration of political and military questions and organization.

In February 1895, Martí orchestrated simultaneous uprisings across the island. His initial efforts in western and central Cuba failed; Spanish forces moved quickly and ruthlessly to stamp out insurgent support in these better developed provinces. In the east, however, Martí succeeded, and the new rebellion survived. By April of 1895, Generals Maceo and Gómez were both on the ground organizing *insurrectos* in eastern Cuba. Spain quickly realized both the seriousness of the revolt and the need to end it as quickly as possible. Thus, Spain assigned General Arsenio Martínez Campos the mission of suppressing Cuba's latest revolutionary movement. The general had served Spain successfully as both a soldier and a diplomat as one of the principle negotiators in the Peace of Zanjón, the treaty that ended the Ten Years War.[12] Thus, by April 1895, Spain and Cuba's *insurrectos* prepared for another long struggle for control of the island's future.

Initially, Martínez Campos sought to isolate the rebellion in eastern Cuba, defeat insurgent bands in the field where he could and negotiate with the rebel leadership once these efforts had exhausted the *insurrectos* revolutionary fervour. This formula had worked perfectly in the Ten Years War. To this end Martínez Campos re-established the Júcaro-Morón *trocha* (a series of fortified blockhouses overlooking a trench) intended to quarantine eastern Cuba from the rest of the island.[13] The general, however, manoeuvred with real disadvantages. Spanish forces on the island were undermanned and were short in every class of supply.[14] Moreover, Spanish forces on the island were often the least experienced and least well-trained men in Spain's already diminished empire. Spanish officers detested service in Cuba to such an extent that to meet the growing demands for officers, the army offered early commissions to its cadets and even commissioned non-commissioned officers.[15] Most everyone, soldier, officer or recently conscripted civilian, paid whatever they could to avoid service on the island.[16] Aware of the gravity of the situation, Martínez Campos pressed the government in Madrid for more men, and they began to shuttle reinforcements into the island almost immediately.

The rebels in the opening stage of the rebellion also focused on applying their own lessons from the Ten Years War. The PRC's civil and military leadership agreed, even before the revolution began, that the new bid for independence had to be an island-wide effort.[17] To that end, Martí had orchestrated uprisings in western and central Cuba that local Spanish troops had crushed almost immediately.[18] Cuba's revolutionaries had to adjust their strategic methods if they hoped to make the rebellion island-wide as originally intended. Fortunately, by the summer of 1895, the PRC's military strength had grown to such an extent in eastern Cuba that Gómez embarked upon a new and bold strategy for the revolution: he would use the Cuban Liberation Army (CLA) to spread the revolution to the rest of the island. To facilitate this aim, Gómez reorganized the CLA into two columns: the Army of Invasion (commanded by Gómez) and the Army of Liberation (commanded by Calixto García). The Army of Invasion would invade western and central Cuba while García consolidated the revolution's gains in the east with the Army of Liberation. Gómez hoped that a Western invasion would allow him to tap into the greater resources and population of Cuba's more developed western provinces.[19]

Invading the west would also facilitate another important component of Cuban strategy: namely, the deliberate destruction of private property on the island. Gómez envisioned Cuba's renewed revolutionary struggle as requiring more sacrifice than the Ten Years War. The root of the problem, he believed, lay in Cuba's prosperity.[20] Inspired by the original inhabitants of Cuba, Gómez believed Cuba's natural wealth and agricultural fertility were 'the cause of her bondage'.[21] Gómez repeatedly asserted to his troops that the only way that the island could ever be truly free was to destroy everything of value.[22] Nor was this an idle rhetorical device. Gómez issued repeated instructions beginning in 1895, often overriding the dicta of the PRC when necessary, to carry out a war against the economic infrastructure of the island. Gómez mandated that all sugar plantations had to be 'destroyed' and that anyone who attempted to grind cane would be treated as a traitor. Gómez ended his circulars thus, 'Let all chiefs of operation of the Liberating Army comply with this order, determined to unfurl even on ruins and ashes, the flag of the Republic of Cuba.' Gómez's goal, in his own words, was the 'the total paralysation of all labour in Cuba'.[23] Although Cuba had sugar and other cash crops located sporadically throughout the island, the most intensive areas of sugar and tobacco cultivation were in the west. Thus, if Gómez's Army of Invasion could penetrate Spanish defences and begin to operate in the west, Gómez could apply his sustained assault on Cuba's economic infrastructure with far greater effect than might otherwise be the case.

The campaign in 1895: Invasion and devastation

As the PRC debated the wisdom of Gómez's plan for invading the west and destroying the island's sugar, the Spanish army prepared to take the field. Martínez Campos rebuilt and reinforced the Júcaro-Morón *trocha* (which absorbed the bulk of the island's field forces). It would be many months though before the *trocha* would be the barrier Martínez Campos envisioned. The soldier-diplomat also dispatched Spanish troops to garrison the largest sugar plantations to thwart insurgent interference with the sugar harvest and made halting progress towards developing a small field force with which to pursue the rebels. By May 1895, Martínez Campos had cobbled together a modest number of flying columns that when combined, numbered approximately 20,000 men and began furtive attempts to bring Gómez to battle. These efforts, however, proved frustrating. Spanish forces were too ill-equipped, under-supplied and utterly ignorant about the location of insurgent field forces to fix, let alone destroy Gómez's army.[24]

In mid-December 1895, Gómez left the security of the *Oriente* (eastern Cuba) and marched west with approximately 4,000 men and another 1,200 *impedimenta* (civilians who performed the manual labour necessary to support Gómez's army).[25] Despite Martínez Campos's efforts to revitalize the Júcaro-Morón *trocha*, major vulnerabilities continued and Gómez's army easily passed through the fortified trench system that summer. Martínez Campos detected the movement and began a groping pursuit, manoeuvring his forces in almost total ignorance of the enemy's size or location. Gómez's disparate columns often humiliated their erstwhile pursuers by literally running circles around them only to return to previous locations to complete the destruction of the local strategic and economic infrastructure like rail and telegraph lines.[26] Even where Martínez Campos's subordinates got the battle they craved, it was only on Cuban terms and were often disastrous for Spanish morale.[27] Cuban forces fought brilliant rear-guard actions that decimated their pursuers and made Spanish forces hesitant to aggressively make contact with the rear of Gómez's columns. With the successful passing of the Júcaro-Morón *trocha*, the revolt was now island-wide.

Even worse, this manoeuvre allowed the *insurrectos* to operate in Cuba's central and western provinces just as the sugar harvest was about to get underway.[28] Gómez's men lost no time in exercising their full authority over the local peoples and most importantly the economic productivity of the region. Gómez circulated notices to the region's sugar plantations that they were to cease all harvesting and grinding of the year's crop.[29] Many planters, comforted by the relative proximity of Spanish garrisons, ignored CLA warnings and continued their normal operations. When discovered by Gómez's troops, insurgent bands targeted these plantations for destruction.[30] By the end of fall of 1895, Gómez's men and their torches had succeeded in achieving their second strategic goal of paralyzing the island's most important economy activity: its sugar production.[31] Further compounding the sense of panic on the island was the fact that Gómez's forces had advanced right to the outskirts of Havana itself, something virtually unthinkable a few months before.[32] One French observer summarized the situation thus, 'Maximo Gomez has absolutely played with the Spanish generals. ... If anyone had told us four months ago that he would be able to stop the crushing of the cane in the Province of Havana, or even in Matanzas, we would have laughed in his face.' Now, the author concluded, 'not a planter dares disobey his orders.'[33] The rebellion had reached a critical mass and seemed unstoppable.

Martínez Campos appeared almost as demoralized by events as his men. Militarily, Martínez Campos believed that he had performed reasonably well but that fortune had turned against him. The political situation, the other element in Martínez Campos's strategic approach, had also stalled. Martínez Campos lamented that his strategy of combining active campaigning while negotiating with the rebel's leadership had been fatally undermined by the island's Peninsular Spanish. The Cánovas ministry instinctively sided with the island's Spaniards and refused to allow Martínez Campos to offer reforms in his negotiations with the rebels. Militarily, he did not have the resources required to win and political alternatives were off the table.

This left Martínez Campos pessimistic about Spain's chances, 'Here will be fulfilled what is historical in Spain: the loss of the Americas by the Spaniards themselves. The general who wishes to govern under the direction of corner g[r]ocers [sic] is lost, as is Cuba, if the Spaniards do not submit and obey the Government, for the enemy commands many elements.'[34] In other words, the real reason for the success of the *insurrectos* was the island's flawed politics, not his inept management of the military elements of the war. If Martínez Campos could not reform the island's politics, he theorized a sterner hand would be needed to implement less ethical alternatives. Privately, Martínez Campos counselled Cánovas's ministry that he found such expedients ethically unpalatable and unwise to boot.[35] Martínez Campos declined to lead such a campaign and volunteered as much to the prime minister.

Spain's conservative ministry in Madrid, disgusted with Martínez Campos's inability to end the insurrection, relieved him in December of 1895 and contemplated who to send to replace him. The cabinet invited General Valeriano Weyler to join them in their strategic deliberations about the situation on the island. Weyler was career soldier in the Spanish army and a military academy graduate. What made Cánovas hesitate was Weyler's politics. He had joined Martínez Campos's efforts to restore the Bourbons late enough that the government in Madrid remained suspicious of his political loyalties. Still he had a reputation for personal bravery, aggressive leadership, and had already seen extensive service in the Spain's small guerrilla uprisings (including the Ten Years War). As Weyler and Cánovas's ministers listened to the army's reports on conditions in Cuba, Weyler developed the genesis of the plan that he believed could crush the Cuban Army and deliver total military victory for Spain.[36]

Weyler's campaign plan had three major components. First, Weyler wanted to create powerful mobile columns capable of hunting down and destroying insurgent bands in the field. He would achieve this not only by continuing his predecessor's build-up of the army on the island but also by abandoning strategically useless positions and removing troops from guarding sugar plantations. Second, Weyler aimed to improve upon Martínez Campos's use of *trochas*. He would strengthen the Júcaro-Morón *trocha*. Weyler also eyed creating a new line of fortified blockhouses from Mariel to Majana to isolate western and central Cuba from each other. These *trochas* would be the anvil onto which the hammer of Spanish mobile columns would smash Gómez's forces. The final element of Weyler's vision was the use of population relocation.[37] Weyler understood that, despite having total political and military control of the island, the nearly 200,000 soldiers that he commanded would still not be enough to secure the entire island simultaneously. By relocating the population, Weyler would be able to better protect Spanish loyalists, reduce the political demands on the Spanish army to protect every plantation and village while simultaneously denying the labour and rations that rural Cubans might provide local insurgent groups. If he could implement these elements of his strategic vision, Weyler promised the Spanish government that he could win a complete military victory for Spain.

Operationalizing this vision was the challenge. Weyler, already familiar with the basic terrain in Cuba, thought that the westernmost province of Pinar Del Río would be the best place to begin. He would then clear the remaining provinces from west to east.[38] The implementation of Weyler's vision was to be both deliberate and gradual. Only once a province was clear would the next province to their east be isolated and then secured. Cánovas's government approved Weyler's conditions and dispatched the general with additional reinforcements to the island hoping to bring the war to a speedy conclusion.

The campaign of 1896: War answered with war

As Weyler embarked for Cuba, a Spanish newspaperman asked Weyler how he intended to win the war in Cuba and Weyler reportedly answered, 'War should be answered by war.'[39] He meant what he said. Weyler firmly believed that Martínez Campos's misguided attempts at political conciliation had brought Spain to the brink of ruin and the island's new governor general did not intend to continue Martínez Campos's efforts at administrative reform and diplomacy. Instead, Weyler believed that Martínez Campos had things backwards, the rebels first had to suffer total military defeat and only then would he pursue potential political reforms and negotiation.[40]

As the island's new governor general took stock of the situation in February 1896, he recognized that Gómez's army had developed critical military and political momentum, and Weyler believed that any further delay in implementing his strategic vision would result in a fait accompli by the insurgents. Weyler decided to take immediate action to reverse the momentum and authorized the recruitment of a 'Corps of Volunteers' from Cuba's Peninsular population in order to help Spanish troop's intelligence and manpower.[41] Weyler himself, during the Ten Years War, had led such a unit with great success, and he looked to duplicate that model on a larger scale.[42] Moreover, Weyler ordered the consolidation and abandonment of indefensible or strategically worthless positions and forbade further detachments to protect private property outside of the confines of Spanish garrisons. Weyler also mandated the continued reinforcement of the Júcaro-Morón *trocha* and construction of another *trocha* from Mariel to Majana in an effort to separate the most active *insurrecto* regions from the more prosperous and stable portions of western and central Cuba.[43] The general also moved swiftly to introduce reconcentration of Cuba's population from the unprotected interior of the countryside. Several problems, however, resulted from Weyler's decision to begin relocation.

In theory, relocation was supposed to be an orderly process. Civilians would arrive at nearby Spanish garrisons, and local municipalities were ordered to receive these refugees and place them in temporary shelters and provide them with plots of arable land so that the relocated people could, after a few months, become self-sustaining.[44] The reality of relocation, however, was much different. Much of the plan's implementation and its effectiveness remained deeply influenced by the operational environment (terrain, disease and the enemy situation) as well as Spain's limited logistical capacity.

To mitigate some of these problems Weyler had to first set the conditions necessary for relocation to be implemented. In the east, where the rebellion was most active, Weyler declared Santiago, Puerto Principe and Sancti Spiritus as the first regions to have their populations relocated.[45] Relocation in these regions, however, remained beyond Spanish means for the moment. Instead the relocation order for these provinces was intended to allow Spanish forces to operate with more freedom in these regions and encourage local commanders to pursue insurgents with more aggression. The first real test case for population relocation was in Pinar Del Río in October of 1896 once the Mariel to Majana *trocha* was complete.[46] The *trocha* now isolated Cuba's western most province from the rest of the island, and Weyler could concentrate his forces into large powerful columns and then force the relocation en masse of the province's inhabitants.

While Weyler's engineers worked to isolate Pinar Del Río, Weyler and Maceo's forces shadow-boxed. Maceo fought when he had ammunition and retreated when he did not. By March of 1896, Weyler's forces had ground down or dispersed Maceo's insurgents until only about 250–500 remained active in the province.[47] Initially, the CLA was effective either in avoiding the columns or in some instances successfully giving battle. Soon, though, as the Mariel-Majana *trocha* became increasingly impenetrable, the province's insurgents began to run out of ammunition. Only infrequent landings from American filibusters continued to provide the CLA ammunition and supplies. Without ammunition, giving battle remained out of the question, and this left Maceo's supply areas vulnerable.

Upon the completion of the *trocha*, in October 1896, Weyler issued a *banda* (a legal decree) that ordered the inhabitants of Pinar Del Río to report to Spanish-held fortifications or towns within eight days or to be treated as traitors. Food stocks were to be confiscated by Spanish troops for the use of the army or destroyed. Any property or people found outside of Spanish-controlled areas were considered fair game by Spanish guerrillas or troops.[48] The order was published with such haste that in most instances most of the civilians who the order applied to only heard about the order when their farms or homes were visited by Spanish troops or guerrillas (the local name for Spanish affiliated irregular groups) mandated their evacuation. Spanish forces were notoriously unsympathetic to the people living in Cuba's countryside, and the people were driven into the province's cities often times within only the clothes on their back.[49]

Further complicating matters, the CLA and Spain's Volunteers had also been practising their own informal versions of population relocation before Weyler had even set foot in Cuba.[50] Insurgent second-in-command Antonio Maceo had, in two months, set fire to more than 59 towns and driven more than 15,000 refugees into Spanish-held cities for their failure to embrace the Cuban independence movement.[51] Other CLA columns in other provinces throughout the island likewise destroyed towns and deliberately herded local civilians who declined to join the insurgency's ranks into Spanish-held cities. Gómez's men also removed civilians who traded with the besieged towns.[52] Thus, Spain was never entirely in control of the process from the very beginning of the operation.

By the end of 1896, Weyler had more than 60,000 soldiers in Pinar Del Río.[53] Large Spanish columns combed the province and harried Maceo's forces. Unable to give battle, the CLA tried with increasing difficulty to avoid Weyler's columns.[54] Maceo himself became a victim of Weyler's successful application of containment and continual pressure. Eyeing the growing pressure with alarm, Gómez ordered Maceo to abandon the province. In December, after multiple failed attempts at penetrating the Mariel-Majana *trocha*, Maceo gave up and sailed around it only to be killed in a clash with a Spanish cavalry patrol a few days later.[55] Weyler had his first major success, only token insurgent forces remained in Pinar Del Río and he had killed one of the most important figures in the insurrection.

Events in the remaining western and central provinces (Havana, Matanzas, Las Villas and Santa Clara) played out with similar dynamics. Like Maceo, Gómez fought back but quickly found himself unable to maintain his position due to a lack of supplies (also like Maceo, he was short on ammunition). Grudgingly, beginning in March of 1896, Gómez's columns retraced their route of invasion this time headed east, harried by Spanish mobile columns the entire way. As Gómez retreated, he tried to summon reinforcements and supplies from the east only to have those orders countermanded by the PRC who diverted his supplies and men to Calixto García. By December of 1896, Gómez too had been forced to abandon western and central Cuba to Weyler.[56] Although Gómez had been pushed out, token insurgent forces remained, and although greatly diminished, they would emerge to damage Spanish property and infrastructure periodically.[57]

In eastern Cuba, a different scenario played out. Although isolated and under pressure, the combination of excellent tactical and operational leadership with adequate resources kept the revolution alive. Calixto García, a veteran of the Ten Years War, used the supplies Gómez coveted to excellent effect and fought a series of brilliant battles and ambushes that eliminated Spain's ability to manoeuvre into the countryside of eastern Cuba.[58] Insurgent groups continued to maintain supply areas that grew food and made basic pieces of equipment.[59] Although the population's enthusiasm for revolution waned as the war seemed to drag on, at no time were Spanish forces as close to eliminating the insurgent groups as their counterparts in western and central Cuba.[60] Indeed, Gómez and García rebuilt the CLA and increased its lethality and effectiveness, adding artillery and machine guns to their arsenal and used them to seize the town of Las Tunas in October of 1897.[61] Eastern Cuba was and would remain Cuba Libre.

Weyler's tactics had reversed the war's military momentum to a substantial extent. When Weyler arrived in theatre, insurgent bands under Gómez, Maceo and García roamed the island at will. Weyler's methods (the combination of using *trochas*, flying columns and population relocation) had at first stalled and then reversed insurgent momentum. By the end of 1897, Gómez could no longer maintain an army of any size outside of eastern Cuba. With the migration of between 295,000 and 365,000 civilians into Spanish-held garrisons, the prospects of Gómez's unaided return seemed slim.[62] From a relative perspective, the tactics seemed to have worked.

And yet even Weyler did not believe that relocation had completely eliminated the *insurrectos*. When members of the press asked Weyler if western Cuba was pacified, he replied 'almost, almost'. Never giving much thought to how his enemies might use these statements to discredit him, Weyler was dubbed overnight 'General Almost Pacified' and the nickname stuck since it seemed to embody nearly everyone's frustration with the seemingly interminable war in Cuba.[63] The capture of Las Tunas demonstrated that eastern Cuba remained beyond Weyler's capability to control. The war had stalemated, and when an anarchist shot Prime Minister Cánovas, Weyler's primary political patron, Madrid ran out of patience.

General Ramon Blanco relieved Weyler in the waning days of 1897. Although Blanco would not end the use of camps completely, by and large, Spain's forced relocation of civilians was over. Instead of trying to subdue the insurrection by force, Blanco remained interested in negotiating an end to the conflict and in trying to maintain Spanish rule on the island in whatever modified form he could win in negotiations with the insurgents. The majority of the rebels, however, were not in the mood to negotiate and instead continued the war in an all-out bid for independence. Population relocation had failed to deliver the total military victory Weyler promised. Worse still, the effects of using reconcentration were just beginning.

Relocation: The causes of failure

Although logistics often play a critical role in conventional wars, in Cuba from 1895 to 1898, sustainment (or the lack thereof) was a critical element in Spanish military failure to subdue the insurrection and make reconcentration work as intended. Spanish logistical challenges contributed to its defeat several ways. First, Spain's leadership could not adequately supply and sustain an army of the size and operating on the scale required to subdue the insurrection in Cuba. Second, the inability of the Spanish army to provide for itself left its ability to provide for the logistical necessities of the Cuban people completely inadequate to the task that confronted it. Cuba's climate, terrain, size and diseases would have challenged any conventional Western powers attempting to project force on the island. The Spanish army of the late nineteenth century lacked the resources and leadership necessary to adapt to these conditions, and it fatally undermined the efforts of Spanish troops to contain the island's violence and bring it to a speedy conclusion.

From the very onset of the war, inadequate logistics hobbled the effectiveness of the Spanish army. The 20,000 Spanish soldiers in Cuba in 1894 were ill-prepared to contain an island-wide insurrection. Cuba's population of 1.6 million people were dispersed over 44,000 square miles of unevenly developed terrain.[64] The initial deployment of Spanish forces reflected the severe shortcomings of Spanish fiscal administration of the army on the island. The forces in theatre were both undermanned and underequipped with shortages in every class of supply.[65] Spain's neglect of the army left Cuba vulnerable to an expanding insurgency due to the inability of the army to pay and supply its forces in theatre. As Spain continued the build-up of the army on the island, Spanish fiscal administration of the army never adequate to begin with, only grew worse with the increase in troops. As Spanish numbers approached 200,000 from 1895 to 1896, even when Spain had adequate financial resources to pay its soldiers, it lacked the administrative ability to do so. By 1896, soldier pay was more than five months in arrears due to the administrative difficulties entailed in the rapid expansion of troops in theatre. The administrative and financial strain on paying for the expansion of the Spanish army forced Spain to rely on other expedients in order to manage the tenfold expansion in manpower. When Spanish soldiers were paid at all, the Spanish government paid in increasingly debased paper currency.[66]

While the inability to pay an army is bad enough, Spanish leaders often failed to be able to provide adequate food for their soldiers. This was both true systemically and in the case of individual operations and both had major effects on Spain's ability to effectively carry out population relocation. One American correspondent with Spain's army observed that the Spanish did not seem to possess 'a commissariat train in the whole army of occupation'.[67] On another occasion, the same correspondent moving with the Spanish army along its rail line from Havana to Santa Clara saw that the more the 1,800 troops participating in the movement had nothing other than raw sugarcane to eat.[68] Spanish resilience in the face of such criminal neglect led one Spanish officer to lament, 'Our soldier is a martyr for his sufferings, the most disciplined in the world, the most tractable, with good direction and fine chiefs, the most valiant. ... If only I could feed them!'[69]

Food and pay, however, were not the most pressing problems that Spanish logistics inadequately addressed. When an American correspondent travelling with Máximo Gómez asked the old general who his favourite subordinates were, he replied, 'June, July, and August'.[70] Gómez's tongue in cheek joke about the role of disease belied one of the most lethal elements of operations in Cuba. Disease was a critical, if not decisive, element in Spain's failure at population relocation. Disease impacted Spanish efforts to implement population relocation in several key aspects. The most obvious way disease reduced Spain's ability to execute population relocation effectively was by lowering the overall effectiveness of Spanish forces operating in theatre. As Martínez Campos attempted to stymie the growth of the insurrection on the island, from March to December 1895, he also had to deal with the growing medical crisis within his own ranks. Spanish military leaders reported more than 49,000 soldiers hospitalized during this period, which is more than double the total number of soldiers Spain had deployed to the island in 1894.[71] Spanish medical authorities on the island did not have the supplies on hand to contain the diseases ravaging their army. Often times, Spanish surgeons lacked access to basic antiseptics, let alone more specialized medicines like quinine.[72]

Nor did the situation improve with time. As Weyler subsequently deployed additional troops into theatre and began to execute their strategy of occupying the defunct *trochas* across the island, the epidemics afflicting Spanish soldiers grew still worse. The *trochas* themselves became vectors of disease. The mission of the soldiers occupying the blockhouses meant that they were often located in the most remote and inhospitable areas of Cuba. In some cases, during the rainy season, the primitive outposts themselves were flooded, yet still occupied, by Spanish soldiers.[73] Unsurprisingly, the number of Spanish effectives able to campaign and take part in Weyler's strategy of relocation dwindled. In 1896, Spanish military authorities, at the height of Spain's relocation efforts, reported that more than 232,000 troops had been hospitalized from disease.[74] At any given time, more than 50,000 soldiers on the island were medically unfit for duty.

Nor were these medical problems limited to the men manning Spain's blockhouses across the island. The field forces attempting to operationalize Weyler's relocation strategy also suffered from the ravages of disease. In the province of Pinar Del Río, Weyler allocated 32,000 men to field operations, the main effort for Spain's ground forces in 1896. Ten days into operations, Weyler's columns reported more than 9,000 men incapacitated from disease, a staggering loss of 28 per cent of his total strength without any action at all from the enemy. Without a doubt, the loss of almost third of his operational strength limited his ability to gain contact with Maceo while simultaneously searching out and destroying any base areas the CLA had developed in the province. Thus, even before relocation began, Spanish logistics were already under considerable strain. Spain could not pay, feed, or care for their soldiers.

The implementation of relocation would only exacerbate many of these problems. Before the war, most of island's cities and the regions surrounding them developed a cash crop-based economy. Much of Cuba's agriculture was located in the island's interior. This made Cuban cities, where the projected camps were soon to be located, vulnerable to any disruption in the food supply chain. At the outbreak of the rebellion, this fundamental basis of Cuban agriculture remained the same. Cities imported the overwhelming bulk of their food from the interior, areas that the Spanish were now deliberately turning into sterile and unproductive regions in order to keep food out of the hands of insurgent forces.[75] Spain would have to develop alternative sources of food to compensate for the destruction of these food networks. That network would have to be via Spain's tenuous supply system.

Once inside these cities, theoretically, Spanish authorities had a plan in place to care for civilians who were forcibly relocated. Spanish officials, however, ineptly managed Weyler's plan. A committee of local elites was supposed to assess the needs of each arriving family and was to find them suitable shelter and assign them a small plot of land that the family could farm to sustain themselves.[76] Nevertheless, these local officials neglected relocated families or believed that they deserved their plight.[77] In localities where municipal officials and charitable organizations did attempt to improve conditions for relocated civilians, they found the needs of these civilians far exceeded what they had on hand to give them.[78]

Given the outright hostility that many of the local civil committees had for their charges, utter neglect of basic shelter was almost inevitable. In virtually every major Spanish garrison, the relocated civilians were often placed in the least sanitary portions of each city. One American observer speculated that the only reasonable explanation for this decision was not indifference but fear of contagion.[79] *Reconcentrado* shelters ranged from abandoned buildings to improvised shelters made of local rubbish, leaves and cloth. The only thing they had in common was that in all cases, virtually all of the shelters provided to refugees were inadequate.[80]

While failure to provide shelter was a major problem, equally problematic was the inability of the Spanish government to develop a sustainable plan to feed the *reconcentrado* population. Although the government intended to allocate plots of land to the relocated refugee population, local elites oversaw the implementation of this programme, and, if they allocated any land at all, they typically gave the refugees the least arable land in the city's environs. Further complicating the efforts at developing self-sustaining *reconcentrado* communities was the fact that Weyler's orders did not provide the *pacificos* with seed with which to begin their food plot and tools with which to farm. Relocated civilians tended to be mostly women and children, population groups who had the least experience with agriculture in Cuba's gendered division of labour. As a consequence, even where local Spanish officials followed the intent of Weyler's strategy, a lack of means (seed, tools and knowledge of agriculture) undermined the effectiveness of the Spanish programme.[81] More typical, however, was the failure of the Spanish government to ensure that the local committees responsible for the *reconcentrados* designated any land at all. In Havana, less than 20 per cent of *reconcentrados* had access to any form of land at all.[82] That meant that in Havana alone, where there were more than 70,000 *reconcentrados*, 56,000 people were completely reliant upon the Spanish government for food.[83] Needless to say, sustaining this large a number of indigent people indefinitely would have been challenging for any late nineteenth-century military.

With the collapse of the original sustainment plan for the reconcentrated population, Spanish authorities turned to other methods to try to feed Cuba's starving masses. One approach was to feed the relocated civilians with the leftovers of Spanish soldier messes.[84] Soldiers provided the local civilians with leftover bones and beans.[85] When it became obvious that this was going to be completely inadequate, Spanish officials attempted to distribute aid directly to the refugees. Even this, however, often times fell well short of the mark. Corruption all along the aid distribution chain by Spanish officials meant that of the few supplies that the Spanish government could provide, went instead to the black market.[86] In the end, none of these efforts were sufficient. Outside observers foresaw massive death from starvation and disease unless some large-scale relief was undertaken quickly.[87]

Just as Spain's logistical means were being taxed to their fullest extent by the scale of the relocation effort, Cuba's insurgent leadership consciously decided to push those means past the breaking point. The CLA's decision to take active measures to worsen the situation in Spanish-held cities further amplified the misery in these camps and made any Spanish attempts to correct the supply situation woefully insufficient.

Gómez's legions took two important actions that exacerbated the already dire conditions inside Cuba's cities: Gómez's troops forced Spanish authorities to implement relocation faster and with greater intensity than was planned for and Gómez's embargo of food products into Spanish-held cities was far more effective than reciprocal Spanish efforts to deprive the CLA of access to food. Both factors contributed to both the scale and intensity of the misery of the relocated populations in Spanish-held cities. In Cuba's western and most economically developed province, Pinar Del Río, this meant that virtually the whole province was subject to CLA destruction. From 1895 to 1896, Maceo's troops crisscrossed the province, and any towns that failed to enthusiastically embrace the Cuban Revolution met with insurgent torches. Maceo's troopers alone were responsible for the destruction in Pinar Del Río of fifty-nine towns.[88] Any plantation owner or farmer that dared defy Gómez's orders found their crops and their buildings subject to CLA torches.[89] In the process of such systematic destruction, CLA torches created massive waves of refugees into Spanish garrisoned towns. Within Pinar Del Río alone, Maceo's operations within 60 days of operations created 15,000 refugees.[90]

While Weyler's plans had included plans to resettle refugees created by relocation, it had an important controlling mechanism that might have mitigated the worst of the circumstances: timing. Weyler's original orders called for a staggered implementation of population relocation that was supposed to progress in Cuba from west to east. In theory, as Weyler's ground forces pacified the interior of the Cuban countryside, civilians in the now pacified province could return to their homes and provide for themselves again while newly established *trochas* would keep insurgents out of the previously cleared areas. Weyler's programme of population relocation would then move to the next eastern-most province.[91] Had Weyler's implementation proceeded as planned, the numbers of refugees requiring government support might indeed have been manageable.

Instead, insurgent strategy and resilience thwarted his implementation. Gómez's legions herded neutral or loyalist Cubans into the cities, rendering Weyler's assumptions about relocation in manageable successive stages inoperable before the ink on the plan was even dry. Even in Pinar Del Río, the first stage in Weyler's successive plan to clear provinces from west to east, insurgent torches remained active. Nor was this an exception, the insurgency still maintained token forces in each province.[92] The CLA, although considerably less potent than before, could still manage to instil fear and destruction. This left Weyler's logistics, already taxed to the breaking point supporting a tenfold increase in the build-up of Spanish soldiers on the island, past its limit. Although it is impossible to distinguish between CLA methods and wilful compliance with Weyler's orders to implement relocation, we know that somewhere between 295,000 and 365,000 civilians moved into Spanish-held garrisons.[93]

Making the situation even worse, the CLA in western Cuba still maintained an effective embargo of Spanish-held cities. Gómez's forces often intercepted merchants who possessed foodstuffs headed to Spanish-held cities. If these merchants held passes from other CLA leaders or PRC members, Gómez often only seized their goods. If they did not have any mitigating paperwork at all, they were executed.[94] The CLA treated desperate foraging parties of *pacificos* from Spanish-held cities even worse combining both humiliation and terror.[95] Gómez's embargo remained.

The final element of Weyler's sustainment of reconcentration, locally administered food plots, failed when the CLA realized that Spanish garrison troops and field forces were inadequate to protect the locally grown crops set aside to feed Spanish garrisons and the *reconcentrados*. Despite mounting difficulties in maintaining large bodies of troops in the west, Gómez's troops found that it only took a handful of insurgents to destroy these food plots. Just a few men, with surprise and a torch, could eliminate several weeks' worth of agricultural progress in a few minutes. And this the insurgents did to devastating effect. Nearly every Spanish-held garrison struggled to protect *reconcentrado* food plots. In an ironic turn of events, the CLA used these same protected food plots for their own forage and often referred derisively to the *pacificos* as their commissary.[96] In combination with Spain's other logistical challenges, Gómez's successfully prosecuted embargo of Spanish-held cities pushed its logistics past the breaking point in mid-1896.

Catastrophe soon followed. Spain's ineffective efforts at managing relocation soon led to widespread starvation and disease. Even the best camps, like Cascorro Hill in Matanzas that had an ideal location for a relocation camp, reported twenty-five to thirty civilians died each day in 1896.[97] The numbers were much worse where the shelter and drainage were less adequate. The aggregate numbers tell the tale. Almost 10 per cent of Cuba's pre-war population or between 55,000 and 170,000 civilians died as a result of population relocation.[98]

And what had Spain gained in return? Even Weyler himself readily conceded that the best that could be said was that Cuba's western provinces were almost pacified.[99] Although almost pacified was a remarkable improvement from the military situation that Weyler inherited when he arrived in February 1896, Weyler's tactics had created a political firestorm in Cuba, Spain and in the United States. The political fallout from the mismanagement of reconcentration is ultimately what doomed Spanish efforts to maintain their empire.

The consequences of reconcentration

Death on such a large scale, in full view of the world, had unintended political consequences that nullified the limited success that such tactics brought Spanish arms in 1896–7. Among them, reconcentration led to two mostly unintended consequences: it destroyed any possibility for a negotiated settlement with Cuba's rebels and American coverage of reconcentration was an important factor in tipping American public support in favour of intervention.

Cuban domestic politics had been radically reshaped by population relocation. Before Weyler and reconcentration, the Autonomist Party in Cuba had hoped that the violence might be ended with some combination of political reform and modest military success. The PRC used the inhumane conditions maintained in the camps to inflame Cuban resentment of Spanish rule and by proxy illustrated the bankruptcy of any policy that left Spanish rule on the island intact. The unfolding humanitarian disaster of the relocation camps radicalized many Autonomists and made them into reluctant supporters of independence. Although General Blanco restored the party's legality, attacked from outside and from within, the Autonomists never recovered. Thus, Spain's incompetent management of the relocation camps helped the PRC destroy any negotiated compromise other than total independence for the island.[100]

While reconcentration had broadened Cuban domestic support for independence it also had international effects. In the United States, virtually every major national news outlet covered conditions in Weyler's camps, and although much of their reporting was highly dramatized and unreliable, the net effect of the negative press coverage of camp conditions gradually swung US public support in favour of recognition of Cuban belligerency and/or independence. Later, this public support extended to US military intervention.[101] Absent the mismanagement of population relocation, the build-up to American intervention, if it happened at all, would have taken much longer and would almost certainly have become a partisan issue much like the decision to annex the Philippines later became. In short, Spanish neglect of the camp's political effects placed them on the strategic trajectory to defeat.

Conclusion

It was clear by the end of 1897 that Weyler's strategic approach to counterinsurgency in Cuba had not achieved the effects he sought. Unable to win, yet still powerful enough not to lose outright to Cuba's rebels, Spain would grimly hang on until the United States intervened in April of 1898. After almost 400 years of Spanish rule in Cuba, Spain's military failure warrants closer examination. If Spain ever had a chance to tamp down the insurgency, it never had a better chance than during Weyler's administration of the island from 1896 to 1897. Spain committed almost 200,000 troops and gave Weyler a virtual free hand to run the island; however, he saw fit in order to achieve total victory over the island's revolutionaries. The centrepiece of Weyler's strategic approach was reconcentration.[102]

So, were these methods beneficial? The answer is mixed. Tactically, Weyler regained freedom of manoeuvre over half of the island, a marked improvement over the situation Martínez Campos left him in 1895. Although the insurgents survived in a much-reduced form, Spanish forces held the initiative. In order to survive, CLA bands had to disperse and operate in increasingly smaller numbers, falling from bands of a few hundred to a dozen or less. Had the United States failed to intervene it remains plausible that eventually Spanish pressure would have forced even these remnants of the CLA to surrender.

Out east it was a different story; Cuban forces under Calixto García remained able to keep Spanish forces isolated to their coastal strongholds and to protect his supply areas from Spanish incursions. If Spain had been able to concentrate as many troops as it had against Pinar Del Río, they might have had more success, but this remains speculative. It is important to note that insurgent tactical success often hinged on their supply of ammunition, and CLA forces in the east appear to have never experienced the dire shortages that their compatriots in the west did. This fact, when combined with the even more difficult terrain in the region, most likely would have turned the war there into a war of attrition where total military success for either party was a dubious proposition.

At the strategic level, population relocation hurt more than it helped. Spain had a limited ability to continue the war, and relocation, while temporarily improving Spain's bargaining position, vis-à-vis the rebels, eliminated any chance at a compromise solution. Use of population relocation also foreclosed the idea that Spain would expand its base of political support outside of the Peninsular Spanish within the island. The *reconcentrados* themselves represented a potential pool of people who could be convinced to support continued Spanish rule. After all, many of them, and they numbered in the hundreds of thousands, elected to take their chances in a Spanish garrison rather than to leave for Cuba Libre. The inhumane treatment they received meant that Spain forfeited these people's political loyalties and laid the foundation for independence, aided in effect by Spanish arms and indifference. The inept management of population relocation also made local autonomy a non-starter politically. The Autonomist Party lost its vitality and never regained its lost influence once General Blanco reinstated their legal status. Internationally, the poor execution of relocation was one of the most important factors in American intervention. When all of these strategic elements are considered, relocation's tactical success does not appear to outweigh its political and strategic cost.

The proximate cause of this high political cost was the Spanish army's inept management of its logistics. The army's expansion, more than tenfold in a year, overburdened the meagre logistics Spanish authorities maintained on the island. The army could not pay, equip, care for, or feed soldiers in the numbers required to subdue an island-wide insurrection. When this was combined with Máximo Gómez's strategy of blockading Spanish-held cities and driving in Cuban civilians from the countryside, Spain's logistics already pushed to its limits by the requirements of the army, broke down completely by an unplanned for surge of 300,000 civilians that were totally dependent on the Spanish government for their subsistence. Spanish authorities compounded the problem though through hostile indifference and criminal neglect of the relocated population. The cost of this official indifference is incomprehensible, almost 10 per cent of Cuba's pre-war population died as a result of the war and relocation. The inability of Spanish logistics to adapt to the war's changing circumstances doomed Weyler's efforts to make reconcentration anything other than a major political liability.

Notes

1 Robert Gerwarth and Stephan Malinowski, 'Hannah Arendt's Ghosts: Reflections on the Disputable Path from Windhoek to Auschwitz', *Central European History*, Vol. 42, No. 2 (June 2009), 279–300 (288).

2 John Lawrence Tone, *War and Genocide in Cuba: 1895-1898* (Chapel Hill: University of North Carolina Press, 2006), 223.

3 Louis A. Pérez, *Cuba between Empires, 1878-1902* (Pittsburgh, PA: University of Pittsburgh Press, 1983), 6–12; Rosalie Schwartz, *Lawless Liberators: Political Banditry and Cuban Independence* (Durham, NC: Duke University Press, 1989), 143–4.

4   Pérez, *Cuba between Empires*, 36.
5   Ibid., 10.
6   Ibid., 144.
7   Ibid., 147.
8   Charles Alexander Petrie, *King Alfonso XIII and His Age* (London: Chapman and Hall Ltd., 1963), 52–4.
9   Schwartz, *Lawless Liberators*, 147–8.
10 Petrie, *King Alfonso XIII*, 54.
11 David F. Healey, *The United States in Cuba: Generals, Politicians, and the Search for Policy, 1898–1902* (Madison: University of Wisconsin Press, 1963), 8.
12 Pérez, *Cuba between Empires*, 42–5.
13 Ibid., 47.
14 Ibid., 74.
15 Charles J. Esdaile, *Spain in the Liberal Age: From Constitution to Civil War, 1808–1939* (Oxford: Blackwell Publishers, 2000), 187; Pérez, *Cuba between Empires*, 77–8.
16 Esdaile, *Spain in the Liberal Age*, 192; Pérez, *Cuba between Empires*, 74.
17 Philip S. Foner, *The Spanish-Cuban-American War and the Birth of American Imperialism, 1895–1902*, Volume 1, *1895–1898* (New York: Monthly Review Press, 1972), 21.
18 Pérez, *Cuba between Empires*, 43.
19 Tone, *War and Genocide in Cuba*, 140–2; Foner, *The Spanish-American-Cuban War*, 27.
20 Grover Flint, *Marching with Gomez: A War Correspondent's Field Note-Book Kept During Four Months with The Cuban Army* (New York: Lamson, Wolfee and Company, 1898), 124, 190; Pérez, *Cuba between Empires*, 127; Foner, *The Spanish-American-Cuban War*, 21.
21 Flint, *Marching with Gómez*, 198.
22 Ibid.
23 Quoted in Foner, *The Spanish-American-Cuban War*, 22.
24 Tone, *War and Genocide in Cuba*, 113–14.
25 Ibid., 139–41; Teresa Prados-Torreira, *Mambisas: Rebel Women in Nineteenth Century Cuba* (Gainesville: University of Florida Press, 2005), 121.
26 Tone, *War and Genocide in Cuba*, 113, 137; Flint, *Marching with Gomez*, 62.
27 Two major battles were fought by the pursuing Spanish army. At Mal Tiempo, the CLA defeated an isolated Spanish column under Colonel Salvador Arizón, and this victory allowed the CLA to invade Matanzas, Havana, and Pinar Del Río. See Tone, *War and Genocide in Cuba*, 123–5; At Coliseo, Martínez Campos finally caught Gómez and forced him to retreat, but Gómez tricked Martínez Campos into believing his temporary withdrawal signalled an end to the campaign. When Martínez Campos redeployed his army to block Gómez's feigned retreat, Gómez continued his

invasion westward, towards Havana, now uncovered by Martínez Campos. See Tone, *War and Genocide in Cuba*, 137.

28 Pérez, *Cuba between Empires*, 49; Jack Cameron Dierks, *A Leap to Arms: The Cuban Campaign of 1898* (New York: J.B. Lippincott Company, 1970), 11.
29 Flint, *Marching with Gomez*, 123;
30 Cristobal N. Madan to Ramon Williams, 24 January 1896, NARA 2, Record Group 59, Consular Dispatches from Havana, Cuba.
31 *El Boletin Comercial of Havana*, 3 January 1896, NARA 2, Record Group 59, Consular Dispatches from Havana, Cuba; *The Journal*, 'Bombs exploded in Havana's Streets', 7 January 1896, Library of Congress; Foner, *The Spanish-American-Cuban War*, 106.
32 Ramon Williams to Edwin Ulel, 22 January 1896, NARA 2, Record Group 59, Consular Dispatches from Havana, Cuba.
33 'Extract from a Letter', 22 February 1896, Philip Phillips Family Papers, Library of Congress.
34 Martínez Campos to Ramon Williams, 24 January 1896, NARA 2, Record Group 59, Consular Dispatches from Havana, Cuba
35 *La Lucha*, 18 January 1896, NARA 2, Record Group 59, Consular Dispatches from Havana, Cuba.
36 Tone, *War and Genocide in Cuba*, 156–8.
37 Pérez, *Cuba between Empires*, 54–5; Tone, *War and Genocide in Cuba*, 159–60; Foner, *The Spanish-American-Cuban War*, 78; Valeriano Weyler, *Memoria de un general: De caballero cadete a general en jefe* (Barcelona: Ediciones Destino, 2004), 202–4.
38 Weyler, *Memoria de un general*, 202–4.
39 Weyler is quoted in Louis A. Pérez, *Between Reform and Revolution* (Oxford: Oxford University Press, 1988), 165.
40 Weyler, *Memoria de un general*, 232.
41 Pérez, *Cuba between Empires*, 54–5.
42 Tone, *War and Genocide in Cuba*, 155–6.
43 Pérez, *Cuba between Empires*, 53–5. Tone, *War and Genocide in Cuba*, 160–1.
44 Foner, *The Spanish-American-Cuban War*, 112–16.
45 *Gaceta De La Habana*, 18 February 1896, NARA 2, Record Group 59, Consular Dispatches from Havana, Cuba.
46 Weyler, *Memoria de un general*, 202–4.
47 Foner, *The Spanish-American-Cuban War*, 82–3.
48 Ibid., 77; Tone, *War and Genocide in Cuba*, 205–9.
49 Foner, *The Spanish-American-Cuban War*, 112–13;
50 Tone, *War and Genocide in Cuba*, 206.
51 Ibid., 203–4; Foner, *The Spanish-American-Cuban War*, 67.

52 Tone, *War and Genocide in Cuba*, 197–9.
53 Foner, *The Spanish-American-Cuban War*, 83.
54 Tone, *War and Genocide in Cuba*, 168–9.
55 Ibid., 185.
56 Ibid., 164.
57 Averell Garr To Assistant Secretary of State, 21 May 1897, RG59, Dispatches From U.S. Consuls in Cienfuegos, NARA2; Tone, *War and Genocide in Cuba*, 172.
58 Tone, *War and Genocide in Cuba*, 171.
59 Flint, *Marching with Gomez*, 244–8.
60 Pulaski Hyatt To State Department, 15 November 1897, RG59, Dispatches From U.S. Consuls in Santiago, NARA2.
61 Tone, *War and Genocide in Cuba*, 234.
62 Ibid., 223. Tone places the number at 295, 357 using the numbers cited by Cuban officials charged with tracking *reconcentrado* numbers. He, however, excluded Havana from his analysis given lack of confirmed municipal data from Havana; Prados-Torreira, *Mambisas*, 122. Prados-Torreira estimated that Havana had received at least 70,000 relocated civilians.
63 Quoted in Tone, *War and Genocide in Cuba*, 189.
64 US War Department, *Census of Cuba Taken under the War Department* (Washington, DC: Government Printing Office, 1900), 11.
65 Pérez, *Cuba between Empires*, 74.
66 Ibid., 78.
67 Stephen Bonsal, *The Real Conditions of Cuba To-Day* (New York: Harper & Brothers Publishers, 1897), 11–12.
68 Ibid., 104.
69 Quoted in Pérez, *Cuba between Empires*, 73.
70 Pérez, *Cuba between Empires*, 77.
71 Ibid., 75.
72 Bonsal, *The Real Conditions of Cuba*, 81.
73 Pérez, *Cuba between Empires*, 77.
74 Ibid.
75 Tone, *War and Genocide in Cuba*, 202.
76 Ibid., 207.
77 Foner, *The Spanish-American-Cuban War*, 112–13.
78 Bonsal, *The Real Conditions of Cuba*, 112.
79 Ibid.
80 Foner, *The Spanish-American-Cuban War*, 112–13.
81 Tone, *War and Genocide in Cuba*, 199.
82 Ibid., 207.

83 Prados-Torreira, *Mambisas*, 122. Prado-Torreira estimated that Havana contained 70,000 relocated civilians. Tone, *War and Genocide in Cuba*, 207. Tone estimated that only 20 per cent of the refugees in Havana were designated food plots.
84 Foner, *The Spanish-American-Cuban War*, 112–13.
85 Prados-Torreira, *Mambisas*, 122.
86 Foner, *The Spanish-American-Cuban War*, 114–15.
87 Bonsal, *The Real Conditions of Cuba*, 23.
88 Foner, *The Spanish-American-Cuban War*, 67.
89 Flint, *Marching with Gómez*, 123–4.
90 Tone, *War and Genocide in Cuba*, 203–4.
91 Weyler, *Memoria de un general*, 204–5.
92 Foner, *The Spanish-American-Cuban War*, 119.
93 Tone, *War and Genocide in Cuba*, 223.
94 Flint, *Marching with Gómez*, 171.
95 In order to discourage further foraging, the CLA in one instance randomly executed five of the adult men with the party and stripped the remaining foragers (including women and children) naked and sent them back to the garrison from whence they came, depriving them of even the one thing that even the unsympathetic Spanish troops had allowed them to retain. See Ada Ferrer, *Insurgent Cuba: Race, Nation, and Revolution, 1868–1898* (Chapel Hill: University of North Carolina, 1999), 170.
96 Flint, *Marching with Gómez*, 253.
97 Foner, *The Spanish-American-Cuban War*, 116.
98 Tone, *War and Genocide in Cuba*, 223.
99 Ibid., 189.
100 Ferrer, *Insurgent Cuba*, 153.
101 Tone, *War and Genocide in Cuba*, 224.
102 For recent commentary on Weyler's methods by journalist Andrea Pitzer, see Pitzer, *One Long Night*, 17–40.

4

A howling wilderness: America in the Philippines

Dr Ethan H. Harding

*Take up the White Man's Burden – The savage wars of peace
Fill full the mouth of Famine And bid the sickness cease.*

The White Man's Burden
RUDYARD KIPLING, 1899[1]

Introduction

Although fought centuries ago, the Philippine-American War, with particular emphasis on how the US military approached the dynamics of populations in the islands brings credible lessons to light – many of which apply to contemporary population-centric counterinsurgency operations. The value of this study to contemporary operations is best found in the operations of J. Franklin Bell and his Third Separate Brigade on Luzon and Jacob Smith and his Sixth Separate Brigade on Samar. In the simplest terms, Bell's approach serves as a unique comparison to the concept of coordinating the modern employment of the Instruments of National Power – diplomacy, information, military and economics.

As a result of the Treaty of Paris that ended the Spanish-American War, the United States inherited many of Spain's colonial possessions – including the Philippines. Early on, American military leaders, in their design of a campaign of pacification, had to work with some challenging constraints and restraints; the United States was a reluctant imperialist – ruling an empire was simply not in keeping with the American ideals of self-determination. An active press, paired-with a population suspicious of anything that smelled of an empire created a complex problem for President William McKinley. With a looming re-election campaign in 1901, he needed a pacified Philippines – quick and without scandal. Lucky for him, he had leaders who could produce wins. Unfortunately, most failed to grasp the larger political dynamics that drove operational requirements. In their defence, most uniformed leaders lacked sufficient experience in fighting insurgencies. The US Army's only recent counterinsurgency experience was fighting Native Americans. Unfortunately, this experience led many veteran leaders to misplace those lessons in situations where they did not fit well in the Philippines.

With these factors, a plan for quick pacification and eventual exit of troops was devised: in areas where tribal structure existed, the United States would co-opt those leaders and their existing tribal government structure. With the credibility of tribal leaders, the US military would assist the fledgling national government in Manila to extend its reach into remote areas.[2]

The White Man's Burden[3]

In his famous poem, *The White Man's Burden, 1899, The United States and the Philippines*, Rudyard Kipling attempted to explain to the American public the obligations and consequences of its newly acquired colonial Philippine territories.[4] The American experience in the Philippines Islands began when, in late April 1898, Commodore George Dewey's fleet smashed the Spanish Fleet at Manila Bay. This, in turn, caused President William McKinley to send ground troops there to take control of the archipelago. As in Cuba, the Spanish were then wrestling with a full blown rebellion in the islands, and Commodore Dewey had actually assisted a Tagalog rebel leader named Emilio Aguinaldo by bringing him back from exile in Hong Kong to the Philippines.[5] The United States formally gained sovereignty over the entire archipelago on 10 December 1898, with the signing of the Treaty of Paris. President McKinley then moved rapidly to establish an administrative apparatus that effectively made the Philippines an American colony. Unfortunately, the United States lacked a colonial office or a ministry of the marine that was prepared to take on the mission of 'benevolent assimilation' as McKinley called the process of annexation and, thus, the job of governing the Philippines fell to the US Army.[6]

The first US Army commander in the islands was Major General Wesley Merritt, who conquered Manila from the Spanish. His tenure was short lived, and he was replaced in late August 1898 by Major General Elwell S. Otis, a Civil War veteran, who was known for his rigidity and poor judgement. As it became clear that the United States did not intend to liberate the Philippines, nationalist leaders such as Aguinaldo turned against the Americans, and by February 1899, the US Army was at war with Filipino insurgents. Otis struck hard against them and was initially successful because Aguinaldo attempted to fight a conventional war with the Americans. Unable to fill its new overseas commitments with the tiny force of 65,000-strong US Army, Congress authorized a further 35,000-strong volunteer force, which was enlisted for two years exclusively for service in the Philippines.[7] This force was very well trained and led, and began to arrive in the Philippines in November 1899. By January 1900, Otis had 63,000 men in seventeen regular and twenty-four volunteer infantry regiments, as well as three cavalry regiments, with which to pacify the islands. The strength of the American force caused Aguinaldo and other Philippine leaders to abandon conventional tactics shifting to guerrilla warfare instead. Otis commanded the Division of the Philippines and also served as military governor. He divided the islands into four departments, Northern Luzon, Southern Luzon, the Visayas, and Mindanao and Jolo. To his credit, while simultaneously fighting the insurgents, Otis organized local government and established a fair judicial code.

The militarization of colonialism

From November 1899 through April 1900, the US Army fought 671 engagements and lost 196 dead and 634 wounded.[8] Many of the battles were fiercely fought, and the American 1st Division commander, Major General Henry W. Lawton, was killed at San Mateo in December. The army claimed to have killed 3,200 and wounded 700 insurgents in the same period, while capturing 2,900 more.[9] General Otis felt successful enough to request relief from his assignment, and he was relieved in May 1900 by the 2nd Division commander, Major General Arthur MacArthur.

It was under MacArthur's leadership that American counterinsurgency policies in the Philippines began to gain notoriety because of harsh methods. This began as MacArthur's continuation of Otis's policies failed to produce rapid and decisive results, which, in turn, pushed the secretary of war to pressure MacArthur. On 20 December 1900, MacArthur issued a proclamation that placed the Philippines under martial law.[10] The legal basis for the declaration of martial law lay in General Orders 100, issued by the US War Department on 24 April 1863 (also known as the Lieber Code).[11] The Lieber Code laid out specific criteria for the identification of combatants and defined allowable behaviour when the army was fighting rebels and partisans. The code was a product of the American Civil War and was designed around the idea of fighting and governing occupied territory. It was quite harsh and, under certain circumstances, permitted the starvation of civilians, retaliation, summary execution and the use of no quarter.[12]

MacArthur's declaration was nowhere nearly as specific as General Orders 100, but it defined what constituted a rebellious act and outlined the penalties for transgressions. While harsh, it is sometimes forgotten that the proclamation also extended protection to those Filipinos, who chose to support the rule of law. According to historian Brian Linn, 'MacArthur believed that his proclamation marked the beginnings of an entirely new campaign ... based on the central idea of detaching towns from the immediate support of guerrillas in the field, and thus also precluding the indirect support which arose from indiscriminate acceptance by the towns of the insurrection in all its devious ramifications.'[13] Concurrently, American troop strength rose to a peak of 70,000 men, and MacArthur proceeded to put the insurgents under relentless pressure with a combination of tactics. American troops were teamed up with locally recruited military units known as Native Scouts and provinces were swept of guerrillas. In some locations, the population was concentrated into camps and a system of US Army provost courts was established. Many villages came over to the Americans, especially when the locals were allowed to harvest the crops of their neighbours who had been identified as insurgents. Aguinaldo himself was captured in March 1901 and other top leaders surrendered in some numbers. By late spring, MacArthur judged that many provinces were, in fact, pacified. His tour ended shortly thereafter, and MacArthur was replaced on 4 July 1901, by Major General Adna R. Chafee.

At the same time that Chafee took command, William H. Taft arrived as the new civil governor, a move that enabled Chafee to refocus the army on primarily military tasks. This division of effort was the result of MacArthur's successes which, in combination with increasing uneasiness about the harshness of military occupation, led some in Washington to think that the Philippines were ready for civilian-led rule. Operationally, the reorganization allowed Chafee to 'replace civil-military organizations with purely military ones, and thus divorce the army from civil administration'.[14] Acting as an accelerant to his action was a combined attack by guerrillas and townspeople on an isolated American garrison at Balangiga, Samar on 28 September 1901. On that day, insurgents attacked seventy-four American soldiers of the Company C, 9th US Infantry Regiment early in the morning in what has been termed a massacre. In hand-to-hand fighting with knives and clubs, forty-eight Americans were killed, including all of the company's officers. Only four soldiers remained unwounded and the attack shocked the American public. The massacre spurred Chafee to action, and he immediately authorized local retaliation. Following this he dissolved the old geographical departments, and in October, Chafee formed two divisions and seven separate brigades. These army units were assigned sectors and given missions to eradicate the remaining resistance through military means. Meanwhile, US troop strength in the islands had steadily dropped to 48,000 men in July and to 37,349 on 1 December.[15] In terms of maximizing his declining strength, Chafee's concept of untying his army from geography did much to restore the mobility of his few remaining troops.

Relocation: Decisions and effects

Unfortunately, Chafee's reassignment of command responsibilities led to what many contemporary observers and later historians have termed as atrocities. Of his subordinates, two officers were particularly linked to practices that today would be considered as war crimes. They were Brigadier General J. Franklin Bell, who commanded the 3rd Separate Brigade on southern Luzon, and Brigadier General Jacob H. Smith, who commanded the 6th Separate Brigade on Samar. Both officers took up their commands in November 1901.

Bell had 2,600 soldiers under his command to control a population of over 600,000 people.[16] Bell's campaign on Luzon was methodical and was based on forcing the insurgents to want to make peace, which meant imposing drastic measures on the general population. While Bell focused on making life impossible for the insurgents and their supporters, in fairness, he also focused on fair and considerate treatment for those Filipinos who abided by the rule of law. Bell began his programme on 8 December by ordering his commanders to establish 'Zones of Protection' within the physical limits of towns into which all Filipinos had to move no later than Christmas.[17] His men then collected up all the foodstuffs in the area from 26 December to 31 December. Once this was accomplished, Bell's brigade began to sweep through the operational area hunting the insurgents. In essence the American strategy on Luzon rested on a basis of the Cuba-like reconcentration of the population in order to deny support to the rebels, and his overall aim was to separate the guerrillas from the people (over 300,000 were relocated).[18] Bell's measures were extreme; houses were burned, Filipino prisoners were executed in retaliation for the killing of American soldiers, and sometimes men found outside the Zones of Protection were shot on sight.[19] Nevertheless, these ruthless tactics and the relentless pursuit led directly to the surrender of the primary insurgent leader, Miguel Malvar, and his men on 6 April 1902.

Meanwhile on Samar, Brigadier General Jacob Smith instituted an even more brutal counterinsurgency regime than Bell had established on Luzon, earning him the nickname 'Howling Jake' Smith. The island of Samar had a population of 202,000, and it was rugged in the extreme, making travel and manoeuvre very difficult.[20] As on Luzon, Smith quickly reconcentrated the people and began to hunt down the insurgents; however, the brutality of the Balangiga massacre apparently served to enrage Smith (many of the dead Americans had been mutilated beyond recognition).[21] Smith's nickname derived from his instruction to US Marine Corps Major Littleton Waller to make Samar 'a howling wilderness'.[22] Waller's orders, moreover, contained specific instructions to take no prisoners and burn and kill everything in sight.[23] Smith's tactics were brutally effective, and he successfully pacified the island within six months. Both Smith and Waller were later tried by courts-martial for these activities, although Waller was acquitted on a technicality. On 4 July 1902, President Teddy Roosevelt declared the insurgency to be over but, in truth, the insurgency continued for years afterward. About 4,200 American soldiers died of the 126,500 men who served in the islands during the insurrection while 16,000 to 20,000 insurgents died as well as about 34,000 Filipino civilians, who died as a direct result of the war.[24] Another 200,000 Filipino civilians died in the cholera epidemics that accompanied reconcentration and deprivation.[25]

The United States' suppression of the Philippine Insurrection left a bitter taste in many American's mouths. Its brutality served as grist for the propaganda mills of the anti-Imperialists in the United States, and American abuses were the subject of a number of congressional commissions and inquiries. Interestingly for modern Americans in the post-9/11 world, the issues of torture and a coercive practice called the 'water cure', which were used to extract information from prisoners were subjects of interest to the congressional committees.[26] Independence for the islands would not come until 1946 and, ironically, at the hands of Arthur MacArthur's son, General Douglas MacArthur.

America's suppression of the Philippine Insurrection lasted about four years and, in the near term, might be classified as generally successful. The American operational design shared many features with that used by Weyler in Cuba; however, the employment of *trocha* was unnecessary in the Philippines because the islands themselves were compact enough to be treated as single sub-sectors. To suppress the insurrection, the United States initially deployed a substantially larger force that was well equipped and well trained. But, as American troop strength in the islands dropped, the Americans turned increasingly to harsher methods that exceeded the brutality seen in Cuba under Weyler.[27]

The consequences of relocation

In application, this plan proved difficult; many remote areas – especially those with Muslim majorities – were suspicious of outsiders and resistant to subordination to centralized rule. In attempting to colonize the Philippines, the Spanish encountered this dynamic and never fully secured power in these areas. Compounding the existing difficulties of a schizophrenic application, where experiences from the Indian Wars – particularly those related to separating insurgents from the populace undermined the goals required to set conditions for central government control and an exit of US troops – in time for President McKinley to leverage this in the coming election.

In attempting to separate insurgent from popular support, while still aiming to leverage tribal structure to pacify remote areas – a vision of success that drove US Army Brigadier General John Bates to enter the US government into a treaty with the sultan of Sulu. Under this arrangement Moro leaders accepted US authority, while Moro authority was largely preserved. In attempting to capitalize on this diplomatic momentum, American forces and their Filipino partners took two approaches.

In the first case, the 1901 forced relocation of populations from areas vulnerable to insurgent influence to areas easily protected by American forces and Filipino allies. Once resettled, American soldiers attempted to prioritize resources into these 'protected zones' – resulting in significant public works programmes, designed to improve access to quality food, medicine and education.[28] The idea of prioritizing resources towards service provision in these protected zones was conducted knowing that relocation could cause upheaval, and the relocated population could either suffer or benefit from their proximity to US garrisons (with deep analysis, we can trace the DNA of the contemporary Provincial Reconstruction Team back to the concept of service provision in protected zones – minus the population relocation portion).[29] Unfortunately, execution of this plan proved difficult – food shortages, poor hygiene practices and insufficient medical care eventually resulted in a cholera epidemic in 1902.[30]

In the second case, forced relocation by circumstances (fighting) – in areas outside of protected zones, where Filipino insurgents could find support, American forces engaged in 'slash and burn' campaigns, where they would destroy anything of value that could enable insurgents to stay in the field.

Legacies and lessons

These misplaced lessons immediately surfaced in 1899 – many veterans from the Indian Wars advocated for a strategy that divided the highly mobile insurgents from the logistics they enjoyed in population centres (see Chapter 2). The legacies of these Indian Wars-based approaches are witnessed by the large number of Native American reservations in the United States today. Results of relocation to protected zones:

From a tactical perspective, the separation of insurgent from population seriously impacted guerrilla activity. At the individual level, insurgents suffered greatly – lack of supplies left insurgents in need of medical care upon capture. This weakening of insurgent forces enabled American and Filipino forces to attack insurgents with great advantage,[31] eventually degrading insurgent operational capabilities to a point where US forces could begin a transfer of operational responsibility to the Filipino Constabulary.

Two critical non-kinetic legal precedents were employed or imposed during the course of the American campaign in the Philippines. These were the Hell Gate Treaty of 1855, which legally deprived Native Americans in

Oregon of their land and General Order 100 – a relic of the post-Civil War Federal occupation of the Confederacy.[32] The former aimed at securing an agreement that could enable the fledgling Manila government to establish control in the outlying areas of the islands. The latter sought to establish what are today called Rules of Engagement for fighting insurgents, and ensuring the protection of civilians.

As a strategic approach both resettlement methods were employed to deny logistical support to the enemy. Unfortunately, these approaches did little to move the United States towards its goal of co-opting the existing power apparatus to support the establishment of a national government – one able to extend governance from Manila throughout the islands.

Relocation, and subordination to American supremacy, put all levels of Moro leadership in a position where they risked discredit.[33] The Moro culture respects fighting prowess, and demands its leaders ensure the well-being of the tribe. The schizophrenic application of relocation and 'slash and burn' operations, and the suffering that resulted, undermined the authority of top leaders. Compounding this dynamic was the loss of many mid-level leaders, who could have rose to inherit roles vacated by more senior tribal leaders.[34] These younger leaders were either dead or moved – with their families to fortified villages, where they were again exposed to highly destructive campaigns waged by American forces.

In terms of what are today called Joint Operations, the US Army and the US Navy operated in ways that greatly complimented the efforts of the other service. While a lack of professional accounts present obstacles in understanding if these results were planned, accidental or opportunities seized at the junior officer level – as many successes were, we will never truly know, but the results point to navy ownership of ports effectively interdicted insurgent access to goods, while further-separating the populace, who were driven to army-controlled areas in order to obtain better access to food and other necessities. Accidental or not, the army and navy succeeded in controlling the flow of basic needs into contested areas.[35] More than anything else, control separated the populace from the insurgent. Across many studies, regardless of terrain, ethnicity, culture or other factors, ensuring a population can fulfil the *Fundamentals of Social Stability* is what was decisive.[36]

Conclusions

In the past decades, as leaders sought to better understand how to best employ resources, counterinsurgency during the Philippine-American War was often discussed. For learning purposes, the best lessons are drawn from Bell's use of Zones of Protection – a technique that built native trust in working with US forces, while simultaneously reinforcing the authority of the tribal leaders needed to establish links from village-provincial-national governments. The carrot of providing needs fulfilment not only served the purpose of separating the populace from the insurgent but did so in a way that ensured positive reaction by a suspicious American domestic population – until disease broke out in camps. Rather than forcible relocation, the counterinsurgent can best separate the population from insurgents by creating conditions favourable to the population. Another lesson applicable for contemporary counterinsurgency operations is the over value of 'kill, capture, and interdict operations'. Many resources are rightly applied to destroying insurgent structure. The reduction of insurgent capacity in Luzon created manoeuvre space for Bell's forces to fill – both inside and outside – the protection zones.[37] However, the culminating point (a military term for a tipping point or an inflection point) of any campaign is when the supporting counterinsurgent and the supported government can set conditions for fulfilment of the *Fundamentals of Social Stability* better than the shadow government.[38] The American campaign in the Philippines also witnessed the common mistake of not understanding enemy networks, overvaluing the elimination of leaders, followed by a premature transition to indigenous forces and leaders. This dynamic occurred in 1901, with the capture of Emilio Aguinaldo – the most visible insurgent leader. American leadership mistook Aguinaldo's capture as an opportunity to execute President McKinley's desired drawdown of American troops prior to the upcoming presidential campaign. Overvaluing the control Aguinaldo had over other insurgent elements, American forces were either pulled from the field or yielded operational responsibility to the Filipino Constabulary.[39] This premature move nearly overwhelmed the native Filipino forces, and left them operationally inconsequential.

Notes

1 Edward J. Erickson, *A Soldier's Kipling: Poetry and the Profession of Arms* (Barnsley: Pen and Sword Publishers, 2018), 138–41.

2 Ethan H. Harding, *Identifying the Pillars of Stability Operations: Using Social Science to Bridge the Gap in Operational Doctrine* (Fort Leavenworth, KS: CGSC Foundation Press, 2010), 44.

3 I am grateful to the editor for allowing me to extensively extract material for the following three sections from his work, Edward J. Erickson, *Ottomans and Armenians, A Study in Counterinsurgency* (New York: Palgrave Macmillan, 2013), 85–9.

4 Erickson, *A Soldier's Kipling*, 138–41.

5 Brian McAllister Linn, *The U.S. Army and Counterinsurgency in the Philippine War, 1899–1902* (Chapel Hill: The University of North Carolina Press, 1989), 5–6.

6   Ibid., 9.
7   These forces were known as US Volunteer formations and comprised twenty-five regiments of infantry and one of cavalry. See Linn, *The U.S. Army and Counterinsurgency in the Philippine War*, 13–14 for an excellent summary of the raising of these forces.
8   Robert D. Ramsey III, *Savage Wars of Peace: Case Studies of Pacification in the Philippines, 1900–1902* (Fort Leavenworth, KS: CSI Press, 2007), 22.
9   Ibid.
10 For a complete copy of MacArthur's proclamation of 10 December 1900 (which was issued ten days later), see Ramsey, *Savage Wars of Peace*, Appendix C, 159–62.
11 For a complete copy of General Orders 100, 24 April 1863, see Ramsey, *Savage Wars of* Peace, Appendix B, 135–57.
12 Ibid.
13 Linn, *The U.S. Army and Counterinsurgency in the Philippine War*, 24. Linn cited US War Department correspondence between Brigadier General Thomas H. Berry and the commanding general, Division of Northern Luzon for this quotation.
14 Linn, *The U.S. Army and Counterinsurgency in the Philippine War*, 26.
15 Ramsey, *Savage Wars of Peace*, 96.
16 Frank L. Andrews, 'The Philippine Insurrection (1899–1902): Development of the U.S. Army's Counterinsurgency Policy' (Louisiana State University Master's Theses, Baton Rouge, LA, 2002), 16.
17 Ibid., 97–8.
18 Ibid., 165.
19 John J. Tierney Jr., *Chasing Ghosts, Unconventional Warfare in American History* (Washington, DC: Potomac Books, Inc., 2006), 132.
20 Division of Insular Affairs, *Report of the United States Philippine Commission to the Secretary of War, For the Period January 1, 1900 to October 15, 1901* (Washington, DC: United States War Department, 1901), 591.
21 Ibid., 131.
22 Mark Oswald, 'The Howling Wilderness Courts-Martial of 1902' (US Army War College Master's Theses, Carlisle Barracks, PA, 2001), 9.
23 Tierney, *Chasing Ghosts,* 132.
24 Ramsey, *Savage Wars of Peace*, 103.
25 Ibid.
26 Henry F. Graff (ed.), *American Imperialism and the Philippine Insurrection (Testimony taken from Hearings on Affairs in the Philippine Islands before the Senate Committee on the Philippines-1902)* (Boston, MA: Little, Brown and Company, 1969), 64–88. The testimony of Robert Hughes, Charles Riley and Daniel Evans regarding the 'water cure' makes interesting comparative reading with regard to the contemporary American practice of 'water boarding' in order to extract information from prisoners.

27 For recent work on the subject of American operations in the Philippines by journalist Andrea Pitzer, see Pitzer, *One Long Night*, 40–53.
28 Kalev I. Sepp, 'Resettlement, Regroupment, Reconcentration: Deliberate Government Directed Population Relocation in support of Counterinsurgency Operations' (US Army Command and General Staff College Master's of Military Arts and Sciences Theses, Ft Leavenworth, KS, 2002), 31.
29 Harding, *Identifying the Pillars of Stability Operations*, 39–40.
30 Sepp, 'Resettlement, Regroupment, Reconcentration: Deliberate Government Directed Population Relocation in Support of Counterinsurgency Operations', 31-2.
31 Ibid.
32 Ibid., 29
33 Harding, *Identifying the Pillars of Stability Operations*, 40.
34 Ibid., 43.
35 Eric Weyenberg, 'Population Isolation in the Philippine War: A Case Study', (Monograph) (School of Advanced Military Studies, Ft Leavenworth, KS, January 2015), 10.
36 Harding, *Identifying the Pillars of Stability Operations*, 85.
37 William Putnam, US Army, 'COIN Lessons Ignored: The Philippines Campaign (1899–1902)', *Small Wars Journal*, (2012), 3.
38 Ibid.
39 Sepp, 'Resettlement, Regroupment, Reconcentration: Deliberate Government Directed Population Relocation in Support of Counterinsurgency Operations', 30.

5

Methods of barbarism:

The Boer War

Dr John Sheehan

When is a war not a war? When it is carried on by methods of barbarism ...
SIR HENRY CAMPBELL-BANNERMAN
London, 14 June 1901[1]

Introduction

'War is an extension of politics by other means' is the standard reduction of Carl von Clausewitz's definitive analysis of Napoleonic, that is, modern warfare. That dictum may indeed be applied to the Boer War, or as it is now referred to as the South African War (Map 5). Formerly described as 'the last gentleman's war', 'the first white man's war' and the last of Queen Victoria's 'little wars', these 'little wars', waged on the cheap, were won with archaic methods of proto-industrial military might that in the space of a few decades had overrun, despite setbacks, vast swaths of the poorly equipped and mutually antagonistic indigenous peoples that inhabited several continents.[2] The stereotype of the Boer War, which pitted a rural, strictly covenantal people against an expanding, mercantile empire, which at its germ is true, must be teased apart to see the many layers of strategy and geopolitics involved in the decisions, and the outcomes of those decisions, in Clausewitz's paradigm. How did Germany, Russia, France, the United States and Dynastic China play roles in the realm of Grand Strategy?

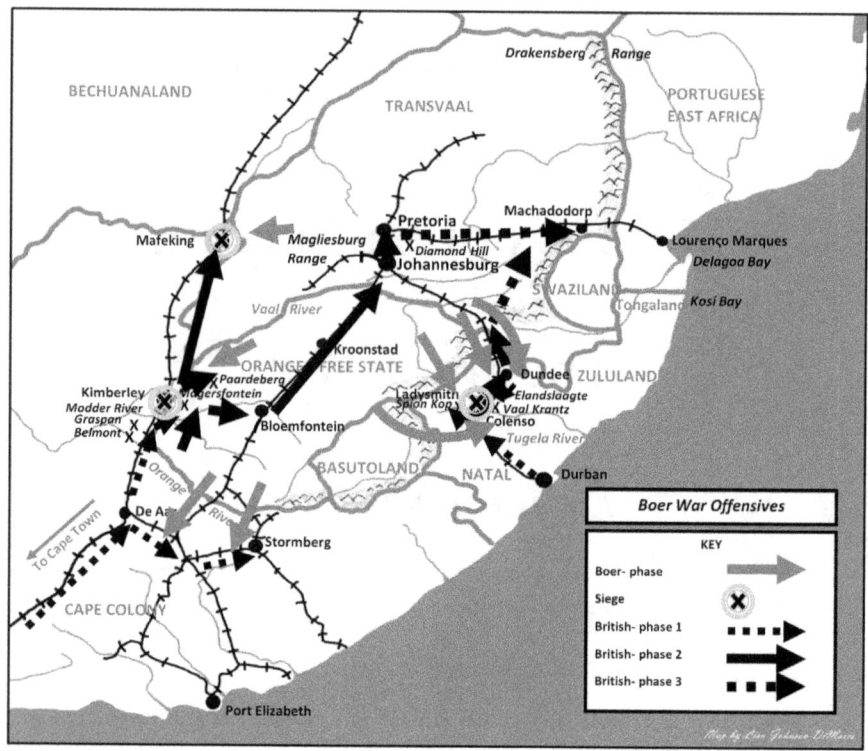

MAP 5 *The Boer War. The Second Anglo-Boer War began as a conventional war and ended as a guerrilla war between the British army and Boer commandos. In order to defeat the Boers, British commanders forcibly relocated the Boer civilian population to concentration camps and drove the guerrillas to destruction against blockhouse and barbed wire lines.*

How could an imperial mantra that promulgated the proselytization of the 'white man's burden' to the savage races of blighted lands result in making those lands even more blighted through 'scorched earth' tactics, removing an entire population to concentration camps and savaging the white race it was meant to promote, while ensuring the subjugation of the black tribes it was meant to enlighten? Recent studies have included the contributions of the local black populations in the struggle – hence the term 'South African War' – and this necessary inclusion will better explain the antecedents, the course and the consequences of the war.[3]

The thesis

Returning to Clausewitz, if war is utilized as a last resort to induce a political point of view on another, who is that other? Ethnicity is defined as those common cultural characteristics shared by a people. Race is of the body; ethnicity is of the mind. Physical traits of personhood, such as racial and sexual characteristics, are not essential to one's ethnicity, but through the course of history, often have been. It is important to state this, because during the Boer War these ideas will intrude greatly into the military extension of political thought and cause seismic shifts in strategic thinking before the treaty ending the war was signed, and the unforeseen consequences of that drying ink became manifest. The purpose of this book, and hence of this chapter, is to use precise analysis to discern the 'razor's edge' of strict military efficacy in using displacement and internment of peoples as a valid Clausewitzian concept. That is a herculean task, and I will first broaden the scope of the thesis to examine the peoples that engaged in combat in the Boer War, and then examine the decisions that ultimately led to the wholesale internment of civilians in concentration camps. Maslow has demonstrated how resources determine behaviour in a strict hierarchy of needs. From basic survival to contemplative enlightenment, the access to resources determines cultural constructions and political 'truths'. In times of fear and dearth, Clausewitz tells us how to transcend politics.

The British

What impelled Great Britain to engage in warfare in southern Africa in late 1899? The little nation of shopkeepers' that had beaten Napoleon never adhered to the nineteenth-century nation-in-arms military ethos that the nations on the continent had, and, as a result, her army was starved of money and men. Britain, Shakespeare's 'fortress made by Nature for herself', via a 'the moat defensive to her house' – the English Channel – favoured her navy, those 'wooden walls' that afforded her a 'splendid isolation' from the cesspit of continental politics and enabled her to win her 'little wars' and gain control over a quarter of the planet's surface. The timeless, hierarchical cant of aristocracy, gentry and commoner was metamorphosing under the pressures of industrialization. The Victorian Compromise, of creeping democratic reforms over the period of half a century, 'progressed' by fits and starts. The nuclei of the British army, the regiments, were clans and tribal groups writ large. A regiment was a tightly knit family of Gordons, Coldstream Guards, Black Watch Highlanders and so on. It may have been a small army with a mobile reserve of only 50,000 men, but it was spirited. This was 'Mr. Kipling's Army',[4] upon whose sinews the White Man's Burden was to be evangelized:

> Take up the White Man's burden – Send forth the best ye breed –
> Go bind your sons to exile, To serve your captive's need;
> To wait in heavy harness, On fluttered folk and wild –
> Your new caught, sullen peoples, Half-devil and half-child.[5]

Edward Said has written about how imperialists promulgate their civilizing missions; they must 'primitivise', if not demonize, the other. The hardening on one's heart among the alien other will lead to dire consequences in the Boer War, whether the other was an unseen sniper, an artful guerrilla, his wife or his child. To muddy the waters further, Darwinian iconoclasm was gnawing at the edges of deified morality, and traditional religion would bare its fangs and fight back with 'Muscular Christianity'. Despite the steady secularization of the nineteenth century,[6] most Britons were reliably Protestant and duly inculcated with the morals of their day as they marched across the veldt in South Africa.[7]

The latter half of the nineteenth century was a disorienting time. It would be termed the fin de siècle, and in it the British army would be caught flat-footed. The army was taught to stand up to Indians with bravery, order and endurance, but in South Africa it would need brains and skill. I will discuss the nature of the Boer Republics before addressing how the 'blood and iron' politics of the German Second Reich upended the balance of power in Europe. It was a horrifying time when Britain's obsolete army could not think of matching Germany's twenty-five army corps in land battle, and the overnight obsolescence of Britain's 'wooden walls' left her island fortress vulnerable to the new steel navies that Germany and France now raced to produce which threatened Britannia's dominance of the seas.

The Boers

In 1652, the Dutch East India Company had set up an entrepôt in the area soon to become known as Cape Town for its mercantile fleets sailing to and from Indonesia. The enclave was quickly populated by Dutch Calvinist pilgrims, who despite their schisms, tended to lean towards fundamentalist doctrines and rites. They were a wandering chosen people who had been delivered unto a promised land. Most Afrikaners acquiesced until 1834, when Britain outlawed slavery, which drove 5,000 of the more covenant-minded Boers – *Voertrekkers* – along with their slaves and other transportable property, northward across the liminal boundaries of the Orange and the Vaal rivers. Though lacking a formed state, their *volk* weltanschauung provided them with a cultural grid, and as Lord Roberts would find out in his mistaken strategy of 'capital seizing' – like Napoleon had done before him at Moscow – Bloemfontein and Pretoria were contradictions to the Boer mindset. There was no central nerve nexus that could be taken with which to throttle the Boer into submission. Each Boer was his own priest and his own general. Their commandos either gave battle or ran away by council, down to a man. At Spion Kop, General Louis Botha had to remonstrate with his reluctant burghers with the most urgent appeals to get them to re-ascend the kopje – hillock – to drive off the British.[8]

During the war, Boer women faithfully provided intelligence to their husbands in the hills and resupplied them when they briefly visited their homesteads. Kitchener would have no qualms burning down her buildings, driving off or killing her animals and leaving her and her children alone amid the smouldering ruins of her veldt farmstead. Within five days of assuming command from Roberts, he said:

> There is no doubt the women are keeping up the war and are far more bitter than the men. ... Every farm is an intelligence agency and a supply depot so that it is almost impossible to surround or catch the enemy.[9]

Misunderstanding the character of the Boer, British intelligence had miscalculated when it advocated a 'scorched earth' policy: 'It was thought that pressure might be brought to bear on the commandos through their womenfolk and that they would not be able to bear separation from their families.'[10] When news of the burnings and depredations reached the commandos, Deneys Reitz related:

> It was borne in on us that a more terrible chapter of the war was opening. The intention was to undermine the morale of the fighting man, but the effect was exactly the opposite. ... Instead of weakening, they became only the more resolved to hold out, and this policy instead of shortening the war, prolonged it by a year or more.[11]

In the end, over 30,000 farms and 40 towns were burned. Of the 260,000 Boers at the conflict's commencement, 115,000 women, children and non-combatant men would be corralled in 45 concentration camps, and due to starvation and disease, 26,000 of them – one tenth of the Afrikaner population – would perish in these camps. Of these, 20,000 would be children. One hundred and fifteen thousand blacks would also be detained in camps, but this time by both the British and the Boers, and 18,000 would die as a result. As the war and the ravages dragged on, Boer society became riven into three distinct groups: the 'bitter-enders', those die hard Boers who would suffer through several seasons of increasing privation and desperation to fight for a peace that guaranteed Boer independence; the 'hands-uppers', those Boers who had fought through the campaigns that had ground up the British field armies, but surrendered when their loved ones and their property suffered grievously at the hands of the counterinsurgent yeoman; and the 'joiners', those Boers who did not own their own land and were the despised lowest dregs of Boer society. It was the joiners who betrayed their own holy seed by fighting with the British for Esau's wages, and who were executed as traitors when caught by the bitter-enders. Fifteen thousand hands-uppers, 27 per cent of the available grist for the commandos signed capitulations after the fall of Pretoria.[12] Many would rejoin after the burnings started. The Boers would not soon forget the 'destructions' of the war. And when the British army began recruiting black auxiliaries, who knew the land, to scout and harass the Boer commandos and the stricken civilians, vengeful acts occurred. After the war, when the British accorded the Boers autonomy, Boer 'memory' sprouted as the bitter harvest of apartheid.

Imperialism and the Great Game

Indeed, if one would pinpoint the fundamental cause of the Boer War, it would be the fight for the acquisition and dominance of the diamond and gold fields of South Africa by the European and local hyper-capitalists of their day.[13] Cecil Rhodes, a messianic British race evangelist, made his fortune by investing in, sabotaging rivals of and unscrupulously fielding a paramilitary force in the diamond fields of Griqualand. Griqualand was originally under the suzerainty of the Boers until Great Britain annexed the territory in 1874. Rhodes again used his paramilitaries avariciously when he acquired the mineral rights within the Ndebele kingdom – present-day Zimbabwe – from Chief Lobengula for a few baubles.[14]

What had worked against the blacks should work against the Boers, Rhodes reasoned, when he loosed his band of irregulars into the Transvaal in 1895 – the Jameson Raid – to incite rebellion among the British *uitlanders* residing there, and seize the gold fields. The fait accompli failed and an international crisis was foisted upon the British government. Tribal black politics were as Machiavellian as anything cooked up by the imperialistic whites. When 40,000 Boers galloped off to war in 1899, 8,000 mounted black attendants – *agterryers* – rode with them, each managing several horses when the commandos dismounted, thus enabling the Boers to put most of their numbers into combat. By the end of the war, when Kitchener's 'scorched earth' and 'ethnic cleansing' tactics had eroded Boer numbers from 60,000 to 15,000, the number of black irregulars mobilized by the British had reached 30,000, a 2:1 ratio of strength against the Boers that emboldened a Zulu military force to fight and inflict 57 casualties upon the burgers at Holkrans. It would be news of Holkrans that would persuade Jan Smuts and his fellow negotiators to make peace with the British.[15]

Emotionalism supplanted rationalism, and patriotism equated to 'jingoism'. 'We don't want to fight, but by Jingo if we do, we've got the ships, we've got the men, and got the money too.' Music halls that staged performances of 'Tommy Atkins' and 'Soldiers of the Queen', to packed houses, proffered the promise of approved sexual pursuit in the Victorian Age: 'Jolly good luck to the girl who loves a soldier!' When war broke out and Kipling's reserve army had been siphoned off to be shot down on three black battlefields in southern Africa in December 1899, it was the common soldier, seeking a lassie and virtuous muscular adventure – the hero of these plays – who answered the call.[16] Yet, duty beckoned. It was the clerk, who could ride a horse, that would torch farmsteads across the veldt, and it was the factory worker that would succumb to the dearth of vivifying resources in the hospital. The war would claim the lives of 22,000 British soldiers, compared to 2,280 Boer casualties. There would be 46,400 Boer civilian deaths.[17]

South Africa in Grand Strategy

The Great Game commenced when Germany unified and threatened to dominate the sport of neo-imperialism in men, material and munitions within a handful of decades. It was to stifle the possible *volk* alliance between the Boers and the Germans, who hoped to develop Kosi Bay into a Teutonic naval base on the Indian Ocean – a dagger pointed at India – that Britain would annex Tongaland. Thereafter, the Pretoria-Laurenço Marques railway would be developed and protected like an only child. But that was all still nebulous; in South Africa in 1899, the strength of the British Empire would be tested in the first 'white man's war' there, and a potentially hostile Germany was prepared to intervene to protect its mercantile and cultural interests with the Afrikaner *volk*. The Boers rallied around their most extremist covenanters in 1881, and under the leadership of Paul Kruger ambushed the meagre troops of Mr Kipling's army in several small engagements, before finally humiliating Major General George Colley at Majuba Hill. The Boer states regained their status as independent nations in 1882.

The uneasy status quo that resulted was overturned altogether when the largest gold deposits in the world were discovered in the Rand region of the Transvaal in 1886. By 1895, more than 54,000 prospectors and speculators had inundated the sleepy 6,000 Afrikaners of Johannesburg, which exploded malignantly into the seething metropolis of infamous renown it was to become. Recognizing that for the Boer nations to survive they needed to modernize, Kruger gladly accepted the taxes and duties provided by these *uitlanders* mucking about in the gold fields. At the same time, he tried to slowly starve British exploitation of the gold profits by restricting the development of rail links to the Cape Colony, and blocking access to the wagon fords – drifts – that crossed the Vaal. This vexed British imperialists. Simultaneously, he wooed German investors to build the Laurenço Marques railroad through Portuguese East Africa and develop 'Teutonic' industry and finance in the Transvaal. Thusly, would Kruger play the Briton off the German in the Great Game. To counter the fatuous ideal of a British federation, he floated that of a South African federation of Afrikaners in its stead, dominated by the *volk*-bond of the Free State, the Transvaal and a reunited Cape state. Stiffened by a *volk*-bond alliance with Germany, it seemed feasible. The solvency of the Transvaal appreciated, and flush with funds, the Boers scoffed up the best rifles in the world, the German Mauser, by the tens of thousands, and mountains of smokeless rounds of ammunition, as well as the latest artillery pieces that money could buy. Kruger was so successful at his brinksmanship that there were naval stand-offs between German and British naval cruisers in Delagoa Bay.[18]

These developments were all too much for the temperament of a man like Rhodes. He would use his paramilitaries to seize Johannesburg once and for all. Hence, in 1895, Jameson and several hundred freebooters were dispatched into the Rand. The new overtly imperialistic Chamberlain government, freshly enfranchised over the ire of the growing German threat, hurriedly dispatched Alfred Milner, as High Commissioner of South Africa, to pick up the pieces of the wreckage of the Jameson Raid. Milner, a freshly minted British race imperialist of the ilk of Rhodes and Chamberlain, would do more than that; he would inveigle a war with the Boers to settle the question once and for all, and he was as adroit at the Great Game as Kruger was. He seized upon the shadow-side of the foreigner to paint Kruger into a corner. Either enfranchise the foreigner/*uitlander*, on the foreigner's terms, or war. It was never enough, until, pounding the conference table in a final outburst of outrage, a tear-swollen Kruger thundered: 'It is our country you want!'[19] It was to be war. Britain simply needed to control the international gold standard.

The war: 1899–1902

During the period of 'phony-peace' in the summer of 1899, both sides prepared and dithered. The British, due to the neglect of their army at the expense of the navy practised 'forward projection' of power to confront potential threats. The ten-million-strong Russian army was confronted by a 350,000-strong British-led army at the portals of the Hindu Kush in Afghanistan. From these cadres, the 'Indian ring' of officers, who were to be shunted over to serve in Africa, would push brinksmanship as a strategic means to achieve political ends. It was the policy designed to contain a European power with predominantly local forces. Roberts – Kipling's darling – and Kitchener were part of this clique. Field-Marshal Lord Garnet Wolseley and General Sir Redvers Buller were part of the 'African ring' that wanted to keep the mass of indigenous blacks on the sidelines through strong defensively strategic positions, and let naval developments settle international issues, before venturing forth on imperial offensives. The plan was to augment the 10,000 troops that garrisoned South Africa from the Cape to Kosi Bay with another 10,000 culled from garrisons in India, Malta, Crete and Egypt – it was to be a 'white man's war' after all – and dispatch these 10,000 to the Natal frontier. Wolseley, the Africanist, was too old to lead, so the Indians under his command, White and Symons, led the advance. Not only did they project too far forward, but they divided their force in the face of the enemy to protect the two avenues of *debouchment* from the Transvaal border, at Dundee and Ladysmith. Wolseley did forecast a 50,000-strong army to finish the job and had dispatched the single reserve corps from Britain under Buller to do just that. Bothering about expensive mule and horse transport could wait until a conflict actually started. It was to be a 'tea-time' war, and the tea-time warriors and forward-projectionists had, to their satisfaction, called Kruger's bluff and prepared. Kruger was not bluffing, but neither was he prepared. To win the latest 'little war' Mr Kipling's army would have to metastasize into an industrial giant, and eventually 250,000 men would sweep across the veldt at the staggering cost of over 240 million pounds.

During the apprehensive build-up to the war, the covenanters drew up no strategic plans other than, once mobilized, to await deliverance via a deus ex machina *denouement* on the battlefield. Only General Jan Smuts conceived a plan. Knowing that war was imminent after the British had dispatched 10,000 men to South Africa, and had just voted for sending 50,000 more, Smuts called for a simultaneous Israeli-like, 'hourglass', offensive to make his numbers strategically multiply in the few weeks that the Boers would hold the military advantage. Of the potential 60,000 effectives that could be mobilized, the Boers initially fielded 40,000 men. Smuts's 'blitzkrieg' was this: the main thrust of 27,000 men would push into Natal, deal with the meagre forces there and drive on to Durban, thus denying the British a port and protecting the Boer international access to supplies via Delagoa Bay. This would protect the eastern flank. The remaining 13,000 would advance in four columns, two of which would advance on Kimberley and Mafeking, which would sever the rail line through Bechuanaland and deprive the British not only of the revenues of the Rand gold fields but also of the diamond mines. By this move, which also cut off communications with Rhodesia, the Boer western and northern flanks would be secured. The other two columns would penetrate into the Cape Colony itself and sever the lateral rail lines running between De Aar and the eastern ports of Durban and Port Elizabeth, while inciting insurrection among the Afrikaners living there. Thusly would the southern flank become secure.

Several things frustrated Smuts's plan. The biggest was the equivocation of Marthinus Steyn, the president of the Orange Free State, who wasted the 'hourglass' opportunity by hoping that further concessions would appease the British. They would not. By the time Steyn recognized his folly, Natal had been reinforced by the British, and the 50,000-men reserve was almost at the docks of Cape Town. With the Boers now fully committed to conflict, Kruger delivered an untenable two-day ultimatum to the British on 9 October. The jingoists had been delivered a casus belli, but their joys at the outbreak of another 'little war', waged on the cheap, or so they envisioned, would be short-lived when the mounted commandos rolled forward forty-eight hours later.

On 20 October at Talana Hill, overlooking Dundee, the British scored a victory, albeit costly, by charging straight at the Boers with their infantry and charging the flank with cold-steel cavalry – *l'arme blanche* – in tried-and-true fashion. The invading Boers, however, had dispersed their commandos into nine columns. Blunted at Talana, and again the next day at Elandeslaagte by Lieutenant General Sir George White, where a threatening penetration was again defeated using the same tactics, the hydra-like tentacles of the Boers forced Brigadier General James Yule, who replaced the mortally wounded Major General Sir William Symons at Talana, back towards Ladysmith, and the combined force of 13,000 Britons was surrounded and besieged there. There would be several attempted stormings by the Boers, who were averse to such tactics, and breakouts by the British, who could not dislodge the Boers in defensive mode, over the next few months, but nothing availed. Commandant-General Piet Joubert, the stolid crony of Kruger, committed too much force to hemming in Ladysmith, which effectively took the steam out of a follow-up dash to Durban. It was too late already. Steyn's hesitation allowed Buller, who landed at Cape Town on 31 October with the reserve, to dispatch forces to Durban and save Natal. Dislodging the intransigent Boers from it, however, would be another matter. On the offensive, the Boers would balk in an assault, but when they went to ground in defence, they came into their own. Joubert would soon die, and the defence in Natal passed into the hands of General Louis Botha.[20]

It was to be the same on other fronts. On 12 October, Boer general Andries Cronje, another one of Kruger's old birds, advanced on Mafeking, where the British rifles gave as good as they got from the Boer Mausers, and another impasse led to Colonel Robert Baden-Powell with a small, spirited force becoming besieged within it. The same scenario played out at Kimberley. Cronje then destroyed the railroad lines through Bechuanaland and crossed the Modder River to the south to confront the expected British advance after Buller had landed. In the invasion of the Cape, the commandos demolished the lateral railroad links that severed Cape Town from Natal. About 10,000 Afrikaners arose to join the Boer raiders, but most elected to stay loyally British and the conflagration was contained.

Confronted with the strategic wreckage of the anaemic British strategy, Buller wanted to advance upon the strategic axis of the Boer Republics, by a concentrated drive on Bloemfontein and Pretoria. But, under intense political pressure to relieve both Kimberley and Ladysmith, he decided to divide his 47,000 effectives into four forces. The first, of 10,000 men under Lieutenant General Lord Paul Methuen, would advance up the rail line from Cape Town to drive directly on Kimberley. The second, of 20,000 men, under himself, would advance from Durban and drive on Ladysmith. The two latter forces, roughly 3,000 men each under Lieutenant General Sir William Gatacre and Major General John French, would liberate and repair the lateral rail links and tamp down the fires of insurrection in the northern Cape. This strategy, which diluted British strength over exterior lines, would enable the Boers to utilize their interior lines and shunt troops from one threatened sector to another as exigencies arose.

Methuen moved off first on 21 November. Cronje would adopt a defence-in-depth strategy to fight him. In a Cowpens- and Guilford Courthouse-like manner, he would shoot and withdraw both tactically and strategically against the British at Belmont on 23 November, at Graspan on 25 November and at the Modder River on 28 November. Each time gallant British infantrymen would carry the field in frontal assaults, leaving bullet-ridden corpses in their wakes as the Boer mounted infantry retreated to the next position. At the Modder, a strategic barrier, the Boers dug-in on the near side of the river and drilled the approaching British with crossfires, while the unimaginative British artillery shelled the far side, 'where the enemy ought to be'. Here, the smokeless rounds of the Boers would come into their own. No one knew where the enemy 'snipers-en-masse' were. Yet, despite these galling fights, Methuen crossed the river, and Kimberley lay barely two dozen miles away.

Following the rail line from Durban, Buller advanced on Colenso and prepared to assault the dug-in Boers on the far side of the Tugela River by 15 December. Buller planned a typical battle: a preparatory barrage to soften up the enemy to be followed by infantry assaults that would crack open the way to Ladysmith, which would then be liberated in the pursuit that followed the battle by the cavalry. Instead, the long range of the modern artillery and rifles possessed by the Boers immobilized the British artillery that had drawn up too close to the front. Ad hoc relief columns had to be dispatched piecemeal into the maelstrom by Buller to extricate the guns, thus unravelling the entire plan. One unfortunate column had floundered into a cul-de-sac of the river and was shot to pieces. This was one of a triad of battles fought between 9 December and 15 December, the casualties of which were to horrify the British government, the people and the press. 'Black Week' it would be called. To pour salt into the wounds, the Boxer Rebellion had broken out in China in November, and a vulnerable India, already shorn of troops, lay under the jowls of the Russian Bear. That predator, however, smelled fresher blood in China, and Britain gave Japan a green light to contest Korea with the Russians. This they would avidly do. And Germany was palliated with the sop of a naval base in Samoa.[21] Britain could concentrate on South Africa, but things got even darker.

After the Modder River, there was one last hill, at Magersfontein, that prevented the British from debouching into the plain and relieving Kimberley. There was no more room for a defence-in-depth strategy for the Boers. The young-blood, General Jacobus De la Rey, talked Cronje into deploying his troops at the base of the hill in interlocking fields of fire from trenches and rifle pits. Let the British artillery plough up the unoccupied hillside and let our rapid firepower decimate the British yet again. Both Cronje and the British obliged. Magersfontein was the second calamity of Black Week. Gatacre would supply the third. A soldier of the good old sort, containment was not his forte. He would project his small column forward to dislodge those bloody Boers from the strategic railroad junction of Stormberg, by jingo! Alas, he got lost in the dark and stumbled into a double ambush from the two hills of a valley as the Romans had done at Caudine Forks. It was the third disaster of Black Week, and when all was tallied, the British had lost 2,776 killed, wounded and captured. The beloved regiments of the Highlanders were decimated. There were no more trained 'whites' left for a 'white man's war'. Europe was delighted and the Kaiser sent his Christmas greeting off to the Court of Britain. The Prince of Wales replied: 'The British Empire is now fighting for its very existence, as you know full well. ... We must therefore use every effort in our power to prove victorious in the end.'[22] From then on, the spigots would be opened. The first phase of the British offensive was over, and the second would commence.

Great Britain responded with the Indian ring, Roberts and Kitchener. The slums of Britain would be scoured for the fodder that would swell the ranks of the army in the field and be spearheaded by a 60,000-strong column that adopted Buller's pigeon-holed strategy, a steamroller advance across the veldt to Bloemfontein and Pretoria. This would be augmented by an 8,000 to 10,000-strong body of yeoman mounted infantry that would do admirably well in beating the Boers at their own game. The only fly-in-the-ointment was the lack of transport animals. The four quarters of the empire would be gleaned for draft animals, and they were slow in coming and quick in dying. The single railroad that linked Cape Town with Pretoria was an Achilles Heel, and the wagon-drawn columns that radiated from it in sweeps were tethered to an evanescent umbilicus.

Like Buller before him, Roberts knew that Kimberley had to be relieved. With more resources for his own front, and with Buller, of the African ring, stymied below the escarpments dominating the Tugela, Roberts played his hand. Let Buller pin down Botha; bad luck to him if he did not have the troops to relieve Ladysmith. Roberts opened his advance on 15 February 1900 via a brilliant sidle past Cronje, who was now outflanked. Cronje pulled up stakes and retreated towards Bloemfontein, thus unmasking Kimberley, which was relieved on the 15 February. Nipping at Cronje's heels, Roberts cornered the Boer at Paardeberg. Cronje erected a bristling star-shaped laager, and Kitchener's troops, especially, shed bled heavily in a week-long assault on the camp. It was God's cue for Boer deliverance. Deliverance did not come and Cronje surrendered. The largest Boer army had capitulated and had a gaping hole been torn not only into the covenanters' heartland but also into their heart. Bloemfontein was rolled into on 12 March, and it was here that the supply problem caught up with the British. Insufficient food, shelter, medicine and, most of all, water led to a typhoid epidemic that killed thousands of British soldiers.

Meanwhile, Botha, with more parity of force with Buller, stalled several British attempts which used the same ineffective tactics, to cross the Tugela, first at Acton Homes in the west on 18 January; then a sidestep to the right at Spion Kop, where stalwart British infantrymen momentarily broke through on 23 January, only to be repulsed the next day; and finally at Vaal Krantz in the east on 6 February. After so many bludgeoning, Buller finally hit upon the idea that was to become, from then on, the classic formula for a modern infantry assault: creeping barrages in the front of an advancing infantry force, which attacks a disoriented foe before he can recover, consolidation of the ground gained and repetition as needed. The cavalry, reconfigured as mounted infantry, could exploit breaches, hold positions and pursue a stricken foe. With this new tactical scheme, Buller again sidled eastwards, stretching Botha to his limit and gained Hlangwane Hill on 19 February. Pieter's Hill – the last obstacle – was won on 27 February. Ladysmith was relieved the following day.

Roberts regrouped and trundled his supply-hobbled colossus forward again in mid-April, routed a half-hearted Boer force – collected from the collapsing front everywhere – at Kroonstad and captured Johannesburg on 31 May. Pretoria capitulated on 5 June, but not before Kruger suffered a final forlorn defeat at Diamond Hill and fled to Delagoa Bay on his beloved German railroad. He carried the Transvaal's treasury with him en route to exile in Europe. Mafeking had been relieved by a secondary column on 17 May. With the Boer capitals acquired, and generous terms being proffered to the burghers in arms, 15,000 'hands-uppers' came in. The war was too expensive and it was high time that it ended. Their mission accomplished, the war was now over, declared Roberts and the press. The Conservatives seized the day and called for an election – 'The Khaki Election' – in which they won a resounding victory. With that endorsement, the Conservatives annexed the Transvaal. The hands-uppers tore up their capitulations, and with the old leaders, Kruger, Cronje and Joubert gone, the young bloods took over the reins. This ended the second phase of the conventional British offensives. The third phase began when the Boer high command split up the commandos into roving guerrilla bands which were untethered from fixed bases and towns. Sending them to fan out across the eastern and western Transvaal and the Orange Free State, the guerrillas raided and destroyed the tenuous British lines of communication.

The relocation decision

Although initially and famously successful in conventional operations against the initially clumsy British offensives, the Boers were relentlessly pushed back. As Roberts and his army approached the Boer capital of Pretoria the under armed and outnumbered Boers recognized that they could not stop the British using conventional military means. On 17 March 1900, the Boer leadership decided to shift the army's tactics away from conventional battles to disrupting British communications through the use of guerrilla tactics.[23] After the fall of Pretoria, Boer Commander in Chief, General Louis Botha ordered his field commanders to destroy the British railways, and on the night of 6/7 June, General Christiaan DeWet's commando launched several successful attacks on bridges and junctions. DeWet's raids caused over £100,000 damage and cut off Pretoria for an entire week.

This act galvanized the British into action leading to a policy of relocation. The extreme sensitivity of the British to Boer attacks on their lines of communications is evident from a proclamation by Roberts on 16 June that held local civilians accountable for aiding and abetting Boers, who destroyed or cut railway and telegraph lines.[24] Roberts authorized the burning of Boer homes and the taking of civilian residents as prisoners of war. A subsequent proclamation three days later further authorized the fining of civilians for damages, the destruction of farms, the forced placement of civilians on trains (the modern term for this is 'human shields'), and placing civilians under the authority of martial law.[25] In spite of these harsh measures, Boer attacks on the railways increased in July in frequency and intensity.[26]

The mechanics of the relocation and concentration of Boer civilians began on 18 June, when Roberts's chief of intelligence, Colonel Colin Mackenzie, recommended that Boer families, whose men were on commando, be 'sent to be supported by their own people at Lydenburg'.[27] The particular problem then facing Roberts in Pretoria was how to feed the enemy population with the railways being cut. Roberts, however, was disinclined towards removal of civilians and the idea died. Later, on 17 July, the military governor of Pretoria, Brigadier John Maxwell, revived the idea and ordered that families without means of subsistence 'be deported to a place or places beyond the British lines to be hereafter to be determined by me'.[28] The first 412 women and children were sent out of the town several days later to Boer lines rather than to camps where the British would have to feed them.

This pattern of relocation continued throughout the remainder of 1900. The exact date of the establishment of camps for Boer civilians is contested. Some accounts asserted that the earliest actual camp existed outside Mafeking, as early as July 1900, but officially, the British established the first camps in January 1901.[29] Nevertheless, by 25 July, David Lloyd George speaking in the House of Commons stated, 'It seems to me that in this war we have gradually followed the policy of Spain in Cuba.'[30]

This was followed on 20 August 1900 by an article that appeared in a London newspaper advocating the employment of Weyler's methods to deal with the Boers.[31] Alfred Milner, the High Commissioner for South Africa, wrote to Roberts three days later recommending the establishment of camps in the Cape Colony. The impetus to establish camps supervised by the British military gathered as Roberts announced that Boers, who surrendered voluntarily would be treated honourably as prisoners of war rather than as criminals. By the early winter, a number of camps were established in the Orange River Colony and in the Transvaal.

With Pretoria captured, the Boer army defeated and the beleaguered towns relieved, the war appeared all but won. On 29 November 1900, Kitchener succeeded Roberts, who had asked to be relieved in September. Britain had about 230,000 soldiers in South Africa when Kitchener assumed command, and the War Office believed that they were opposed by 8,000 Boers, who remained active in the field.[32] Unfortunately for Britain and Kitchener, the Boers ignored these odds and chose to continue fighting. Moreover, their leaders resolved to conduct guerrilla warfare in an attempt to wear out the British in the vastness of the South African veldt. In order to relieve British pressure on the commandos the Boers invaded Cape Colony on 16 December, thereby expanding the scope of the war and thoroughly alarming the British. Determined to end Boer resistance once and for all, Kitchener decided upon a strategy similar to that of General Weyler in Cuba. The heart of this was the construction of barbed wire fences along railways, roads and across the veldt with interlocking blockhouses, the construction of which began in early 1901 (Weyler had called these *trocha*). These barriers were, at first, hastily constructed and porous, but as time went on they became more comprehensive.

By the end of the war there were 3,700 miles (6,000 km) of lines with 8,000 blockhouses manned by 50,000 British troops and 16,000 Africans.[33] Kitchener then reorganized his army into columns, led by aggressive young commanders, who were given the mission to drive the Boer commandos onto the blockhouse lines. In this manner, entire sectors could be cleared of guerrillas and then be brought under control. At first, it was easy for the Boers to slip thorough the blockhouse lines, but by mid-1901, this was becoming increasingly difficult, as Kitchener organized about 50,000 men into columns of 1,000 to 5,000 horsemen. These self-sufficient highly mobile columns, often containing pom-poms and artillery, were turned loose inside the ever-increasingly restricted blockhouse lines to hunt down the Boers.

The columns were also charged with the responsibility of sweeping up Boer civilians and destroying their property, including livestock, in order to deny the commandos logistical support. By March 1901, the drives were in full swing, large numbers of Boer civilians were arriving in camps and vast areas of the Transvaal were swept clear of livestock and people.[34] By the end of the month, there were over 20,000 Boers in camps in the Transvaal and another 2,500 in camps in Natal.[35] The scope of the sweeps was staggering and sometimes netted huge numbers of livestock. In one sweep lasting about a month the British seized 7,000 horses, 38,000 sheep (of which 15,000 had to be slaughtered as they could not be moved efficiently) and about 6,000 head of cattle.[36] Farm burning and the deliberate devastation of property turned the Boer landscape into a wasteland. Kitchener distanced himself from the devastation by encouraging the Boers to surrender and by attempting to hand over control of the camps to civilian authorities.[37]

The first use of the phrase 'concentration camp' also came in March from radical MPs C. P. Scott and John Ellis, who took it from Weyler's programme of reconcentration camps in Cuba.[38] Parliamentary interest accelerated and, by April, the House was demanding statistics and information about the treatment of Boers incarcerated in British camps.[39] As more Boers were brought in from the drives, camp numbers increased to about 50,000 by May 1901. The handover of camp control to civilian authorities, who had few resources with which to manage and sustain the camps, envisioned by Kitchener went badly, and conditions inside the camps rapidly deteriorated. Rations and water supplies were inadequate, medical care was sporadic or non-existent and sanitary conditions were abysmal. As a result, mortality rates in the camps shot up.

By September 1901, the British had confined over 100,000 white civilians in thirty-three camps, most of which contained about 3,000 to 5,000 people. Alert to the racist policies of the Boers, the British segregated whites and blacks into separate camps, and about 66,000 blacks were incarcerated by September, as well. Mortality rates in the camps for both races soared as diseases such as typhus and dysentery swept through the crowded tents. Sadly, mortality rates among children were particularly high and approached 30 per cent in many camps.[40] The horrific conditions inside the concentration camps became a cause célèbre in England and activist Emily Hobhouse's scathing indictments of Britain's neglect of Boer civilians scandalized the country.

> Hobhouse's reports described a catastrophe of near genocidal proportions conducted by the British Army under Kitchener. They showed that the British, incapable of protecting the health of their own troops, thousands of whom died of disease, were totally at a loss in dealing with problems of malnutrition and mass disease that spread like wildfire in the cramped and insanitary conditions of the concentration camps.[41]

As a result of this adverse publicity, and belatedly, British authorities began to improve conditions with the camps but death rates continued to rise in the white camps peaking in October 1901 and in the black camps peaking in December. British politicians frantically began to distance themselves from Kitchener's policies and called for parliamentary investigations. Kitchener, for his part, informed London that the government should not complain unless it was in a position to do better, but after December, few additional whites were sent to the camps.[42] Blacks, however, continued to be swept up and by May 1902, there were about 107,000 blacks confined to the camps. The total number of dead remains contentious. The most comprehensive estimates come from a post-war Boer government investigator, who asserted that almost 28,000 white Boers died in the camps.[43] An accurate number for black victims will probably never be known, but certainly exceeded the total number of whites.

With the destruction of the Boer farmsteads, logistical support for the Boer commandos began to constrict and many abandoned their German rifles and began to use captured British rifles and ammunition. Similarly, the capture of British food and supplies became equally important for the commandos. In spite of this, the defeat of the Boer guerrilla forces in the field took eighteen months and a huge effort by Kitchener's columns. In the end, there was nowhere for the surviving Boer 'Bitter Enders' to hide and most of the surviving commandos were run to ground and killed or captured. A peace agreement was signed on 31 May 1902, at which time in addition to the civilians held in concentration camps, the British held some 30,000 prisoners of war.[44] In Parliament Henry Campbell-Bannerman thundered, 'When is a war not a war? When it is carried on by methods of barbarism in South Africa.'[45]

Conclusions

Did resorting to interning civilians in concentration camps and scorching the earth of years of labour hasten the end of the war? Was it a wise military option in Clausewitzian terms? Like Grant's options when he pinned Lee by the nose to his entrenchments in Petersburg and loosed Sherman and Sheridan to scorch the earth and make war upon the Confederate population, he did ensure that the war was extended by another year, but he also ensured that it was over in a year. So too did the scorched earth policies of Roberts and Kitchener extend and end the war by a year. Pathetic in terms of strategic benefit as scorched earth and civilian atrocity was in Sun Tzu's eyes, what other option than those utilized by the 'Butcher' Grant and the 'Barbarous' Kitchener could guarantee that guerrilla warfare would not become an interminable haemorrhage on men, morale and material like the War on Terror is today. In my view, the war's end was hastened by the internments in cold strategic terms, but the 'benefits' were entirely tactical and short-term. Britain safeguarded her interests in India and China and gained the richest spot on the planet in South Africa. But in doing so, did Britain not harden her heart towards the 'other' and sow the malignant seeds that would be reaped when her non-white colonial populations would throw off the 'burden' of their white mentors? And were Russia and Germany not set on the path to embittered confrontations towards the British Empire in two world wars and one cold war by the strategic needs of 'other' imperialists?

Notes

1 John Wilson, *CB, A Life of Sir Henry Campbell-Bannerman* (London: Constable and Company Limited, 1973), 349.
2 Between pages 364–71, Byron Farwell lists 164 little wars; the Boer War is the 5th from the last. Byron Farwell, *Queen Victoria's Little Wars* (New York: W. W. Norton and Company, 1972).

3 See especially Bill Nasson, *The South African War: 1899–1902* (London: Oxford University Press, 1999), Martin Bossenbroek, *The Boer War* (New York: Seven Stories, 2012), and Martin Meredith, *Diamonds, Gold, and War* (New York: Public Affairs, 2007).

4 Rudyard Kipling was the poet laureate of the British soldier in the Victorian Era. His heart belonged to the British army in India. For the British army and regimental system in the nineteenth century, see Byron Farwell, *Mr. Kipling's Army* (New York: W. W. Norton and Company, 1981).

5 For the Kipling poems and a cultural analysis of European imperialism, see John Sheehan, *The Warrior Messiah: The Cultural Roots of European Imperialism* (Saarbrücken, Germany: Lambert Academic Press, 2012), especially 471–2.

6 Ibid., See 426–83 for an analysis of the tension between secularization and muscular Christianity in the British mind in the nineteenth century.

7 Stephen Manning, *Soldiers of the Queen* (Stroud, Gloucestershire: Spellmount, 2009), 203–4.

8 For an analysis of the Boer covenantal mindset, see Donald Akenson, *God's Peoples* (Ithaca, NY: Cornell University Press, 1992), 1–84.

9 Nasson, *The South African War: 1899–1902*, 221.

10 Ibid., 453.

11 Deneys Reitz, *Commando* (New York: Charles Bond Paper Book, 1930), 148.

12 For the numbers of concentration camp detainees, Boer and black, and hands-uppers, see John Gooch, ed., *The Boer War* (London: Frank Cass, 2000), 97–9 and Bossenbroek, *The Boer War*, xii–xiii.

13 Robin Winks, ed., *British Imperialism: God, Gold, Glory* (New York: Holt, Rinehart, and Winston, 1963), 11, 28.

14 See Sheehan, *The Warrior Messiah*, 479, and Steve Attridge, *Nationalism, Imperialism and Identity in Late Victorian Culture: Civil and Military Worlds* (New York: Palgrave Macmillan, 2003), 6 and Sheehan, *The Warrior Messiah*, 478–9.

15 See James Morris, *Pax Britannica* (New York: Harcourt, brace, Jovanovich, 1968), 44. For the 'agterryers', see Bossenbroek, *The Boer War*, xii.

16 For jingoism and the bourgeois morality of the Victorian Age, see Attridge, *Nationalism, Imperialism and Identity in Late Victorian Culture*, 21, 29, and Oren Hale, *Publicity and Diplomacy: With Special Reference to England and German: 1890–1914* (Boston, MA: D. Appleton & Co., 1940), 46–223.

17 Richard Price, *An Imperial War and the British Working Class: Working Class Reactions to the Boer War—1899–1902* (London: Routledge and Kegan Paul, 1972), 231–2.

18 For analyses of the Great Game and its relevance to South African history, see Thomas Pakenham, *The Boer War* (New York: Random House, 1979), 11–99; Meredith, *Diamonds, Gold, and War*; Robert Massie, *Dreadnought* (New York: Random House, 1991); and Paul Kennedy, ed., *The War Plans of the Great Powers: 1880–1914* (Boston, MA: Allen and Unwin, 1980), 79–185.

19 Pakenham, *The Boer War*, 47–70.
20 I pull the bulk of my military analysis, except for where noted, from the following three references: Pakenham, *The Boer War*, Meredith, *Diamonds, Gold, and War*, and John Wisser, *The Boer War: A Military History* (Stratford-upon-Avon, Warwickshire: Coda Books, Ltd., 2013.).
21 For the Boxer Rebellion see Gooch, *The Boer War*, 38–9.
22 Massie, *Dreadnought*, 273.
23 S. B. Spies, *Methods of Barbarism? Roberts and Kitchener and Civilians in the Boer Republics January 1900-May 1902* (Capetown: Human & Rousseau, 1977), 101.
24 Ibid., 102.
25 Ibid., 103.
26 Ibid., 106. For example, on 3 July 1900, the Boers destroyed a third of a mile of track near Greylingstad and one mile of track near Valkfontein.
27 Spies, *Methods of Barbarism?* 128.
28 Ibid., 129.
29 See Ibid., 144–5, for commentary on this subject. Emily Hobhouse, an early British woman's rights advocate, who did not arrive until December 1900, maintained that the Mafeking camp existed from a number of eyewitness testimonies.
30 Ibid., 148.
31 Ibid. Kitchener's strength rose to 240,000 by May 1901; however, thousands were locked into garrison and lines of communications duties leaving Kitchener with less than half for active operations in the field.
32 Keith Terrance Surridge, *Managing the South African War, 1899–1902*, (Woodbridge, Suffolk: The Boydell Press, 1998), 113.
33 Eversley Belfield, *The Boer War* (London: Archon Books, 1975), 132. Belfield's chapter on 'Blockhouses and Drives' (129–39) contains valuable information on the construction and manning of the blockhouse lines. For a map of the mature blockhouse lines, see Leopold Scholtz, *Why the Boers Lost the War* (Basingstoke, Hampshire: Palgrave Macmillan, 2005), 120.
34 Spies, *Methods of Barbarism*, 233–4.
35 Ibid., 193.
36 Byron Farwell, *The Great Anglo-Boer War* (New York: W.W. Norton & Co., 1976), 355.
37 Kitchener to Broderick, 7 March 1901, in Wessels, *Lord Kitchener and the War in South Africa*, 79–82.
38 Pakenham, *The Boer War*, 535.
39 For recent work on the subject of British concentration camps by journalist Andrea Pitzer, see Pitzer, *One Long Night*, 54–82.
40 Spies, *Methods of Barbarism*, 215. Spies asserted that in a number of localized camps the per annum mortality rate for children exceeded 100 per cent.

41 Kenneth O. Morgan, 'The Boer War and the Media (1899–1902)', *Twentieth Century British History*, Vol. 13, No. 1 (2002), 11.
42 Spies, *Methods of Barbarism*, 258.
43 Ibid., 265.
44 Farwell, *The Great Anglo-Boer War*, 441. The mortality rates of Boer POWs are almost inconsequential, and about 24,000 of the 30,000 were imprisoned outside South Africa in locations such as Bermuda, Ceylon, India and St. Helena
45 For Hobhouse's visiting the concentration camps see A. Ruth Fry, *Emily Hobhouse: A Memoir* (London: Jonathan Cape, 1929), 108–36, and for Campbell-Bannerman, see 160. For her outrage, see Pakenham, *The Boer War*, 506.

6

Uneven repression:

The Ottoman state and its Armenians

Maxime Gauin

It would be foolish of them [Ottoman Armenians] to nurture again dreams of independence after the events that occurred [in 1895–6]. Any attempted uprising would be fatal to them.
FRENCH VICE-CONSUL IN MARAŞ (ANATOLIA)
Report of 2 January 1897[1]

Introduction

The forcible relocation of a part of the Ottoman-Armenian population in 1915–16 is arguably the most controversial issue of Ottoman and Turkish history, as well as the most disputed of cases studied in this book (Map 6). The subject was discussed among the earliest specialists of Turkey[2] even before the accusation of 'genocide' emerged in mid-1960s.[3] The genocide polemic began in the context of the Cold War with the Soviet Union using the organizations of the Armenian Diaspora to divide the West.[4] Since the 1970s, hot discussions have taken place in academia[5] adding to the inflammatory rhetoric of Armenian nationalist groups (who claim that all Turks – including those who are born after 1915, are guilty of 'genocide'[6]).

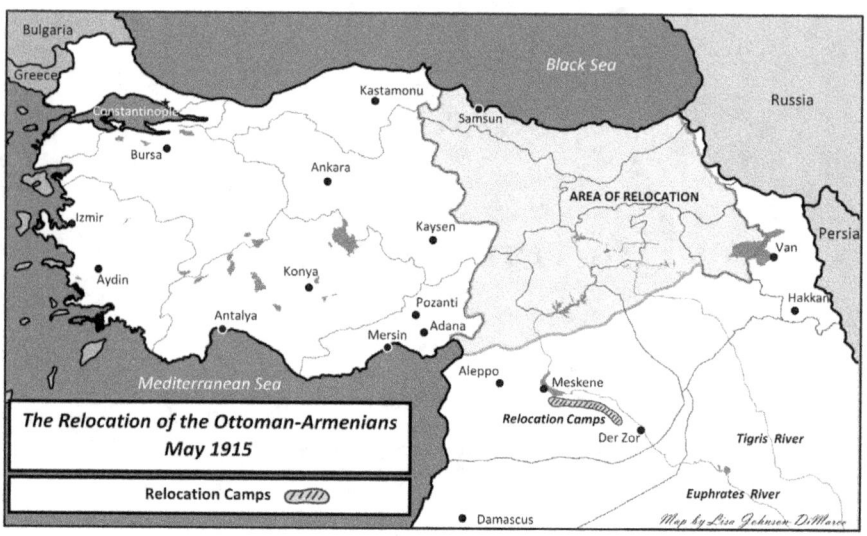

MAP 6 *Ottoman-Armenian Relocations. The Ottoman government forcibly relocated over 500,000 Ottoman-Armenian citizens of six Ottoman provinces in eastern Anatolia, as well as those living in major cities located on the lines of communications, by the decree of 27 May 1915. In the course of the removal to camps in the Euphrates valley thousands of Ottoman-Armenians were killed while in convoys moving south.*

Compounding this was a misconception that writing about the subject was 'taboo' among Turkologists. (However, those asserting so only demonstrated their unfamiliarity with the historiography.)[7]

For too long, the subject has been quantitatively dominated by 'historiography by political committee and committed historians',[8] who have neglected the most basic facts and sources, particularly the scope and the aims of the Armenian nationalist insurrections of 1914–15.[9] Yet, virtually all the relevant archives are available now – except those of the Armenian committees.[10]

This chapter defends the thesis that the relocation decision of the Ottoman cabinet was taken due to national security concerns. The rebellions organized in 1914–15 by the Armenian nationalist organizations were a major and unparalleled threat for the Ottoman military and also for the national existence of the Ottoman Empire. This was made worse by the trauma of the Balkan Wars (1912–13), the loss of territories with a Turkish majority (Macedonia and Western Thrace) and five decades of Armenian nationalist activities against the Ottoman state (1862–1913). Of the cases studied in this book, this is the only one of a mass rebellion having taken place in the core of a sovereign state threatening the very existence of a nation. This chapter challenges the description of the Ottoman-Armenians as a monolithic bloc of powerless victims and also the perception of the

Armenian revolutionary nationalist organizations as simple 'tools' (as if they had no real autonomy) of the Triple-Entente.

The strategic situation

The causes and nature of the Ottoman-Armenian insurgency cannot be understood without a brief overview of the previous half-century. The first nationalist Armenian revolt took place at Zeytun (today's Süleymaniye) in 1862. The model was the Montenegrin insurrections and the aim to provoke a French intervention (similar to Lebanon in 1860), but Paris was not interested and the trusted French vice-consul in Maraş opposed the claims of the insurgents.[11] Zeytun rebelled again in 1878,[12] in the context of the Ottoman-Russian war of 1877–8.[13] Regardless, another conspiracy for an uprising at Erzurum (eastern Anatolia) was discovered by the police before being carried out, in 1882.[14]

After this failure, revolutionary Armenian nationalist parties emerged, namely the Armenakan (later absorbed by the Ramkavar) established in Van and Marseille in 1885, the Hunchaks, created in Geneva in 1887, and the Dashnaks (Armenian Revolutionary Federation or ARF), established in Tbilissi (Russian Empire, at that time) in 1890. The Hunchaks organized rebellions at Sasun (eastern Anatolia) in 1894[15] and again at Zeytun in 1895–6, as well as smaller clashes across eastern Anatolia in autumn 1895.[16] The ARF organized an uprising at Van (eastern Anatolia) in 1896[17] and another insurrection at Sasun in 1904.[18] In these cases, the model was the Bulgarian insurrection of 1876, which had provoked a Russian military intervention leading to the independence of Bulgaria.[19] Bulgaria was a particularly important example: Muslims represented about 45–49 per cent of the population prior 1876[20] proving a minority could affect intervention. The Armenians were in minority in every Anatolian province.[21]

These uprisings had mass terrorism as corollary. In particular, the arson organized by an Armenian group (almost certainly Hunchaks) burned one-third of Salonika (today's Thessaloniki, in Greece, at that time an Ottoman city) in 1890.[22] Then, the hostage-taking incident at the Ottoman Bank by the ARF in 1896 was only a part of a more general scheme to ravage Istanbul completely. That the ARF failed to complete its attack other places (such as the Sublime Porte) came as a result of an informant and the action of the Ottoman police.[23] Similarly, in 1905, an ARF conspiracy to devastate Izmir entirely, by a series of bomb attacks, was discovered in time by the police.[24] It is fundamental to understand that bloody reprisals against innocent Armenian civilians were an essential aim of the revolutionary nationalists. In an interview with former director of the Robert College (American school in Istanbul) Cyrus Hamlin, a Hunchak leader clearly stated that their insurrectional work and their attacks against Kurdish civilians had to provoke counter-killings, as it was the only way to obtain a Russian and/or British intervention.[25] As early as 1896, officials of the Ottoman Bank found the ARF terrorists desired a maximum of collateral victims and were eventually 'happy' to learn that these victims actually had been 'numerous'.[26]

It is true that in 1908, the Young Turk revolution, transforming the autocracy of Sultan Abdülhamit II into a constitutional regime, seemed to change the policy of the Armenian revolutionary nationalists as well. Indeed, the Young Turks (the Committee Union and Progress or CUP) and the ARF cooperated against the Russian Empire – and its policy of Russification – until the first weeks of 1912.[27] Regardless, and beside the fact that the local chapters of the Armenian revolutionary parties, under the leadership of Archbishop Mushegh Seropian, did not accept reconciliation and provoked bloody interethnic clashes in and around Adana in 1909,[28] Russia's Armenian policy completely changed during the year 1912. Forcible assimilation was abandoned and the trial of ARF members ended with a remarkable number of acquittals, but the other defendants were sentenced to light punishments only.[29] At the same time, Italy attacked the Ottoman Empire in 1911–12,[30] followed by the invasions of the Balkan coalition (Balkan Wars, 1912–13),[31] which led to the Russian government asking for a joint intervention of the Triple-Entente (but the French one vetoed the project).[32]

Supporting Russian aggression in the Balkans was Saint Petersburg's demand in 1912 for Armenian 'reforms' in eastern Anatolia. After discussions that are, in themselves, out of the scope of this book, a compromise was reached at the end of 1913. The reforms did not create an autonomous Armenia, but did create a large region in eastern Anatolia supervised by two European inspectors-general (leaving to the Ottoman cabinet the possibility to choose and dismiss the other high civil servants).[33] The agreement was formally signed on 8 February 1914. What is fully relevant, however, is the fact that this Russian initiative was clearly perceived as a first step towards a military intervention. A Russian 'journalist', named Antuan Berezovsky-Godinsky (who was rightfully called by the French ambassador, Maurice Bompard, an agent provocateur), delivered a speech in Bitlis, where he stated: 'Reform or occupation of your regions are our [Russia's] responsibility', adding, 'You must arm yourself' to be ready to support a Russian attack and 'you know well, probably, that all our [diplomatic] representatives in Turkey jointly work with the Dashnaks [ARF]'. And, in case these sentences were not clear enough, he added: 'Russia does not want, and never wanted to send you missionaries. She prefers to send you her cannons and soldiers instead of missionaries.'[34]

In and around the French MFA, the Russian initiative was perceived as a major threat to the general peace, as well as against French interests in the region, but a second veto against an essential ally seemed impossible in the context of the growing German threat. Efforts were made, in 1913–14, to find a solution acceptable by Istanbul and Saint Petersburg.[35] On the contrary, as the Russian ambassador in Paris observed on 13 March 1913, 'in this affair' the Armenian parties, including the Ramkavar of Boghos Nubar (an influential Egyptian-Armenian leader), 'have the firm intention to follow, in all things, the indications of the Russian Government'.[36] One of the clearest proofs was the assassination of Bedros Kapamaciyan, the Armenian mayor of Van and a staunch supporter of the CUP (the Young Turks), by the ARF, in December 1912.[37] Yet Boghos Nubar was aware of the risk of 'sinking' in playing the game with Russia, but he did so,[38] and Arshak Vramian, a key ARF leader, told the French Vice-Consul in Van: 'It does not matter if the Armenians are killed instead of living as they are living! We are determined to restart the revolutionary action we had suspended for four years; for every assassinated Armenian we will kill ten Kurds, and if necessary, we will attack higher [characters]: valis [governors], ministers and even the sultan.'[39]

It is clear that the Armenian nationalists' insurrections of 1914–15 were far from being spontaneous. A last point to clarify is the allegation of the necessity for 'self-defence'.[40] The British Vice-Consul in Van, Ian Smith observed in January 1914: 'Since the arrival of the present vali, Tahsin Bey, strong measures have been taken [in the province of Van] against various Kurdish brigands, so at present the Armenians have little to complain in this respect.'[41] The French Vice-Consul wrote in October of the same year that Tahsin was a 'civil servant of the highest value', who restored order everywhere.[42] Correspondingly, in July 1914, the British consul in Erzurum reported that 'public security seem[ed] admirable between Erzurum and Erzincan, and in the neighbourhood of Erzincan town'. Similarly, the French Vice-Consul in Mersin noticed previously (in May 1913) that the ceremonies of Easter 'took place in the utmost calm' and that that were no solid basis for 'the concerns of the Armenians'.[43] Regardless, there is a tendency among the advocates of the 'Armenian Genocide' claims to extrapolate a threat to Ottoman-Armenians in the whole eastern Anatolia based on problems of banditry in Van and Bitlis and to ignore the radical improvement of public security in these provinces in 1913–14.[44] The Armenian revolutionary committees remained armed for putative 'self-defence' but this disguised a coherent strategy, emerging in 1912, based on the belief that Russian interventions would prevail.

After the Italian-Ottoman War and Balkan Wars, the CUP leadership certainly was traumatized and frustrated, but its policy remained pragmatic. In mid-1913, the cabinet attempted to conclude an alliance with Sofia considering it more efficient than pushing the Bulgarians into the arms of the Russians. Correspondingly, in 1914, the CUP cabinet tried, in vain, to sign a Balkan alliance with Greece. The Ottoman Empire entered the First World War in November 1914, without popular enthusiasm, only after having resisted for months German demands and pressure.[45] The CUP leadership had very limited war aims, the end of capitulations (the special legal statutes of foreigners); the recovery of Batumi, Kars, Ardahan (lost in 1878); and, more generally, the weakening of Russia. Contrary to what is often claimed,⁴⁶ the CUP never had pan-Turkist (union of the Turkish peoples, from the Balkans to eastern Turkestan) or pan-Turanist (the same, added to Hungary and Finland) plans.⁴⁷ In fact proponents of such an expansionist policies were repressed in 1913 by the CUP.⁴⁸

Russia, on the other side, had the most ambitious war aims, taking the Straits and, as much as possible, territories in eastern Anatolia.⁴⁹ In such a context, Armenian nationalism was materially integral to these goals; however, the sole Russian interest remained expansionism.⁵⁰ Armenian insurgents and volunteers were even more needed as the Russian army faced serious difficulties of mobilization in 1914.⁵¹ Moreover, the Russians prioritized the front against Germany, wrongly expecting a quick collapse of the Ottoman Empire.⁵²

The Armenian insurgency erupts

The first action of the Armenian revolutionary nationalists in favour of the Triple-Entente was the recruitment of volunteers. An unknown number of Istanbul Armenians applied to the British and French consulates as early as July 1914,⁵³ even before the war began and some weeks later, a committee in Marseille began to recruit Armenians of the Diaspora for the Foreign Legion (*Légion étrangère*) (the total was about 400 men).⁵⁴ These actions remained symbolic in absolute terms and in comparison with the Armenian recruitment for the Russian army. Large-scale recruiting started before the Ottoman Empire entered the First World War and was organized from Tbilisi by an Armenian National Committee under a joint initiative of all the revolutionary nationalist parties. The political leader was Alexander Khatissian, mayor of the city,⁵⁵ but the military chief was Garegin Pasdermadjian, the former head of the group that had attacked the Ottoman Bank in 1896.⁵⁶

Alerted to the beginning of this recruitment, the CUP proposed to the ARF the creation of an autonomous post-war Armenia forged from both Ottoman and Russian territories. The ARF refused. Officially, the party proclaimed its neutrality, but in practice, it continued to work for Russia.⁵⁷ As early as 29 October 1914, just before the entry of the Ottoman Empire in the war, the British Consul in Batumi estimated the total of Armenian volunteers for the Russian army to be almost 45,000.⁵⁸ Correspondingly, by autumn 1914, the desertions of Armenian soldiers from the Ottoman army in Erzurum became haemorrhagic: 6,000 crossed the boundary in October and at least 3,500 of them subsequently received military training from the Russian army.⁵⁹ The total deserters, from the Erzurum garrison alone, were about 50,000.⁶⁰ It is true that the German consul, Max Erwin von Scheubner-Richter (who was not a professional diplomat), denied the existence of insurrectional preparation in this province, but the Russian consul in the same city, who was precisely in charge of providing weapons to the Armenian revolutionaries of Erzurum, reported the opposite.[61] The forthcoming events confirmed the first attack by an Armenian guerrilla unit in the province of Erzurum took place in October 1914.[62] Yet, as it had already seen, the British consul in Erzurum called 'admirable' the state of the public safety in the province in July 1914. In fact, these activities had nothing to do with 'self-defence'.

Not surprisingly, the Armenian nationalists were even more active in the province of Van (which had a higher density of Armenians). The British vice-consul there had observed in January 1914 the considerable effort of the ARF to arm the Armenian population,[63] and this effort intensified in October of the same year, according to one of the men in charge.[64] The strategy of local Armenian leader, Aram Manukian, was to arm not only the urban but also the rural population (a choice that makes him a precursor of Mao Zedong in this regard). Uprisings took place in the countryside in February and March 1915, intensifying during the first days of April, with the cutting of the road connecting Van city to Bitlis. Trying to behead the rebellion, Governor Cevdet ordered the arrest of Arshak Vramian (the same Vramian who told the French vice-consul in December 1912: 'We are determined to restart the revolutionary action'), but his men missed the most important military leader – Manukian. The revolt of Van city erupted in April 1915, in connection with the insurgents of the countryside, supported by the Russian army and more particularly military units of Armenian volunteers. The city and most of the province were captured quickly by the Russian army[65] followed by the Tsar himself congratulating the Armenian revolutionary nationalists.[66] The only regret of the Russian leadership was the 'indiscriminate slaughter' of Muslims in the province of Van, by both Armenian insurgents and volunteers, because it made the domination of the region difficult.[67]

In effect, 'the Van uprising acted as a catalyst' igniting other uprisings, particularly in Sivas, where Armenian insurgents attacked the corridor between Erzurum and that city (which was located strategically deep in the Ottoman Third Army's rear areas).[68] A ciphered message from the governor of Sivas on 22 April 1915 noted that 15,000 Armenian deserters from the province of Sivas had joined the Russian army and 15,000 others had formed guerrilla units.[69] In the province of Diyarbakır, also located in deep in the strategic rear areas, the authorities were more proactive: 'A great amount of explosives, 50 bombs, plenty of ammunition and weapons, state property and dynamite powder were captured' on 26 April as well as twelve Armenian revolutionary leaders and, during the previous ten days, 1,000 Armenian deserters had been apprehended.[70]

At Zeytun, the insurgents, mostly members of the Hunchak party, did not need the example of the ARF at Van to revolt. In continuity with the uprisings of 1862, 1878 and 1895–6, a new revolt began as early as February 1915,[71] followed in March by the rebels capturing the gendarmerie armoury, killing several gendarmes and destroying the telegraphic lines.[72] 'At the head of the movement might be placed the same persons who directed the movement of 1895.'[73] Because of the central location of Zeytun, the insurgents planned to threaten the lines of communications with Erzurum. They also wished to help an Anglo-French landing at Mersin and/or Iskenderun from Cyprus (occupied by Britain since 1878). Indeed, several plans were presented in 1914–15 by British and French officials,[74] as well as by Armenian nationalists (in particular Boghos Nubar for the Ramkavar and Mikael Varandian for the ARF).[75]

The Mediterranean coast was a hotbed of Armenian insurrectionary activity. From 19 December 1914 to the beginning of February 1915, the HMS *Doris* commanded by Captain Frank Larkin attacked the gulf of Iskenderun. Among other damages, Larkin's vessel destroyed five bridges and landed men who cut a telegraphic line. Larkin reported, on 27 December, 'The Armenian railway officials themselves smashing the electric batteries on the telegraph lines with particular satisfaction.' Correspondingly, six Armenian villages of the Musa Dagh mountain range prepared an uprising.[76] The Committee of the Armenian National Defence (Ramkavar) estimated the number of Armenian insurgents to be 25,000 in Çukurova and 15,000 in 'the neighbouring regions'.[77] In January 1915, two French vessels, the *Requin* and the *D'Entrecasteaux* conducted operations similar to the HMS *Doris*, in front of the ports of Iskenderun and Mersin.[78] For the British and the French, the goal was to cut the railway connecting Anatolia and the Arab provinces. For the Armenian revolutionary nationalists, beside this military goal, there was the project of establishing an 'integral Armenia', from the Black Sea to the Mediterranean Sea.[79]

These actions came to nought when the British cabinet gave the priority to the operations at Gallipoli[80] while the French vetoed in February an increase of the British activities around Iskenderun.[81] Indeed, and beside the simple rivalry between the two powers, during the first half of 1915, Paris was, unlike London, opposed to the partition of the Ottoman Empire.[82] Moreover, a number of French officers noticed with some concern the absence of links of their government with the Armenian insurgents. For both strategic (a landing in Lebanon would have been easier than Iskenderun) and political reasons (the population was mostly made of Christian Arabs, who were historical clients of France), these French officers advocated a landing in Beirut[83] (or at least both in Lebanon and in Çukurova).[84] These conflicting hesitations were one of the main reasons why there was no mass landing in support of Armenian nationalists in the Ottoman Empire during the year 1915. That having been said, these hesitations did not prevent the Armenian revolutionary nationalists in Bursa from helping the landing at the Dardanelles, in organizing insurrections, threatening the communications between Istanbul and the battlefield.[85]

The operational situation

The total number of Armenian insurgents is unknown today, but they might be estimated to be 25,000 in Van, according to US ambassador Henry Morgenthau, who was far from being a friend of the Turks and still less an enemy of the Armenians.[86] An Armenian nationalist leader, who was in direct contact with his counterparts in the Caucasus, gave the estimate of 30,000 for the province of Bitlis.[87] As it has already been explained, there seem to have been 15,000 in Sivas, 15,000 in Zeytun and 25,000 in Çukurova. These figures do not include the insurgents of Bursa, Urfa and other locations with large Ottoman-Armenian populations. In these conditions, and until a systematic investigation in the Ottoman and Russian archives is conducted, 100,000 rebels (without counting the volunteers of the Russian army) is a conservative estimate. While it certainly was not the majority of the Ottoman-Armenian population, it was huge number of enemies for an army already battling on several fronts. The counterinsurgency method traditionally used against Armenian, Macedonian, Arab and Kurdish insurgents, from 1878 to 1914, namely, the mobilization of large-scale units, was impossible in the context of 1915.

The most obvious example is the rebellion at Van – the Ottoman army lost the control of most of the province because it had simply not enough combat soldiers. The Ottoman army was organized on the German model and logistical support units in the empire's interior had no significant protection against guerrillas. Armenian nationalist attacks on the communication lines, such as the few strategic paved roads of north-eastern Anatolia, or the only railroad connecting Istanbul to the Arab provinces, or the communications between Istanbul and the frontline at Gallipoli (on the Dardanelles), where the Ottomans had no combat units,[88] were a major threat to Ottoman national security in 1915.

Making the relocation decision

The Ottoman decision to relocate the Ottoman-Armenians was taken in several steps. The first relocations were local operations, near Dörtyol in March 1915. Zeytun followed the next month, efficiently suppressing these two local revolts, as they were designed to do by the local military commands, the Ministry of War and the Ministry of the Interior.[89] Also in April 1915, the Ministry of the Interior closed down the remaining Armenian nationalist committees. Minister of Interior Talat's circular explained the decision stating, 'The last revolutionary movements in Zeytun, Bitlis, Sivas and Van, which took place at a moment when the country was engaged in war' and which 're-confirmed [the] treacherous aspirations' of the Armenian nationalists.[90] Talat finished his circular in explicitly forbidding any kind of implementation of these measures 'which might result in mutual massacre of Moslem and Armenian elements'.⁹¹

The corollary of these police operations was the arrest of 235 suspected Armenian nationalists in Istanbul on 24 April. In addition, the Ottoman police seized, during these operations in Istanbul 19 Mauser rifles, 74 Martini rifles, 111 Winchester guns, 3,591 pistols and 45,221 pistol bullets.⁹² This combination of local relocations and local operations remained the Ottoman policy until the end of May. As late as 2 May 1915, in a letter to Minister of the Interior Talat, Minister of War Enver considered the relocation of the Armenians living around the lake of Van and still hesitated on the method (either expelling them to Russia or relocating them to the Arab provinces).⁹³ It was not until the law of 27 May 1915 that the relocations expanded to larger parts of Anatolia.

As a result, it appears that the relocation was not the mechanistic effect of the revolt at Van, but the consequence of the fear that several other similar revolts (at least in their effects to the one of Van) would take place if a massive counterinsurgency strategy was not immediately put in place. In the current state of our knowledge, the main decision-makers were Minister of War Enver but more so Minister of the Interior Talat, who prepared the bill of 27 May 1915. The implementation of the relocation campaign involved the two ministries, and it was carried out by gendarmerie and the governorates. The communication between two of the main leaders of the Ottoman Empire confirms the counterinsurgency nature of the operations of 1915 and parts of it must be quoted directly to illustrate the direct evolution of a clearly articulated relocation policy.

> Unfortunately, while the means to bring about a final solution to this problem [by reforms] is being worked out, some of the Armenians living in places close to the battlefields have recently become involved in activities aimed at creating difficulties for our army in its fight against the enemy to protect the Ottoman borders. *Those Armenians are trying to impede the operations of the army, and the transfer of supply and ammunition.* They are combining their aspirations and activities with those of the enemy's and are fighting against us in the ranks of the enemy. Within the country, they dare to carry out armed attacks against the military forces and the innocent civilians, to become involved in acts of murder, looting and plundering in the Ottoman cities and towns, to provide supplies to the enemy's navy and to inform them of the places with fortified posts. *The conduct of such rebel elements has rendered it necessary to remove them from the area of military operations and to evacuate the villages serving as operational bases and shelters for the rebels* (emphasis added).⁹⁴

The relocation of Ottoman-Armenians resulting from counterinsurgency policies remains contested, and there are other interpretations of these events. For example, sociologist and author Taner Akçam affirms that the note of Talat to Grand Vizir Sait Halim shown above 'is the clearest possible refutation of the official Turkish version of the events of 1915, which insists that the policies toward the Armenians were the result of the wartime exigencies'.[95] In fact, Akçam's selective emphasis of the word 'final solution' is an example (among many others) of deliberate manipulation of a source to support the allegation of 'genocide'.[96] The concerns of Talat are clearly exposed in this note. They were: the revolts and the attacks against the lines of communication, the use of Armenian villages by the insurgents and the safety of Muslim civilians. Akçam takes inflammatory phrases out of context. He and other authors even stoop to use known forgeries, such as the 'Ten Commandments' attributed to the CUP,[97] the book of Mevlanzade Rifat (a Kurdish nationalist who pretended to have been a CUP leader but never was),[98] or the 'Andonian documents',[99] to support the genocide accusation.[100] In fact, there is nothing in the Ottoman archives linking the Ottoman government to crimes committed against the relocated Armenians.[101] Moreover, the extensive British investigation against 144 ex-Ottoman officials interned in Malta after the war (1919–21) also failed to discover authentic evidence against them as individuals or against the Ottoman state.[102] The record clearly shows that thousands of Ottoman-Armenians were killed deliberately in localized instances of mass murder and intentional neglect. This is not a denial of genocide but rather points out that authentic evidence of a plan to exterminate the Ottoman-Armenians is conspicuously absent from the historical record.

Another method used today to negate the primacy of national security concerns in the 1915 relocation is to emphasize – and to distort – the policy of the CUP towards other non-Muslim communities. Fuat Dündar, who writes from a Kurdish nationalist perspective, affirms the existence of a 'demographic engineering policy' that also targeted Greeks by moving them from eastern Thrace and Western Anatolia to inner Anatolia. This thesis is also based on a distortion of documents, for example, leading to a confusion between relocation in other parts of the same provinces and relocation to central Anatolia.[103] More generally, to say the very least, the empirical evidence of the CUP cabinet's improvised policies regarding the resettlements of Muslim refugees during the Balkan Wars and the First World War does not corroborate at all the speculations on 'demographic engineering'.[104] Even more strikingly, perhaps, in summer 1914, refugees from the Caucasus were concentrated – against their will – in central Anatolia, particularly Konya, namely where the Turkish majority was the most overwhelming and probably the oldest, instead of being left in eastern Anatolia and of diluting the share of Greeks, Armenians and Kurds.[105]

Another approach to explaining the Armenian relocations is to allege a general 'anti-Christian' policy of the CUP thereby conflating Ottoman-Armenians and Ottoman-Greeks. In such a perspective, the relocation of Greeks from the Black Sea in 1916–17 is presented as a persecution,[106] or even as an extermination.[107] In fact, the Greek archbishop of Samsun – in absolute contrast with his counterpart of Trabzon, a prudent man who preserved the safety of his coreligionists – organized guerrilla activities against the Ottoman state as early as 1914, and these activities increased in summer 1916, in the context of successful Russian offensives. In fact, this counter-insurrectional relocation was carried inside Anatolia and without massacres.[108]

The Assyrian case is also increasingly used to support the thesis of an 'anti-Christian' policy, with the same kind of disregard for authentic historical sources.[109] Indeed, as early as 1913, French Vice-Consul Zarzecki (Van) reached the conclusion that Mar Shimoun, the Nestorian patriarch was 'one of the most active agents of Russia' in the region.[110] Moreover, at the beginning of the First World War, Shimoun ordered the assassination of his own uncle, who was a loyal Ottoman citizen and opposed to any revolt.[111] Then, Shimoun organized an uprising that led to violent battles with local Kurds followed by a mass exodus to Iran, in the worst possible conditions.[112] The appreciation of Colonel Pierre Chardigny, the French attaché in the Caucasus, is one of the most accurate: 'It is certain that Russia is responsible for the woes of the Assyrian people. ... It was Russia that provoked the revolt of the Nestorian Assyrians of Mar Shimoun.'[113]

The relocation campaign

Beside the local relocations of March–April 1915, the main campaign took place from June to August. A second wave took place in September 1915, as a result of a second series of insurrections, which was not a 'resistance' against the relocation but rather a coordinated attack against the Ottoman lines of communication, during the summer and the beginning of autumn.[114] One of the most relevant cases was Urfa. The Armenian community of this city was initially exempted of relocation, and even saved in August by the Ottoman authorities from Kurdish gangs which wanted to attack local Armenians.[115] Yet, the month after, the Armenian nationalists launched a well-planned uprising, which was defeated by heavy artillery attacks, and the majority of the community was expelled.[116]

Archival sources, as well as survivor memoirs, indicate that at least 350,000 to 400,000 Ottoman-Armenians, and more likely 500,000, were exempted from relocation and remained in their homes throughout the war.[117] It is, in itself, strong evidence that relocation was a national security measure conducted in a designated geographic area. Geographically, the main exemptions were for most of the Armenians of the western cities and provinces of Istanbul, Izmir,[118] Kütahya,[119] Konya,[120] and Kastamonu, as well as in the Syrian city of Aleppo.[121] Beside these provinces, Armenians in various places who were deemed loyal, for example, civil servants,[122] members of families of soldiers, Catholics and Protestants,[123] were also exempted. Many thousands of Ottoman-Armenian men served in the Ottoman army through the end of the war.[124] It also bears noting that the relocation never included Armenians from the Ottoman Parliament, for example, Artin Boşgezenyan remained the CUP deputy of Aleppo, Onnik Ihsan an independent deputy of Izmir, Dikran Barsamian an independent deputy of Sivas[125] and Manuk Azarian a senator of Istanbul.[126] In this regard, the forcible relocation of Ottoman-Armenians was far less systematic and inclusive than the one of Japanese and Japanese-Americans during the Second World War (see Chapter 8).

A key issue in today's discourse is the identification of the units in charge of the forcible relocation. It is often claimed[127] that the Special Organization (SO), an elite force of the Ottoman army, was in charge, but the Ottoman archives do not confirm this claim at all.[128] Noted historian Guenter Lewy has exposed an impressive series of the manipulation of sources, used by Vahakn Dadrian, to support this allegation.[129] In particular, in one note, Vahakn Dadrian gives three published sources to confirm the participation of the SO,[130] but in fact, none of them corroborate anything of this kind, as they do not mention this unit at all.[131] Moreover, the assertions of Taner Akçam regarding the SO rely almost exclusively on Vahakn Dadrian's work and cite the same manipulated sources, thereby compounding the errors.[132] In the current state of our knowledge, the main force in charge of the relocation was the gendarmerie, or more exactly what remained of the gendarmerie after the mobilization, assisted by locally recruited groups of Muslim and Kurdish tribesmen.[133]

The concrete conditions of the relocations are another essential question. The two main destinations were (1) western Syria and Lebanon and (2) the Euphrates valley in eastern Syria and what is now Iraq. Even historian Hilmar Kaiser, a supporter of the 'extermination' charge, now admits the diversity of the situations, and more particularly the efficiency of protective measures taken by Cemal Paşa (No. 3 of the CUP regime) in Western Syria and Lebanon. Dr Kaiser's criticism of French (and Ramkavar) historian Raymond Kévorkian (who blames Cemal for a 'genocidal' intent, neglecting the relevant sources) is quite interesting,[134] but his own remarks on the policy of the central government are not based on a sufficient research.[135] Importantly, in the areas under the control of Cemal, there is no evidence of systematic killings.[136] Furthermore, the individual perpetrators of crimes were, as much as the authorities could, held to account for their crimes: 1,397 were sentenced to imprisonment or execution from October 1915 to January 1917.[137] It also bears noting that civil servants and provincial officials received orders to provide food and supplies to relocated Armenians. Furthermore, American missionaries were allowed to distribute additional rations to the relocated persons.[138] Those who raise the question 'Is it possible that the Ottoman campaign to pacify eastern Anatolia was both counterinsurgency and genocide?'[139] should consider these mitigating acts of the central government.

The military outcomes

In operational, tactical and strategic terms, the forcible relocation of Armenians in 1915 was a nearly complete success. The insurgencies of the Armenian nationalists were almost completely extinguished. Only a handful of gangs continued their activities after 1915.[140] In this regard, the campaign was more effective, for example, than the Spanish army's in Cuba, and the Ottoman army obtained decisive results faster than the British in South Africa or that of the US Army in the Philippines. It may be partly due to the fact that these three armies fought colonial campaigns, unlike the Ottoman army, which was fighting for the survival of the nation in its own homeland. Noted Middle Eastern historian Bernard Lewis observed, 'For the Turks, the Armenian movement was the deadliest of all threats', because 'to renounce these lands [from the Black Sea to the Mediterranean Sea] would have meant not the truncation, but the dissolution of the Turkish state'.[141]

During the entire war, in the Çukurova sector, there was no mass landing by the Entente. This absence is certainly due not only to the continuous hesitations between Entente partners regarding the ports of Mersin, Iskenderun and Beirut as places appropriate for a landing[142] but also to the reinforcement of the Ottoman forces in the area in 1916[143] and to the almost complete end of the Armenian nationalists' insurrections – as this end deprived the Entente of any hope of significant military support from the interior. In Bursa, the risk of a blockade of the communication lines was totally eliminated thus helping make possible the allied victory at Gallipoli.[144]

In north-eastern Anatolia, the counterinsurgency campaign and relocations did not stop the Russian offensives of 1915 and 1916 completely, but they did contribute in preventing the Russian army from penetrating to Ankara. Moreover, the scenario of Van (the capture of a city by internal insurgents leading to the loss of an entire province) was avoided. To a certain extent, the situation could be compared to the Marne battle in 1914: the enemy was stopped before obtaining a decisive victory, but not repulsed back to his territory. In brief, it is essential to distinguish the scope of the danger in April–May 1915 and the scope of the actual results in the end. Precisely because the Ottoman army reacted as it reacted, Van was the only province lost as a result of an Armenian insurrection.

This military success certainly had a human cost, but this cost has yet to be honestly studied and balanced against authentic sources and evidence. Yves Ternon claims that Arnold Toynbee estimated the losses to be 1,200,000 and the number of survivors to be 600,000,[145] but in fact, Toynbee's conclusion is the reverse: 600,000 Armenians died and 1,200,000 survived.[146] It has also been claimed by Yves Ternon and more recently by Taner Akçam that Mustafa Kemal (Atatürk) endorsed the figure of 800,000 deaths.[147] Actually, Atatürk called it 'a slander'.[148] The best estimates for the total wartime losses are around 600,000 to 642,000 (about 37 per cent of the pre-war Ottoman-Armenian population),[149] and this total includes 150,000 who died during the relocation of about 300,000 Ottoman-Armenians by the Russian army (to the Caucasus)[150] as well as 50,000 others who died during the epidemics at Yerevan in 1918–19.[151] These figures have to be compared with the losses of Anatolian Muslims: around 2,500,000 (18 per cent of the pre-war population; 62 per cent in the province of Van),[152] including more than 500,000 killed by Armenians and Cossacks.[153] The death toll of the 500,000 Ottoman-Armenians relocated from six Eastern Anatolian provinces in the 1915 counterinsurgency campaign is unknown today. Estimates range from 20 per cent to 100 per cent but, knowing that thousands survived, 40–50 per cent might be a fair estimate.

Conclusion

Few events prove the need for dispassionate and scholarly history engaging the various authentic sources more than the Armenian case in 1915–16. The politicization of historical writing has led to the arbitrary use of political explanations where, actually, the relocations were a military solution to a military problem. The Armenian revolutionaries neglected the demographic balance, ignored the lessons of the past and wrongly believed (after the independence of the Christian Balkan states, the Balkan Wars and the Ottoman defeat at Sarikamis in December 1914–January 1915) that it was their turn. The Ottoman state reacted with an effective but heavy-handed response they did not expect – and similarly, they did not expect the reaction of the Turkish people, led by Mustafa Kemal (Atatürk) from 1919 to 1923.[154]

Notes

1 Archives du ministère des Affaires étrangères (AMAE), La Courneuve, microfilm P 16738.

2 Yusuf Hikmet Bayur, *Türk İnkılâbı Tarihi* (Ankara: Türk Tarih Kurumu), Volume II-3, 1951, 18–100, III-3, 1957, 35–59; Eleanor Bisbee, *The New Turks. Pioneers of a Republic, 1920–1950* (Philadelphia: University of Pennsylvania Press, 1951), 49; Ernest Jackh (Ernst Jäck), *The Rising Crescent: Turkey Yesterday, Today and Tomorrow* (New York and Toronto: Farrar & Rinehart, 1944), 41–4; Esat Uras, *Tarihte Ermeniler ve Ermeni Meselesi* (Ankara: Yeni Matbaa, 1950).

3 Henry Bidou, *Histoire de la Grande guerre* (Paris: Gallimard, 1936), 317–18; Maurice Larcher, *La Guerre turque dans la guerre mondiale* (Paris: Chiron, 1926), 395 and 602; Morgan Philips Price, *A History of Turkey* (London and New York: George Allen & Uwin/MacMillan, 1956), 68–9, 76–7, 79, 90–1 and 99.

4 Bernard Lewis, *Notes on a Century. Reflections of a Middle Historian* (London: Weidenfeld & Nicolson, 2012), 286–7; Gaïdz Minassian, *Guerre et terrorisme arméniens* (Paris: Presses universitaires de France, 2002), 18–20, 36 and 38–40.

5 Christopher Walker and Gwynne Dyer, 'Correspondence', *Middle Eastern Studies*, Vol. 9, No. 3 (1973), 376–85; Richard G. Hovannisian, Stanford Jay Shaw, and Ezel Kural Shaw, 'Forum: The Armenian Question', *International Journal of Middle East Studies*, Vol. 9, No. 3 (1978), 379–400; Türkkaya Ataöv and Norman Ravitch, 'The Armenian Question', *Encounter* (May 1982), 91–4; Vahakn N. Dadrian and Malcolm E. Yapp, 'Correspondence', *Middle Eastern Studies*, Vol. 33, No. 3 (1997), 640–2; Guenter Lewy and alii, 'Genocide?', *Commentary*, (February 2006), 3–10; Joseph A. Kéchichian, Keith David Watenpaugh, and Michael M. Gunter, 'Notes and Comments', *International Journal of Middle East Studies*, Vol. 39, No. 3 (2007), 509–18; Vahagn Avedian, Pulat Tacar, and Maxime Gauin, 'EJIL: Debate!', *European Journal of International Law*, Vol. 27, No. 3 (2012), 797–835.

6 Yervant Khatanasian, 'Genocide and the Armenian Case', *Armenian Review*, Vol. 17, No. 4–68 (1964), 3–7; Armand Sammelian, « Tel père, tel fils », *Armenews.com*, avril 27, 2017, Available at http://armenews.com/article.php3?id_article=141126

7 David Gutman, 'Ottoman Historiography and the End of the Genocide Taboo: Writing the Armenian Genocide into Late Ottoman History', *Journal of the Ottoman and Turkish Studies Association*, Vol. 2, No. 1 (2015), 167–83; Donald Quataert, 'The Massacres of Ottoman Armenians and the Writing of Ottoman History', *Journal of Interdisciplinary History*, Vol. 26, No. 2 (2006), 249–59.

8 Andrew Mango, 'Historiography by Political Committee and Committed Historians: Review Article', *Middle Eastern Studies*, Vol. 25, No. 4 (1989), 531–62. See also Gilles Veinstein, « Trois questions sur un massacre, » *L'Histoire* (avril 1995), 40–1.

9 For a critical overview of this neglect: Jeremy Salt, 'The Narrative Gap in Ottoman Armenian History', *Middle Eastern Studies*, Vol. 29, No. 1 (2003), 19–36.

10 'The Strange Case of Yektan Turkyilmaz', *Duke Magazine*, (November–December 2005), http://dukemagazine.duke.edu/article/strange-case-yektan-turkyilmaz; Yücel Güçlü, *Historical Archives and the Historians' Commission to Investigate the Armenian Events of 1915* (Lanham, MD: University Press of America, 2015), 119–28.

11 Dépêche du vice-consul de France à Maraş, 6 août 1862, Centre des archives diplomatiques de Nantes (CADN), microfilm 2 Mi 2566; Louise Nalbandian, *The Armenian Revolutionary Movement* (Berkeley, Los Angeles, and London: University of California Press, 1963), 66–76.

12 A French translation of documents seized after this revolt has been forwarded to the Quai d'Orsay by the Ottoman embassy in Paris on 19 May 1879: AMAE, 75 ADP 41.

13 On this war: Hakan Yavuz and Peter Sluglett (ed.), *War and Diplomacy The Russo-Turkish War of 1877–1878 and the Treaty of Berlin* (Salt Lake City: University of Utah Press, 2011).

14 Dépêche du vice-consul de France à Erzurum, décembre 22, 1882, AMAE, P 801.
15 Justin McCarthy, Cemalettin Taşkıran, and Ömer Turan, *Sasun. The History of an 1890's Armenian Revolt* (Salt Lake City: University of Utah Press, 2014).
16 P. Pisani, « Les affaires d'Arménie, » *Le Correspondant* (10 novembre 1895), 420–6; Idem; Kâmuran Gürün, *The Armenian File* (London, Nicosia, and İstanbul: K. Rüstem & Bro./Weidenfeld & Nicolson, 1985), 142–54.
17 Justin McCarthy, Esat Arslan, Cemalettin Taşkıran, and Ömer Turan, *The Armenian Rebellion at Van* (Salt Lake City: University of Utah Press, 2006), 54–77.
18 Le vice-consul de France à Kharpout au ministre des Affaires étrangères, mai 26, 1904, AMAE, P 16741.
19 William L. Langer, *The Diplomacy of Imperialism. 1890–1902* (New York: Alfred A. Knopf, 1960), 150–60, 204–10 and 349–50; Guenter Lewy, *The Armenian Massacres in Ottoman Turkey* (Salt Lake City: University of Utah Press, 2005), 16–30; Jeremy Salt, *Imperialism, Evangelism and the Ottoman Armenians, 1878–1896* (London and Portland: Frank Cass, 1993), 22–136.
20 Ömer Turan, *The Turkish Minority in Bulgaria (1878–1908)* (Ankara: Türk Tarih Kurumu, 1998), 79–98.
21 Justin McCarthy, *Muslims and Minorities: The Population of Ottoman Anatolia and the End of the Empire* (New York and London: New York University Press, 1983), 47–88; Meir Zamir, 'Population Statistics of the Ottoman Empire in 1914 and 1919', *Middle Eastern Studies*, Vol. 17, No. 1 (1981), 85–106.
22 Stephen Bonsal, *Heyday in a Vanished World* (New York: W. W. Norton & C°, 1937), 286–9.
23 Lettre du chargé d'affaires à Constantinople au ministre des Affaires étrangères, septembre 3, 1896, AMAE, P 949; Idem; Gaston Auboyneau, *La Journée du 26 août 1896 à la Banque impériale ottomane* (Villeurbanne: Imprimerie Chaix, 1912).
24 Maxime Gauin, 'The Missed Occasion: Successes of the Hamidian Police against the Armenian Revolutionaries', *Review of Armenian Studies*, No. 30 (2014), 121–5.
25 Langer, *The Diplomacy of*, 157–8.
26 Auboyneau, *La Journée du*, 28 and 34.
27 Michael A. Reynolds, *Shattering Empires: The Clash and Collapse of the Ottoman and Russian Empires, 1908–1918* (Cambridge and New York: Cambridge University Press, 2011), 98–102.
28 Le vice-consul de France à Mersin et Adana au ministre des Affaires étrangères, 23 octobre 1908, AMAE, P 16742; Dispatch of consul Bie Ravnal (Mersin) to the Under-Secretary of State, 6 May 1909, National Archives and Records Administration (NARA), College Park, RG 84, Records of Foreign Service Posts, Diplomatic Posts Istanbul, vol. 216; Kemal Çiçek (ed.), *The Adana Incidents of 1909 Revisited* (Ankara: Türk Tarih Kurumu, 2011); Yücel Güçlü, *The Armenian Events of Adana in 1909: Cemal Paşa and Beyond* (Lanham, MD: Hamilton Books, 2018).

29 Despatch of the British consul in Erzurum, October 14, 1913, The National Archives, Kew Gardens (London), FO 195/2450; Richard Hovannisian, *Armenia on the Road to Independence. 1918* (Berkeley, Los Angeles, and London: University of California Press, 1967), 22–3 and 31; Gaïdz Minassian, *Géopolitique de l'Arménie* (Paris: Ellipses, 2005), 15.

30 Jean-Louis Miège, *L'Impérialisme colonial italien de 1870 à nos jours* (Paris : SEDES, 1968), 81–97.

31 Edward J. Erickson, *Defeat in Detail. The Ottoman Army in the Balkans* (Westport, CT: Praeger Publishers, 2003); Hakan Yavuz and Isa Blumi (ed.), *War and Nationalism* (Salt Lake City: University of Utah Press, 2013).

32 Maurice Paléologue, *Au Quai d'Orsay à la veille de la tourmente. Journal, 1913–1914* (Paris: Plon, 1947), 173–5.

33 Le chargé d'affaires à Constantinople au ministre des Affaires étrangères, décembre 31, 1913, AMAE, P 16745; Idem; Joseph Heller, 'Britain and the Armenian question, 1912–1914. A study in Realpolitik', *Middle Eastern Studies*, Vol. 17, No. 1 (1980), 8–20.

34 Le vice-consul de France à Van au ministre des Affaires étrangères, mai 2, 1913, AMAE, P 16744.

35 Robert de Caix, « La question des réformes arméniennes, » *L'Asie française* (août 1913), 336–7; S. Zarzecki, « La question kurdo-arménienne, » *La Revue de Paris* (15 avril 1914), 873–94. Zarzecki was the Vice-Consul in Van in 1912–1913. De Caix was an *éminence grise* of the MFA.

36 René Marchand (ed.), *Un livre noir. Diplomatie d'avant-guerre d'après les documents des archives russes, 1910–1917*, Volume II (Paris : Librairie du travail, 1923), 47–8.

37 Hasan Oktay, 'On the Assassination of Van Mayor Kapamaciyan by the Tashnak Committee', *Review of Armenian Studies*, No. 1 (2002), 79–89; Kapriel Serope Papazian, *Patriotism Perverted* (Boston, MA: Baikar Press, 1934), 69.

38 L'ambassadeur de France à Constantinople au ministre des Affaires étrangères, octobre 20, 1913, AMAE, P 16745.

39 Le vice-consul de France à Van au président du Conseil, ministre des Affaires étrangères, décembre 19, 1912, AMAE, P 16743.

40 For an example of this allegation: Vahakn N. Dadrian, 'The Secret Young-Turk Ittihadist Conference and the Decision for the World War I Genocide of the Armenians', *Holocaust and Genocide Studies*, Vol. 7, No. 2 (1993), 194–5.

41 Report of 10 January 1914, in Muammer Demirel (ed.), *British Documents on Armenians* (Ankara: Yeni Türkiye, 2002), 634.

42 Le vice-consul de France à Van au ministre des Affaires étrangères, octobre 10, 1914, AMAE, P 16745.

43 AMAE, P 16744.

44 Yves Ternon, *Les Arméniens, histoire d'un génocide* (Paris: Le Seuil, 1996), 200–2.

45 Feroz Ahmad, 'Great Britain's Relations with the Young Turks 1908–1914', *Middle Eastern Studies*, Vol. 2, No. 4 (1966), 323–5; Mustafa Aksakal, *The Ottoman Road to War* (Cambridge and New York: Cambridge University Press, 2008); Kemal Karpat, 'The Entry of the Ottoman Empire into World War I', *Belleten*, Vol. 68, No. 253 (2004), 687–738. Taner Akçam, *A Shameful Act* (New York: Metropolitan Books, 2006), 112 claims the opposite without knowing the relevant sources.

46 Akçam, *A Shameful Act*, 112; Peter Balakian, *The Burning Tigris* (New York: Perennial, 2004), 147 and 162–6; Hans-Lukas Kieser, *Talaat Pasha. Father of Modern Turkey, Architect of Genocide* (Princeton, NJ and Oxford: Princeton University Press, 2018), XI, 9, 11–12, 17, 98–104 and *passim*; Raymond Kévorkian, *The Armenian Genocide* (London and New York: I. B. Tauris, 2011), 195–200 and 699–714; Ronald Grigor Suny, *They Can Live in the Desert, but Nowhere Else* (Princeton, NJ and Oxford: Princeton University Press, 2015), 152–3 and 206; Zarevand, *United and Independent Turania: Aims and Designs of the Turks* (Leiden: E. J. Brill, 1971), translated from Armenian by Vahakn N. Dadrian.

47 Feroz Ahmad, 'Book Review', *Middle Eastern Studies*, Vol. 6, No. 1 (1970), 104–5; Lewy, *The Armenian Massacres*, 45–7; Michael A. Reynolds, 'Buffers, Not Brethren: Young Turk Military Policy in the First World War and the Myth of Panturanism', *Past and Present*, No. 203 (May 2009), 137–79.

48 Paul Dumont, « Bolchevisme et Orient, » *Cahiers du monde russe et soviétique*, Vol. 17, No. 4 (1977), 379.

49 Sean McMeekin, *The Russian Origins of the First World War* (Cambridge, MA and London: Harvard University Press, 2011), *passim*; C. Jay Smith, 'Great Britain and the 1914–1915 Straits Agreement with Russia: The British Promise of November 1914', *The American Historical Review*, Vol. 70, No. 40 (1965), 1015–34.

50 Stéphane Yerasimos, « Caucase, la grande mêlée (1914–1921), » *Hérodote*, n° 54–55, 4ᵉ trimestre 1989, 155–9.

51 Norman Stone, *The Eastern Front. 1914–1917* (London: Penguin Books, 1998), 213.

52 Ozan Arslan, 'The 'Bon Pour l'Orient' Front: Analysis of Russia's Anticipated Victory over the Ottoman Empire in World War I', *Middle East Critique*, Vol. 18, No. 2 (2014), 175–88.

53 Memorandum of Captain Torkom, August 1915, FO 371/2485/126836.

54 Aram Turabian, *Les Volontaires arméniens sous les drapeaux français* (Marseille: Imprimerie nouvelle, 1917), 5–34.

55 Ibid., 40.

56 Garegin Pasdermadjian, *Why Armenia Should Be Free* (Boston, MA: Hairenik Press, 1918). Balakian, *The Burning Tigris*, 199, criticizes the 'naïve romanticism' of Pasdermadjian in 1914 but does not provide any development on his action at that time. Vahakan Dadrian, *History of the Armenian Genocide* (Providence, RI: Berghahn Books, 2004) is silent on the activities of Pasdermadjian during the First World War.

57 Morgan Philips Price, *War and Revolution in Asiatic Russia* (London: George Allen & Uwin, 1918), 243–5. See also Onur Önol, 'The Eighth World Congress of the Dashnaktsutyun and Its Aftermath', in Hakan Yavuz and Feroz Ahmad (ed.), *War and Collapse. World War I and the Ottoman State* (Salt Lake City: University of Utah Press, 2016), 781–99.

58 Demirel, *British Documents on*, 665.

59 Undated military report from Van (March 1915), in *Armenian Activities in the Archive Documents* (Ankara: ATASE), Volume I, 2005, 110–11.

60 McMeekin, *The Russian Origins*, 154.

61 Ibid., 278, n. 75 (criticizing Akçam, *A Shameful Act*, 197–9).

62 Gürün, *The Armenian File*, 196.

63 Report of 10 January 1914, in Demirel, *British Documents on*, 635–6.

64 Haig Gossoian, *The Epic Story of the Self Defense of Armenians in the Historic City of Van* (Detroit, MI: General Society of Vasbouragan, 1967 [1930]), 13.

65 McCarthy, Arslan, Taşkıran, and Turan, *The Armenian Rebellion*, 176–232 and 258.

66 Gabriel Korganoff (Gorganian), *La Participation des Arméniens à la guerre mondiale sur le front du Caucase (1914–1918)* (Paris: Massis, 1927), 26 and 28.

67 Reynolds, *Shattering Empires*, 157–8.

68 Erickson, *Ottomans and Armenians*, 168.

69 *Documents on Ottoman Armenians*, Volume II (Ankara: Directorate General of Press and Information, 1985), 80–1.

70 Ciphered message from the governor of Diyarbakır, 27 April 1915, Ibid., 83.

71 Note de l'ambassadeur de Russie à Paris, février 23, 1915, in Arthur Beylerian (ed.), *Les Grandes Puissances, l'Empire ottoman et les Arméniens dans les archives françaises (1914-1918)* (Paris: Publications de la Sorbonne, 1983), 7.

72 Yusuf Sarınay (ed.), *Osmanlı belgelerinde Ermeni İsyanları* (Ankara: Başbakanlık Basımevi, 2008), Volume IV, 105–8 and 113–15. Thanks to Sümeyye Hoşgör (Middle East Technical University, history department) for the translation.

73 Answer of the Russian government to the British one, 17 April 1915, FO 371/2484/22083/46942.

74 Pierre Roche, Note relative aux conditions topographiques et climatériques d'une attaque française contre Alexandrette et Alep, et aux immédiats résultats de guerre de l'occupation des deux villes, décembre 1914 ; Extraits d'un rapport de M. Marteaux, directeur de l'exploitation du chemin de fer Damas-Hama et du port de Beyrouth, décembre 28, 1914 ; Rapport sur un projet soumis par Lord Kitchener à son gouvernement, novembre 13, 1915, Service historique de la défense (SHD), Vincennes, 16 N 3198.

75 Memorandum of Nubar to the British authorities, 3 February 1915, in Vatche Ghazarian (ed.), *Boghos Nubar's Papers and the Armenian Question, 1915–1918: Documents* (Waltham, MA: Mayreni, 1996), 3–5; Copie d'une communication du ministre français à Sofia, 3 mars 1915, in Arthur Beylerian

(ed.), *Les Grandes Puissances*, 12–13; Memorandum of Mikael Varandian to Sir Edward Grey, 20 February 1915, FO 371/2484/37609; Ciphered telegram of the British minister in Sofia to the Foreign Office, 3 March 1915, in Demirel (ed.), *British Documents on*, 667.

76 Edward J. Erickson, 'Captain Larkin and the Turks. The Strategic Impact of the HMS Doris in Early 1915', *Middle Eastern Studies*, Vol. 46, No. 1 (January 2010), 151–62; Stanford Jay Shaw, *The Ottoman Empire in World War I* (Ankara: Türk Tarih Kurumu), Volume II, 2008, 876–0.

77 Note to the British government, July 1915, in Jean-Claude Montant (ed.), *Documents diplomatiques français. 1915*, Volume III, *15 septembre–21 décembre* (Berne: Peter Lang, 2004), 98.

78 État-major de l'armée, service historique, *Les Armées françaises dans la Grande guerre* (Paris: Imprimerie nationale, IX-1, 1936), 10–12.

79 A. Tchobanian, Les aspirations arméniennes, avril 7, 1915, in Hasan Dilan (ed.), *Les Événements arméniens*, Volume II, 152–67; Hasan Dilan (ed.), *Les Événements arméniens dans les documents diplomatiques français (1914–1918)* (Ankara: Türk Tarih Kurumu, 2005), Volume IV, 368–72; Letter of Tchobanian to Sir Edward Grey, 13 April 1915, FO 371/2484/43561.

80 Christopher M. Bell, *Churchill and Sea Power* (Oxford and New York: Oxford University Press, 2013), 59–75.

81 James Barr, *A Line in the Sand. Britain, France and the Struggle That Shaped the Middle East* (London and New York: Simon & Schuster, 2011), 15.

82 Note confidentielle complémentaire sur les questions soulevées par le forcement des Dardanelles, 5 mars 1915, in Dilan (ed.), *Les Événements arméniens*, Volume I, 71–4 ; Lettre du ministre des Affaires étrangères au ministre de la Guerre, avril 28, 1915, SHD, 7 N 2150.

83 Projet de débarquement d'un corps expéditionnaire en Orient, janvier 20, 1915, SHD, 16 N 3198.

84 Le général de brigade Baumann, ex-chef de la Mission militaire de réorganisation de la gendarmerie en Turquie, à Monsieur le général commandant en chef des armées françaises, janvier 4, 1915, SHD, 16 N 3195.

85 Devlet Arşivleri Genel Müdürlüğü, *Aspirations Et Agissements Revolutionnaires Des Comites Armeniens Avant Et Apres La Proclamation De La Constitution Ottomane* (Ankara: Devlet Basımevi, 2001), 213–14.

86 Erickson, *Ottomans and Armenians*, 166–7. On the discrepancies between Morgenthau's documents and his book published in 1918: Heath Lowry, *The Story Behind 'Ambassador Morgenthau's Story'* (İstanbul: The Isis Press, 1990).

87 Turabian, *Les Volontaires arméniens*, 40–2.

88 Edward J. Erickson, *Ottoman Army Effectiveness in World War I. A Comparative Study* (London and New York: Routledge, 2007), 14–60.

89 Telegram of Talat to the governor of Adana, 1 March 1915, in Hikmet Özdemir and Yusuf Sarınay (ed.), *Turkish-Armenian Conflict*, 11; Yücel Güçlü, *Armenians and the Allies in Cilicia (1914–1923)* (Salt Lake City: University of Utah Press, 2010), 81; Yusuf Halaçoğlu, *Facts on the Relocation of Armenians (1914–1918)* (Ankara: Türk Tarih Kurumu, 2002), 58–60.

90 Salâhi Sonyel, 'Armenian Deportations: A Re-Appraisal in the Light of New Documents', *Belleten*, Vol. 36, No. 141 (January 1972), 59. The original text and the translation by the Foreign Office can be checked (as it has been done by the author of this chapter) in FO 371/4241/170751.

91 Sonyel, 'Armenian Deportations'.

92 Yusuf Sarınay, 'What Happened on April 24, 1915? The Circular of April 24, 1915, and the Arrest of Armenian Committee Members in Istanbul', *International Journal of Turkish Studies*, Vol. 14, No. 1 & 2 (2008), 78.

93 The full letter is translated in Gürün, *The Armenian File*, 199.

94 Özdemir and Sarınay (ed.), *Turkish-Armenian Conflict*, 58–9.

95 Taner Akçam, *The Young Turks' Crime against Humanity* (Princeton, NJ and Oxford: Princeton University Press, 2012), 136–7. Kieser, *Talaat Pasha*, 431, n. 15, calls Taner Akçam's book 'an insightful recent study on the Armenian genocide, largely based on Ottoman documents'. Such a sentence is self-explanatory.

96 Maxime Gauin, 'Review Essay—"Proving" a "Crime against Humanity?"' *Journal of Muslim Affairs*, Vol. 25, No. 1 (2015), 141–57; Lewy, *The Armenian Massacres*, 43–128 and passim; Kent Schull, 'Book Review', *The Journal of Modern History*, Vol. 76, No. 4 (December 2014), 975–6.

97 Akçam, *The Young Turks'*, 197; Balakian, *The Burning Tigris*, 189–90; Vahakn N. Dadrian, 'The Secret Young Turk', 173–8; Kévorkian, *The Armenian Genocide*, 242. Donald Bloxham ('Donald Bloxham Replies', *History Today*, Vol. 55, No. 7 [July 2005], 68) calls the 'Ten Commandments' a text 'at best dubious' but the same Donald Bloxham wrote a praise for the cover of Raymond Kévorkian's book. This is contradictory.

98 Vahakn Dadrian, 'The Convergent Roles of the State and Governmental Party in the Armenian Genocide', in Levon Chorbajian and George Shirinian (ed.), *Studies in Comparative Genocide* (New York: St Martin's Press, 1999), 100; Fatma Müge Göçek, *Denial of Violence* (Oxford and New York: Oxford University Press, 2014), 571, n. 327; Kévorkian, *The Armenian Genocide*, 247; Akaby Nassibian, *Britain and the Armenian Question 1915–1923* (London and Sydney: Croom Helm, 1984), 90.

99 Akçam, *The Young Turks'*, 272; Balakian, *The Burning Tigris*, 346–7.

100 Regarding these forgeries see Dyer, 'Correspondence', 377–82; Bernard Lewis, *From Babel to Dragoman: Interpreting the Middle East* (Oxford and New York: Oxford University Press, 2004), 389; Ömer Engin Lütem and Yiğit Alpogan, 'Review Essay: "Killing Orders: Talat Pasha's Telegrams and the Armenian genocide"', *Review of Armenian Studies*, No. 37 (2018), 45–82; Şinasi Orel and Sürreya Yuca, *The Talât Pasha 'Telegrams': Historical fact or Armenian fiction?* (Nicosia and Oxford: K. Rüstem & Brothers/Oxford University Press, 1986).

101 Odile Moreau, *La Turquie dans la Grande guerre. De l'Empire ottoman à la République de Turquie* (Paris : SOTECA/Belin, 2016), 209.

102 Letter of R. W. Woods, of behalf of the Prosecutor of His Majesty in England and Wales, to the Foreign Office, July 29, 1921, FO 371/6504/E 8745; Letter of Judge Lindsay Smith to the British High Commissioner in İstanbul, Horace Rumbold, August 29, 1921, FO 371/6504/E 10023.

103 Ahmet Efiloğlu, 'Fuat Dündar and the Deportation of the Greeks', *Middle East Critique*, Vol. 23, No. 1 (2014), 89–106; Ahmet Efiloğlu, 'The Exodus of Thracian Greeks to Greece in the Post-Balkan War Era', in Hakan Yavuz and Feroz Ahmad (ed.), *War and Collapse. World War I and the Ottoman State* (Salt Lake City: University of Utah Press, 2016), 330–70. Mr Dündar has left this criticism unanswered.

104 Sinan Kuneralp (ed.), *Une ambassadrice de France à Constantinople. Les souvenirs de Gabrielle Bompard de Blignières, 1909–1914* (İstanbul: Les éditions Isis, 2016), 74–6; Xavier de Planhol, *Les Nations du Prophète* (Paris: Fayard, 1993), 692–9; Shaw, *The Ottoman Empire*, Volume I, 2006, 567–77.

105 Shaw, *The Ottoman Empire*, Volume I, 571.

106 Akçam, *The Young Turks'*, 63–96; Suny, *'They Can Live'*, 330.

107 Balakian, *The Burning Tigris*, 286 and 339; Kieser, *Talaat Pasha*, 257–8 and 355.

108 Efiloğlu, 'Fuat Dündar and', 104–5; Stéphane Yerasimos, « La question du Pont-Euxin (1912–1923), » *Guerres mondiales et conflits contemporains*, n° 153 (janvier 1989), 10–16.

109 Kieser, *Talaat Pasha*, 154, 185, 203–5, 234, 239–40 and passim; Suny, *'They Can Live'*, XVI, XIX, 118 and *passim*.

110 Le vice-consul de France à Van au ministre des Affaires étrangères, mai 24, 1913, AMAE, P 16744.

111 Nicolas Gasfield, « Au front de Perse pendant la Grande guerre – Souvenirs d'un officier français, » *Revue d'histoire de la Guerre mondiale*, II-3 (juillet 1924), 129; Bülent Özdemir, *Assyrian Identity and the Great War* (Dunbeath: Whittles Publishing, 2012), 51–3.

112 Yonca Anzerioğlu, 'The Revolts of Nestorian Christians Against the Ottoman Empire and the Republic of Turkey', *The Muslim World*, Vol. 100, No. 1 (2010), 48–51 ; Florence Hellot, « L'ambulance française d'Ourmia (1917–1918) ou le ressac de la Grande guerre en Perse », *Studia Iranica*, Vol. 25, No. 1 (1996), 50–1 and 60.

113 Le colonel Chardigny, chef de la mission militaire française au Caucase, à M. le ministre de la Guerre, avril 13, 1919, CADN, 1SL/1V/138.

114 Erickson, *Ottomans and Armenians*, 200–9.

115 Report of Samuel Edelman, U.S. Consul in Aleppo, 26 August 1915, NARA, RG 59, M 353, reel 44 (867.4016/23).

116 Erickson, *Ottomans and Armenians*, 207–8.

117 Ibid., 216–17 (the list provided here does not include the Armenians of İstanbul, and contains underestimates, about İzmir, for example).

118 Report of Lewis Heck, secretary of the American embassy in İstanbul, 7 February 1918, 23, NARA, RG 59, M 353, reel 7 (867.00/813); Letter of Charlton Whittal (British businessman settled in İzmir) to general Townshend, 10 February 1921, FO 371/6499/2265; S.R. Marine, Turquie, n° 833, juin 14, 1919, SHD, 1 BB^7 232.

119 Yusuf Halaçoğlu, *The Story of 1915: What Happened to the Ottoman Armenians?* (Ankara: Türk Tarih Kurumu, 2008), 91.

120 O. J. Campbell, Report on the Vilayet of Konya, p. 8, Hoover Institution Archives, Stanford University (California), Paris Peace Conference (1919–1920), U.S. territorial section, box 4; S.R. Marine, Turquie, n° 1351, 25 novembre 1919, SHD, 1 BB⁷ 235.

121 Lewy, *The Armenian Massacres*, 191.

122 Francis Gutton, *Prisonnier de guerre chez les Turcs. Une captivité pas comme les autres (1915–1918)* (Paris : Bibliothèque de la captivité, 1976), 52.

123 SR Marine, Turquie, n° 747, juin 6, 1919, SHD, 1 BB⁷ 232; Kemal Çiçek, *The Great War and the Forced Migration of Armenians* (Belfast: Athol Books, 2011), 80–81.

124 Erickson, Ottoman Army Effectiveness, 129–30 and Ottoman Army Headquarters 2nd Division to the Office of Personnel Affairs, June 28, 1917, in Armenian Activities in, Volume II, 72–80.

125 Mehmet Biçici, 'Osmanlı Meclis-I Mebusânı'nda Ermeni Mebuslar ve Faaliyetleri (1914–1918)', in *19.-20. Yüzyıllarda Türk-Ermeni İlişkileri* (İstanbul: İstanbul Üniversitesi/Türk Ocakları, 2015), Volume I, 357–9 and 366–7.

126 S.R. Marine, Turquie, n° 532, 4 avril 1919, CADN, 36 PO/1/7.

127 Akçam, *A Shameful Act*, 59, 151–7 and passsim; Donald Bloxham, *The Great Game of Genocide* (Oxford and New York: Oxford University Press, 2005), 69–70; Dadrian, *History of the of the Armenian Genocide*, 237–45 and *passim*; Göçek, *Denial of Violence*, 22 and 154; Kévorkian, *The Armenian Genocide*, 38, 180–7 and passim; Kieser, *Talaat Pasha*, 248–58; Suny, 'They Can Live', XX, 190 and 219.

128 Edward J. Erickson, 'Armenian Massacres: New Records Undercut Old Blame', *The Middle East Quarterly*, Vol. 13, No. 3 (Summer 2006), 67–75; Polat Safi, 'History in the Trench: The Ottoman Special Organization – Teşkilat-ı Mahsusa Literature', *Middle Eastern Studies*, Vol. 48, No. 1 (2012), 89–106.

129 Lewy, *The Armenian Massacres*, 82–8.

130 Dadrian, *The History of the Armenian Genocide*, 244, n. 9.

131 Falih Rıfkı Atay, *Zeytindağı* (1930; İstanbul: Pozitif, 2012), 37–8; Sonyel, 'Armenian Deportations: New', 60; Arnold J. Toynbee, *The Western Question in Greece and Turkey* (London, Bombay and Sydney: Constable & C°, 1922), 280.

132 Erman Şahin, 'Review Essay: A Scrutiny of Akçam's Version of History and the Armenian Genocide', *Journal of Muslim Minority Affairs*, Vol. 28, No. 2 (August 2008), 309–12.

133 Halaçoğlu, *The Story of 1915*, 44; Lewy, *The Armenian Massacres*, 225–6; *Le Capitaine Sarrou, un officier français au service de l'Empire ottoman* (İstanbul : Les éditions Isis, 2002), 45.

134 Hilmar Kaiser, "Regional Resistance to Central Government Policies: Ahmed Djemal Pasha, the Governors of Aleppo and Armenian Deportees in the

Spring and Summer of 1915', *Journal of Genocide Research*, Vol. 12, No. 3/4 (2010), 173–218.

135 Maxime Gauin, 'The Armenian Forced Relocation: Putting an End to Misleading Simplifications', *Review of Armenian Studies*, No. 31 (2015), 111–12.

136 Lewy, *The Armenian Massacres*, 163–6 and 180–7.

137 Shaw, *The Ottoman Empire*, Volume II, 1098–9.

138 Regulation of 30 May 1915, in Hikmet Özdemir and Yusuf Sarınay (ed.), *Turkish-Armenian Conflict*, 80; Letter of the U.S. missionary station of Antep (Gaziantep) to William Peet, 13 August 1915, American Board of Commissioner for Foreign Missions (ABCFM) archives, Harvard University, Cambridge (Massachusetts), Houghton Library, 16.10.1, box 8; Letter of Leslie A. Davis, ex-U.S. consul in Elazığ, to the American Committee for Armenian and Syrian Relief, 3 October 1917; Letter of Ambassador Abram Elkus to Charles Vickrey, 5 October 1917, Library of Congress, manuscript division, Woodrow Wilson papers, reel 337; Henry Riggs, *Days of Tragedy in Armenia* (Ann Harbor, MI: Gomidas Institute, 1997), 158 et 174–5.

139 Richard Outzen, 'Between Counter-Insurgency and Genocide', *War on the Rocks*, 18 September 2014, https://warontherocks.com/2014/09/between-counterinsurgency-and-genocide/, Ahsan I. Butt, *Secession and Security, Explaining State Strategy against Separatists* (Ithaca, NY and London: Cornell University Press, 2017), 125–62 tries to answer positively, but without knowing the primary sources.

140 Copy of cable from Adana gendarmerie regiment command, 7 February 1917, in *Documents on Ottoman*, Volume II, 1983, 111.

141 Bernard Lewis, *The Emergence of Modern Turkey. Third edition* (Oxford and New York: Oxford University Press, 2002), 356.

142 Le ministre de France au Caire au président du Conseil, ministre des Affaires étrangères, 26 juillet 1917; État-major général de l'armée—Groupe de l'avant—3ᵉ bureau, Note sur une action éventuelle de la France en Syrie, 18 juillet 1917; Conditions d'une intervention de la France en Syrie, 5 août 1917; Plages et points de débarquement possibles sur la côte syrienne, 5 août 1917, SHD, 16 N 3195, dossier 4.

143 Le ministre de France au Caire au président du Conseil, ministre des Affaires étrangères, décembre 23, 1916, in Dilan (ed.), *Les Événements arméniens*, Volume I, 156–7.

144 Edward J. Erickson, *Gallipoli. Command under Fire* (Oxford: Osprey Publishing, 2015).

145 Ternon, *Les Arméniens*, 300.

146 *The Treatment of Armenians in the Ottoman Empire, 1915–1916* (New York and London: G. P. Putman's Sons, 1916), 650–1; Toynbee, *The Western Question*, 342.

147 Akçam, *A Shameful Act*, 183.

148 Şahin, 'Review Essay', 309.

149 McCarthy, *Muslims and Minorities*, 121–30.

150 Hovannisian, *Armenia on the*, 67.
151 Colonel Chardigny, « La question arménienne, » octobre 30, 1919, SHD, 16 N 3187, dossier 4.
152 McCarthy, *Muslims and Minorities*, 133–7.
153 Jeremy Salt, *The Unmaking of the Middle East* (Berkeley, Los Angeles, and London: University of California Press, 2008), 67–8. Göçek, *Denial of Violence*, 216 and 250 gives lower figures, but without any source.
154 On the Armenian (and Greek) issues during this period: Maxime Gauin, 'Revisiting the Fire of Izmir', *Journal of South Asian and Middle Eastern Studies*, Vol. 41, No. 1 (Fall 2017), 31–53.

7

From the Pale:

The Russians and the Jews

LtCol Kevin D. Glathar

> *In fact, a survey sent to leading army officials (Russian) found that nearly all of them shared a presupposition that Jews were disloyal and should be treated as spies.*
> ERIC LOHR, *The Russian Army and the Jews*[1]

Introduction

The 1964 musical 'Fiddler on the Roof' by Jerry Bock continues to enjoy a global audience. Based on the book by Joseph Stein, son of Jewish immigrants from Poland, this story captures the essence of the relocation of the Jewish population living in the Settlement of Pale by the Russian Army (Map 7). Like many other civilian populations affected by the First World War, Jews in Russia were caught between their religion and their Orthodox Christian rulers. However, the Jews in the Pale had been living in this precarious position for literally centuries before the war began.[2] Surrounded by a zealous Russian Orthodox Christian population, the Jews in the Pale had been marginalized for years in the wake of increasing anti-Semitism seeded by the Reformation and Enlightenment. Many historians argue the Pale, and specifically the plight of the Jewish population inhabiting this area, was a result of economic and nationalistic factors instead of anti-Semitism. Regardless of reasons, the Jewish inhabitants of the Pale in 1914

MAP 7 *The Pale 1915. After 1492, displaced Jews increasingly moved north into Eastern Europe which was then controlled by the Russian Czar. According to the Russian census of 1897, over 4,000,000 Jews lived in the area known as the Pale Settlement, which they were prohibited from leaving. They were frequently subjected to violent* pogroms *during the nineteenth century. Thought to be sympathetic to the Germans in the First World War, the Russians Jews in the Pale Settlement were forcibly relocated to cities and towns in the interior.*

were a primary focus for the Russian civilian leadership, and more so, the army because Jews in the Pale had generally been viewed as unaccepting of the Czarist-ruled Russian Empire. Moreover, the impending invasion of the German army exaggerated this view point assigning further the label of spies to Jews in the Pale. This chapter describes the Russian army policies and directives that called for the forced relocation of no less than 300,000 Jews from Western Russia.[3]

The thesis of this chapter is that, in military terms, the relocation of Jews in the Pale was a part of a Russian counter-German invasion campaign influenced by centuries old socialpolitical motivations rather than the formation of an insurgency and Russian national security concerns. The probability of a German invasion into the western parts of the Russian Empire after 1914 was a real threat and could not be ignored by Russian political and military leadership.[4] Considering the successful gains by and relative strength of the Austro-Hungarian and German campaigns in 1914–15, the likelihood of a successful invasion of the Russian heartland was assumed inevitable. The predominately Orthodox Christian leadership of the Russian Empire had failed to remove Jews long before Catherine the Great created the Pale in 1791, and an impending invasion by the German army provided a convenient excuse to relocate some 300,000 Jews living in the Pale.[5]

The Jews and the Pale

This section focuses on the historical events that brought Jews to Europe and Western Russia. These events also shed light on the anti-Jewish sentiment that influenced Russian decisions to relocate Jews from the Pale Settlement during the First World War. The remaining portion of this section will outline the events inside Russia leading to the formation of the Pale Settlement and events outside Russia influencing their participation in the First World War, more specifically the Eastern Front.

To understand the underlying sentiment against the Jews in the Pale, one must first examine how they came to settle in Eastern Europe and Western Russia. While a long and sorted history, it is useful to examine the events leading to the original expulsion of the Jews from their original homeland in what is the modern-day Middle East. In doing so it will be apparent to the reader that a pattern emerges with respect to how, and why, other ethnic groups and nations dealt with Jewish populations. In addition to striking defeats of the Russian army along other portions of the Eastern Front during the First World War, this long-standing feeling towards Jews heavily influences the Russian army's plan for relocation of Jews in 1915.[6]

Although expulsion of the Hebrews had occurred a number of times in the pre-Christian era (notably the Exodus from Egypt in the twentieth century BCE and the Babylonian Exile in 722 BCE), the Jewish revolt in 66–70 CE led to a long-lasting expulsion of the Jews from Judea.[7] While some Jews remained behind, the bulk of the population fled to what would become Spain, Portugal and the Mediterranean littoral. In 1492, King Ferdinand completed the *Reconquista* of Spain and expelled the Moors from the peninsula. He also expelled the Sephardic Jews as well and subjected those who remained behind to the Inquisition.[8] While some of the expelled families went to Constantinople, many fled northeast into what became Germany and Poland. There they joined an earlier wave of refugees fleeing from Muslim and Christian oppression (many of these fleeing people became Ashkenazi Jews and adopted a Yiddish language and culture). In Poland and the Baltic's, the Jews lived a precarious existence which alternated between periods of relative acceptance and safety and period of oppression and hostility. By 1648 and the Treaty of Westphalia 60 per cent of the world's Jewish population lived in Poland. Despite a series of brutal wars by 1750, some 750,000 Jews lived in Poland (60 per cent of the world population).

The Prussians, Russians and Austrians first partitioned Poland in 1772, and most of Jews living there were brought under Russian rule. Subsequently, two more partitions in 1792 and 1795 extinguished the country called Poland until after the First World War. In 1791, under Catherine the Great, Jews were permitted to live in the newly annexed areas taken from the Ottoman Empire on the Black Sea and would the next year be allowed to remain in the former regions of Poland. Under the residential provisions for Jews their merchants were prohibited from trading in other provinces in Russia. The Czarist government sought thus to reduce the number of Jews participating in commerce within the annexed areas of Poland. This was primarily intended to serve national and economic interests by preventing competition by Jews with Russian merchants and encouraging settlement in more remote and sparsely populated areas in southern Russia. Catherine's decree of 1791 was finally ratified in 1794 and applied to the second partition of Polish annexation. The third partition of Poland was followed in 1799 by the annexation of Courland and came to known as the Pale Settlement. These areas, under a 'Jewish Statute', the province of Astrakhan and the northern Caucasus in 1804, Bessarabia in 1812 and in 1868 an area known as the Vistula Region, also generally included the Pale Settlement. Overall, the intent of Czarist legislators under Catherine II and Alexander I for Jews living in newly acquired areas added to the Pale Settlement to serve colonization interests.

The Pale Settlement covered an area approximately 390,000 square miles from the Baltic Sea to the Black Sea. The census of 1897 reported 4,899,300 Jews lived there accounting for 94 per cent of the Jewish population in Russia and 11.6 per cent of the general population of the Pale Settlement. It may seem surprising but Jews were a minority in every portion of the Pale. In the Pale 82 per cent of Jews lived in the towns and villages but only accounted for 36.9 per cent of the urban population. In essence, the Pale Settlement was a territory within the borders of Czarist Russia that allowed legal residence for Jews. The settlement predated the Polish partition and came into being when Russia was confronted with a Jewish element within its borders that had been excluded since the end of the fifteenth century. Within this area Jews were afforded similar freedom of movement as had already been given to other persons of similar social and economic standing. However, during this time, most of the inhabitants of lesser social standing in Russia, including townsmen and merchants, were deprived freedom of movement and confined to their places of residence, so this was not a particularly broad change.

Under Czar Alexander II changes to restrictions within the Pale Settlement included increases in freedom of movement for non-Jews in Russia while restrictions on the movement of Jews beyond the Pale remained in force. Anti-Jewish legislation by the Czarist government was spurred by a growing impatience of Jewish society as well as a general negative public opinion of Jews in this portion of Russia. In 1827 severe restrictions were imposed on the densely populated Jewish quarter of Kiev. Under Nicholas I, who is credited with coining the term 'Pale of Settlement', Courland (modern Lithuania) was removed from the Pale in 1829. By 1835 the provinces of Astrakhan and the northern Caucasus are also excluded. In 1843 Nicholas I ordered the expulsion of the Jews from an area thirty-three miles wide along the border with Prussia and Austria. The Russians had a difficult time applying this edict and were forced to redraft it in 1858 reducing the area to include only those Jews settled in the immediate border zone. However, the roots of relocation had been sown.

In 1859, additional residential rights were granted to merchants and in subsequent years these rights were extended to university students, those engaged in the medical profession and various craftsmen, if they were able to pay registration fees. Rights of residence were also granted to those who remained Jews and whose children were part of the 'Nicholas soldiers'. Jews were optimistic that these changes were progressing towards abolition of the Pale Settlement. This would not be the case, and in 1881, all of the residential rights granted under Czar Nicholas I were rescinded as part of the general reaction of the public in Russia at this time. In addition to rescinding previously granted residential rights, the 'Temporary Laws' of 1881 prohibited any new settlement by Jews outside towns and small residential areas in the Pale. Jews living in villages before the publication of the decree were authorized to remain only in those villages. Adding insult to injury, peasants in the Pale were granted rights that allowed them to demand expulsion of Jews living among them. Along with the new decrees came additional administrative burdens, brutality by local authorities and systematic acceptance of bribery by lower administrative officials badly penalized the Jewish residents of Russia. By 1892, thousands of Jewish craftsmen and their families were expelled from Moscow adding to the validation of relocation as a way to deal with Jews.

Early in the twentieth century political and economic pressure from Jews on the Czar's government afforded relaxation of the 'Temporary Laws' in most portions of Russia. Some areas with increased Jewish populations were granted rights of residence. Subsequently by the beginning of the First World War approximately 300 settlements were opened to Jewish residence. In January of 1905, troops of Russian Czar Nicholas II opened fire upon peaceful demonstrators in St. Petersburg killing hundreds in what was called 'Bloody Sunday'. Other demonstrations and riots broke out in the country.

The organizers of the demonstrations and riots were Marxists and socialists, many of whom were highly educated Russian Jews. Later in 1905 Russia suffered military defeats by a newly industrialized Japan, which further inflamed Russian nationalism and an already existing anti-Semitism. In 1910, Jewish members of the Constitutional-Democratic Party proposed a bill abolishing the Pale. However, a lack of cohesion between liberals and reactionaries in the party made the proposal of demonstrative value only. In turn the conservative parties on the 'Right' responded with a counter-motion 'to expel the Jews from Russia'. This motion came to vote in February 1911 but failed to pass and never saw a plenary session of the legislature.

Anti-Semitism, Russification and the Jews

There are a number of threads which need to be wound together in order to understand why the Russian Jews were vilified and why anti-Semitism was so strong in Russia. The spread of anti-Semitism began in the Medieval Ages and spread to Russia. This combined with efforts to create a homogeneous population via Russification led to the isolation of Russian Jews. Resistance to Russification led directly to, and inflamed the infamous violent campaigns against the Jews known as pogroms. In turn, the pogroms created a willingness to resist and to support revolutionary change within the Russian Jewish communities.

The term 'Russification' came about in the 1770s through the writings of Sergey Uvarov, who advocated 'autocracy, Orthodoxy, and "Russian-ness"'. The Czars embraced the movement, which was relatively benign until the reign of Czar Alexander III. Under Alexander II the policy became punitive and forced such things as changing religion to Orthodox Christianity, adopting the Cyrillic alphabet and the Russian language and changing one's name to a Russian name. The policy did not just affect Russian Jews, it also affected Catholic Poles, Caucasian Muslims and Cossacks. In addition to the police and secret police, the Russian government organized private gang-like organizations to enforce Russification locally. The infamous Black Hundred gangs, in particular, were violently anti-Semitic and targeted Russian Jews. In the fall of 1905 through the spring of 1906, Black Hundred gangs were responsible for killing some 21,000 Jews in the Ukraine for being 'anti-Russian'. Naturally the Czar's efforts to force change were met by strong resistance by ethnic and religious minorities living within the Russian Empire. The Russian Jews reacted strongly and resisted Russification to the point of dying.

The nineteenth century also saw the implementation of pogroms, which began in Odessa in 1821. The word 'pogrom' in Russian is a derivative word meaning 'to destroy, to wreak havoc, to demolish violently, its literal translation is to harm'. More pogroms followed but the assassination of Czar Alexander II in 1881 led to a four year wave of terror of over 200 pogroms.

Russian Jews were thought to have been deeply involved in the conspiracy to kill the Czar. Thousands of Russian Jews were killed or injured and many were expelled from the homes. An even bloodier wave of twentieth-century pogroms occurred between 1903 and 1906, this time moving to areas inhabited by Russian Jews who lived outside the Pale. Russian Jews were also implicated in the uprisings of 1905.

It is important to consider the impact of the early secret terrorist organizations on the Russian government and the Russian psyche. Many Russian Jews were prominent in these organizations as well as in revolutionary societies. In the 1880s, the Anarchist movement erupted in Europe and spread to Russia. The Anarchists were committed to political change brought about by violent terrorist incidents ('propaganda by deed') designed to provoke heavy-handed government responses.[9] The Nihilists also sprang up about the same time as the Anarchists, and famously on 26 August 1879, Russian Nihilists sentenced Czar Alexander II to death.[10] Unlike the Anarchists, who desired political change, the Nihilists were committed to the destruction of society, but they also embraced terrorism as their vehicle for change. The twentieth century brought a new terrorist organization to Russia called the Socialist Revolutionary Party, which like Marxism, advocated socialism of the land and society. Many of the influential Socialist Revolutionary leaders were Russian Jews, including Mikhail Got, Mary Andreyevich Natanson and Ilya Rubanovich. The Socialist Revolutionaries were very well organized with a tight cell-like structure, and they had strong ties to the Armenian Revolutionary Federation (see Chapter 6).[11] Czar Nicholas and the *Okhrana* (the Czar's secret police) waged a determined campaign to eradicate the Socialist Revolutionary Party but failed in the end. It is fair to say that, in the years immediately preceding the First World War, the Russian government was convinced that terrorist revolutionary activity was alive and well in Russia and that its adherents included Russian Jews.

The First World War

On 28 June 1914, Archduke Franz Ferdinand, heir to the Austrian throne, visited Bosnia. He and his wife narrowly miss being killed by a bomb that was thrown at their automobile, and they continued their visit only to be shot and killed a short time later by a nationalist member of the Serbian secret revolutionary society known as the Black Hand. Knowing the assassin to be a Serbian nationalist on 23 July 1914 Austria-Hungary, with the backing of Germany, delivered an ultimatum to Serbia. Two days later Austria-Hungary severed diplomatic ties with Serbia and began to mobilize its troops. On 28 July 1914, the Austro-Hungarian Empire declared war on Serbia. The following day Britain called for international mediation to resolve the worsening crisis but the Russians began partial troop mobilization as a precaution and urged Germany to use restraint. The Germans saw Russia as posturing for advantage and began to mobilize themselves. Reacting to the Austrian attack on Serbia, Russia began full mobilization of its troops on 31 July and Germany demanded they cease mobilization. This sets the scene strategically, and on 1 August 1914, Germany declared war on Russia. France and Belgium began full mobilization. On 3 August Germany declared war on France and invaded neutral Belgium. Britain then sent an ultimatum to withdraw from Belgium which was rejected by the Germans. On 4 August Great Britain declared war on Germany. The First World War had begun.

The strategic situation in 1914

The strategic situation for Russian civilian and military leaders as the country entered into the First World War was grim to say the least. Russia could be characterized as politically weakened by an internal revolution, militarily inept compared to most Eastern and Western powers, economically depressed and lacking growth potential, socially prejudiced against Jewish populations, industrially stagnant and viewed in general as a nation with a large under-educated population with small appetite for progress and change. When the Ottoman Empire mobilized in August 1914 (but did not enter the war until November on the side of Germany) Russia's major ports in the Black Sea joined its Baltic ports in being isolated from Russia's European allies.

Early Russian operational level offensives into East Prussia were defeated by the Germans, who took the offensive and destroyed two entire Russian armies in the Tannenberg and Masurian Lakes campaigns.[12] Although the Russians had been very successful against the Austro-Hungarians in Galicia, by November 1914, the Russian army was already in decline. The Germans decided to capture Łódz located in western Poland, which fell in December with the loss of another Russian army. This forced the Russian general staff to transfer forces from Carpathia, weakening their armies there. In early 1915, the Germans pushed through the Masurian lakes threatening Grodno. By May, the Russians had taken huge losses, which they could not replace and, moreover, were almost out of artillery ammunition.[13] On 10 May the Germans broke through the front and the Russians executed frantic, but unsuccessful counter-attacks along the San River. According to the Russian chief of staff, 'The strategic position is quite hopeless.'[14] In combination these poor Russian decisions, and even poorer tactical execution, led to staggering losses on the Eastern Front and, in turn, atrocities in the Pale Settlement.

The geographic isolation of the Russian Empire caused by the German blockade of the Baltic Sea and the Ottoman blockade of the Black Sea imposed a crippling penalty on the Russian economy. Effectively cut off from marketing its agricultural exports in the fall of 1914 the Russian balance of trade suffered immediately. Moreover, the greatly reduced flow of imported industrial materials such as steel and manufactured components immediately constricted the production of weapons. Although the far eastern port of Vladivostok remained open to trade, the port lay at the end of a single track 5,000 mile rail road. Thus, as the war progressed into 1915 and 1916 the Russian government had almost no income and a failing capacity to care for its citizens displaced by war.

The operational situation regarding Russian Jews

As the Russian armies went down in defeat the German army advanced into Russian Poland adjacent to the Pale. This increasingly became a concern for the Russians, particularly with regard for the Jewish inhabitants of the Pale. Jewish men had been conscripted into the three armies fighting on the Eastern Front, for example 18 per cent of the reserve officers in the Austro-Hungarian army were Jewish[15] while Germany commissioned 2,000 Jewish officers during the war.[16] Although thousands of Jews served loyally in all three combatant armies, the Russians and Germans in particular viewed them with pronounced anti-Semitism, General Ludendorff believed the Polish Jews were 'particularly backward' but blamed the Russian administrators for their condition.[17] Anti-Semitism aside, he also believed that 'generally, the Jews of Poland favoured the Germans – the alternative was rule by Russia, where pogroms against were relatively commonplace'.[18] In addition ethnic Poles encouraged this view: a leading Polish politician declared that '90 percent of the Jews are traitors and 10 percent are spies'.[19]

As early as 31 August 1914, stories circulated among German soldiers on the Eastern Front that the Russian army was 'mistreating civilians, especially Jews'.[20] When the Austro-Hungarian army abandoned Lemberg to the Russians on 2 September, most of the city's Jews fled rather than welcome the Russians (28 per cent of the city's population was Jewish).[21] When the Austro-Hungarian fortress-city of Przemyśl (in Poland) fell to Russians in the spring of 1915, the Russians launched a fresh pogrom to drive them into submission.[22] Those who refused were expelled, and 17,000 Jews were forced to leave the city. After the capture of Warsaw the German governor general issued instructions for the 'severe treatment of the Russian population, excepting Jews'.[23]

The relocation decisions

Russian Jews were mistrusted and were said to spy for both sides.[24] Noted British historian, John Keegan noted that Russian Jews living in occupied

Poland, who 'being often German-speakers, were regarded (by the Germans) as useful instruments of occupation policy'.[25] In Russia, Gregory Rasputin, confidant of the Czarina, was known to have been financed 'by certain Jewish bankers who were, for all intents and purposes, German agents'.[26] Petrograd, in particular, was infested with enemy agents and sympathizers, many of whom were thought to be Jewish. Many figures in the Russian high command made no secret of their anti-Semitism, including General Nikolai Yanushkevich, the chief of the general staff. 'Many wished to remove all Jews from occupied parts of Galicia and a policy of deportations was implemented across the region.'[27]

Violence against Russian and Baltic Jews began almost immediately after the start of the war. According to German army rabbi Arthur Levy, who reported in December 1914 on conditions near Radom, Poland,

> Levy counted pogroms in 215 places and 'no end of this terror is in sight'. In Stasew eleven Jews in their praying shawls and shrouds had been hanged in the synagogue on Yom Kippur. In Bechawa near Lublin, 78 Jews had been hanged in one day on charges of espionage. In Łódź, 15,000 small tradesmen had their property taken from them and were left destitute.[28]

The relocation decisions appear to be evolutionary as a result of the advances of the German army in 1915. In January 1915, or about the same time as the Ottomans began to relocate the Armenians, the Russian army began a coordinated large-scale forced relocation of Jews living near the front line area of the Eastern Front. The Russian 'army command convinced itself that Russia's Jews were unreliable, that they had close ties to their kin abroad, that they were more attracted to the Austrian and German cultures than to the Russian, and that Jews shirked military service and engaged in spying and espionage on a broad scale'.[29] 'On 25 January 1915, Yanushkevich took the first major step in this direction, sending a circular to army commanders throughout the front zone authorizing the expulsion (*vyselenie*) of "all Jews and suspect individuals" from the entire region of military activity where troops were present.'[30] In February, the Russians passed a 'Liquidation Law' allowing the seizure of land within 160 kilometres of the frontier belonging to Jewish citizens of the Central Powers[31] (Germany and Austro-Hungary).

In March 1915, Grand Duke Nikolai, the supreme commander of the Czar's armies, ordered that Jewish civilians 'should be driven toward the German lines – they would either be killed by German fire or become refugees on the German side of the front'.[32] After the Austro-German offensive broke the Russian Third Army at Gorlitz in April 1915, entire eastern provinces of the Russian Empire were emptied of their Jewish populations in an expanded area west of a line running north-south from Riga to Kovno. By now there was a general policy to expel Jews from the major towns as the Russians approached.[33] These measures were justified by the publication of stories of the alleged Kuzhi Incident, which took place in modern Lithuania. Published on 28 April 1915, the story alleged that Russian Jews, called *zhids* in the text, signalled the advancing Germans and then helped them snipe at Russians.[34]

On 3 May a massive deportation began from Kovno province, which in a two-week period, resulted in approximately 150,000 Jews being forcibly removed from their homes.[35] On 15 May, Ivan Goremykin, chairman of the Council of Ministers, told a colleague that the recent deportation orders applied to 300,000 Jews.[36] In addition to forced relocation, the Russian army began officially sanctioned hostage-taking in order to insure compliance. As in the Ottoman Empire, the relocated persons became prey for brigandage, notably by Cossacks. The scale of the forced expulsions was unprecedented in the Russian Empire, and the area of Poland and White Russia known as the Pale was emptied of its Jewish population. As many as 100,000 Jews died in the process.[37] The Russian army often used accusations of sabotage or espionage as a reason to move 'unreliable Jews'[38] en masse to the interior.

While the deportations had been going on for several months, General Mikhail Alekseyev, commander of the Northwestern Front issued a comprehensive army policy on 30 June 1915 towards Jews, titled 'Rules on the Deportation of Jews from Military Districts of the Northwest Front'.[39] This far-reaching order allowed army commanders to deport Jews from operational areas and, moreover, to take hostages in order to insure their compliance. One historian noted that about 100,000 Jews from forty towns in the vicinity of Warsaw were forced to migrate.[40] Another historian called these 'a continuous series of massive, arbitrary, wholly unnecessary expulsions of the civilian Jewish population-now predominately composed of women, children, the elderly and the infirm'.[41] In addition to the relocation of Jews suspected of collusion with the enemy, thousands of Russian-subject Muslims in the Caucasus were likewise relocated to places in the interior.[42] Tatars in the Crimea and ethnic Germans in the Ukraine, both groups of which were Russian citizens but not ethnically Russian, were subjected to similar treatment.

The mechanics of relocation

Unlike the other cases in this book Russian and Polish Jews who were relocated from the Pale and the Baltics were not sent to refugee or internment camps. Neither were they packaged into vulnerable foot convoys as the Ottomans had moved the Ottoman-Armenians. Instead the Jews were transported deep into the vast interior of Russia. There is a fair amount of irony here as people identified as a threat to national security were moved to areas of the Russian Empire that had previously been forbidden for them to live in; whereupon to be released. The mechanisms for relocation simply brought evicted Jews together in near railway stations and terminals where they were temporarily camped.⁴³ When enough railway cars were available, the Jews were loaded and sent east to whatever destination the train happened to be going to. Commingled with the Jews were hundreds of thousands of relocated Ukrainian Germans, Gypsies as well as thousands of Russian refugees who fled the war zones. It is important to understand that 'Refugeedom is something spontaneous; but forced resettlement is arbitrary behavior' (wrote one Russian doctor in April 1916).⁴⁴

> In April-May 1915, the third phase commenced with larger scale mass evacuations: in this case the deportees were assigned destinations in advance and the journeys were better organized with the use of trains and the help of civilian officials. In May, the expulsions took on extreme proportions and were extended by General Nikolai Radkevich to the whole of Courland, to the province of Kaunas and part of Grodno and Suwałki: 200,000 Jews (40,000 from Riga) were expelled and treated as deportees.⁴⁵

By the fall of 1915, some 1/5 of the available rolling stock was tied up moving these vast numbers of people eastward and the overloaded system began to break down. Railway traffic jams became common and build-ups of displaced people became commonplace in the stations all along the rail lines leading into the interior. Conditions on the trains were 'squalid and demoralizing and refugees sometimes spent days in the company of decomposing corpses, the victims of cholera, dysentery, or pneumonia. Trainloads of Jewish refugees were sometimes pelted with stones by hostile onlookers encouraged by local army commanders.'⁴⁶ State and local officials formed refugee committees to assist the people who were relocated with food, housing, sanitary needs and clothing but in wartime Russia, isolated from the west and world trade by the war, these efforts were woefully insufficient. At the operational level the Russian state had no centralized plans for where these people would ultimately go. Thousands of Russian and Polish Jews found themselves in such unlikely cities as Saint Petersburg, Moscow and Ekaterinberg, which had previously been forbidden to Jews.⁴⁷ As these places were filled with refugees and relocated Jews, those arriving were pushed even farther east beyond the Ural Mountains to Siberia and the Russian Far East.

Numbers of those affected vary considerably – one historian estimated that 300,000 Jews were evicted from the Pale in 1914–15.⁴⁸ Historian Aaron Levine asserted that over 600,000 Jews were displaced from the Pale alone by the summer of 1915 when far larger numbers were additionally relocated.⁴⁹ Levin continued, 'However, it can be said with some confidence that the Jewish population and refugees suffered most acutely from the discriminatory treatment they faced during the first years of the war.'⁵⁰ At least half of the Jewish population of Russia, some three million people, almost all of whom lived in the Pale or the Baltics, were relocated.⁵¹ The historians working in this area have not fully tabulated the death toll of relocated Jews, but one historian has estimated that at least 100,000 Jews died as a direct consequence of relocation.[52]

Conclusion

This chapter has outlined the chronology and major events leading to the decisions to relocate and do violence against the Jewish population in the Pale Settlement and other areas of the Russian Empire. It has only been recently that researchers have pieced together enough evidence to better understand the events surrounding the evacuation and relocations of this population in 1914–15. The body of work dealing with this subject reveals an underlying anti-Semitic sentiment, rather than authentic security concerns, drove military plans and actions to relocate Russian Jews. In truth fears of Jewish support for Germany and Austria-Hungry were overblown and based more on opinions than hard facts. However, in light of other population displacement in the Russian Empire at the outbreak of the war on the Eastern Front, especially the Ukrainian ethnic Germans, one should consider broader strategic and operational decisions by civilian and military leadership respectively. What is clear from the broader set of evidence is that majority of relocated civilian populations in Russia were not inclined to participate in activities that would have been detrimental to Russian efforts to protect the homeland. This was even true of ethnic Germans, whose families had lived in Russia since Catherine the Great's time, who were largely unsympathetic to the war aims of the Central Powers and were far more concerned with maintaining the status quo. It also seems that the anti-Semitic sentiments and general disdain for Jews by Russians overshadowed any prejudicial feelings or treatment of other people groups living in Russia. This resulted in Jews suffering disproportionately more than other refugee groups.

There was certainly a tremendous amount of ambiguity in Russian policy regarding the empire's Jews. In the Eastern Front's war zone, operational commanders clearly regarded the Baltic Jews and Jews from the Pale as a threat. Even small numbers of Jews involved in sabotage, espionage and terrorism against the Russian military in the Pale or the Baltics would have played havoc with Russian military operations. While there was never an actual Jewish threat, it appeared to Russian decision-makers, who were predisposed to anti-Semitism, that there *might* be a threat. Thus in a pre-emptive move, which in many ways was similar to the American evacuation of Japanese-Americans in 1942 (see Chapter 8), the Russian military went ahead with a massive relocation campaign.

Yet, at the strategic or national level there appears to have been little thought given to how a relocated Jewish population might have negatively affected the Russian war effort in other more western parts of the empire.

Localized violence and pogroms against Jews 'in the relocation pipeline' varied greatly from place to place. It is clear that there was no unified policy at national or regional level penalizing or discriminating against relocated Jews. Moreover, the Russian state did not establish specialized camps to detain the relocated Jewish population and, in effect, simply cast them adrift in locales farther to the east inside the empire. Such concentrations of Jews at the eastern terminus locales of the relocation pipeline tended more to defining them as refugees rather than potential enemies of the state.

Notes

1. Eric Lohr, 'The Russian Army and the Jews: Mass Deportation, Hostages, and Violence during World War I', *The Russian Review*, Vol. 60, No. 3 (July 2001), 404–19, 407.
2. Joanna Sloame, 'Latvia Virtual Jewish History Tour', 1998–2018 American-Israeli Cooperative Enterprise, Available at https://www.jewishvirtuallibrary.org/latvia-virtual-jewish-history-tour (accessed 25 November 2018).
3. Richard Overy, *The Dictators: Hitler's Germany, Stalin's Russia* (New York: W. W. Norton Company, Inc., 2004), 236.
4. Robert K. Massie, *Nicholas and Alexandra: The Last Tsar and His Family* (London: Orion Books Ltd, 1967), 309–10.
5. Robert Drews, 'Religion in Eastern Europe and the Middle East from 1648 through the Reign of Catherine the Great', in *Coursebook: Judaism, Christianity and Islam, to the Beginnings of Modern Civilization* (Vanderbilt University, 2018), 1–19, 14.
6. Lohr, 'The Russian Army and the Jews', 409.
7. Steve Mason, *A History of the Jewish War: AD 66–74* (New York: Cambridge University Press, 2016), Chapter 1 *passim*.
8. Raphael Patai, *The Jewish Mind* (New York: Hatherleigh Press, 2007), 150.
9. Max Boot, *Invisible Armies, an Epic History of Guerrilla Warfare from Ancient Times to the Present* (New York: W.W. Norton & Company, 2013), 226–34.
10. Ibid., 235.
11. Ibid., 243.
12. See Dennis E. Showalter, *Tannenberg, Clash of Empires* (Washington, DC: Brassey's Inc., 2004), *passim*.
13. Stone, *The Eastern Front 1914–1917*, 130–5.
14. Ibid., 139.
15. Prit Buttar, *Collision of Empires, the War on the Eastern Front in 1914* (Oxford: Osprey Publishing, 2014), 69.
16. Dennis E. Showalter, *Instrument of War, the German Army 1914–18* (Oxford: Osprey Press, 2016), 180.

17 Buttar, *Collision of Empires*, 315.
18 Prit Buttar, *Germany Ascendant, The Eastern Front 1915* (London: Hutchinson, 1998), 302. (Oxford: Osprey Press, 2017), 169.
19 Tracey Hayes Norrell, *Shattered Communities: Soldiers, Rabbis, and the Ostjuden under German Occupation: 1915–1918* (PhD diss., University of Tennessee, 2010), 57.
20 Buttar, *Collision of Empires*, 260.
21 Ibid., 261.
22 Buttar, *Germany Ascendant*, 143.
23 Stone, *The Eastern Front 1914–1917*, 82.
24 Buttar, *Germany Ascendant*, 131.
25 John Keegan, *The First World War* (London: Hutchinson Publishing, 1998), 303.
26 Buttar, *Germany Ascendant*, 397.
27 Ibid., 230.
28 Norrell, *Shattered Communities: Soldiers, Rabbis, and the Ostjuden under German Occupation: 1915–1918*, 86.
29 Eric Lohr, *Nationalizing the Russian Empire, The Campaign against Enemy Aliens during World War I* (Cambridge, MA: Harvard University Press, 2003), 137.
30 Lohr, 'The Russian Army and the Jews', 409.
31 Buttar, *Germany Ascendant*, 262.
32 Ibid., 397.
33 Ibid.
34 Ibid., 308–9.
35 Lohr, 'The Russian Army and the Jews', 410.
36 Lohr, *Nationalizing the Russian Empire*, 140.
37 Ibid., 150.
38 Alexander V. Prusin, 'The Russian Military and the Jews in Galicia', in Eric Lohr and Marshall Poe (eds.), *The Military and Society in Russia 1450–1917* (Leiden: Brill, 2002), 537.
39 Lohr, 'The Russian Army and the Jews', 413.
40 Lohr, *Nationalizing the Russian Empire*, 139.
41 David Vital, *A People Apart, the Jews in Europe 1789–1939* (Oxford: Oxford University Press, 1999), 653.
42 Lohr, *Nationalizing the Russian Empire*, 153.
43 Peter Gatrell, *A Whole Empire Walking, Refugees in Russia during World War I* (Bloomington: Indiana University Press, 1999), 21.
44 Ibid., 31.
45 Giuseppe Motta, *The Great War against Eastern European Jewry, 1914–1920* (Cambridge: Cambridge Scholars Publishing, 2017), 22.

46 Gatrell, *A Whole Empire Walking*, 29.
47 Ibid., 54–5.
48 Pavel Polian, *Against Their Will, The History and Geography of Forced Migrations in the USSR* (Budapest: Central European University Press, 2004), 25.
49 Aaron Levine, 'Russian Jews and the 1917 Revolution', *Primary Source*, Vol. IV, No. II (Spring 2014), 17.
50 Ibid., 18.
51 Serena Tiepolato, 'The Jews in the Eastern War Zone' [edited transcript of American Jewish Committee (eds.), *The Jews of the Eastern War Zone* (New York: American Jewish Committee, 1916)], DEP n.7 / 2007, 179.
52 Prusin, 'The Russian Military and the Jews in Galicia', 537.

8

They are our enemies:

The Japanese-American internment

Dr Edward J. Erickson

Korematsu was not excluded from the Military Area because of hostility toward him or his race. He was excluded because we are at war with the Japanese Empire.

KOREMATSU v. UNITED STATES, MAJORITY OPINION

US Supreme Court, 18 December 1944

Introduction

The US Supreme Court decided (in a 6–3 split) to uphold the conviction of twenty-three-year-old Fred Korematsu for violating federal laws restricting Japanese-Americans in 1942.[1] The minority opinion, written by Associate Justice Robert Jackson, held that Korematsu's individual rights were compromised because of his Japanese ancestry (Map 8).[2] Americans today would agree with Justice Jackson and point to the removal of over 100,000 Japanese-Americans from the west coast in 1942 as de facto evidence of racism and prejudice. Congressional investigations in the 1980s reached similar conclusions.[3] Indeed, the contemporary American narrative about the relocations stresses the denial of civil rights of minorities

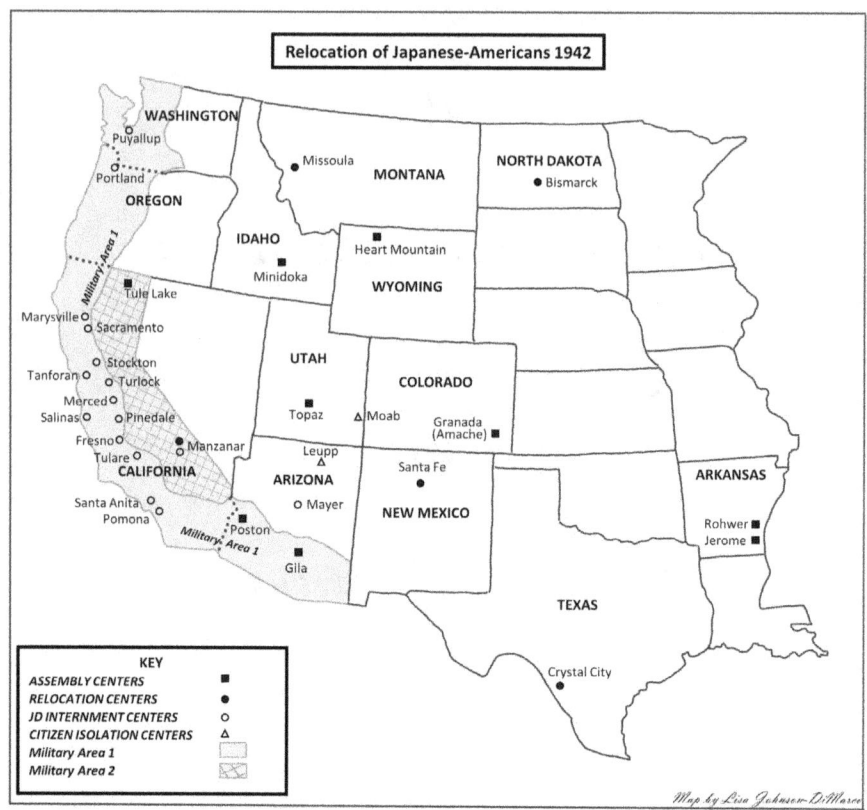

MAP 8 *Japanese-American Internment 1942. US Army and government officials forcibly relocated over 100,000 American citizens of Japanese ancestry to internment camps in the continental interior. With no credible evidence the American decision-makers believed that the Japanese-Americans constituted a fifth column threat. Although well treated, the relocated Japanese-Americans lost much of their property and businesses to unscrupulous white Americans.*

rather than examining the military aspects of the relocation decisions.[4] This chapter will not re-examine the civil liberties issues nor will it recapitulate the profound effects and impact of the relocations. Rather, this chapter re-examines the zeitgeist and the information available at the time which was used by the US military to reach recommendations and relocation decisions at the operational level. The purpose of this chapter is not to justify the relocation decisions but to track the major elements of military decision-making which led an infamous and flawed policy of population removal in wartime.[5]

The thesis of this chapter is that, in military and operational terms, the forced relocation of Japanese-Americans in 1942 is best understood as a counter-fifth column campaign. This chapter outlines the story of relocated people who were not in rebellion and who did not support the enemy. Like the Russian Jews in 1915 (see Chapter 7) bigotry, racism and fear rather than facts enabled the decision-makers to construct a case leading to forced relocation.

At the beginning of the war the military problem to be solved on the American west coast was how to protect vital installations (mostly aircraft factories) from sabotage and/or aerial attack coordinated by subversives.[6] This problem was nested within a contemporary context of a racially prejudiced society compounded by professional and popular 1940s understandings regarding fifth column operations (defined as traitors within the population who actively assisted the enemy). As this chapter shows, American military assessments in 1942 about such a fifth column considered capability and assumptions of intent rather than observed activities or fact-based intelligence.

Actual military planning to deal with potential fifth columnists began in mid-July 1941 with an agreement between the Justice Department and the War Department, and as war approached, joint threat assessments resulted in coordinated plans for observing and controlling enemy aliens (which across the country included Germans, Italians, Japanese and others). After Pearl Harbor on 7 December 1941, the War Department, the Justice Department and state civil authorities developed a racially and fear-based appraisal of the internal fifth column threat to the American west coast and to Hawaii, which resulted in plans to remove aliens, some naturalized individuals, and notably the entire Japanese and Japanese-American population from certain designated war zones. American army commanders and their staffs were responsible for the recommendations to relocate these categories of people. These recommendations were ratified by executive and congressional decisions in February and March 1942 legalizing the removal and internment of Japanese-American citizens.

The strategic situation

American strategic planning prior to Pearl Harbor focused on the Western Hemisphere and its defence. The famous Rainbow Plans (numbered One to Five) established defending the Western Hemisphere as the primary missions of the US Army and US Navy before which offensive operations would be launched overseas. All five versions of the plan identified the continental United States as the defensive 'main position' which lay behind an 'outpost line' consisting of Alaska-Hawaii-Panama-Puerto Rico that shielded the main position.[7] The Philippines, Guam and Samoa remained outside this perimeter and plans for these territories fluctuated during the pre-war period. In theory the outpost line and America's formidable Pacific Fleet kept the Japanese at bay well away from continental United States. At the strategic level, defence planning was conducted by a Joint Planning Committee (JPC) composed of army and navy officers. Planning for the land defence of the United States was conducted in the War Plans Division (WPD) of the US Army's general staff. Conceptually, for army planners, defence planning envisioned forming two components of equal size; mobile ground and air forces in the interior formed into a strategic reserve, and seacoast defences in fixed locations.[8] This thinking created a strategic dilemma in the allocation and positioning of troops and material, which by 1941, continued to plague strategic planners.

The fall of France in June 1940 turned the defined world of the army and navy planners upside down because the Anglo-French alliance had provided a certain shield against Axis aggression in Europe. However, with Britain standing alone, Axis-aligned French colonies in Africa and the Caribbean theoretically provided Germany and Italy with the means to attack directly the continental United States. Although the Italian fleet was confined to the Mediterranean and the German surface fleet reduced to irrelevance, the US Navy shifted significant forces to the Atlantic to deal with the threat of German submarines and the occasional German surface raider.[9] This left the hitherto powerful Pacific Fleet vis-à-vis the Japanese navy with near parity in battleships and inferiority in all other types including aircraft carriers. The Pearl Harbor disaster further weakened the Americans.

The war in the Pacific went very badly for the allies over the next six months as the victorious Japanese conquered Hong Kong, Wake Island, Guam, Malaya, Singapore, the Philippines and the Dutch East Indies, and on 7 June Japanese troops landed on Attu and Kiska Islands in Alaska. The Royal Navy, US Navy and the Netherlands navy lost dozens of ships in the South China and Java Seas, including HMS *Prince of Wales* and the HMS *Repulse*. An American victory in the Coral Sea in early May 1942 slowed the Japanese onslaught, but it was not clear to Americans that the tide was beginning to turn in the Pacific. The clear-cut and widely publicized American victory a month later at Midway, in early June 1942, decisively ended Japan's possession of the strategic initiative, but it would take the United States until mid-1943 to wrest the operational initiative away from the enemy (with the conclusion of the Guadalcanal campaign). It is fair to say that until early-1943 Japan remained a real and compelling operational threat to America's west coast.

The fifth column

An understanding of the term 'fifth column' is vital in understanding the zeitgeist affecting the strategic situation in early 1942 in the United States. The term originated during the Spanish Civil War in 1936 when rebel General Francisco Franco proclaimed that he had four columns marching on Madrid and a 'fifth column' of secret sympathizers already in the city.

The term was immediately acquired in the vernacular of Americans. In 1938 popular American author Ernest Hemingway published *The Fifth Column and the First Forty-Nine Stories* which became a best seller (*The Fifth Column* was Hemingway's only, and not well received, play).[10] The concept of deliberate fifth column activities gained credence among military professionals as an actual operational concept in 1940 when the details of the German invasion of Demark and Norway were reported. In Norway, a pro-German nationalist army major named Vidkun Quisling and pro-Nazi Norwegians actively paved the way for the invading German forces.[11] Like the term 'fifth column' the term 'Quisling' entered the American vocabulary to mean a traitor embedded in a nation's military that was willing to help the enemy. These terms were a part of the American discourse of the 1940s and counter fifth column operations, as will be described below, became part of American defence plans.

Targeting Japanese-American citizens began before the war. As early as 1932, American law enforcement and military agencies were 'providing a cooperative and clandestine surveillance of the Japanese community' in the United States and its territories.[12] Most of the surveillance was conducted by the Office of Naval Intelligence (ONI) which, because of the large Pacific Fleet, had more of an interest in this than its army counterpart, the Military Intelligence Division (MID or the G-2). The ONI reported the presence of a Japanese espionage ring in Seattle and Portland in October 1935 and, moreover, reported that active spying was ongoing in Hawaii. A State Department report in 1936 asserted that Japan had agents in every large city in America and on the west coast.[13] President Franklin D. Roosevelt wrote to the chief of naval operations in 1936 that every Japanese citizen or non-citizen on Oahu, Hawaii ought to be definitely identified and put on a list.[14]

As war approached in 1939, Roosevelt directed (on 26 June) that the Federal Bureau of Investigation (FBI), ONI and the MID jointly investigate, control and deal with all espionage, counter-espionage and sabotage matters.[15] Structurally, the three agency directors composed a committee of co-equals but a year later Roosevelt placed the FBI in overall charge.[16] The FBI director, J. Edgar Hoover (who was an extremely strong personality) quickly ran into an institutional quagmire when all three agencies claimed responsibility for surveillance of fifth column activities.[17] Much information was gathered by the three agencies but there was no centralized authority or office charged with integration and analysis of intelligence. This lack of what is today called all-source intelligence remained a problem for American decision-makers throughout the coming war. Despite this the three agencies managed to collaborate and send the names of over 2,000 Japanese aliens to the Justice Department, which established a consolidated list under the supervision of a 'Special Defence Unit'.[18] This list was known as the 'ABC List' and categorized individuals according to risk; for example, those ranked in Group A were 'known dangerous' making them likely fifth columnists.[19]

In March 1941, a clandestine break in by the ONI (known as the Ringle raid) of the Japanese consulate in Los Angeles led to new names added to the list and confirmation of many names already on the list. This information led to the arrest in June of a Japanese naval officer masquerading as a student and the destruction of a small espionage ring. The story of American naval code breaking as it relates to the defeat at Pearl Harbor as well as to the victory at Midway six months later is well known. In fact, American naval intelligence officers had broken many of the Japanese codes; the resulting intelligence was known as 'Magic'[20] but they remained focused on operational matters in the western Pacific rather than on espionage activities. As war approached both intelligence and law enforcement agencies in California and Hawaii continued to focus on perceptions rather than facts regarding internal threats.

Operational planning

Competing demands forced American military planners to delineate and prioritize their conceptions of current national and military policies. They named hemisphere defence as the first and basic policy.[21] The Joint Board's estimate articulated a policy of the 'preservation of the territorial, economic and ideological integrity of the United States and of the remainder of the Western Hemisphere'.[22] The execution of these responsibilities lay in the hands of four US field army headquarters supervised by the army's newly activated General Headquarters (GHQ). In March 1941, the four field armies were also designated as 'Defence Commands'. The eastern United States was designated as the Eastern Defence Command, under First Army Commander, Lieutenant General Hugh A. Drum, while the western United States (including the states of Washington, Oregon, California, Idaho, Nevada, Utah and Arizona) was designated as the Western Defence Command under Fourth Army Commander, Lieutenant General John L. DeWitt.[23] Then on 3 July 1941, GHQ received authority over the Defence Commands/Field Army for defensive planning (in addition to their training responsibilities).[24] The bulk of the army's combat forces, nineteen of thirty-four infantry, armoured, and cavalry divisions, lay in the interior assigned to the Second and Third Armies for training and as a strategic reserve. These orders established the operational architecture for the defence of the continental United States against external and internal enemies.

Operational planning for the defence began much earlier and included actions against internal threats such as fifth column operations. Planners were concerned especially about the diversion of 'combat troops from field operations to internal security missions'.[25] Sabotage by a fifth column was another concern as was the spreading of fear and uncertainty among civilian populations. Following the fall of France in the summer of 1940,[26] the G-2 (the army staff section responsible for intelligence and security) became concerned about such threats and began to study measures for protection against sabotage that had been approved by the Civilian Defence Bureau (an agency within the War Department).[27] These measures were then consolidated into an army-level counter-fifth column plan, which was approved by the War Department on 22 October 1940.[28] On 1 November the army directed corps commanders to quietly gather state and local plans for dealing with fifth columnists. By August 1941, all corps commanders had completed tactical-level fifth column plans, which were tested in October in the I Corps area (New England). Following the success of the tests the War Department transferred responsibility for implementing the counter-fifth column plans to the army's provost marshal general that month as well. However, due to the slow activation of military police battalions, corps commanders were forced to use combat troops for counter-fifth column plans which consisted in the main of guard duty for key military, infrastructure and industrial sites. The War Department also established a special force called the US Guards to provide guards for fixed sites but this organization also fell far behind its schedule of activations leaving the field army to fill the gap.

In concert with the development of plans, identification of potential fifth columnists began by examining the data from the 1940 US census for names and addresses of German, Italian and Japanese residents and adding to the existing ABC Lists. An agreement on 18 July 1941 between the War Department and the Justice Department gave Justice the responsibility for controlling enemy aliens in the event of war.[29] Of the 126,947 living in the continental United States, 112,353 persons of Japanese ancestry lived in the three west coast states (California alone had 93,717). On the west coast there were 40,869 Japanese aliens (called Issei) and 71,484 Japanese-American citizens (called Nisei).[30] An additional 58,000 Italian and 22,000 German aliens resided in the Pacific states (many of whom were Jewish refugees from the Nazis).

The operational situation

As early as February 1941, General George C. Marshall, US Army chief of staff, warned his Hawaiian commander about sabotage.[31] The War Department sent war warnings to the Philippine, Hawaiian and Caribbean commanders on 27 November 1941 as well as to General DeWitt on the west coast. The Department of the Navy's war warnings specifically directed commanders 'to take appropriate measures against sabotage'.[32] A separate anti-sabotage alert went to DeWitt, as Fourth Army commander, on the same day.[33] DeWitt promptly notified his army air and navy counterparts, as well as his subordinate commanders, and he implemented counter fifth column measures. About noon Washington time on 7 December 1941, Marshall sent his Pacific commanders a final war warning, which arrived too late to help American commanders in Hawaii. Three days after the Pearl Harbor attack, Marshall designated DeWitt's Western Defence Command (including the territory of Alaska, and the Second and Fourth US Army Air Forces) as an active theatre of war (Drum's command on the Atlantic coast received similar authority). Subject to certain restrictions on air movements and deployments DeWitt was now the de facto military theatre governor of seven American states as well as an operational-level field army commander.

Army and navy commanders in the outpost line and garrisons of the Pacific received separate war warnings on 27 November 1941 to which responses were varied. All commanders received instructions to implement the activities of the Japan-specific parts of the Rainbow Five war plan. The US Army commander in the Hawaiian Department was Major General Walter C. Short, who was directly responsible for the air warning systems and air defences of the fleet anchorage at Pearl Harbor. On 28 November Short issued orders which included that 'all necessary measures be taken to protect military establishments, property, and equipment against sabotage, against propaganda affecting Army personnel, and against all espionage'.[34] In the Hawaiian Department Short's plans included three levels of alert tailored to the threat. 'Alert No.1 was "a defence against sabotage, espionage, and subversive activities without any threat from the outside"; Alert No. 2 encompassed No. 1 plus defence against air, surface, and submarine attack; No. 3 was "a defence against all out attack".'[35] According to historian Gordon Prange, Short became preoccupied with the notion that the 170,000 Japanese and Japanese-Americans living in Hawaii (of whom 37,500 were foreign born) constituted a fifth column threat. Short also believed the fifth column activities of the Nazis in the early days of the war would reappear in Hawaii. Short's 'fixation persisted although not a single case of Japanese sabotage occurred while he commanded the Hawaiian Department'.[36] The War Department, Hawaii's governor, Honolulu's mayor and leading citizens concurred in Short's assessment.

During the numerous post-attack congressional and military investigations Short repeatedly justified his alert status by noting that after the war warnings of 27 November, he properly notified the War Department of his actions and his alert status. Nevertheless, because of Short's interpretation of the threat, his aircraft remained lined up wingtip-to-wingtip and unarmed making them easy targets on the morning on 7 December 1941. A number of official inquiries examined Short's actions and universally found him guilty of severe errors in judgement. In particular, Short was severely criticized for his decision to place his command in an alert condition based on the probability of sabotage rather than the probability of aerial attack.[37]

On the west coast, under the Rainbow Five Plan, General DeWitt was responsible operationally for coastal defence, air defence and air warning, and for guarding non-military installations of significant importance to the rearmament effort in seven western states. In particular, the War Department identified the aircraft factories in coastal cities (Boeing in Seattle, Douglas and Lockheed in Los Angeles and Consolidated in San Diego) as vital for the national defence.[38] In fact, half of all American aircraft production and almost all heavy bomber production (B-17s and B-24s) came out of just eight plants in the Los Angeles area.[39] Naval yards and shipbuilding in Puget Sound, Portland, San Francisco Bay, Los Angeles and San Diego, as well as the California oil industry 'were of only slightly less importance to the future conduct of the war'.[40] The importance of California in the American war effort cannot be overstated.

General DeWitt's Fourth Army headquarters was located at the Presidio of San Francisco, California, and comprised the III Corps headquarters at the Presidio of Monterey, California (composed of the 7th, 35th, and 40th Infantry Divisions) and the IX Corps headquarters at Fort Lewis, Washington. (Composed of the 3rd and 41st Infantry Divisions, however, the 3rd Infantry Division was detached for amphibious training and unavailable.)[41] In addition he had coast artillery regiments, anti-aircraft regiments and a large number of smaller units. Overall, the Western Defence Command had about 172,000 officers and men available for duty of which 121,000 were assigned to the ground forces. Navy, Marine Corps and Coast Guard personnel added another 75,000 men to the security of the west coast but remained outside DeWitt's authority. The army forces assigned to DeWitt conformed to the requirements of the Rainbow Five war plan which assumed raids on the mainland rather than major attacks. DeWitt's most serious weakness was his five anti-aircraft regiments which lacked two-thirds of their equipment.[42] DeWitt requested more ground troops but these requests were denied until the Pearl Harbor attack. However, by February 1942, the 3rd Infantry Division returned to his control, and the War Department reinforced him with a cavalry brigade and nine more anti-aircraft regiments, giving DeWitt over 250,000 soldiers.[43] The air forces were also reinforced with three pursuit and three bombardment groups but they remained very short of bombs and ammunition.

While these forces and numbers appear large, given the huge expanse of territory, two international borders, some 1,400 miles of coastline and a large number of installations and key industrial plants, DeWitt was continually hard-pressed to find personnel to meet all operational and tactical requirements.[44] Major General Joseph Stillwell, commanding III Corps and the Southern California Sector of the WDC, noted in his diary on 20 December 1941 that he was expected to provide guards not only for obvious vital infrastructure such as aircraft factories, oil wells and refineries, and dams and railroad bridges but also for civilian radio stations, hospitals, federal office buildings and aqueducts.[45] Stillwell continued in his diary that four of his seven infantry regiments were deployed on these kinds of guard duty. In fact, General DeWitt's theatre equalled an area equivalent to Europe west of the Vistula, and a quarter million men were woefully insufficient to his needs.

The relocation decision

By today's standards Lieutenant General John L. DeWitt would clearly be termed a racist and the extant literature about these events represents him as such. The most vivid character portrait of DeWitt is found in the work of Peter Irons, who painted DeWitt in raw terms which offend our modern sensibilities.[46] Irons noted that DeWitt was sixty-one years old when he assumed command of the Fourth Army on 5 December 1939 and that he had spent his entire life in uniform or living on army posts. He argued that DeWitt had a 'long career in a segregated army' that 'had infected him with the virus of prejudice against blacks and Asians'.[47] Irons continued with, 'his service in the Philippines could hardly have shielded him from the virulent anti-Asian racism that pervaded the occupying American army'. Irons quoted a number of direct racially insensitive remarks made by DeWitt which added weight to his assessments. However, Irons completes his analysis of the Fourth Army commander by ironically asserting, 'It was not bald prejudice that clouded DeWitt's military judgment in the days after Pearl Harbor as much as fear.'

It is important to note at this point in the narrative that the United States in the 1940s was a profoundly conservative society in which discrimination by race, ethnicity, gender and sexuality was deeply embedded in both American law and culture. The military and naval services were segregated and tightly compartmentalized in an exclusive micro-society outside mainstream America.[48] John DeWitt was a man of his times and his biased thinking and world views were characteristic and representative of his class and profession. Certainly his Hawaiian counterpart, Major General Walter Short, saw the world in similar terms. My own conclusion is similar to Peter Irons's in that DeWitt had certain prejudices, but these do not fully explain his decisions. Whatever DeWitt's personal sensibilities, it is a fact his WDC had competing priorities including conventional defensive responsibilities, counter-fifth column and counter-sabotage responsibilities, and training and readiness responsibilities, all of which weighed on him and occupied his mind.

The Pearl Harbor attack shocked the country, and Americans immediately embraced the idea that Japan executed a 'sneak attack' before actually declaring war. Those paying attention to Japan knew that the Japanese navy had conducted a similar surprise attack on the Russian Pacific Fleet lying at anchor at Port Arthur before declaring war in 1904.[49] It did not take long for this fact to lodge in the consciousness of the American public. At 3.30 pm Washington time, 7 December, General Marshall ordered General DeWitt to 'round up all suspicious characters listed' in cooperation with the FBI and for army corps commanders to notify manufacturers to take all special measures against sabotage.[50]

On 7 and 8 December 1941, Roosevelt issued presidential proclamations which provided a basis for immediate action against German, Italians and Japanese aliens (actually predating American declarations of war) that constituted a danger to the United States. Three days later General DeWitt placed his command in a higher defence category than required under Rainbow 5 (moving it from Category B to Category C). The WDC also implemented civil defence plans, counter-fifth column plans and counter-sabotage plans. By 13 December, the Department of Justice (DOJ) had interned 831 enemy aliens in the Pacific states (595 Japanese, 187 Germans and 49 Italians).[51] During the next three weeks there were many false reports of Japanese naval and air flotillas off the west coast including a Treasury Department report that an estimated 20,000 Japanese in the San Francisco area 'were ready for organized action'.[52] On 19 December DeWitt recommended to GHQ that all adult enemy aliens be removed to the interior. In a telephone conversation with Major General Allen W. Gillion, the provost marshal general of the army, DeWitt mentioned that he had been visited by a representative of the Los Angeles Chamber of Commerce who had asked that all Japanese in the Los Angeles area 'be rounded up'.[53] DeWitt then told Gillion (who was in agreement with him) that 'such actions would alienate the loyal Japanese ... and the authorities should watch for suspicious activities and then take necessary steps ... rather than try and intern them'. DeWitt ended the call by asserting that he believed that 'we could weed out the disloyal ... and lock them up if necessary'.

Later in the month the DOJ announced regulations requiring enemy aliens surrender radio receivers, transmitters and certain types of cameras by 5 January. The DOJ also had concerns about the specific mechanisms for dealing with west coast aliens and arranged for a conference to be held in San Francisco. The conference was held on 4–5 January 1942, and in attendance was an individual who would figure heavily into the unfolding narrative; he was Major Karl R. Bendetsen, the chief of the Provost Marshal's Aliens Division. General DeWitt opened the conference by declaring his serious concern about the alien situation and his distrust concerning the loyalty of the Japanese population; aliens and citizens alike.[54] He explicitly noted the threat to defence installations on the west coast, including naval yards, 'but primarily the aircraft factories – Boeing up north and a large number in the Los Angeles and San Diego area'.[55] DeWitt continued asserting that he was holding a large number of troops guarding these installation and that the threat was constant and growing more dangerous every day. Participants recorded that DeWitt was opposed to a mass evacuation. The conference concluded with a plan of action that included rapid alien registration, regulations for FBI searches, and for the designation of strategic areas by the army from which enemy aliens would be barred (with exact descriptions for cause) by the attorney general.

General DeWitt moved quickly and designated the boundaries of the strategic areas on 9 January but coordination with the navy (which wanted him to exclude not only enemy aliens but also certain Japanese-Americans who could not prove severing allegiance with Japan) delayed sending his final lists to the attorney general until 21 January 1942. DeWitt's recommendations called for eighty-six Category A exclusion zones and eight Category B pass and permit zones. His staff computed that 7,000 enemy aliens, 40 per cent of whom were Japanese, would have to be relocated. The secretary of war, Henry L. Stimson, forwarded DeWitt's recommendations to Francis Biddle, the attorney general, on 25 January with additional comments from a telephone conversation with DeWitt the previous day. In the call, DeWitt expressed great apprehension over the presence of many thousands of enemy aliens; moreover, he asserted that interceptions and attacks on US shipping from the west coast were 'undoubtedly coordinated by intelligent enemy control' involving shore-to-ship radio communications.[56] DeWitt ended the call by insisting on immediate and stringent action. In fact Japanese submarines sank two oil tankers and one freighter off California in December 1941 and army bombers reported sinking (erroneously) a submarine off Oregon on 24 December. However, no American ships were sunk off the Pacific coast in January, which in retrospect makes General DeWitt's assertions quite problematic.

On the same day the administration published what is called the 'Roberts Report', and it landed like a bombshell on the American public. It owed its origins to an 18 December 1941 executive order from Roosevelt forming a commission to find out what happened and who was responsible for the Pearl Harbor disaster. The commission is generally known as the 'Roberts Commission' after its presiding officer US Supreme Court Associate Justice Owen J. Roberts. The commission arrived in Hawaii on 22 December 1941 and returned to the mainland on 10 January 1942. The commission interviewed 127 witnesses, examined a large number of documents, and the Roberts Report was published publically by the US Senate on 25 January 1942.[57] Among other things the report concluded that espionage had been a factor in the defeat and that it had been widespread by Japanese consular agents and by Japanese residents on Oahu. This inflammatory accusation was proven false after the war.

On 4 February 1942, Colonel (now promoted) Bendetsen sent a memorandum to the provost marshal general outlining his recommendations for the steps leading to relocation. It is fair to call Karl Bendetsen the architect of relocation because the operational concept surfaced in this memo for the first time. He recommended three sequential steps: first, the issuance of a presidential executive order authorizing the secretary of war to designate military areas; second, General DeWitt would designate military areas; third, the immediate evacuation from the designated military areas of all persons not proposed to be licensed to remain.[58] Bendetsen also noted that if all of DeWitt's Category A areas were designated as exclusion areas that about 30,000 people would have to be relocated. General Gullion forwarded a revision of Bendetsen's memo (with all references to General DeWitt removed) to the assistant secretary of war as his department's recommendation on 6 February. Over the next five days there was a flurry of correspondence and conversations between the attorney general, the DOJ and the War Department concerning the questions to be determined in order for the president to make a decision. On 11 February Secretary Stimson telephoned the president and briefed him on the proposals, the results of which were relayed to Bendetsen as carte blanche to proceed ahead with his plans.

The famous American newspaper columnist and political commentator Walter Lippman now entered the debate with a 12 February 1942 article in *The Washington Post*; the headline of which read, 'The Fifth Column on the Coast'.[59] Lippman had met DeWitt and Bendetsen at the Presidio of San Francisco earlier and the article reflected the military's thinking about the problem. Lippman asserted that the administration in Washington was unwilling to adopt policies of mass relocation and mass internment. He also fed fuel to the fire by insisting, 'it is a fact that communications take place between the enemy at sea and enemy agents on land'.[60] Lippman dismissed the evidence that no sabotage had occurred nor had any espionage agents been apprehended by suggesting that these enemy assets lay in waiting for a well-organized blow to be struck with maximum effect. These inflammatory assertions reflected contemporary thinking about fifth column operations. Lippman was a Pulitzer Prize winner, widely read in America, and his piece was immediately picked up and republished in hundreds of newspapers across the country.

Within naval intelligence circles, Commander Ringle (of the Ringle raid) reported in early February that only a very small minority (less than 3 per cent) of alien and citizen Japanese were so fanatically loyal to the emperor that they could be expected to act as saboteurs or spies.[61] However, Ringle also asserted that a larger majority might be 'passively disloyal' if given the opportunity. Ringle's report reinforced the point that sabotage and subversion did not require a large number of participants to achieve a deadly effect.

By this time, General DeWitt had second thoughts about the plans, and on 14 February, he sent revised recommendations by airmail which advised the additional relocation of Japanese-Americans from the areas he had previously identified as Category A. In this memorandum General DeWitt explicitly stated his 'estimate of possible and probable enemy activities as the following: a) naval attack on shipping, b) naval attack on coastal shipping and vital installations, c) air raids on vital installations, d) sabotage of vital installations throughout the Western Defence Command'.[62] Very importantly DeWitt continued, 'Hostile naval and air raids will be assisted by enemy agents signalling from the coastline and the vicinity thereof; and by supplying and otherwise assisting enemy vessels and by sabotage.' This sentence was effectively inclusive by identifying Japanese-Americans, not only as saboteurs but also as fifth columnists actively assisting in all four of the threats that he had advanced.

DeWitt's 14 February recommendations also included his concepts for designating strategic areas for exclusion as well as stating that all aliens and suspected persons be included in exclusion measures. Three days later DeWitt then added to his appreciations in a telephone conversation with General Gullion by stating explicitly that he was 'opposed to any preferential treatment to any alien irrespective of race'.[63] DeWitt's recommendations were passed around the War Department until sent on to GHQ at 5.00 pm on 18 February. The next day the GHQ non-concurred with DeWitt's recommendations and decided instead to recommend that only enemy alien leaders be arrested and interned, rather than relocating the entire Japanese-American population from certain designated areas.[64] However, this decision came about too late to have an effect.

Earlier on 13 February 1942, a Pacific coast congressional subcommittee on aliens and sabotage had recommended that all persons of Japanese lineage, aliens and citizens alike, be deemed dangerous and evacuated from strategic areas. This recommendation was sent to the president on 16 February who asked Stimson to reply. In the meantime, Colonel Bendetsen rushed to Washington by air to attend a conference on 17 February with Secretary Stimson, General Gullion, Major General Mark Clark (plans chief at GHQ) and Mr John McCloy (Stimson's deputy). General Clark protested vigorously against mass evacuations because it would involve too many troops and resources. That evening McCloy, Gullion and Bendetsen met with Justice Department representatives at the home of attorney general Biddle. General Clark was not present for reasons that are unclear, but perhaps obvious, today. McCloy was in possession of a memo from General Marshall expressing serious concerns for the safety of the west coast industrial plants and reaffirming the dilemma this placed on General DeWitt regarding troop utilization.[65] At the meeting Gullion 'pulled from his pocket and read the draft of a proposed Presidential Executive order that would authorize the Secretary of War to remove citizens and aliens from areas he might designate'.[66] Biddle accepted the draft and after several more meetings between Justice and the army, President Roosevelt signed Executive Order 9066 on the evening of 19 February 1942.

Knowing that the presidential order authorizing the relocation of Japanese-Americans was in the works enabled McCloy, Gullion and Bendetsen between 18 and 20 February to draft explicit instructions to General DeWitt. These War Department directives issued on 20 February surprised General DeWitt, who wanted all enemy aliens, including Germans and Italians, as well as American-born Japanese moved out of strategic areas, because the directives only applied to Japanese aliens and citizens. (DeWitt had clearly stated earlier that he was opposed to any sort of preferential treatment for German and Italian aliens.) On 21 February, Stimson finally replied to the congressional subcommittee assuring them that plans for a partial or complete evacuation were being formulated. The War Department and the Justice Department officials co-wrote a draft of legislation backing up the executive order, which was forwarded to Congress on 9 March. After a brief debate the draft became Public Law 503, passing by voice vote in both houses on 19 March and signed into law two days later by President Roosevelt.

Operationalizing the decision

On 23 February the Imperial Japanese navy submarine I-17 surfaced off Santa Barbara and sent thirteen shells from its deck gun at oil installations (the damage was negligible). This shifted American coast and air defences into the highest state of alert, and on the night of 24/25 February, over-anxious gunners fired thousands of rounds into the air over Los Angeles against supposed Japanese aerial raiders. This comic opera event became known as the 'Battle of Los Angeles' and served to highlight the nervousness and fear on the west coast. Unfortunately the media blended fact with fiction creating an overly exaggerated picture of the actual threat to the west coast which inflamed public opinion in the Pacific states against Japanese-Americans. Popular commentators on the Mutual Broadcasting Company's radio programmes became particularly strident in calling for evacuations. In addition to the demands of elected congressional and state officials, groups like the American Legion, the California Farm Bureau Federation, the Growers-Shippers Association and the Native Sons and Daughters of the Golden West began to vigorously and publically advocate for the removal of ethnic Japanese.[67] The sincerity of these groups, which benefitted financially from the removal of Japanese-Americans from the agricultural sector of the west coast economy, is obviously suspect today.

On the same day as the shelling of Santa Barbara Colonel Bendetsen arrived back in San Francisco to serve as the liaison officer between General DeWitt and Assistant Secretary of War McCloy and to assist in the implementation of the relocation directives. Before the war Bendetsen had practised law and he helped General DeWitt draft the first proclamations informing the public about the mechanics of the relocation. On 2 March the first press release and first proclamation were released. The proclamation established two defined military areas which divided the west coast into manageable sectors based on the number and vulnerability of critical installations contained therein.[68] The most important sector was Military Area No. 1, which covered the western halves of the three Pacific coast states and southern Arizona. The greatest number of the Fourth Army's critical installations, including the vital aircraft factories, lay in this area. Military Area No. 2 covered the eastern halves of the three states and northern Arizona. The press release forecast the exclusion of persons of

Japanese ancestry from Military Area No. 1 and the exclusion of German and Italian aliens from some parts of Area 1 as well.

General DeWitt had hoped that relocation would be voluntary, and his press release urged Japanese-American to move out voluntarily of the defined areas and into the interior. He hoped that voluntary cooperation would ease the administrative burden of relocation. Previous efforts encouraging voluntary relocation in late February simply moved about 15,000 Japanese-Americans from one restricted zone to another and only about 2,000 people had actually voluntarily moved out of Area No. 1.[69] Colonel Bendetsen, the architect of the strategic plan, now provided the brains behind the operational plan.

Meanwhile, in Washington, the scope and scale of Roosevelt's executive order began to sink in. At a cabinet discussion on 27 February the president expressed his concern over transportation and resettlement and asked for opinions and recommendations on the path forward. According to Secretary Stimson's notes the meeting was confusing and, based on DeWitt's assessments that relocation would degrade of his ability to defend his theatre, the president decided that 'the work should be taken off the shoulders of the army'.[70] The result of this discussion was that a single agency was established to handle relocation and a Department of Agriculture official, who had been working informally on the evacuation problem (many Japanese-Americans worked in the agriculture industry), was identified to supervise it. On 18 March 1942, Roosevelt named Mr Milton S. Eisenhower (the older brother of the soon to be famous American general) as the director of the newly established War Relocation Authority (WRA). Three days later Bendetsen recommended termination of voluntary relocation, which both DeWitt and Eisenhower supported. On 29 March, DeWitt ended voluntary relocation and prepared to begin controlled compulsory evacuation under WRA supervision.

On DeWitt's northern flank the Canadian government had reached similar conclusions and announced plans on 14 January 1942 to remove partially persons of Japanese ancestry from the Pacific coastal areas of British Columbia.[71] However, perceptions of the threat evidently intensified because on 26 February the Canadian government announced a complete evacuation of British Columbia's 22,000 persons of Japanese descent. Over the next eight months the government relocated 21,000 ethnically Japanese residents, of whom three quarters were Canadian citizens, to camps in the interior. Farther north the secretary of war (on 6 March 1942) extended Executive Order 9066 to include the territory of Alaska, which contained 230 ethnic Japanese, half of whom were American citizens.

It was General Witt's intent, as late as 8 May 1942, to carry out the evacuation and the detention of German and Italian aliens from prohibited zones in his theatre.[72] He faced strong opposition from politicians in Washington, from the War and Justice Departments and even from within his own staff. DeWitt's assistant chief of staff for civil affairs, Lieutenant

Colonel William E. Boekel, recommended that mass evacuation of German and Italian aliens was 'neither necessary nor desirable'.[73] The obviously prejudiced Boekel justified his argument by pointing out about Japanese-Americans that 'their oriental habits of life, their and our inability to assimilate biologically, and what is more important, our inability to distinguish the subverters and saboteurs from the rest of the mass made necessary their class evacuation on a horizontal basis'.[74] Nevertheless, DeWitt proceeded to ask the War Department on 10 May for authority to conduct collective, but measured and limited, evacuation of German and Italian aliens from Military Area No. 1. DeWitt explicitly noted that the evacuation of Germans and Italians were justified on the grounds of military necessity.[75] Stimson and McCloy disagreed and refused his request to which DeWitt insisted, if his recommendations were denied, the War Department would issue him definite instructions to the contrary that would exempt him from all responsibility for the consequences. General DeWitt was covering himself and had previously said to the mayor of Los Angeles he 'was not going to be a second General Short'.[76] By this time the unfortunate Hawaiian Department commander (Major General Walter Short) had not only been disgraced and involuntarily retired from active duty but the Roberts Report accused him of dereliction of duty and severe lapses of judgement.

Final instructions of authority came from the War Department to General DeWitt on 22 May 1942. These did not relieve him of responsibility but did provide him with broader authority to remove German and Italian aliens on a case-by-case basis based on the general's estimate of the military necessity of the situation.[77] On 27 May DeWitt placed the Western Defence Command on special alert, and three days later the Operations Division of the army staff notified him of the War Department's 'conviction that surprise attacks on the west coast are a possibility from now on'.[78] Although the opposing fleets were about to collide at Midway there were other troubling events demonstrating Japan's offensive capabilities. Between 3 and 6 June 1942, Japanese troops invaded and occupied Attu and Kiska (two islands in the Aleutian chain) and naval air forces bombed Dutch Harbor, Alaska. On 20 June Japanese submarine shelled a Canadian radio station on Vancouver Island, and the following night a Japanese submarine surfaced and shelled Fort Stevens at the mouth of the Columbia River in Oregon; physical damage was inconsequential but the resulting publicity was not. The last direct attack by the Japanese navy happened on 9 September 1942 when a small aircraft, launched by the Japanese submarine I-25, bombed a mountain slope near Brookings, Oregon, causing a small forest fire. As late as December 1942 a US Navy patrol erroneously reported an unidentified group of 10 to 20 vessels 500 miles off the California coast. These attacks served to confirm Japan's capability to attack the west coast.

While self-serving and racially motivated economic interests helped drive removal of Japanese-Americans from California pragmatic economic interests kept them in Hawaii, Major General Delos Emmons, General

Short's replacement in Hawaii, who was now responsible for the defence of the islands, assured the 98,000 Japanese-American citizens and 20,000 Japanese in the islands of fair treatment if they remained loyal to the United States. This was because ethnically Japanese workers provided the bulk of the skilled labour in the islands. Emmons personally 'expressed little faith in their loyalty in the event of an invasion but he believed them indispensible (Sic) unless they could be replaced by an equivalent labour forces from the mainland'.[79] However in Washington, Frank Knox, the secretary of the navy, also advocated for their restriction leading to a number of cabinet discussions about evacuation. The War Department sided with a pragmatic approach based on the need for skilled labour while the navy, which had no actual responsibilities for the defence of the islands, advocated removal. Stimson and Marshall began to plan for an evacuation of Japanese-Americans from Hawaii. McCloy visited Oahu in late March and learned that both army and navy commanders in Hawaii opposed evacuation, preferring instead 'to treat the Japanese in Hawaii as citizens of an occupied foreign country'.[80] The interdepartmental debate raged for several months, eventually involving the direct engagement of the president (who generally sided with the navy in such army–navy squabbles).

Over the summer of 1942 the War Department hedged its bets by coordinating with WRA to move up to 15,000 evacuees from Hawaii to relocation centres in the continental United States. The debate continued and General Emmons received conflicting instructions over the summer but was finally directed to identify and evacuate about a thousand of the Japanese and Japanese-American residents whom he considered as dangerous. Partial evacuation of Japanese-Americans began previously in April, and by 7 June the Western Defence Command had evacuated more than 100,000 persons of Japanese ancestry from Military Area No. 1. Removal from Military Area No. 2 was complete in early August, and the last movement from an army assembly centre to a relocation centre occurred on 3 November 1942 after which the WRA took over general responsibility for the care of the relocated persons. Between November 1942 and March 1943, General Emmons evacuated 1,875 Hawaiian residents to WRA relocation camps on the mainland.[81]

General DeWitt's final report on the Japanese evacuation

General DeWitt's staff compiled a final report which was sent to Secretary of War Stimson through General George Marshall on 19 July 1943. In its published form DeWitt's final report comprises 618 pages of text, maps and charts. Henry Stimson's Foreword provided the seedbed for the idea that national security concerns override civil liberties. Stimson wrote, 'It was unfortunate that the exigencies of the military situation were such as to require the same treatment for all persons of Japanese ancestry, regardless of their individual loyalty to the United States. But in emergencies, where the safety of the nation is involved, consideration of the rights of individuals must be subordinated to the common security.'[82] Herein lay the rationale for the Korematsu decision eighteen months later.

DeWitt's final report can only be called a whitewash and a massive fraud and apologia for a relocation programme that, by 1943, was increasingly viewed with scepticism by many Americans. The first sentence in the report is accusatory and read, 'The evacuation was impelled by military necessity.'[83] DeWitt then asserted that 'intelligence services records reflected the existence of hundreds of organizations in California, Washington, Oregon and Arizona, which prior to 7 December 1941, were actively engaged in advancing Japanese war aims'. He continued by insisting that thousands of American-born Japanese had returned to Japan before the war for indoctrination and that 'Emperor worshipping ceremonies' were common among Japanese-American communities in the western United States. He characterized Japanese-Americans cultural groups as funded by a Japanese war chest and insisted that they constituted a menace that had to be dealt with. DeWitt finished his polemic by asserting that it was better to have 'this protection and not needed it rather than to not had it and needed it – as we have learned to our sorrow'.[84] In fact, none of these *ex post facto* allegations were true nor had any of them been advanced before the war.

It is hard for a modern American to read DeWitt's final report which characterized the Japanese-American population as willing puppets of the Japanese military that were ready to spring at the throats of unwary Americans immediately on orders from Tokyo. DeWitt's staff, led by Colonel Bendetsen, proceeded to include dozens of unproven accusations, such as the 'Emperor worshipping ceremonies', none of which appear in the actual historical record of the decision-making process. Bendetsen also assembled monumental sets of tabular data showing how and where the relocated persons went, and showing that few died or became sick en route or in camps. Moreover, DeWitt's report contained dozens of photographs depicting well cared for and smiling interned Japanese-Americans in the internment camps of the nation's interior. These photographs are obviously posed, and they remind the author of the staged Nazi photographs and films of the showcase Theresienstadt Concentration Camp in what is now the Czech Republic, showing healthy, smiling and contented inmates and their families engaged in productive work and cultural activities. Almost none of the first part of DeWitt's report (titled *Evacuation – Its Military Necessity*) portraying Japanese-Americans as a threat was in any way based on factual information and authentic intelligence. One political scientist subsequently characterized the report as a 'suppression of evidence'.[85] In essence, DeWitt's final report was simply a white washed argument by assertion unsupported by evidence. Unfortunately for the United States, DeWitt's final report was accepted at the time as factual and figured heavily in wartime US Supreme Court cases dealing with the civil liberties of Japanese-Americans. According to an official US Army historian's writing in 1959, 'In fact, no proved instances of sabotage or of espionage after Pearl Harbor among the west coast Japanese population were ever uncovered.'[86]

In September 1943, General John L. DeWitt was relieved of command of the WDC and transferred to command the Army and Navy Staff College in Washington, DC. He had held this command for almost four years, and although there is some speculation that DeWitt was moved as a consequence of his decisions about relocations, the author believes that it was more a matter of army personnel policies. General Delos Emmons, the Hawaiian Department commander, replaced DeWitt at the Western Defence Command. John DeWitt retired in 1947 and lived until 1962. As for the Japanese-Americans President Roosevelt rescinded his executive order in January 1945 and most of the internees returned home by the end of war (although some remained until 1946).

'Interpretations tested by consequences'[87]

It is difficult today to consider the actions of the US government, its departments and the military in relocating an entire class of persons as justified in any way. It is incontestable that an actual evidence-based case was never made at the time to legitimize or justify the relocation of the West Coast Japanese-American population. In the post-war years, Americans became aware that the Japanese-Americans remained loyal and that no record of subversion or sabotage existed. In fact, antagonistic public opinion regarding Japanese-Americans actually began to evaporate in 1944 when the story of the 'Nisei Japanese' as they were popularly known became publicized.

At the time of Pearl Harbor, numbers of Japanese-Americans were serving in the Hawaiian National Guard. They were called into federal service in 1940, but in May 1942, officers and men of Japanese ancestry were withdrawn from units and formed into a provisional battalion. On 5 June 1942, the soldiers were shipped to the mainland and reorganized as the separate battalion.[88] On 22 January 1943, the manpower-stressed War Department directed that a Japanese-American regimental combat team activate at Camp Shelby, Mississippi in February.[89] The Hawaiian guardsmen transferred there and were joined by volunteers from Hawaii and from the mainland. These men became the famous 442nd Regimental Combat Team (RCT); an all-arms independent unit comprised of infantry regiment, field artillery, combat engineers and supporting services. These units were sent to the European theatre for obvious reasons and landed in Italy in 1943. By June 1944, the Nisei Japanese had piled up an incredible record of medals for battlefield heroism, and the War Department belatedly recognized the public relations value of their service. A 28 June message from General Marshall to General Jacob Devers, commander of American forces in the Mediterranean, read:

> Operations reports show the 442nd Infantry and the 100th Battalion Japanese in action on the 5th Army front against heavy resistance. If military reasons do not preclude, it would be beneficial to give publicity to aggressive action of these Japanese troops. It has tremendous value, not only from the propaganda side, but helps materially in our handling of the American-of-Japanese-descent problem in this country, particularly on the west coast.[90]

The assertions in the last sentence of the passage above came about by requests from the Department of the Interior, which in conjunction with the WRA, was encountering non-cooperation, dissent and violent disturbances in the relocation camps confining increasingly angry Japanese-American citizens.[91] Within days the US Fifth Army, commanded by the famously publicity hungry General Mark Clark (who early 1942 had opposed relocation), dispatched specialist photographers and journalists to interview and film the Nisei units.[92] The resulting publicity fed the national appetite for heroes and the 'Nisei Japanese' earned a reputation as some of most distinguished and highly decorated American fighting men in the Second World War. This favourable publicity unleashed a tidal wave of admiration, sympathy, and support for the Nisei soldiers which, in turn, belatedly turned into wide spread recognition that, despite internment, Japanese-Americans were loyal citizens.

Critical interpretations of the responsibility for the relocation decision mostly descend on General John L. DeWitt and President Franklin D. Roosevelt as the most culpable, followed closely by the 'architect of relocation' Colonel Karl Bendetsen. However, the prevailing understandings of fifth column activities in 1942, the lack of resources of guard vital installations and the actual danger presented by the Japanese fleet compounded by the presence of a definable population of enemy ethnicity near strategic points illustrate the ease with which these decisions were made. General DeWitt made it his business to indentify aliens and first generation immigrants as potential fifth columnists, and then by listing Japanese naval forces as a present threat, DeWitt irrevocably, but incorrectly, identified Japanese-Americans as a latent enemy threat in being.

It would be improper to conclude this chapter without mentioning several other specious rationales advanced as justification for relocation. One of the oddest early justifications appeared in a November 1942 letter from the assistant secretary of the army to General Hugh Drum, which turned the argument inside out by suggesting that Japanese-Americans should be relocated for their own safety because 'direct action might be taken against the Japanese as a result of the rather antagonistic attitude of the local population'.[93] Later, in the US Army's official history of the relocation, historian Stetson Conn asked, 'What were the reasons that impelled the Army to carry out the mass evacuation of Japanese residents from the west coast?'[94] Conn skirted around his own question but noted, 'Although little support for the argument that military necessity required a mass evacuation of the Japanese can be found in contemporary evidence, it might be contended that the co-operation of the white population of the Pacific states in the national defence effort could not have been otherwise assured.'[95] Frankly, both of these explanations are ridiculous and border on the absurd.

Conclusion

This chapter has outlined the chronology and major events leading to the decisions to relocate Japanese-Americans from the west coast in 1942. The evidence available at the time did not support mass relocation and nothing has come light since which reinforces the extant evidence. However, it is important to consider the effect of racism, fear and precautionary courses of action in strategic and operational decision making. How much did the issue of race figure into these decisions? Readers should form their own opinions but unquestionably race was a factor in the decisions. The fact that the government did not relocate Germans and Italians en masse provides a counterpoint for this conclusion; however, in fairness neither Germany nor Italy possessed the naval capability to attack the continental United States. Readers must also consider, however, that fear of espionage, sabotage and fifth column activities remained important concerns of the decision-makers, especially General DeWitt. Greatly flawed in their zeitgeist-based and racially prejudiced assumptions, American decision-makers presented the relocation of Japanese-Americans as a counter-fifth column campaign vitally necessary for the defence of the west coast in 1942.

Notes

1 Department of the Interior, War Relocation Authority, *WRA: A Story of Human Conservation* (Washington, DC: Dept of the Interior, 1946), 25. There are a number of terms which blur together; the WRA called relocated individuals 'evacuees', the evacuees entered the relocation pipeline at local assembly centres and were transported to reception centres. From there they were finally settled in relocation centres (of which Manzanar is probably the most well-known today). There were ten WRA centres all located using the US Army's terminology 'at a safe distance from strategic locations' (see page 20 of *WRA*).

2 Dissenting Opinion, Korematsu v. United States, 323, US 214 (18 December 1944).

3   *Report of the Commission on Wartime Relocation and Internment of Civilians*, published as *Personal Justice Denied* (Civil Liberties Public Education Fund and the University of Washington Press, 1997).

4   See, for example, Morton Grodzins, *Americans Betrayed: Politics and the Japanese Evacuation* (Chicago, IL and London: University of Chicago Press, 1949); Jacobus tenBroek, Edward N. Barnhart and Floyd Matson, *Prejudice, War and the Constitution* (Berkeley: University of California Press, 1954); Roger Daniels, *The Politics of Prejudice* (Berkeley: University of California Press, 1962).

5   Petra to Dorothy, '*The fifth column people. The people who fight us from inside the city*'. Dorothy to Petra, '*They are our enemies*'. (Act Two, Scene Three), Ernest Hemingway, *The Fifth Column and Four Stories of the Spanish Civil War* (New York: Charles Scribner's Sons, 1938), 71.

6   'Conference with General De Witt' at Office of Commanding General, Headquarters Western Defense Command and Fourth Army; 4 January 1942, 1. National Archives, Folder 2–4, Box 383.

7   Stetson Conn and Byron Fairchild, *United States Army in World War II, The Framework for Hemisphere Defense* (Washington, DC: Center for Military History, 1960), 16.

8   Ibid., 18–19.

9   Samuel Eliot Morison, *The Rising Sun in the Pacific 1931-April 1942* (Boston, MA: Little, Brown and Company, 1950), 57. In April–June 1941, the three modernized *New Mexico* class battleships, the fleet carrier USS *Yorktown*, and supporting smaller ships shifted to the Atlantic, which reduced the Pacific Fleet by 20 per cent.

10 Ernest Hemingway, *The Fifth Column and the First Forty-Nine Stories* (New York: Charles Scribner's Sons, 1938).

11 Richard Petrow, *The Bitter Years, The Invasion and Occupation of Denmark and Norway April 1940-May 1945* (New York: William Morrow and Company, 1974), 4–6.

12 Peter Irons, *Justice at War, The Story of the Japanese American Internment Cases* (Oxford: Oxford University Press, 1983), 19.

13 Ibid.

14 Ibid., 20.

15 Ibid.

16 Ibid.

17 Ibid., 21.

18 Ibid., 21–2.

19 Ibid.

20 Gordon W. Prange, *At Dawn We Slept, The Untold Story of Pearl Harbor* (New York: McGraw-Hill Book Company, 1981), 80–2.

21 Maurice Matloff and Edwin M. Snell, *Strategic Planning for Coalition Warfare 1941–1942* (Washington, DC: Center for Military History, 1953), 60–1.

22 Joint Board Estimate of 11 September 1941 cited by Conn and Fairchild, *The Framework of Hemisphere Defense*, 144.
23 Stetson Conn, Rose C. Engelman and Byron Fairchild, *United States Army in World War II, Guarding the United States and Its Outposts* (Washington, DC: Center for Military History, 1960), 28–9. To this day Conn, Engelman and Fairchild's volume of the US Army's official histories remains the most comprehensive and well-sourced publication regarding the military situation in 1941–1942 and the fullest explanation of the military decisions regarding the wartime relocation of Japanese-Americans.
24 Kent Roberts Greenfield, Robert R. Palmer, and Bell I. Wiley, *United States Army in World War II*, The *Organization of Ground Combat Troops* (Washington, DC: Center for Military History, 1947), 119.
25 Conn and Fairchild, *The Framework of Hemisphere Defense*, 65.
26 Radio message No. 1, Marshall to MG Van Vorheesis, 20 June 1940 (NA/RG 165) Army chief of staff George Marshall warned his general staff about the danger of sabotage to the Panama Canal and other vital installations. See Larry I. Bland (ed.), *The Papers of George Catlett Marshall, Volume 2, July 1, 1939-December 6, 1941* (Baltimore, MD: The Johns Hopkins Press, 1986), Facsimile on 250.
27 Ibid., The CDB's approved Civil Defence Plan of 18 March 1940 formally handed general supervision for civil defence planning to the War Department.
28 Conn, Engelman and Fairchild, *Guarding the United States and Its Outposts*, 74–5.
29 Kent Roberts Greenfield (ed.), *Command Decisions* (Washington, DC: Office of the Chief of Military History, 1960), 126–7.
30 Ibid.
31 Message, Marshall to Short, 7 February 1941 (NA/RG 165), Bland, *The Papers of George Catlett Marshall, Volume 2*, 411–13.
32 Charles A. Beard, *President Roosevelt and the Coming of the War 1941, a Study in Appearances and Realties* (New Haven, CT: Yale University Press, 1948), 525.
33 Conn, Engelman and Fairchild, *Guarding the United States and Its Outposts*, 80.
34 Report of the Commission Appointed by the President of the United States to Investigate and Report the Facts Relating to the Attack on Pearl Harbor by Japanese Armed Forces (Washington, DC: Senate Documents, 23 January 1942), Section IX. This report is generally known as the "Roberts Report" (or the "Roberts Commission") after its presiding officer Associate Justice Owen J. Roberts, US Supreme Court.
35 Gordon W. Prange, *Pearl Harbor, the Verdict of History* (New York: McGraw-Hill Book Company, 1986). Prange cites the *Hearings before the Joint Committee on the Investigation of the Pearl Harbor Attack: Congress of the United States*, Part 27, page 125.
36 Ibid., 348.

37 Prange, *Pearl Harbor, The Verdict of History*, 348–62. The title of Prange's chapter about Short's state of mind and operational considerations is titled "Alerted to Prevent Sabotage."
38 Wesley Frank Craven and James Lea Cate (ed.), *The Army Air Forces in World War II, Plans and Early Operations January 1939-August 1942* (Washington, DC: Office of Air Force History, 1948), 280.
39 Conn, Engelman and Fairchild, *Guarding the United States and Its Outposts*, 82.
40 Ibid.
41 Steven E. Clay, *U.S. Army Order of Battle, 1919–1941* (Fort Leavenworth, KS: Combat Studies Institute Press, undated), 137–240.
42 Conn, Engelman, and Fairchild, *Guarding the United States and Its Outposts*, 83–5.
43 Ibid.
44 Message, Marshall to Stimson, 28 March 1941. The subject of diverting federalized troops to guard industrial plants had come up in March 1941, which Marshall preferred to avoid because of the deleterious effect in would have on mobilization. Bland, *The Papers of George Catlett Marshall, Volume 2*, 457.
45 Ibid., 77–8.
46 Irons, *Justice at War*, 24–8. For another example see Jeffery F. Burton, Mary M. Farrell, Florence B. Lord, and Richard W. Lord, *Confinement and Ethnicity, An Overview of World War II Japanese American Relocation Sites* (Tucson, AZ: The National Park Service, 1999), "DeWitt had a history of prejudice against non-Caucasian Americans, even those already in the Army, and he was easily swayed by any rumour of sabotage or imminent Japanese invasion."
47 Ibid.
48 Edward M. Coffman, *The Regulars, the American Army 1898–1941* (Cambridge: President and Fellows of Harvard College, 2004), 318–20, 354–71, 406–17.
49 Denis and Peggy Warner, *The Tide at Sunrise, a History of the Russo-Japanese War, 1904–1905* (New York: Charter House, 1974), 3–20. The opening chapter in the Warner's book is titled "The First Pearl Harbor."
50 Larry I. Bland (ed.), *The Papers of George Catlett Marshall, Volume 3, December 7, 1941-May 31, 1943* (Baltimore, MD: The Johns Hopkins Press, 1986), 9.
51 Conn, Engelman and Fairchild, *Guarding the United States and Its Outposts*, 116.
52 Ibid., 117.
53 Ibid.
54 Ibid. 119.
55 "Conference with General De Witt" at Office of Commanding General, Headquarters Western Defense Command and Fourth Army; 4 January 1942, 1. National Archives, Folder 2–4, Box 383.

56 Conn, Engelman and Fairchild, *Guarding the United States and Its Outposts*, 120. See this page for the transcript of this conversation.
57 Report of the Commission Appointed by the President of the United States to Investigate and Report the Facts Relating to the Attack on Pearl Harbor by Japanese Armed Forces (Washington, DC: Senate Documents, January 23, 1942).
58 Conn, Engelman, and Fairchild, *Guarding the United States and Its Outposts*, 128.
59 Irons, *Justice at War*, 60–1.
60 Ibid.
61 Conn, Engelman, and Fairchild, *Guarding the United States and Its Outposts*, 148.
62 Memorandum for the Secretary of War from the Commanding General, Western Defense Command, 14 February 1942, Appendix to Chapter III, Final Report: Japanese Evacuation from the West Coast 1942 (Presidio of San Francisco: WDC, 1943), 33–8.
63 Conn, Engelman, and Fairchild, *Guarding the United States and Its Outposts*, 136.
64 Ibid., 133.
65 Bland, *The Papers of George Catlett Marshall, Volume 3, December 7, 1941– May 31, 1943*, 111–12.
66 Conn, Engelman, and Fairchild, *Guarding the United States and Its Outposts*, 135.
67 *Report of the Commission on Wartime Relocation and Internment of Civilians*, published as *Personal Justice Denied*, 67–72.
68 Conn, Engelman, and Fairchild, *Guarding the United States and Its Outposts*, 139.
69 Ibid.
70 Ibid., 140.
71 Ibid., 143.
72 Ibid.
73 WDC Memo of 4 May 1942, Boekel to Bendetsen, cited by Conn, Engelman, and Fairchild, *Guarding the United States and Its Outposts*, 144.
74 Ibid.
75 Conn, Engelman, and Fairchild, *Guarding the United States and Its Outposts*, 146.
76 Grodzins, *Americans Betrayed*, 278.
77 Conn, Engelman, and Fairchild, *Guarding the United States and Its Outposts*, 146.
78 Ibid., 91.
79 Ibid., 208.
80 Ibid., 211.

81 Ibid., 214.
82 Headquarters, Western Defense Command and Fourth Army, Final Report: Japanese Evacuation from the West Coast 1942 (Washington, DC: US Government Printing Office, 1943), v.
83 Ibid., vii.
84 Ibid., vii.
85 Irons, *Justice at War*, See Chapter 8, 'The Suppression of Evidence', 186–281.
86 Greenfield, *Command Decisions*, 138.
87 Beard, *President Roosevelt and the Coming of the War 1941*. The phrase "Interpretations Tested by Consequences" is Beard's title for the epilogue (Chapter XVIII) of his book.
88 Conn, Engelman, and Fairchild, *Guarding the United States and Its Outposts*, 212.
89 Orville C. Shirey, *Americans, The Story of the 442d Combat Team* (Washington, DC: Infantry Journal Press, 1946), 19. The integration of African-Americans into combat units of the US Army at about the same time also reflected the general shortage of quality manpower for the ground forces.
90 Ops Division, War Department message to Commanding General, USA Forces, 28 June 1944, Online, Available at: http://www.the442.org/battlehistory.html (accessed 11 February 2018).
91 See, for example, 'The Manzanar Disturbance', Department of the Interior, *WRA: A Story of Human Conservation*, 49–50.
92 HQS, Army Air Forces Mediterranean, Caserta, Italy message to Commanding General, Allied Forces, Algiers, 30 June 1944, Online, Available at: http://www.the442.org/battlehistory.html (accessed 11 February 2018).
93 Conn, Engelman, and Fairchild, *Guarding the United States and Its Outposts*, 149. Assistant Secretary McCloy's letter to Drum listed three reasons why Japanese-Americans should be relocated: (1) the west coast's proximity to the war zone, (2) the large concentration of ethnic Japanese, followed by his absurd third assertion quoted in the text.
94 Ibid., 147.
95 Ibid., 148.

9

A collective measure:

Population resettlement in the Malayan Emergency

LtCol Gregory J. Reck

It is at this 'heart' that we must aim to eliminate the Communist cells among the Chinese population to whom we must give security and whom we must win over.

Appreciation of the Situation in Malaya
LTG SIR HAROLD BRIGGS, 10 April 1950

Introduction

The roots of the Malayan Emergency (1948–60) lay not in the process by which Malaya was inhabited, but by the character of some in the Chinese diaspora, who lived there (Map 9). At the core of the discontent within a section of Malayan Chinese was a long-held belief that their people had suffered grievous wrongs at the hands of differing governing powers and that their fate was always to be as second-class citizens. Malaya was a country that was home to a large diaspora of ethnic Chinese, who left the mainland to earn money mining tin and harvesting rubber. However, while many found inclusion and integration in the cities, a disproportionately large number found themselves as squatters along the periphery of the jungles. These were

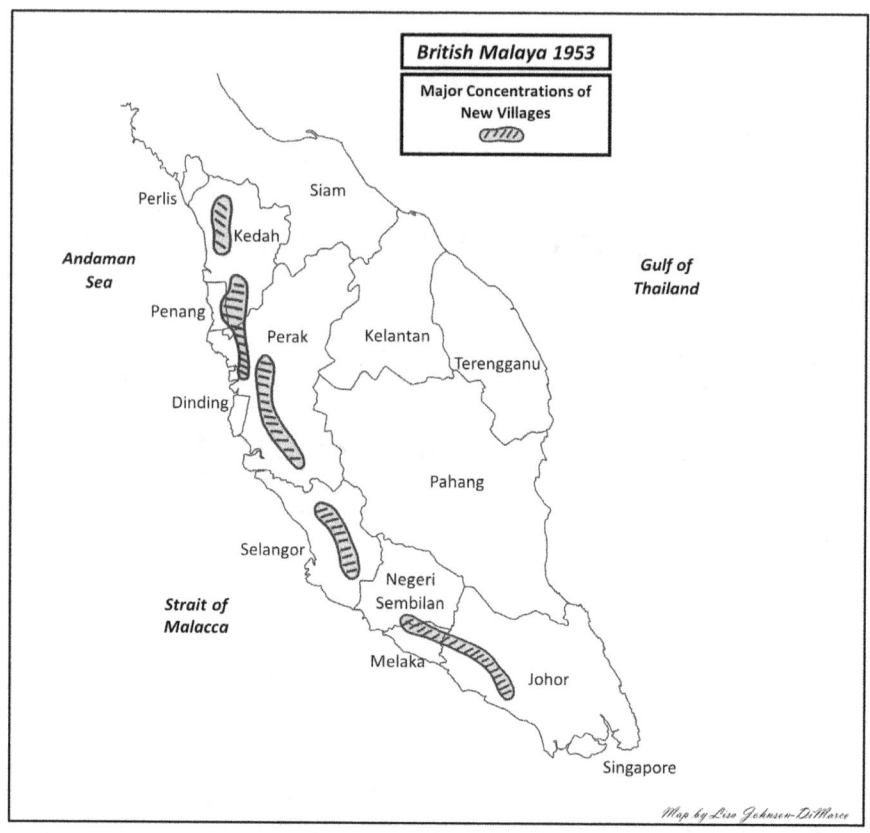

MAP 9 *British Malaya 1953. In an effort to separate ethnically Chinese guerrillas from popular support, British General Sir Gerald Templer forcibly relocated hundreds of thousands of Chinese Malays. After being resettled in New Villages, Templer successfully managed the counterinsurgency campaign by sweeping defined sectors clear of the weakened guerrillas.*

the people, who were low-skilled and agrarian farmers before they came over and could not afford their own land and suffered from the bigotry of the natives and earlier immigrants. It was from these demographics that the Malayan Communist Party (MCP) exploited for money, food and recruits. Since these people lived in the fairly ungoverned areas, the MCP was able to operate relatively free from harassment by security forces.[1]

Many in the diaspora remembered or knew of the Japanese attacks against mainland China in the late 1920s and into the 1930s. Furthermore, while the British were a relatively fair colonial power, the Malay population still bucked under the yoke of its rule. What didn't alleviate the simmering animosity was that many in the diaspora also recalled the British massacre of Chinese workers and students in 1925 in Singapore.[2] The British did little after the Second World War to assuage this discontent, and it was further exacerbated by the lingering ethnic stratification of the population that left many out of the political and economic process.

The British garrison defending *Fortress Singapore* surrendered in February 1942 to the Imperial Japanese military; it shattered the perceived invulnerability of the British Empire.[3] That loss, coupled with the subsequent occupation by Imperial Japanese forces, which continued the debasement of ethnic Chinese during their administration, facilitated the guerrilla warfare that was followed by the Malayan People's Anti-Japanese Army (MPAJA). This guerrilla force, which was permeated with members and leadership from the MCP, received training and material from the British, and this provided the means and methods for the future struggle against the British colonial government almost immediately following the end of the Second World War, laying the groundwork for the future insurgency.[4]

Even though the MCP lacked the support of the greater part of the various demographics in Malaya and its support was drawn from the Chinese squatters, who lived on the periphery of Malayan society, critical weaknesses in the British administration's intelligence and security forces facilitated early insurgent successes.[5] The insurgents made their bases in the jungles of Malaya out of necessity, which provided them with security from normal security force patrols and concentrated presence. In addition, these jungle bases were in proximity to squatter villages, where the insurgents could gather needed resources. With the weapons and ammunition cached from British forces during the Second World War and a well-trained cadre, courtesy of that same British Special Operations Executive (SOE), insurgent launched attacks from these bases and quickly began to overwhelm the rubber plantations that were closest to the insurgent bases, and were most vulnerable.

The government's understanding of the insurgency was poor, and it was because of several factors: lack of intelligence, misunderstanding of the growing threat and disconnected leadership. In fact, intransigence to concerted action against the insurgents by the government lasted until well into 1950, and was mostly a result of fractious power sharing and disbelief in the strength of the insurgency. In 1950, Britain appointed Major General Sir Harold Briggs the director of operations. He recommended and began the institution of an approach to countering the insurgency that focused on harnessing the concerted efforts of the entire government's, not just the military's or security forces', 'secure the population' capabilities to hinder the growth of the insurgency and eventually to starve them of resources. This plan reinvigorated the floundering resettlement programme and became eponymously known as the Briggs Plan.[6]

The Briggs Plan was a relatively simple, but comprehensive plan that held very closely in nature to earlier British counterinsurgency doctrine. To understand the Briggs Plan, an understanding of insurgency is necessary. An insurgency is a struggle for political power, which is nearly always the end, not the way or means, of the insurgents' strategy and tactics. Even the theorist Carl von Clausewitz recognized and postulated that '*War is not an independent phenomenon, but the continuation of politics by different means*'.[7] He correctly deduced that warfare was not solely the purview of a government, but can also be of and by the people/population.[8] This was clearly the case with the MCP, who created a fighting force from the disenfranchised Chinese diaspora within Malaya with the intent of overthrowing the British and sultanates in order to establish a unified, but wholly communist, state.

Dr Timothy Lomperis's book, *From People's War to People's Rule*, posited, based on Max Weber's archetypes that all governments govern through a combination of influence, and to some degree coercion from the permission or consent of the populace.[9] From those, legitimacy for that government is obtained and lasts as long as the populace perceives and recognizes that legitimacy. This is critical because legitimacy is a significant indicator of the extent to which the local population accepts systems of authority, decisions and conduct. Political legitimacy of a government determines the degree to which the population will voluntarily comply with the decisions and rules issued by a governing authority.[10]

When the relationship between the government and the governed breaks down, challenges to legitimacy result. If a significant section of the population, or just an extreme faction, believes it cannot achieve a remedy through established political processes, it may resort to armed insurgency. In his 1934 work, *Imperial Policing*, Sir Charles Gwynn outlined what he recognized as core elements to an insurgency, as it moves to challenge and defeat the legitimacy of the established government: wearing down the determination of a government to counter and prove the powerlessness of the government.[11]

Therefore, the development of an effective counterinsurgency approach starts with the acceptance of the population as key to a counterinsurgency operation.[12] The struggle for legitimacy with the population is typically a central theme of the conflict between the insurgency and the government in relation to which is fit to govern.[13] Governance is the ability to serve the population through the rules, processes and behaviour by which interests are articulated, resources are managed and power is exercised in a society. A state's ability to provide effective governance rests on its political and bureaucratic willingness, capability and capacity to establish rules and procedures for decision making, as well as its ability to provide public services in a manner that is predictable and acceptable to the local population.

To that end, the Briggs Plan was intended to be thorough and long-term, with no expectation of speedy and decisive results. It envisaged clearing the country from south to north, leaving behind strong police and civil authorities once an area was secure. It also sought to isolate insurgents from rural populations to enable them to come forward with information. Moreover, it aimed at depriving the Communists support and forcing them into the open. Briggs realized that in order to do so, the government must establish proper administrative control in Malaya and re-establish legitimacy, the government must accomplish the following: resettle the Chinese squatters and provide oversight by police and auxiliary police; group local labour in mines and on estates, which would attenuate potential interaction with insurgents and reduce the necessity for high levels of security forces in those areas; expand the recruitment and training of criminal investigation and special branch personnel; establish a minimum level of military troop strength throughout the country to support local security forces and concentrate forces for clearing priority areas; ensure that police and army collaborated and operated in accord, with joint operational control on all levels and close integration of police and military intelligence. The Plan went into effect on 1 June 1950, and Briggs created state and district war executive committees (SWEC and DWEC), whose members made joint decisions and issued orders to subordinates through their respective services' chains of command to ensure complete integration of actions to support the civil power.

Yet, the British government's overall counterinsurgency programme impact, and their eventual defeat of the insurgents did not come about simply because of population resettlement. Scholarly work published on the resettlement agree that resettlement was a large part of the successful execution of the counterinsurgency plan,[14] but the greatest benefit to the counterinsurgency effort was in the success of the other facets of the British government's counterinsurgency efforts that the resettlement enabled. It is then therefore the thesis of this chapter to demonstrate that the resettlement programme under the Briggs Plan facilitated the successful conclusion of the counterinsurgency efforts by means of isolating the insurgents from the population, legitimizing the government and creating a more inclusive Malaya.

Malaya and its demographics

Malaya is on the far southern point on a peninsula that originates from Burma and part of Thailand. Bounded in the East by the South China Sea and in the West by the Straits of Malacca, Malaya is in Southeast Asia. It is approximately the size of New York State, covering 50, 690 square miles, with almost four-fifths of it being dense rainforest and swamp.[15] Mountains range north-south with the highest point being Mount Gunong Tahan. Monsoons occur twice a year in December through January and May through October with substantial rainfalls in excess of 250 inches a year. This mountain range has created many small valleys and alluvial plains between them and the lowlands and together has helped create terrain that can become tremendously difficult to travel or access by anything other than foot.[16]

Prior to the Second World War, Malaya was a collection of small, separate kingdoms or sultanates. Because of its location and rich natural resources, the Strait of Malacca became a popular trade passage between the East and West. This resulted in bringing many Arab, Chinese and Indian traders into the region for over 1,500 years, some of whom settled there. This migration profoundly influenced Malaya's evolution and resulted in a highly diverse population reflected by the demographic breakdown during the Emergency: 50.4 per cent of Malaysia's population is Muslim Malay, 23.7 per cent is Chinese, 11 per cent is indigenous Malay, 7.1 per cent is Indian and the remaining 7.8 per cent comprised by other ethnic groups.[17] Despite the fact that these groups had many decades of living together, native Malayans did not give equal rights to immigrant groups, no matter how long they had lived there. The Chinese immigrants were being the lowest caste in the system.

Islam had become the primary religion in Malaya and was introduced to Southeast Asia by Muslim traders; most of the indigenous population adopted the religion during the ensuing years. Because of its rich resources, especially rubber and tin, and strategic positioning, Malaya became an important asset in the eyes of the dominant European powers. In the eighteenth and through the mid-nineteenth century, various sultanates on the Malayan Peninsula and northern Borneo fell under British colonial rule. Britain administered Malaya by supporting local leaders and eventually persuaded them to create the Federated Malay States in 1895.[18] The consolidation of the sultanates and British rule, however, did nothing to ameliorate ethnic tensions and seemed to only heighten the desire for self-rule.

The strategic situation – South East Asia

The seeds for discontent in Malaya took root sometime in 1925 after the founding of the South Seas Communist Party, which was later reorganized as the MCP.[19] The start of the Second World War was not the beginning of the insurgency, but it was a major catalyst. The end of the Second World War saw the world become divided between Western and Communist ideologies. While Western powers' attention lay in Europe, Nationalist China's government was in the twilight of its existence, as Mao Zedong's communists were increasing their control in the rural countryside and moving on Chiang Kai-shek's seat of power. In Malaya, the overall goal for the MCP was to spread the communist ideology through the recruitment of Malays, Chinese and Indians,[20] but mitigating factors, such as varying levels of satisfaction with the government, economic well-being and a mistrust of the Chinese by the other ethnicities, created a political environment through which the MCP evolved predominantly into an ethnically Chinese organization.[21] With a large Chinese diaspora, many of whom did not find the economic successes that they had hoped when they emigrated, Malaya offered a vulnerable population for communist propaganda to exploit. The fact that Malayan Chinese remained the lowest caste under the British,

Japanese Imperial governments, and by that of other Malayans, only increased ethnic Chinese vulnerability to exploit further.[22]

The jubilation at the end of the Second World War quickly faded as the battle for political ideologies took centre stage. In Europe, Communist forces were quickly consolidating their holds on occupied lands. In China, where the Soviets were relative newcomers to that theatre, occupying Soviet forces pillaged to what some scholars estimated at approximately $850 million.[23] Despite the monetary loss and damage, Chinese Communists and Soviet leadership established military relations, which would later be of great assistance to the Chinese Communists' eventual victory.[24]

The Chinese Revolution coupled with the Soviet occupation of many European countries gave the communist brand a great deal of prestige on the world stage. Communist insurgencies would soon begin springing up across the globe, that is, the First Indochina War, the Greek Civil War, the Iran crisis of 1946 and the Korean War to name but a few. With the Soviet Union dominating in the West and creating what was to become known as the Iron Curtain, the Communists in China and then Communist China hoped to extend the Bamboo Curtain,[25] and took up the responsibility of forwarding social revolution in the period of decolonization after the Second World War in the East.[26]

The strategic situation – Malaya

Prior to the Second World War, the MCP (aka the Communist Party of Malaya) began operating under British colonial rule in 1930, built from the remnants of the Chinese South Seas Communists Party that began in 1924.[27] After a slow recovery, the MCP gained momentum and greater influence under the young party leader, Lai Teck, who focused on influencing the trade union movement and establishing workers' committees at numerous workplaces.[28] To check increased communist influence in Malaya, British authorities and local security forces fielded a rapid response that was as brutal as it was effective: many ethnic Chinese strikers were deported to China, where the Chinese Nationalist government often executed them as Communists.

In 1941, when the Japanese invaded Malaya and forced the surrender of British forces under the command of Lieutenant General Arthur E. Percival, the MCP quickly built up strength in numbers and general popularity from across Malaya under the guise of an anti-Japanese resistance force that became the MPAJA. In something of a cruel twist, the Japanese were not interested in punishing local Malay or Indian population and focused their ire on Malayan Chinese.[29] During this period, British resistance leaders, John Davies, Richard Broome and SOE's Major Fredrick Spenser Chapman were hard-pressed to wage effective war against the Imperial Japanese military and turned to the MCP as a potential ally both during and after the war.[30]

MCP volunteers were trained and equipped by British officials as guerrillas under Force 136 and operated behind enemy lines in Malaya.[31]

Although the British lent advisers and logistical aid to the MCP, a firm mutual trust never developed, aggravated by MPAJA emphasis on fighting rival political factions instead of the Japanese. At war's end, the British managed to demobilize the MPAJA, but because of its wartime service, the British officially recognized the MCP in Malaya. Over the next three years, the MCP openly extended its influence into numerous ethnic Chinese student clubs, schools and labour groups. In addition, the MPAJA established an 'Old Comrades Association' with branches in every town.[32] Race riots between native Malays, Chinese and Indians (representing 50.4 per cent, 23.7 per cent and 7.1 per cent, respectively) became common, as old tensions grew anew over the issue of Malayan nationalism and independence. Nevertheless, the MCP failed to attract other Malayans into their organization because of the long history of animosity and racial tensions.[33]

In 1946 the British announced the Malayan Union Proposals, which would have led to the granting of citizenship to the Malayan Chinese, and would have attenuated nascent violence that the MCP was propagating. The proposals were, however, extremely unpopular with the wider Malay population, so the British withdrew them. This about-face enraged the Malayan Chinese. Some of them, abandoned protests and strikes, began a campaign of violence that included intimidation, sabotage and selective assassination of government and local community leaders.

The operational situation

The year 1948 was a year of many communist uprisings and the desire for action grew in the MCP. After the party leader, Lai Teck, left Malaya in 1947, he was accused by the MCP of absconding with MCP funds. Almost at the same time, he was discovered to have been a double agent for the British. The MCP's deputy, Chin Peng, became the new leader. While Lai Teck had desired constitutional inclusion and manoeuvre the MCP along those lines, Chin Peng desired revolution as soon as possible, and he convinced the MCP Central Committee that the opportunity had finally presented itself to create a communist 'people's democracy' with the MCP naturally at its head.[34]

In 1948 the MCP attempting to redirect this tension and violence, decided to convert the struggle against the British into a rural guerrilla war. It was at this point that Chin Peng remobilized the old guerrilla army and ordered the men enrolled in the 'Old Comrades' into jungle camps.[35] At the start of hostilities, the entire insurgency had approximately 3,250 of the Malayan Races Liberation Army or MRLA combatants, 10,000 members of the Minh Yuen (People's Organization, 3,000 members of the MCP and 60,000 active communist members [not MCP]). During its peak, the insurgency was able to field 5,500 combatants, but it is unclear if these were additions or drawn from the other groups.[36]

Small raids, ambushes, kidnappings, bombings and assassinations characterized the guerrilla warfare waged by the MCP's combat arm, the Malayan National Liberation Army (MNLA), often mistranslated as the Malayan Races Liberation Army or MRLA.[37] To achieve this and to raise funds and equip the insurgency, he also directed robberies against government officials, police stations and prominent businessmen and their estates. With less discrimination, they also threw grenades into movie theatres and attacked buses, killing and injuring non-combatants. While the MRLA grew during this period, terrorist actions against political and economic targets, executed to demonstrate the government's inability to provide security, failed to help widen the MCP's base of popular support, and it remained almost exclusively an ethically Chinese party at this point.[38]

From the early stages of the Emergency and up to 1950, a severe lack of intelligence and a lack of unified command and effort hampered the government's response. On the military front, the outnumbered security forces could not effectively fight an enemy moving freely in the jungle and enjoying support from the Chinese rural population. British planters and miners, who bore the brunt of the communist attacks, saw the government as incompetent in the face of this existential threat. As a result, the initial government strategy was primarily an enemy-centric approach[39] to guard important economic targets, such as mines and plantation estates. Furthermore, many of the ethnic Chinese squatters, who were merely accused of providing support to the guerrillas had their homes burned, were deported[40] or killed. These heavy-handed police and military tactics, which were highly publicized using a robust communist propaganda strategy, increased support for the guerrillas in the first two years of the emergency.

In September 1945, the Malayan Security Service (MSS) was re-established as part of the British Military Administration responsible for collecting information on subversive organizations in both Malaya and Singapore. The MSS was plagued by personnel shortages due to significant losses during the Second World War and was only manned at 50 per cent of the authorized level. Furthermore, the MSS had the daunting and time consuming task of rebuilding secret agent and informer networks that existed pre-war while the country was in a politically and physically unsettled state. From April to June 1948 there was increased lawlessness and a series of terrorist attacks, but the MSS provided no early warning about the outbreak of violence and minimal information regarding MCP's strength and plans. As a result of these failures, the colonial office disbanded the MSS and distributed the personnel and functions to the Singapore and Malaya Special Branches Criminal Investigation Departments.[41]

By the time of the declaration of the Emergency in 1948, the British in Malaya were hardly prepared to conduct counterinsurgency.[42] Malaya's forces were minimal and a mixture of various units ranging from military to paramilitary with thirteen infantry battalions in Malaya, including seven partly formed Ghurkha battalions, three British battalions, two battalions of the Royal Malay Regiment and a British Royal Artillery Regiment being used as infantry. At the height of the campaign, military forces rotated in regularly with 22–23 battalions being in theatre and forces totalling 30,000 men to include Special Air Services. The British created a Special Field Force and had up to 3,000 members. Finally, there was the Regular Special Constabulary with about 10,000 officers. These numbers rose steadily throughout the counterinsurgency. At its peak, counterinsurgency forces reached a high, with regular police reaching 36,737, the Constabulary hitting 44,878, the addition of the Kampong Guards and an Auxiliary Police Force with the two forces totalling 47,000 members, and a Chinese Home Guard of 300,000 members.[43]

In contrast, support for the MRLA was mainly based on around 500,000 of the 3.12 million ethnic Chinese then living in Malaya. These 500,000 have been referred to as 'squatters', and the majority of them were farmers living on the edge of the jungles where the MRLA were based. This allowed the MRLA to supply themselves with food, providing a source of new recruits, and as a source of intelligence for the nascent insurgency. The ethnic Malay population supported them in smaller numbers. The MRLA gained the support of the Chinese because they were denied the equal right to vote in elections, had no land rights to speak of and were usually very poor. The MRLA's supply organization was called 'Min Yuen' (Mass Organization). It had a network of contacts within the general population.

The MRLAs camps and hideouts were in the rather inaccessible tropical jungle with limited infrastructure. Most MRLA guerrillas were ethnic Chinese, though there were some Malays, Indonesians and Indians among its members. The MRLA was organized into regiments, although these had no fixed establishments and each encompassed all forces operating in a particular region. The regiments had political sections, commissars, instructors and secret service. In the camps, the soldiers attended lectures on Marxism–Leninism, and produced political newsletters to be distributed to civilians.

In February 1952 General Sir Gerald Templer was appointed the High Commissioner of Malaya after the insurgents killed his predecessor, Sir Henry Gurney, in an ambush. Unlike his predecessor, Templer adopted a population-centric strategy[44] and travelled the country and met with all major communities to help address grievances in the country's policies. Initially, Templer put the weight of his effort on improving the conditions for the Chinese population that were relocated from the jungle fringes to fortified 'New Villages' under the Briggs Plan in 1951. This population provided the most support to the guerrillas because it was the most vulnerable to attacks and was largely neglected lacking proper security, water and sanitation, and both the insurgents and the government knew that a secure population meant no food, no recruits and no intelligence.

Analysis: Government reaction 1948–50

The government's reaction in this and the next stage is perhaps the most important determinant of whether a movement will develop into an insurgency.[45] During these early stages, a potential insurgent group is weak, disorganized and vulnerable to nonviolent government countermeasures, and this was exactly the case with the Malayan Emergency. Efforts by the British government towards greater assimilation of the ethnic Chinese were already underway, as were other programmes that undercut the MCP's narrative.[46] For the aforementioned reasons, however, the government is likely to err in the way that they handled or treated these grievances. The British did not react strongly enough prior to the outbreak of violence and allowed the MCP to seize the initiative.

When they did respond, the British Home Government in June 1948 declared Malaya to be in a 'State of Emergency', and this resulted in several strong counterinsurgency measures by the British federation government. In 1948, 'Emergency Resolution 17' permitted police detention of any suspected insurgents or sympathizers without trial for as long as a year, and could result in deportation. Police forces expanded eventually, intelligence operations intensified and British Commonwealth military units made themselves equal, and later superior, to the MRLA in jungle warfare skills. Security forces deliberately, and with seeming impunity, aimed to coerce the population to support the government through deportation, mass arrests and property destruction.[47] Permission was obtained in 1949 from the Royal Thai government allowing 'hot pursuit' of fleeing MRLA guerrillas up to ten miles into Thailand.

In addition, security forces were experiencing problems in the field because of the large amount of space to control. Even early attempts at food rationing failed. During *Operation Snow White* in 1949, security forces attempted to blockade the Mentakab-Jelebu-Menchis area to prevent further insurgent gains in those areas. The security forces forced locals to sell all private rice stocks/reserves above a certain quantity in order to stop the locals from selling or giving to the insurgents any surplus. The blockage was in place to prevent new supplies of rice from coming into the towns. Security forces patrolled the jungles to hunt insurgents, but were not fully trained in this warfare. The outcome was less than optimal with only three insurgents being eliminated and security forces involved only destroyed several abandoned camps.

There was far too much ground to cover, and at this point, too few security forces to cover so much terrain by foot. Even after Briggs assumed the role of director, security forces continued to experience problems controlling space. What were labelled as *Priority Operations*, by Briggs, which consisted of large-scale operations up to and during 1951, such as *Operations Grasshopper*, *Warbler* and *Sedge*, before the completion of the relocation, still failed to deny the insurgents freedom of movement or stop their activities.⁴⁸ It wasn't until the relocation concluded, when security forces were freed up, and those forces switched to smaller scale patrols and jungle bases that progress were made against the insurgents.

Reasons why the British government initially failed to prevent insurgency

(1) Terrain: Malaya's geography was incredibly difficult to navigate with 'the internal conflict therefore raged fiercest where these farmers and "squatters" had settled, on the fringes of the "jungle wilderness" which blanketed four fifths of a country about the size from north to south, bisecting the country'.⁴⁹

(2) Information: In the period following the Second World War, the British government in Malaya failed to develop an intelligence network in the cities and countryside. This paucity facilitated the MCP's unhindered growth and expansion.

(3) Forces: At the beginning of the armed conflict, government security forces were roughly the same size as the insurgent forces. There were not enough forces to patrol the cities, the plantations and the jungle. Furthermore, they were ill-equipped to conduct deep jungle operations. Lastly, the security forces were not trained to conduct counterinsurgency operations.

(4) Political Fractiousness: The political parties were fractious and did not collaborate well. Because of their intractable positions on many topics, the government had long periods of delayed decision making.⁵⁰

Initial insurgent success

(1) Instability: The Second World War created an atmosphere where normal society, economy and governmental control were all highly disrupted. As a result of this tumultuous period, Malaya experienced high levels of crime and banditry throughout the country. This created a perception by the population of governmental instability and caused them to question the government's legitimacy and its ability to govern.

(2) Diaspora: Because the MCP was primarily ethnic Chinese, there was a more favourable attitude towards them in the Malayan Chinese rural communities and especially among the squatters. Prior to the establishment of the Home Guard and the creation of local governments in the New Villages, there were few Chinese in the government or in its security forces.⁵¹

(3) Terrain: The natural terrain afforded the insurgents initially a relatively safe location from which to conduct their operations. It was the thick jungle into which the insurgents could find sanctuary by building camps and re-establishing communication routes, but still close enough to reach into the squatter community for food, money and recruits.
(4) Government Inertia: Initial government indecision regarding the MCP's role in rising violence and MCP dominance in the unions.

Whole-of-government approach

After Briggs became the director of operations, he set about improving the way that the government fought the insurgents. Briggs and his successors switched to 'a population-centric approach that required a cooperation between the military and the government' to accomplish. It was, and still, is an approach that integrated the collaborative efforts of the departments and agencies of a government: security; political; economic and informational as the base, to achieve unity of effort towards a shared goal in order to control the environment.[52]

Analysis: Resettlement to new villages

In order to control the activities of the Minh Yuen and to reduce the manoeuvrability of the MRLA, the government in 1950 instituted the 'Briggs Plan', which, in part, made provisions to expand and to improve the resettlement programme of the nearly one-half a million Chinese squatters, who had been living close to the jungle, into new villages that could be controlled by the British. The squatter communities (distinct from the long-standing Malay kampongs) had grown up during the Japanese occupation, when the closure of the large tin mines and rubber plantations caused hundreds of thousands of natives to seek survival through subsistence farming on the edge of the dense jungle that covered four-fifths of Malay. In the jungles, where the MCP had their camps and other sanctuaries, the insurgents could not grow enough food to sustain their movement, so they turned to the squatters.[53] In fact, the MCP had to use the Chinese squatters for food production because the jungles were too difficult for the insurgents to cultivate and the aborigines were not agrarian and could not be trained to farm.[54]

The central objective of Briggs's plan was the separation of the MCP rebels from the civil populace, and hence their primary source of intelligence and – most importantly – food. As was discussed, the rugged, mountainous terrain and jungles of the Malayan Peninsula did not lend itself to agricultural development. In fact, two-thirds of the country's rice requirement had to be imported, as was nearly one-third of all of Malaya's food supply at this time.[55] The insurgents were leveraging the Chinese squatters through terrorism to provide them with home-grown food and rice, which Briggs and his team noted.[56] However, in the outset of the Emergency, laws and logistics were neither adequate enough to effectively isolate the squatters nor adequately attenuate insurgent activity against them.[57] Even though a 1948 plan had devised a resettlement programme as a means to address this, local support for this action was lacking. Without this support, the programme made no real progress.[58] Despite the fact that something needed to be done to keep the insurgents from the squatters, it wouldn't be until 1950 when true progress in this area would occur.

In April 1950, London appointed Lt. General Sir Harold Briggs as a director of operations, Malaya. Within one week of arriving, he published a finding that reinforced the necessity to isolate the vulnerable population from the insurgents that was very reminiscent of the 1948 finding. He based his finding on two conclusions: (1) squatters and unsupervised labourers were breeding guerrillas and (2) the Chinese were willing to help defend themselves against the Communists.[59] His plan was ambitious with a tight timeline of 2 years to relocate over 500,000 squatters into new locations and homes. What differed from 1948 was that after over two years of insurgent activity, there was finally support for resettlement.

The decision for relocation

While the British were aware to some degree of the MCP's communist activities prior to 1948, research seems to indicate that they were unaware as to the extent, and also of the creation after the communists' Fifth Plenary Session of the Central Committee of the MCP of the Malayan People's Anti-British Army (MPABA).[60] This newly formed organization once called upon by the MCP leadership undertook a campaign of arson and murder aimed primarily at British citizens, economic interests and supporters.[61]

Malaya at this time was a very important economic interest of Britain because of its rubber and tin manufacturing industries. Post WWII had yet to see the rise of synthesized, and artificial rubber and natural rubber was only found in abundance in a few geographic areas around the globe, of which the British did not hold exclusive rights. Tin was critical post WWII because of its alloy strengthening properties and in many uses such as tinfoil, which was widely used before yielding to aluminium foil. So, with two major economic resources being threatened, Britain was not going easily or willingly to yield Malaya to the insurgents.

Between 1948 and 1952, squatters were taken from their homes and forced into 'resettlement areas' under British control as part of a campaign known as the Briggs Plan, formulated by the director of operations in

Malaya, Sir Harold Briggs. Briggs did not arrive in Malaya until 1950, and while resettlement had been underway before his arrival, Briggs expedited the process and identified the need to render assistance to the relocated in the form of amenities and social welfare programmes. The resettlement areas would be later christened 'New Villages' by Briggs' replacement, Gerald Templar, who later became High Commissioner in 1952.[62]

Resettlement, despite peaceful, but vociferous, protests from the civilians being moved, for the most part went well, and the relocation operations were not interrupted by guerrilla interference or delayed through lack of preparedness by the British forces. There was in fact surprisingly little opposition and very little violence used against government officials responsible for its execution, and John Coates noted and emphasizes 'the kindness and compassion with which most of the troops carried out resettlement'.[63] Resettlement operations were meticulously planned out well in advance and were executed with discipline and efficiency. Villages were surrounded by trucks and soldiers at dawn, with their inhabitants being informed that they were to be moved to a secure location. Any of their possessions that could not be moved, including houses and crops, were destroyed.[64]

The New Village

The layout of a standard New Village represented a new way of living for the relocated squatters. There were many new amenities available to them, and the spatial layout of the New Village was decidedly more organized than where they lived. The police station was either located in the centre of the New Village or else placed at a higher position to enable surveillance of the villagers and their daily activities. Other government buildings, such as community halls, schools, dispensaries, as well as shops and markets, were arrayed close to the police station to ensure quick response should the need arise. Several watchtowers sat at the edge of the village, ostensibly to protect villagers, but invariably functioning as surveillance to monitor villagers' movements. There were two access points, guarded by Malay auxiliary constables, who controlled the movement of people and vehicles in and out of the village. The residential areas were normally designed along horizontal and perpendicular lines in a grid pattern.

The British government established some 500 'New Villages' throughout Malaya and they were of two types. Labourers (miners and plantation workers) were to live in dormitory camps, which were usually added as suburbs to existing towns. Farmers were sent to agricultural villages, over half of which were entirely new and meant to be self-supporting. With the squatter Chinese population separated and protected from the insurgent terrorism and propaganda, the rest of the whole-of-government approach by British authorities was greatly enabled because the control of the population and space instilled security and confidence back into the government.[65]

The human and social consequences

The resettlement programme during the campaign was a central strategy in the British counterinsurgency military operation to defeat the MCP in Malaya. The New Villages were a success for the British and accomplished what they were designed by Briggs to do. However, they far-outlived their strategic purpose and continued to provide shelter for the Chinese community for well over fifty years. Not only did they provide the former squatters with their own lands but these New Village communities also became 'bastions' of Chinese settlement.[66]

The New Villages have served their role eminently in the colonial plan for political survival. Today, they are left more like a neglected step-child than as a testimony to the struggle for building a democratic way of life in the formative stage of nationhood. Many New Villages are losing their social and economic vigour, and can only watch the twentieth-first century go by. While the New Villages had indeed offered 'a great social opportunity' for the inhabitants, it had been lamented that it was 'a pity that better use is not being made of it'.[67]

The implementation of New Villages was not without problems and failure to overcome these problems led to the inevitable marginalization of hundreds of New Villages economically and culturally.[68] While some former squatters returned to their homes, the great majority stayed and helped to produce thriving communities. However, economic development and population growth contributed to the uneven progress of the New Villages in what is now Malaysia based on their location. Those New Villages located in semi-urban and urban peripheries thrived, while the New Villages situated in the rural areas did not. However, taken into context, the overall outcome was generally positive because the squatters did end up better off than had they stayed.

Resettlement effects on civil/military counterinsurgency operations

The government's plan that isolated the vulnerable population from the insurgents, which for the MCP was vital for their survival, was a powerful move that hobbled the MCP. Since the MCP had no success in translating their ideology to the urban centres, and were unable to grow or force the aboriginals to supply them adequately, the MCP relied heavily upon the

Chinese squatters, living in the rural areas. Once deprived of their means of securing food, recruits and information, the MCP forces were opened up for elimination.[69]

While Briggs is given the credit for the programme, relocation had been ongoing prior to his arrival. By making the resettlement programme something that would later become known as 'winning the hearts and minds' evolved into a major change in the way that the world would counter an insurgency. The impact of the relocation/resettlement in Malaya cannot be overstated. As was outlined regarding legitimacy, the Malayan resettlement programme provided the isolation from the insurgents that the government needed to regain the initiative in a whole-of-government approach. Granted, the insurgents made many tactical and strategic errors throughout the war, but based on the analysis of how insurgencies end, the insurgents' defeat was inevitable.

By physically and psychologically isolating the insurgents from the population, the British cut off the MCP's ability to recruit new members, secure food, secure information and a level of freedom of movement. This severally hobbled the insurgency. First, they could not replace food lost by growing their own because the insurgents could not create farms of substantial size without alerting counterinsurgent forces as to their locations and because the insurgents lacked means and method to do so.[70] Second, the insurgency could not develop the aboriginal population to provide for them to any degree because they were only a subsistence farmer and lacked surpluses for the insurgent to exploit.[71] Finally, the MCP was never able to secure external support from any other communist country or country sympathetic to their cause. In the end, the insurgents simply could not sustain their insurgency from a logistical point of view.

Once the population was isolated, the British government was able to focus on a whole-of-government approach to further psychologically distance the insurgency narrative from their target audience. Once the squatters were finally settled into the New Villages during 1952, attacks on and deaths from insurgents dropped dramatically, which signify a more controlled security situation.[72] The government, and then the Chinese themselves, were able to provide more focused security and to expand operations around the New Villages, so that the threat against them was nullified. This enabled another of Thompson's tenants, one that the US military would later designate as 'clear-hold-build'. Once an area was deemed 'white'[73] in terms of security, police and government would be restored to that area, the British government would lift wartime restrictions, and military operations would move to the next priority area. As a result, security forces were also released for new tasks, and retraining of police became possible from 1952 onward.

Under Briggs's leadership, the resettlement programme became a vector for social change. Racial tensions, discrimination and disenfranchisement, especially concerning the Chinese, had created the opportunity for the MCP to grow. In an effort to bring the Chinese more into the government, the

Home Guard was established. Its function was to protect the New Villages. This evolved and discredited the narrative espoused by the insurgents that Chinese were forced into supporting a foreign government because more and more Chinese became part of the government. To further undercut the insurgent messaging, in 1948, the British government signed onto the Federation of the Malaya Agreements with the eleven Malay States. These agreements laid the foundations for progress towards self-rule. In 1952, London sent a directive to General Templer that Malaya should eventually become a fully self-governing nation and a united one.

The second part of that statement is of significance because it directed Templer to be inclusive to non-ethnic Malayans. Later that year, after compromise, Malaya had a new law that extended federal citizenship to 50–60 per cent of the Indian and Chinese population there. The New Villages benefitted from this overall development because they were authorized and empowered to elect village councils and become part of the local government. With this, another spoke in the insurgents' propaganda was eradicated and their credibility was subsequently greatly reduced.

The New Villages were locations where former squatters had the opportunity to attend schools, get health services and other amenities that the former squatters had not had before nor were the insurgents able to provide. Even the jungle outposts, where patrols and security for the aboriginals took place, continued to be maintained after the Emergency, renamed 'Administrative Posts', but still supporting schools, health services and trade. In terms of legitimacy with respect to expectations, the New Villages and the jungle outposts showcased the governments' ability to provide for their people. Again, the insurgents failed even before the establishment of the New Villages because they used a great deal of coercion to get the squatters to provide for them.

Economically, the establishment of the New Villages was a great boon for squatters. Once moved into the Villages and provided land for their own use and ownership, the economy of New Villages. Subsequently focused primarily around agriculture the New Villages began producing vegetables for the urban markets. Yet, many villagers depended on rubber holdings for a living, or worked at the estates or smaller farms as rubber tappers. Others worked in tin mines, timber camps or in fishing and stock rearing. For those New Villages located around larger cities, especially outside Kuala Lumpur, the former squatters worked in the engineering, metal trades or as shopkeepers, hawkers, tailors or clerks. Some even found work in the small-scale industries making food and beverages and various simple manufactured items. From peripheral and subsistence living to becoming part of the economy of a more significantly untied Malaya, New Villagers bettered their lives under the resurgent government and global economy. This again was another area that the insurgents were not able to better in terms of ideology or through action.

Conclusion

Malaya gained its independence on 31 August 1957, and on 31 July 1960 insurgency was declared over by the newly elected Alliance Party's leader, Tunku Abdul Rahman. In the end, 6,698 Communists were killed, 2,819 were wounded and 2,675 were captured. On the government's side, 1,865 were killed, 2,560 captured and none captured. Civilian cost was 2,473 killed, 810 wounded and none captured. The insurgents were not wholly captured, and Chin Peng and approximately 300–400 continued along the Thai border, but were marginalized and wholly ineffectual.[74] It is impossible to say that the resettlement programme was the reason that there were so few people killed, but the resettlement programme did help pave the way for future successes in a whole-of-government approach. In Chin Peng's own words:

> We had much effort to cultivating the Min Yuen in the squatter communities and the supply lines we created were effective. However, as more and more people were herded into the new villages with their high cyclone wire fencing, their barbed wire, flood lights, police guards, constant searches, frequent interrogations and general restrictions on movement, we realized we were facing nothing less than a crisis of survival.[75]

Yet, even though relocation was a part of a greater whole, the resettlement aspect of the Briggs' plan was not the primary reason behind the success of the Malayan government's counterinsurgency efforts, but it was highly instrumental in facilitating that success. As has been mentioned throughout this chapter, and in the research material used, resettlement was already being conducted prior to Briggs' arrival, but with only limited effect on thwarting insurgent activities.

While there is no way to completely validate the next statement, Rand's study entitled *On How Insurgencies End* posited several key characteristics of a failed or failing insurgency that does not include population relocation. Within those parameters, Malaya fit well: length of time of the insurgency (longer is better for the government), use of terrorism, which depicts a potential loss for the insurgent, defections and desertions by the insurgents (Lai Teck and Chin Peng respectively) and failure by insurgents to secure external support and true sanctuary. While there are always exceptions, in Malaya's case, the sum total of the number of negatives point to what became the eventual success by the government over the insurgents. This, the successful execution of a resettlement programme, and the British government's whole-of-government approach, the British government, despite a poor initial response, defeated the MCP convincingly with surprising little loss of life or cost.

Notes

1 John Cloake, *Templer, Tiger of Malaya* (London: Harrap Limited, 1985), 273.
2 Chin Peng, *My Side of History* (Singapore: Media Maters Pte, Ltd, 2003), 41–2.
3 Ibid., 10.
4 Ibid., 75.
5 John Coates, *Suppressing Insurgency: An Analysis of the Malayan Emergency, 1948–1954* (Boulder, CO: Westview Press, 1992), 23.
6 John Nagl, *Learning to Eat Soup with a Knife: Counterinsurgency Lessons from Malaya and Vietnam*, (Chicago, IL: University of Chicago Press, 2002), 71.
7 Carl von Clausewitz, (Edited and translated by Peter Paret and Daniel Moran), *Two Letters on Strategy* (Fort Leavenworth, KS: Combat Studies Institute Reprint, 1992), 21; emphasis mine.
8 Ibid., 17.
9 Max Weber's governmental archetypes are charismatic authority, traditional authority and legal-rational authority. However, further discussion of Weber and his archetypes lay outside the scope of this research.
10 Timothy J. Lomperis, *From People's War to People's Rule: Insurgency, Intervention, and the Lessons of Vietnam*, (Chapel Hill: The University of North Carolina Press, 1996), 31–3.
11 Charles Gwynn, *Imperial Policing* (Edinburgh: R. & R. Clark, 1939, 2nd edition), 11, https://archive.org/details/in.ernet.dli.2015.275121 (accessed 25 October 2018).
12 US Joint Chiefs of Staff, *Joint Publication 2-24: Counterinsurgency Operations* (Washington: Joint Chiefs of Staff, 2009), I-3.
13 Yuri M. Zhukov, *Population Resettlement in War: Theory and Evidence from Soviet Archives* (Harvard: Department of Government, December 3, 2013), 2–5.
14 Ibid., 63.
15 Robert Jackson, *The Malayan Emergency and Indonesian Confrontation: The Commonwealths' Wars: 1948–1966* (London: Routledge, 1991), 1–2.
16 J. M. Gullick, *Malaysia* (New York: Frederick A. Praeger, Publishers 1969), 20–2.
17 Cynthia Hannon and Robert Anna, 'A Successful Counterinsurgency: The British and the Malayan Emergency', *Jackson School Journal of International Studies*, Vol. 6, No. 2 (Spring 2016), 18.
18 Ian E. Rinehart, 'Malaya: Background and U.S. Relations', *Current Politics and Economics of South, Southeastern, and Central Asia*, Vol. 23, No. 2 (2014), 153+. Available at: http://www.questia.com/read/1P3-3492293461/Malaya-background-and-u-s-relations (accessed 25 October 2018).
19 R. W. Komer, *The Malayan Emergency in Retrospect: Organization of a Successful Counterinsurgency Effort* (Santa Monica: The Rand Corporation, February 1972), 1.

20 The Chinese, Malays and Indians represented the three largest and most influential ethnic groups in Malaya.
21 Cheah Boon Kheng, 'The Communist Insurgency in Malaya, 1948–90: Contesting the Nation-State and Social Change', *Singapore: New Zealand Journal of Asian Studies*, Vol. 11, No. 1 (June 2009), 132–4.
22 Hannon and Anna, 'A Successful Counterinsurgency: The British and the Malayan Emergency', 19.
23 Ronald Spector, *In the Ruins of Empire: The Japanese Surrender and the Battle for Postwar Asia* (New York: Random House, 2007), 35.
24 Ibid., 47.
25 Michael R. J. Vatikiotis, 'Catching the Dragon's Tail: China and Southeast Asia in the 21st Century', *Contemporary Southeast Asia*, Vol. 25, No. 1 (2003), 65. Available at: http://www.questia.com/read/1G1-102909260/catching-the-dragon-s-tail-china-and-southeast-asia (accessed 25 October 2018).
26 Tsuyoshi Hasegawa (ed.), *The Cold War in East Asia: 1945–1991* (Washington DC: Woodrow Wilson Center Press, 2011), 5.
27 An interesting note, this party held a conference in 1930 in Singapore, where Ho Chi Minh and the leaders of the party were arrested during a police raid. Nagl, *Learning to Eat Soup with a Knife*, 60.
28 Ibid., 61.
29 Spector, *In the Ruins of Empire*, 77.
30 Richard L. Clutterbuck, *The Long, Long War: Counterinsurgency in Malaya and Vietnam* (New York: Frederick A. Praeger, 1966), 21.
31 Peng, *My Side of History*, 146
32 Clutterbuck, *The Long, Long War*, 22.
33 Robert Taber, *The War of the Flea: A Study of Guerrilla Warfare Theory and Practice* (Sterling, VA: Potomac Books, 2002), 139.
34 Ibid., 29–30.
35 Ibid., 35.
36 Lomperis, *From People's War to People's Rule*, 205.
37 While mistranslated, the majority of material available on The Emergency labels the group 'MRLA' and for the remainder of this chapter, 'MRLA' will be the used.
38 Kheng, 'The Communist Insurgency in Malaya, 1948–90: Contesting the Nation-State and Social Change', 133–4.
39 The enemy-centric approach basically understands counterinsurgency as a variant of conventional warfare. It sees counterinsurgency as a contest with an organized enemy, and believes that we must defeat that enemy as our primary task. There are many variants within this approach, including 'soft line' and 'hard line' approaches, kinetic and non-kinetic methods of defeating the enemy, decapitation versus marginalization strategies and so on. Many of these strategic concepts are shared with the population-centric school of counterinsurgency, but the philosophy differs. Enemy-centric approach

could be summarized as 'first defeat the enemy, and all else will follow'. See U.S. Department of State, *Counterinsurgency Guide* (Washington, DC: U.S. Government Printing Office, January 2009), 14.

40 Under Emergency Regulation 17D, inhabitants of entire villages could be detained/deported at the High Commissioner's discretion. See John Scurr, *The Malayan Campaign: 1948–1960*, Oxford: Osprey Publishing, 1982), 4.

41 Huw Bennett, 'A Very Salutary Effect: The Counter-Terror Strategy in the Early Malayan Emergency, June 1948 to December 1949', *Journal of Strategic Studies*, Vol. 32, No. 3 (2009), 422.

42 Karl Hack, 'The Malayan Emergency as Counter-Insurgency Paradigm', *Journal of Strategic Studies*, Vol. 32, No. 3 (2009), 383–414 (386).

43 Jackson, *The Malayan Emergency and Indonesian Confrontation*, 17–19. Numerous units from across the Empire rotated in and no slight is meant in not listing them here. Furthermore, various sources give differing numbers, but in the end, the numbers of security forces were decidedly in greater proportion than those of insurgent.

44 The population-centric approach understands counterinsurgency as fundamentally a control problem, or even an armed variant of government administration. It believes that establishing control over the population, and the environment (physical, human and informational) in which that population lives, is the essential task. Again, there are many variants within this approach, including some very hard-line methods and some softer approaches, but the underlying philosophy is 'first control the population, and all else will follow'. See U.S. Department of State, *Counterinsurgency Guide*, 14.

45 Bard E. O'Neill, *Insurgency and Terrorism: Inside Modern Revolutionary Warfare* (Dulles: Brassey's, Inc., 1990), 153–4.

46 James Flint, 'Assessing the British Counter-Insurgency Effort in Malaya', *E-International Relations Students*, 11 February 2015. Available at: http://www.e-ir.info/2015/02/11/assessing-the-british-counter-insurgency-effort-in-malaya/ (accessed 25 October 2018).

47 Bennett, 'A Very Salutary Effect', 417.

48 Coates, *Suppressing Insurgency*, 151.

49 Hack, 'The Malayan Emergency as Counter-Insurgency Paradigm', 673.

50 It should not be forgotten, too, that Malayan politics were played out against the background of the Communist Party of Malaya's (CPM) determined uprising to overthrow the Government of Malaya, which affected literally every aspect of Malayan economic and sociopolitical life, and was never very far away in the background at a time when colonial Malaya was just recovering from the effects of the Second World War and the Japanese Occupation.

51 Nevertheless, the MCP did not have overall command of the entire Chinese communities' loyalties because most Chinese were relatively apolitical.

52 Gywnn, *Imperial Policing*, 1, 4, 15.

53 Clutterbuck, *The Long, Long War*, 45.

54 Riley Sunderland, *Resettlement and Food Control in Malaya* (Santa Monica, CA: The Rand Corporation, September 1964), 4–5.
55 Clutterbuck, *The Long, Long War*, 45.
56 Ibid., 26.
57 Ibid., 27.
58 Ibid., 26.
59 Ibid., 35–43.
60 The MCP would later reorganize this group into what was known as the Malayan Races Liberation Party (MRLA). Nagl, *Learning to Eat Soup with a Knife*, 64.
61 Nagl, *Learning to Eat Soup with a Knife*, 62–3.
62 Paul Street, *Malayan New Villages: An Analysis of British Resettlement of Ethnic Chinese People during the Malayan Emergency, 1948–1960* (Kindle: Paul Street, 1st edition, 2014), 118–25.
63 Coats, *Suppressing Insurgency*, 90.
64 Street, *Malayan New Villages*, 118–25.
65 Hack, 'Everyone Lived In Fear: Malaya and The British Way Of Counter-Insurgence', 683.
66 Wen Pingqiang, 'The Chinese New Villages in Malaysia: Impact of Demographic Changes and Response', *Center for Malaysian Studies*, Part 2. Available at: http://www.malaysian-chinese.net/publication/articlesreports/articles/7181.html (accessed 13 June 2018).
67 Ibid., 'Conclusion', Part 3.
68 Komer, *The Malayan Emergency in Retrospect*, 56.
69 Ben Connable and Martin Libicki, *How Insurgencies End* (Santa Monica: The Rand Corporation, 2010), 97.
70 Sunderland, *Resettlement and Food Control in Malaya*, 70–1.
71 Ibid., 71.
72 Karl Hack, 'The Malayan Emergency as Counter-Insurgency Paradigm', *Journal of Strategic Studies* Vol. 32, No. 3 (June 2009), 5–7.
73 An area was considered 'white' when insurgent activities were fully curtailed, so that military forces could concentrate on those areas still experiencing insurgent activity. It was part of Templer's 'stick and carrot' approach because white areas would have wartime restrictions lifted. See Jackson, *The Malayan Emergency and Indonesian Confrontation*, 47 and Nagl, *Learning to Eat Soup with a Knife*, 102.
74 Nagl, *Learning to Eat Soup with a Knife*, 102–3.
75 Peng, *My Side of History*, 268.

10

Centres de Regroupement:

The French in Algeria

Dr James N. Tallon

> *The counterinsurgent faces the decision of resettling. ... Such a radical measure is complicated and dangerous.*
>
> Counterinsurgency Warfare, Theory and Practice[1]
>
> DAVID GALULA, 1964

Introduction

The Algerian War (1954–62) was one of the most bitter and hotly contested conflicts during the 'Wars of Decolonization/Liberation'.[2] In order to deny aid and comfort to the FLN (*Front de libération nationale*) French forces initiated a strategy often known as *Quadrillage* (Gridding or dividing territory into quadrants).[3] This quartering of the insurgent areas of Algeria into manageable sectors, in turn, prompted a massive movement of humanity. This policy resulted in the forced relocation of nearly 30 per cent of the population into new locations, a policy known as *Regroupement* (Map 10).[4]

This programme placed many Algerians into camps/relocation centres called *Centres de Regroupement* where they could not assist nor support the insurgents and simultaneously were not threatened by them. Arguably, in combination with harsh scorched earth tactics on the part of the French armed forces, the insurgency was largely contained by 1959. While there

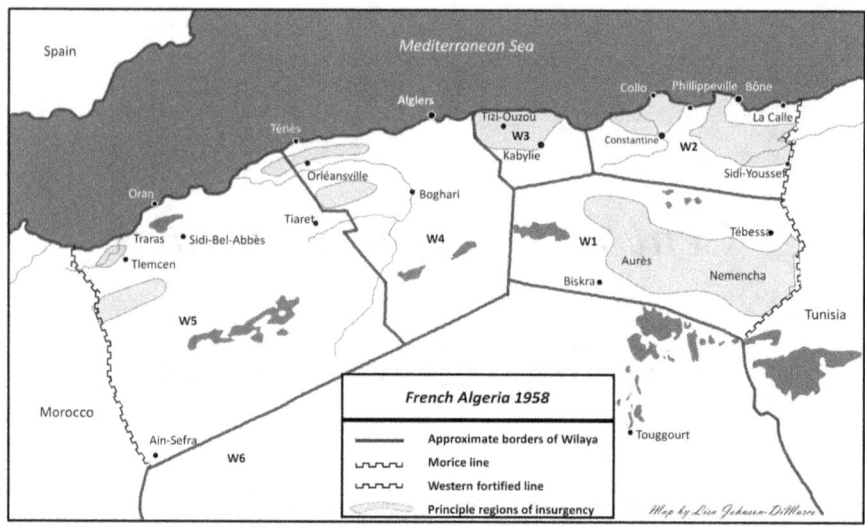

MAP 10 *French Algeria 1958. Under a programme called* Quadrillage, *French commanders in Algeria forcibly relocated 2.3 million Algerians to* Regroupement *centres. At the same time they fortified the eastern and western borders to isolate the area and then swept up the insurgents sector by sector. The French effort took over five years but, in the end, was successful in nearly eradicating the insurgency.*

is truth in this assessment, the massive dislocation bred resentment and despair among many relocated populations. Additionally, politically at home and in Algeria itself, many began to question the French presence in Algeria, especially if such extreme measure were necessary to maintain its existence.

The strategic setting

The French presence in Algeria began in 1830 with a military response to a supposed diplomatic slight towards the French envoy, Pierre Deval, with the 'fly-whisk (fly-swatter) incident'. During this Mr Deval was purportedly hit in the face by Husayn Dey (1818–30) with a fly-whisk.[5] The entire incident arose out of payments in arrears on grain shipments delivered to France during the Napoleonic Wars. This crisis came to a head as Algiers' revenue from corsairing rapidly declined after the 1810s. After this incident Charles X (1824–30) initiated a blockade against Algiers. When this proved ineffective he launched a military operation. The French invasion force made landfall at Sidi Fredj: some 25 kilometres (16 miles) from Algiers, on 14 June 1830, with over 34,000 troops and 100 ships, the Algerine defences were overwhelmed and the road to Algiers was laid open.[6] French forces, after a three-week campaign, captured Algiers on 5 July 1830. Husayn Dey accepted exile in Naples and French forces ransacked the city.

Not long after the capture of Algiers the Bourbon Charles X was overthrown by Louis Phillipe I, which initiated the so-called July Monarchy. This new government needed to bolster its slumping popularity and did so by sanctioning colonial expansion in Algeria. But, the French colonial project was directionless. This meant that commanders on the ground were given a wide berth and allowed to engage in operations as they saw fit. This effectively dragged France into a long-term occupation in Algeria. Many different constituencies within France, both left and right, sought to legitimate and reconcile this seizure, but it became increasingly difficult to hold on to Algeria after the initial occupation. Resistance rallied around new leaders in Algeria. Particularly Muslim religious officials who saw France's takeover of Algiers in terms of a religious/civilizational struggle became the leaders in this movement. From 1830 to 1847, France struggled to solidify and hold the gains of 1830. ʿAbd al-Qādir/Abdelkader and other Muslim leaders openly attacked French forces, and to counter this a full time military presence was required.[7] Along with this commitment to suppressing rebellion, European settlers began to make their way to Algiers in hopes of a better life. This created a tale of two societies living side by side in the new Algeria. This reality accelerated as the French repression of resistance became more brutal. By 1847, many of the main resistance groups, including ʿAbd al-Qādir/Abdelkader's movement, had been defeated and European settlement intensified. Resistance simmered throughout the nineteenth century, but the tide turned in favour of France and the settlers. The seminal moment for the settlers came with the official declaration of the incorporation of Algerian into France on 26 August 1885.

This declaration set a course towards even more settlement and greater discontent between the Muslim population and the *colons*. Despite incorporating Algeria into the Third Republic, Muslims were given no voting rights effectively making them second-class citizens, a slight that would have long-lasting repercussions. This division of status was enshrined in the *Code de l'Indigénat* of 1881.[8] The *Code* bred contempt among the Muslim populations of Algeria. Additionally, because it was applied to all Muslims, this contempt drew many of Algeria's regions and classes together in their dislike of France's colonial system.

Once Algeria became a part of France, settlers began to move in greater numbers into the Algerian coastal cities and their environs. This was encouraged by many different sectors of French society. Many of the *colons* were French, but some also came from Italy, Spain, and Malta. By 1960, the *colons* made up 10% of Algeria's population, some 1.1 million people. This population controlled 30-40% of Algeria's land. That being said, the majority of the *colons* remained relatively poor. Not by the standard of Muslim Algerians, but by the standard of metropole France, few prospered. Thus, the *colons* were an amalgam of southern Europeans, the majority of which were engaged in low-level service jobs and industrialized agriculture. The *colons* were tied to France, but sought autonomy, they resented interference from Paris and many began to believe in their own role in spreading civilization in North Africa.

Many in Algeria, both Muslim and Non-Muslim, rallied to the French cause during the First World War. Particularly for the Muslims it was viewed as a way to get political recognition and break down the *Code de l'Indigénat*. Tens of thousands of Muslim Algerians went to France and elsewhere fighting for the French empire in the hopes of reform and greater political freedom. A political movement 'Young Algeria' emerged and further agitated for better treatment and more rights. Metropole France responded to the post–WWI realities with token reform and even these were railed against by the *colons*.[9] These had largely stalled by the 1930s. The Second World War profoundly altered the colonial order in North Africa. With the defeat of the Third Republic by Germany, the Vichy regime took over in Algiers and became the ally of the *colons*. But, this was quickly wiped away by an Anglo-American invasion in 1942 (Operation Torch). Vichy was overthrown and hope for liberation on the part of Muslims appeared possible. However, the toppling of the old older by Operation Torch terrified the *colons*.

Battered by the Second World War and German occupation, France began to reassess its commitments to its overseas empire. It sought to reassert control in the aftermath of Vichy and Allied and Axis occupation of its territories. In Algeria, in May 1945 violent demonstrations broke out in the hopes of forcing France from Algeria. What resulted was terrible violence visited upon both the Muslim population and the *colons*. As result of this chaos and growing Anglo-American influence in the region, French authorities felt obligated to assert control over the territory again. The settlers for their part began to cultivate a siege mentality that had already been present. Many rural settlers after the violence moved to the coast and the large cities of Algeria. This movement began to transform the *colon* identity into a new conceptualization of the European community in Algeria, the *pied-noir*. This new identity focused on its connection to France and became more anti-Muslim.[10] As the 1950s progressed, tension mounted in Algeria.

This became even more pressing after French reverses in Indochina. The failure to contain the Vietminh offered a vision of how France could be ejected from Algeria. Additionally, throughout the 1950s and 1960s many of France's other territories within Africa slowly became independent. All of these factors shaped Algeria's society and had a profound impact upon the Algerian War.

The operational setting

As the Algerian War began France was forced to contend with the rumblings of independence elsewhere in its empire as well as its commitments to NATO particularly in Germany. Forces were also deployed during the Algerian War to the Suez in 1956, further dividing French attention to the revolution in Algeria. This meant the French army in Algeria was forced to rely upon the forces available and recruit from within the country and draw upon conscripts from France. In this way France had a 'two-tier army' one made up of Algerian and French conscripts and a regular army, which also comprised the French Foreign Legion and Paratrooper units.

In the fall of 1954 at the beginning of the Algerian War the total number of French forces in Algeria stood at around 70,000 including the *gendarmerie* and reservists. French forces reached their largest numbers in 1958–9, with just over 400,000 troops being deployed. In addition to this, there were some 176,000 *gendarmerie*, auxiliaries and police. The total number of French forces who saw service Algeria in 1954–62 was over 1,447,000.[11]

After the initial shock of the revolution, the French were reinforced by units from metropolitan France, from units engaged in NATO operations in Germany and units from Indochina. Many of these were motorized units as well as Foreign Legion units and paratroopers. These reinforcements infused striking power and confidence into French forces in Algeria. With this reorganization, the motorized units, Foreign Legion and paratroopers carried most offensive operations and reservists, and auxiliary forces served as garrison troops and in relocation operations.

Numerous auxiliary forces were utilized by the French during the war. Over 180,000 Muslim reservists, the *harki*, augmented French regular forces throughout the war. In addition to the *harki* other auxiliaries were utilized. These were particularly active in *Quadrillage* operations.

At the beginning of the war in 1954–9, the FLN had a well-organized army within Algeria. Many of the FLN's troops had served in the French army or had been trained elsewhere in the Arab World, particularly Egypt and Iraq. These forces were often known as the *mujahidin/moudjahidine*. They were able to strike at targets in Algeria and intimidate uncertain populations into joining the FLN cause as well as gaining needed supplies. The *Musabbalin/Moussebiline* were auxiliaries and part-time fighters for the FLN. They augmented the operations of the *mujahidin*. The *feda'yin/fidayine* were used for specific operations, sabotage, assassination and so on.[12] There was a great degree of flux in these categories as the war progressed. This was particularly true after the Challe offensive and the French army effectively sealed Algeria's border. The *mujahidin*, the regular forces, were badly mauled by French operations and for intents and purposes collapsed. This was further exasperated by internal divisions within the FLN and feuds between different FLN commanders. Additionally, reinforcement became nearly impossible because of the sealed border. So the FLN's auxiliary forces and volunteers continued the struggle against the French, but did so with less striking power. The FLN was able to arm and maintain regular army formations in Tunisia and Morocco. These forces did tie French units along the border, but they were never effective at breaching the cordon along the border.[13]

The peak of French forces in Algeria was around 400,000 troops, the maximum number of FLN solders was only around 50,000, although the exact numbers for the FLN are difficult to calculate.[14] After 1959, the FLN's army forces were depleted, but the remaining axillaries and volunteers filled in for the soldiers lost. Both the French and FLN saw the composition of their forces change significantly. In a certain sense both France and the FLN both had a 'two-tier' army. Both sides drew significantly from Algeria's population for auxiliary forces, but also maintained a regular army. However, by the end of the war the FLN's regular army, in essence, only existed outside of Algeria.

Touissant Rouge

On the night of 31 October and into 1 November 1954 a series of semi-coordinated attacks were carried out on several civilian and military targets in numerous areas within Algeria. The source of the attacks was an emerging group which became the FLN. This new group unilaterally spoke for all of nationalist groups in Algeria, and in their rhetoric claimed that they now superseded all previous organizations. Only six or seven people died in these attacks, but they represented a mounting dissatisfaction with the Fourth Republic's attempt to re-establish colonial rule in North Africa. Later, this event was imagined to be the beginning of the Algerian War. It's often referred to as *Toussaint Rogue* (Bloody/Red All Saints Day). But, at the time, serious violence was spreading across Algeria's borders in Tunisia and Morocco. Many thought that *Toussaint Rogue* was a result of this neighbouring violence rather than an internal attack. Nonetheless, the FLN attacks in the fall of 1954 changed the dynamic within the Algerian national movement and the way in which France viewed how to deal with this new resistance movement.

Quadrillage and *Regroupment*

Quadrillage succeeded in separating the FLN from the material support of many rural villages and towns.[15] Additionally, the propaganda value of presenting the image of control and normalcy was also valuable to French strategists. However, villages and towns that were surrounded by fences or wire in addition to guard towers and a garrison often felt like prisons. Thus, as a strategy, *Quadrillage/Regroupement* was a mixed bag. It was successful in the short term, denying the FLN material support and drawing large swathes, of Algerian society into a protection scheme dependent upon French military and civilian officials. However, despite significant successes, the cost both in terms of money and in propaganda terms meant that the strategy largely failed. In a certain sense, the *Centres de Regroupement* were unsuccessful as a long-term counterinsurgency strategy, but successful as a demographic engineering project.[16] In the short term, many of the *Centres* were protected from the FLN and remained loyal or at least controlled by France; however, the difficulty, not to mention the cost, of maintaining the *Centres* began to wear on civilian populations and some became more amenable to the FLN. Many Algerians began to feel they were being terrorized by French authorities and amid very poor conditions, grew to miss their homes. The French press began to question the motives of the *Centres de Regroupement* and began to criticize them openly.[17]

Thus, as a short-term tactic, *Quadrillage/Regroupement* was successful. It kept the FLN off balance, provided a respite from reprisals and offered a degree of safety. It showed that France cared about average Algerians and that they were willing to protect them wherever they may be. However, as a long-term strategy *Quadrillage/Regroupement* was a failure. The amount of men, money and resources expended was significant. The lion's share of these went to things that did not directly quell the insurrection nor inflict damage on the FLN. The conscript soldiers assigned to garrison duty in *Centres de Regroupement* often disliked the assignment and felt uninspired by it. Furthermore, the massive numerical advantage that the French had was never fully brought to bear on their enemy. As a result, specialists, particularly paratroopers and French Foreign Legion units, who carried out most of the combat operations, were stretched very thin.[18] In most cases they were quite effective, but by the end of the war, a degree of fatigue set in and they began to question strategy as well as political decisions.[19] This was perhaps the greatest failure of the *Quadrillage/Regroupement* strategy.

The camps themselves were not well-planned and began as an impromptu solution to a growing problem, rather than a grand strategy that was planned in advance. Later, there was greater clarity on how camps should be designed and managed, but it was difficult to deal with hundreds of ad hoc camps already created. In some cases, camp conditions were unsanitary and the housing provided was inadequate. Either way, presenting Algeria as one large French prison became an important propaganda image for the FLN. Finally, and most critically, the populations moved into the camps were left to languish too long. In many cases they remained for several years. This raised the ire of French and international media and became a boon for the FLN. The real or imagined conditions of the camps became a valuable propaganda tool, which rapidly undid most of the strategic gains and trust the French had accumulated.[20]

The architects of *Quadrillage* and *Regroupement*

The immediate predecessors of the *Quadrillage/Regroupement* strategy in the Algerian War had its origins in French Indochina (Vietnam, Cambodia and Laos). Many officers who served in Indochina later served in Algeria. In the late 1940s and early 1950s the French employed a *Regroupement* programme against the Viet Minh, particularly in what is today Cambodia.[21] Furthermore, examples of resettlement in Algeria predated the war of 1954–62. In the original process of 'pacifying' Algeria, a policy of relocation or dislocation had already been employed to move or 'settle' restive and rebellious tribes during the nineteenth century.[22]

French tactics in the Algerian War resembled and, in many ways, inspired the Strategic Hamlet Program of the United States in South Vietnam 1962–4 and the *aldeamentos* (strategic resettlements) and *reordenamento rural* (rural resettlement) programmes of Portugal in Angola and Mozambique 1961–74.[23] They were also similar to the tactics employed by the British in Kenya 1952–64.[24] All of these relocation programmes were at least partly inspired by the 'New Villages' of the Briggs Plan implemented the British during the so-called Malayan Emergency 1948–60.[25] Although, other relevant examples were known before this and in many ways the *Regroupement* programme mirrored previous tactics in Algeria.[26] All of these examples shared colonial strategies of separating or relocating populations from rebellious elements in order to protect settlements.

Discontent in Algeria boiled over in early November of 1954. The political aspirations of several activist groups were stifled by French authorities. In response, splinter groups emerged, most significantly the FLN, which became the prime nexus of resistance.[27] Popular support for the new movement soared and French authorities reacted to the revolt. What became later known as the Algerian War began. As it progressed and spread, the French employed new tactics in an attempt to squelch the surging support for the FLN. By 1956 some 450,000 French soldiers were committed to containing the FLN by dividing up the country into a series of zones. The *Quadrillage/Regroupement* strategy was first utilized to separate civilian populations from the FLN, as a result of creating no-go/forbidden zones, in these areas populations had to be relocated. General Gaston Parlange used this strategy for the first time in November 1954 and into the beginning of 1955 in the Aurès Mountains/Jabal al-Awas. It began as an impromptu *Regroupement*, trying to stifle support for the FLN.[28] By 1957–8, *Regroupement* became a standard procedure.[29] The formal articulation of the strategy came about when the Governor General of Algeria Robert Lacoste and General Raoul Salan designated the policy of *Resserrement des Populations* (contraction/restriction of populations). Camps were to become stable and economically self-sufficient. Moreover, an organization was established to inspect and deal with oversight within the camps, this became known as *Inspection Générale de Regroupement de Populations* (IGRP). The director of the organization was none other than General Gaston Parlange, the architect of the *Regroupment* strategy. As the camps came under greater scrutiny, French authorities had concerns about conditions within the camps as well as future prospects of the camps becoming self-sustaining. The prime moment for *Quadrilliage/Regroupement* and the *Centres de Regroupement* strategy was 1955–9, although it did continue on into 1960–1.

Large numbers of soldiers, mainly draftees, garrisoned strategic points and infrastructure as well as relocated populations. The remainder, principally the French Foreign Legion and Paratrooper units, actively sought out the FLN and attempted to destroy them. The soldiers who were assigned to *Quadrillage/Regroupement* duty often found it tedious and boring. Many complained of this during and after the conflict.

The imposition of *Quadrillage* by French military authorities contradicted the civilian administration of Algeria. This caused tension throughout the war and bred resentment. By the middle of twentieth century, Algeria had been divided by the French civilian authorities into departments, districts and municipalities. The French military instead divided the land into zones, sectors, quarters (*quartiers*) and sub-quarters (*subquartiers*). This upset the local administration of numerous areas. During the *Quadrilliage*, areas were designated as operational zones (*zones opérationnelles*), pacification zones (*zones de pacification*) and forbidden zones (*zones de interdites*). Within the forbidden zones, civilians were forced to evacuate and moved into *Centres de Regroupement*.

Laying down the grid

Initially, French forces utilized a strategy of forbidden zones (*zones de interdites*) in order to concentrate forces on the resettlement process. This briefly gave the FLN free movement in these areas and emboldened them to launch several attacks. Once the relocation process was completed, the French military sent out small patrols to mirror the size of units the FLN possessed. They constantly attempted to harass the FLN's movement, sweeping through encircled areas, ensnaring guerrillas and interdicting their supplies.[30] This was often referred to as *ratissage*, literally raking. These French units were very mobile and were often heliborne.[31] Their raids were made easier due to the relocation of much of the rural civilian population. Another part of this strategy was cordoning, *bouclage*, of the borders of Algeria, especially the Tunisian border.

One of the main cordons was the Morice Line. This 460-kilometre (285-mile) barrier along the Tunisian border was part of the overall counterinsurgency strategy to deny material and moral support to the FLN. This was accomplished, for the most part by September 1957, with the completion of the Morice Line, named for the then minister of defence.[32] This barrier as a part of *Quadrilllage/Regroupement* strategy was very effective in interdicting supplies to the FLN from outside Algeria, particularly from Tunisia. It was a tangle of barbed wire dotted with guard towers and patrolled by thousands of French troops.[33] The entire barrier was also studded with searchlights, radar and millions of anti-personnel mines. Later the Morice Line was strengthened by the Challe Line. In many ways the cordon, particularly the Morice Line, was the most effective element of the entire *Quadrilllage/Regroupement* strategy.[34] Other barriers were deployed along the Moroccan and, to a lesser degree, along the Libyan border.

Although these barriers were expensive to construct and maintain, they represented a miniscule amount of the overall French expenditure, and they were incredibly effective at interdicting supplies from outside Algeria. Additionally, the FLN was drawn into vain attempts to launch large-scale operations to breach these barriers. While small breaches were not uncommon and occasionally successful, the large-scale operations launched by the FLN were generally disastrous. In fact, the largest battle of the Algerian War was fought near the Morice Line. A FLN assault was repulsed and casualties were high. These assaults played into the hands of the French and allowed them to bring to bear their superior resources and weapons in a concentrated area. These offensives cost the FLN dearly in terms of manpower and weapons. Between 1957 and 1959, the FLN lost nearly 10,000 men in addition to the hundreds that were captured, not to mention the significant loss of thousands of weapons.[35]

In contrast to this French success, the most significant failure of the *Quadrilliage/Regroupement* strategy was the *Centres de Regroupement*. By the end of the war an estimated 3,525,000 Algerians were forced from their homes, nearly 30 per cent of the population. Some 2,350,000 were resettled in camps newly created by the French military. Another estimated 1,175,000 Algerians were resettled in pre-existing villages. The total number of individuals that were moved has been debated and described in several different ways.[36] Michel Cornaton's earliest work using principally IGRP data suggested the total number of people relocated near 1,868,545. Later with fieldwork undertaken immediately after the war in 1963–5, he estimated upwards, arriving at the figure of 2,350,000 persons relocated. This amounted to nearly one-third of Algeria's population.[37] Other sources, mainly older ones, estimated that 15–25 per cent of the population were relocated or displaced. In either case, the number of people relocated dwarfed any other relocation project in the same period.

Once large sections of the rural population were relocated, the struggle began to turn the newly created spaces into liveable villages. The initial *Centres des Regroupement* were improvised, many conditions within these camps were poor. Little or no running water and electricity were commonplace.

Nomadic population suffered even more as relocation coupled with unfamiliar living conditions compounded the misery. Additionally, many nomadic groups lost or were forced to give up their flock of herd animals, depriving them of the only livelihood they had known.[38] Many of the relocated populations had their old homes destroyed with or without their permission. In fact, French commanders encouraged their soldiers to force voluntary destruction so that they would not have to compensate the people displaced. These kinds of tactics soured many of the relocated Algerians to the relative safety and the prospect of new housing within the camps.[39] When the nature of these camps was revealed in 1959, a more systematic approach was launched to rehabilitate the image of the camps.[40] The *Mille Villages*/Thousand Villages programme was set in motion by Paul Delouvrier. These were presented as new modern villages that would uplift Algerian society. They were a sign of France's commitment to the Algerian people.[41] Despite this image and some genuine attempts at establishing better living conditions, the international and French media began to detail deplorable conditions and question the programme entirely. The comparison to the Second World War–era concentration camps began to be used frequently. This was a comparison French authority had long tried to avoid and dreaded. But these comparisons became more pervasive and once-muted criticism became much more pronounced.

Later, Charles De Gaulle himself came to Algeria and initiated the Constantine Plan to formalize the aforementioned programmes into a coherent strategy.[42] With the *Mille Village* measures, De Gaulle's Constantine Plan and the establishment of the IRGP, the *Quadrilllage/Regroupement* strategy suffered from a lack of focus and mission creep. Gradually semi-permanent relocation centres became permanent Model Villages. This ratcheted up the cost and put severe strain on camps that were meant to be temporary.

Aside from relocation, many Algerians simply fled the fighting, which caused further strain on the French strategy and Algerian society.[43] All of the major cities in Algeria like Algiers, Constantine and Oran saw a significant increase in their populations during the conflict as rural populations fled the fighting and settled in the relative safety of the urban environment. Yet, as these cities filled many people were forced into *bidonville*/shantytowns.[44]

Going off the grid

As the war brutally dragged on and public opinion in Algeria, France and abroad deteriorated, there was a re-evaluation of the *Quadrilllage/Regroupement* strategy. Despite the French success in securing Algeria's frontiers and the ability of French forces to harass the FLN, there was also a gradual shift to modernization programme. The *Centres des Regroupement* were to become *Nouveaux Villages* after 1960.[45] What had begun as an aggressive military strategy of relocation slowly morphed into a development and propaganda project. Further manpower was diverted to these camps and the focus transitioned from defeating the FLN to winning over the people of Algeria.[46]

Despite the purported uplift that France was delivering to average Algerians in camps, daily newspapers began to characterize the *Centres des Regroupement* as concentration camps and the FLN used this to gain support at home and abroad.[47] Thus, the FLN did not have to pursue an aggressive strategy to attack French forces, but simply had to not be destroyed and allow the millions within the *Centres des Regroupement* and elsewhere grow weary of French efforts. Additionally, international pressure also began to accrue as a result of the relocation strategy. The FLN used this to gain leverage. The Coup of April of 1961 further discredited French efforts and, by comparison, improved the image of the FLN.

With independence, officials of the Algerian state, principally drawn from the ranks of the FLN and other revolutionary groups continued, in some respects, the 'modernization' project of the *Centres des Regroupement*, although with less harsh measures. Moreover, many who had been relocated remained in their new surroundings.[48] This is perhaps the greatest legacy of the *Quadrillage/Regroupement* strategy.

Conclusion

The entire French *Quadrillage/Regroupement* strategy during the Algerian War was an improvised solution to a pressing problem. It built upon previous French experiences in Algeria and Indochina as well as British efforts in the Malay States and elsewhere in the same period. The scale of the French policy relocation during the Algerian War made it stand out from previous relocation schemes, but it did not represent something new or innovative, except for the scale of the relocation and the ways in which it was rationalized. As the strategy progressed some regularization occurred, but the nature of *Centres de Regroupement* continued to develop throughout the war from temporary lodging to model village. This undermined the strategy.

The scale of relocation also presented a problem, in essence, one-third of Algeria's population was voluntarily or involuntarily sequestered in a variety of types of lodging.[49] Still others fled the conflict, heading to the large urban centres of Algeria or abroad, causing confusion in the relocation process. This mass movement of people did initially stifle the efforts of the FLN to get supplies and recruits. But, as temporary housing became permanent and the living conditions of many who were relocated were less than ideal, especially those living in the *bidonville*/shantytowns of the main cities of Algeria, sympathy for the FLN gained steam. Additionally, French military operations often employed scorched earth tactics in order to deny the FLN supplies and shelter, which often meant that 'temporary' housing would become permanent. The discontent of uprooting nearly one-third of Algeria's population far outweighed the short-term gains of stifling the FLN recruiting efforts and denying them supplies.

Notes

1 David Galula, *Counterinsurgency Warfare, Theory and Practice* (Westport, CT: Praeger Security International, 2006, reprint of 1964 edition), 78.

2 This conflict lacks consensus on a name, this work will refer to it as the Algerian War, but it is also known as the Algerian War for Independence or the Algerian Revolution. In French it's referred to as *Guerre d'Algérie* or *Révolution algérienne*, in Arabic it is almost always referred to *al-Thawra al-Jaz'airiya* or the Algerian Revolution.

3 FLN is an abbreviation for *Front de libération nationale*. It was formed in October of 1954, was the national liberation movement within Algeria and remains one of the most powerful political parties in the country. The military arm of the FLN known was the ALN (*Armée de libération nationale*), or in Arabic *Jaysh al-Tahrir al-Watani al-Jaza'ir*. For the sake of clarity, henceforth, these two organizations will simply be described as the FLN.

4 Despite these mass relocations, extant literature on the topic remains limited, although a recent upsurge has occurred. Much of the literature is older see: Pierre Bourdieu and Abdelmalek Sayad, *Le déracinement: la crise de l'agriculture traditionnelle en Algérie* (Paris: Éditions du Minuit, 1964), Michel Cornaton, *Les regroupements de la décolonisation en Algérie* (Paris: Ed. Economie et humanism, 1967), Keith Sutton and Richard I. Lawless, 'Population Regrouping in Algeria: Traumatic Change and the Rural Settlement Pattern', *Transactions of the Institute of British Geographers*, Vol. 3, No. 3 (1978), 331–50. For some newer interpretations of this topic see: Keith Sutton, 'Army administration tensions over Algeria's centres de regroupement, 1954–1962', *British Journal of Middle Eastern Studies*, Vol. 26 (1999), 243–70, Mahfoud Bennoune, 'La doctrine contre-révolutionnaire de la France et la paysannerie algérienne: les camps de regroupement (1954–1962)', *Sud/Nord*, Vol. 14, No. 1 (2001), 51–66. The most recent interpretations see: Moritz Feichtinger, 'Strategic Villages: Forced Relocation, Counter-insurgency and Social Engineering in Kenya and Algeria, 1952–1962', in *Decolonization and Conflict: Colonial Comparisons and Legacies* ed. Martin Thomas and Gareth Curless (London: Bloomsbury, 2017), 137–57, Moritz Feichtinger, '"A Great Reformatory": Social Planning and Strategic Resettlement in Late Colonial Kenya and Algeria, 1952–63', *Journal of Contemporary History*, Vol. 52, No 1. (2017), 45–72. See also: Fabien Sacriste, *Les camps de 'regroupement': une histoire de l'État colonial et de la société rurale pendant la guerre d'indépendance algérienne (1954-1962)* Toulouse 2, 2014, this work was not consulted, but based other publications published by this author and the fact that the dissertation comprises more than 1,300 pages, one can assume there will some valuable material in this work.

5   Jamil M. Abun-Nasr, *A History of the Maghrib in the Islamic Period* (Cambridge: Cambridge University Press, 1999), 249–50.
6   Martin Evans, *Algeria: France's Undeclared War* (Oxford: Oxford University Press, 2013), 9–10.
7   Ibid., 11–14.
8   Ibid., 22–3.
9   Ibid., 38–48.
10 Ibid., 85–93.
11 Charles R. Schrader, *The First Helicopter War: Logistics and Mobility in Algeria, 1954–1962* (Westport, CT: Praeger Publishers, 1999), 39–41.
12 Ibid., 145–58 and Roger Trinquier and Daniel Lee, *Modern Warfare. A French View of Counterinsurgency* (London & Dunmow: Pall Mall Press, 1964), 11–17.
13 Schrader, *The First Helicopter War*, 145–8.
14 For an estimate of the FLN's forces See: Schrader, *The First Helicopter War*, 151.
15 To invoke a frequently utilized Mao quote, 'The guerrilla swims among the people as fish in the sea. Without the support of the people the guerrilla is a fish out of water, it cannot survive.' Mao Zedong, *On Guerrilla Warfare* (New York: Praeger, 1961), 93. *Regroupment* was an attempt to drain the sea and make the FLN a fish out of water.
16 In point of fact, all of the most recent counterinsurgency relocations and concentrations were in the long term unsuccessful. Britain left the Malay States by 1960–2 and the communist insurgency lasted until 1991, the United States left Vietnam and South Vietnam collapsed in 1975 and the Portuguese left Angola and Mozambique in 1975. Indeed, to reiterate and build upon Galula 'such a radical measure is complicated and dangerous'. It is also most often unsuccessful. Galula, *Counterinsurgency Warfare*, 78.
17 Fabian Klose, *Human Rights in the Shadow of Colonial Violence: The Wars of Independence in Kenya and Algeria* (Philadelphia: University of Pennsylvania Press, 2013), 168.
18 Schrader, *The First Helicopter War*, 42. In February of 1959 nearly 39 per cent of French forces were engaged in *Quadrilliage* operations. Around 14 per cent were patrolling Algeria's frontiers or guarding key points of infrastructure. Only about 15 per cent of forces were actively engaging the FLN.
19 This came to a head in April 1961. After a referendum for Algerian independence in January of 1961 was successful, Maurice Challe, Raoul Salan and several other generals rallied paratrooper units to seize control of strategic points in Algeria. This coup defied civilian authority and pitted professional soldiers against conscripts. The coup lost momentum and the conspirators were seized. However, this event illustrates the disconnect many paratrooper units had from mainstream French opinion. See: Pierre Abramovici, *Le putsch des généraux: De Gaulle contre l'armée, 1958–1961* (Paris: Fayard, 2011), *passim*.
20 Feichtinger, 'Strategic Villages: Forced Relocation', 144 and Klose, *Human Rights in the Shadow of Colonial Violence*, 168.

21 Michel Cornaton, *Les regroupements de la décolonisation en Algérie* (Paris: Editions ouvrières, 1967), 38–42.
22 Charles Richard, *Etude sur L'insurrection du Dahra (1845–1846)* (Algiers: Typographie A. Besancenez, 1846), 182–94, Michel Cornaton, *Les camps de regroupment de la guerre d' Algérie* (Paris: L'Harmattan, 1998), 42–53, Jennifer Sessions, *By Sword and Plow: France and the Conquest of Algeria* (Ithaca, NY: Cornell University Press, 2011), 264–308.
23 Miguel Bandeira Jerónimo, 'A Battle in the Field of Human Relations: The Official Minds of Repressive Development in Portuguese Angola', in *Decolonization and Conflict: colonial comparisons and legacies*, ed. Martin Thomas and Gareth Curless (London: Bloomsbury, 2017), 115–36, Brendan F. Jundanian, 'Resettlement Programs: Counterinsurgency in Mozambique', *Comparative* Politics, Vol. 6, No.4 (1974), 519–40, Gerald J. Bender, 'The Limits of Counterinsurgency: An African Case', *Comparative Politics*, Vol. 4, No. 3 (1972), 331–60.
24 Feichtinger, 'A Great Reformatory', 45–72.
25 John Nagl, *Learning to Eat Soup with a Knife: Counterinsurgency Lessons from Malaya and Vietnam* (Chicago, IL: University of Chicago Press, 2005), 71–6, Souchou Yao, *The Malayan Emergency: A Small, Distant War* (Copenhagen: NIAS Press, 2016), 97–115, and Leon F. Comber, *Malaya's Secret Police, 1945–60: The Role of the Special Branch in the Malayan Emergency* (Clayton: Monash Asia Institute, 2008), 173–97.
26 See John Lawrence Tone, *War and Genocide in Cuba, 1895–1898* (Chapel Hill: University of North Carolina Press, 2008) and Andreas Stucki and Laureano Xoaquín Araujo Cardalda, *Las guerras de Cuba: violencia y campos de concentración (1868–1898)* (Madrid: La Esfera de los Libros, 2017).
27 Evans, *Algeria: France's Undeclared War*, 118–23.
28 Cornaton, *Camps de Regroupment*, 63–5 and Alf Andrew Heggoy, *Insurgency and Counterinsurgency in Algeria* (Bloomington: Indiana University Press, 1972), 214.
29 Feichtinger, 'Strategic Villages', 135–57. Using archival material from the *Service Historique de l'Armée de Terre* located in Vincennes, France, henceforth identified as SHAT, see SHAT 1H2030: *Directive Générale 654/SC/RM.10/S, Regroupment de Populations*, 20 September 1957.
30 Sutton, 'Army Administration Tensions', 255.
31 See for example François Denoyer, *Quatre ans de guerre en Algérie: lettres d'un jeune officier* (Paris: Flammarion, 1962), Gérard Périot, *Deuxième classe en Algérie* (Paris: Flammarion, 1962), and Alain Manevy, *L'Algérie à vingt ans* (Paris: B. Grasset, 1960).
32 Schrader, *The First Helicopter War, passim*.
33 André-Roger Voisin, *Algérie, 1956–1962: la guerre des frontières sur les barrages électrifiés* (Charenton-le-Pont: Presses de Valmy, 2002), Jacques Vernet, 'Les barrages pendant la guerre d'Algérie', in *Militaires et guérilla dans la guerre*, ed. Jean-Charles Jauffret, Maurice Vaïsse, and Charles-Robert Ageron, *d'Algérie* (Brussels: Éditions Complexe, 2001),

Charles-Robert Ageron, 'Un versant de la guerre d'Algérie: la bataille des frontières (1956–1962)', *Revue d'histoire moderne et contemporaine*, Vol. 46, No. 2, (1999), 348–59.

34 André Morice (1900–90) served in many French cabinet positions, including minister of defence in 1957. He later became mayor of Nantes 1965–77.

35 A similar barrier was constructed by the Italians during anti-insurrectionary operation 1922–31. It was built to contain the Sanusiyya rebellion. The barrier spanned some 271 kilometre (168 mile) See: Nir Arelli, 'Colonial Soldiers in Italian Counter-Insurgency Operations in Libya, 1922–32', *British Journal for Military History*, Vol. 1, No. 2 (2015), 47–66.

36 For a schematic of the Morice Line, See: Shrader, *The First Helicopter War*, 205.

37 Shrader, *The First Helicopter War*, 217.

38 Cornaton, *Les regroupments*, 103–18.

39 Sutton, 'Army Administration Tensions', Sutton cites SHAT 1H2030 regarding this recommendation.

40 Cornaton, *Les regroupments de la décolonisation en Algérie*.

41 Heggoy, *Insurgency and Counterinsurgency in Algeria*, 213–16. Heggoy draws upon documents from the Centre de Hautes Études Administratives sur l'Afrique et l'Asie Modern (CHEAM) attached to the University of Paris. These sources are often compiled by colonial officials and they can be seen as conservative numbers.

42 M.H. Davis, 'Restaging Mise en Valeur: "Postwar Imperialism" and The Plan de Constantine', *Review of Middle East Studies*, Vol. 44, No. 2 (2010), 176–86.

43 The report was released in the French newspaper *Le Monde* on March 12, 1959. Vincent Duclert, 'Un rapport d'inspecteur des finances en guerre d'Algérie. Des camps de regroupement au principe de gouvernement', *Outre-mers*, Vol. 90, No. 338 (2003), 163–97.

44 The French colonial position is echoed by Maurice Faivre, a participant in the 1000 villages programme. See Maurice Faivre, *Les 1000 villages de Delouvrier: protection des populations musulmanes contre le FLN* (Sceaux: L'Esprit du livre, 2009).

45 Klose, *Human Rights in the Shadow of Colonial Violence* cites SHAT, 1H 2030/D1 May 25, 1960.

46 Sutton, 'Army Administration Tensions', 247–58.

47 Named for Maurice Challe, See: Francois-Marie Gougeon, 'The Challe Plan: Vain Yet Indispensable Victory', *Small Wars & Insurgencies*, Vol. 16, No. 3 (2005), 293–316.

48 Heggoy, *Insurgency and Counterinsurgency in Algeria*, 216.

49 Bourdieu, the population of Algiers increased by 203,000 between 1954–1960, Heggoy, *Insurgency and Counterinsurgency in Algeria*, 208.

11

Counterinsurgency at the 'rice roots' level:

South Vietnam's Strategic Hamlet Campaign

Dr Nathan R. Packard

> *This vast movement, born in the heat of war, is our preemptory reply to the Communist challenge. ... The strategic hamlet is also and primarily the point of impact of a political and social revolution which will serve as a foundation of our economic revolution.*
>
> PRESIDENT NGO DINH DIEM, 1962[1]

Introduction

From 1961 to 1963, the South Vietnamese government of President Ngo Dinh Diem, backed by the United States, implemented the Strategic Hamlet Program. The primary threat to South Vietnam was a communist insurgency known as the National Liberation Front (NLF) or Viet Cong (VC). In a country that was 88 per cent rural, with an estimated 2,500 villages divided into 16,000 self-sustaining hamlets, winning the war in the countryside was essential.[2] The communists considered the villages their centre of gravity and organizing at the village level had been the centrepiece of their strategy dating back to the colonial era. The Strategic Hamlet Program was one of the few strategies pursued by South Vietnamese and the Americans that directly challenged their adversary's programme in the countryside. The intent was to separate the rural population from the insurgents by establishing protected hamlets. In addition to security, the government would hold free elections and provide economic aid, medical facilities and educational services. The ultimate objective was to build support for the government in the countryside thereby reducing the insurgents' influence.

Conceptually the programme called for building defences around existing hamlets. In practice, however, tens of thousands of villagers were forcibly relocated. In time, relocation came to define the programme. This chapter will examine whether or not the Strategic Hamlet Program achieved its military objective of pacifying the countryside by increasing support for the government at the village level. At best, the programme represented a comprehensive, whole-of-government effort to defeat the insurgency at the 'rice roots' level. Despite some initial successes, involuntary resettlement, forced labour and the failure of the government to deliver on its promises bred resentment. The programme ultimately failed to win over the populace and was cancelled following the overthrow of the Diem regime in late 1963.

The Strategic Hamlet Program was not a resettlement campaign per se. In fact, the de facto head of the programme, President Diem's brother and adviser, Counsellor Ngo Dinh Nhu, was adamant that as few villagers be resettled as possible; providing protection and services was the overarching goal. In many hamlets only a small percentage of villagers, such as those living in outlying areas, were relocated. In others, however, local officials forcibly moved entire hamlets. Because relocation decisions were a local matter and most of the forced moves were within existing districts, it is not possible to estimate with any degree of certainty how many peasants were moved involuntarily. Local officials could move villagers at their discretion with no requirement to report. The South Vietnamese government and its American advisers only tracked the total number living in strategic hamlets. When numbers of relocated civilians were recorded, it was usually by journalists or US advisers. The experienced combat correspondent and Asia hand, Keyes Beech, estimated that about 5 per cent of the totals provided by the government represented forced resettlements, which would put the number of civilians forcibly relocated at around 400,000 over the life of the programme.[3] Despite the fact that the majority of strategic hamlets involved building defences around existing hamlets, the entire programme was associated with relocation.

Although relocation was not central to the overall strategy, the Strategic Hamlet Program does provide some insights on resettlement as a counterinsurgency technique. First, forced relocations are incredibly unpopular. They breed resentment among the target population and can be an effective propaganda tool for anti-government forces. Second, implementation is incredibly difficult and requires large numbers of competent local officials. Success or failure was often determined by the skill of local leaders. Unfortunately for the Diem regime, such officials were not available in large numbers and those who did exist were often targeted for assassination. Along these same lines, relocating populations is resource intensive. Throughout the short life of the programme, officials lamented their inability to meet commitments due to insufficient resources, which leads to a third observation – government forces have to come through on their promises for relocation to have any chance of success. Time and again, observers noted that the success of a particular hamlet hung on whether or not the villagers believed that their quality of life had improved; far too often they did not. Ultimately, involuntary relocations during the Strategic Hamlet Program were highly problematic and oftentimes counterproductive.

The strategic situation

The origins of the insurgency in South Vietnam can be traced to the period of French colonial rule over what was then known as French Indochina from 1887 to 1954. The Second World War was a watershed event for the anti-French resistance. On 19 May 1941, Ho Chi Minh founded the 'League for the Independence of Vietnam' (*Viet Nam Doc Lap Dong Minh*). Members of the movement, commonly known as the Viet Minh, pledged to liberate the country from French and Japanese control and improve the standard of living for the peasantry. Following the Japanese surrender, Ho took control of Hanoi, declared Vietnamese independence on 2 September 1945, and announced the creation of the Democratic Republic of Vietnam (DRV).[4]

In the aftermath of the Second World War, France attempted to reassert its colonial dominance, igniting the First Indochina War between France and the Viet Minh. Controlling the rural areas of Vietnam was a cornerstone of the Viet Minh strategy. In much of the countryside, the Viet Minh shadow governments were recognized as the legitimate authorities. French forces controlled only the cities and towns. The French surrender at Dien Bien Phu in 1954 not only resulted in France's withdrawal but also stood as yet another victory for the insurgents on the national level. When assessing the Strategic Hamlet Program, it is important to remember that at the time of its implementation, the Viet Minh had been building its rural base for two decades, conducted successful military operations against two great powers and was recognized as the legitimate government by the majority of the population.

The United States had initially supported the Viet Minh during the Second World War. The onset of the Cold War, however, changed the strategic calculus. Although the Viet Minh claimed to be a national front organization open to people of different political points of view, its leadership, to include Ho Chi Minh, were mostly committed communists. In 1951 the majority of the Viet Minh leadership was absorbed into the Lao Dong (Vietnamese Workers' Party), a communist organization. In accordance with its global containment strategy, US support for anti-communist efforts in Indochina steadily increased throughout the early 1950s. At the time of the French defeat at Dien Bien Phu, the United States was paying 80 per cent of France's military costs.[5] When France withdrew, the United States assumed the role of main ally of non-communist elements in the country.

Following Dien Bien Phu, the parties involved met in Geneva to negotiate an end to the war between France and the Viet Minh. The Geneva Accords granted Vietnam its independence, divided the country provisionally along the seventeenth parallel into northern and southern zones and stipulated general elections in July 1956 to 'bring about the unification of Viet-Nam'.[6] The Viet Minh were recognized as the legitimate rulers of the northern zone, renamed the DRV, while non-communist elements ruled southern zone known as the State of Vietnam, the future Republic of Vietnam. The Accords also called for the separation and regrouping of forces; approximately 90,000 southern Viet Minh moved north while 5,000 to 10,000 cadre remained in the South, most of them with orders to refocus on political activity and agitation.[7] With France's withdrawal, the United States shifted its support to President Ngo Dinh Diem, who had announced the establishment of the non-communist Republic of Vietnam in 1955. Diem, with the support of the United States rejected the provisions on free elections and reunification as outlined in the Geneva Accords.

The DRV expected the Diem regime to fall victim to its own internal contradictions. Diem, however, proved more resilient than anyone expected. He instituted repressive measures against communists and other anti-regime elements throughout the south. The infamous Law 10/59 was the cornerstone of the government's Anti-Communist Denunciation Campaign. It provided severe penalties to anyone convicted of 'infringing upon the security of the State'.[8] The law stipulated that special military tribunals would try suspected offenders and determine appropriate penalties; options included death and life imprisonment. The law's application was not limited to communists but rather it was expanded to persecute anyone who expressed dissatisfaction with the ruling family. As reported by one US Defense Department official, Law 10/59 in combination with the Anti-Communist Denunciation Campaign made 'the central government ... visible – and resented – at the village level as it had never been before in Vietnam'.[9] The law would remain in effect, and remain just as unpopular, throughout the life of the Strategic Hamlet Program.

Not all former Viet Minh accepted Ho Chi Minh's orders to lay low and await peaceful reunification. The Diem regime's anti-communist campaign made the resumption of armed struggle a matter of life or death. Fearing that the southern insurgency would either be eliminated or pursue its own course, Hanoi authorized limited, local, terrorist-type actions in what was referred to as the 'extermination of traitors' campaign beginning in late 1956.[10]

When this course of action proved inadequate, in 1959 the Communist Party adopted Resolution 15 which sanctioned armed force. However, according to Pierre Asselin, a leading expert on Hanoi's decision making during the war, noted the effort was to remain limited. One communist source cited by Asselin noted that Resolution 15 'permitted the active use of military forces only in combination with the political struggle as local circumstances required and not for the purpose of militarily defeating the Diem regime by commencing a large-scale guerrilla war or "people's war"'.[11] For its part, Hanoi would provide limited material support; the source of strength would be southern rural areas, an arrangement that would not change appreciably during the lifetime of the Strategic Hamlet Program.

The NLF, founded in 1960, represented the military expression of the return to armed struggle. It also posed the primary military threat to the Diem regime. Contrary to the regime's claims that the NLF was a tool of Hanoi, the insurgency was indigenous to the South and was in some respects a home-grown reaction to the government's authoritarian tendencies and political oppression.[12] Membership was open to all anti-Diem activists. The Front's stated goals were fairly straightforward: overthrow Diem, establish a democratic coalition government, provide land to the peasants and peacefully reunify Vietnam.[13] Despite the fact that not all NLF members were communists, the Diem regime coined the term 'Viet Cong', a shortened translation of Vietnamese communist, to describe the movement and its members.

The Front provided momentum and structure to the anti-Diem forces. Their tactics were based on Mao Zedong's principles of guerrilla warfare and were similar to those employed by the Viet Minh against the French in the First Indochina War. The insurgents, many of whom were former Viet Minh, established bases in secluded areas and emerged only at night to attack targets of opportunity such as small detachments of government troops, government officials and landlords. In addition, the NLF employed booby traps and mines to spread terror. Overall, the hit-and-run tactics of the NLF proved remarkably effective at frustrating Army of the Republic of Vietnam (ARVN) forces trained in conventional methods by their American advisers.[14]

A second key component of the Front's strategy was to develop support among the peasant population – a group marginalized by the Diem regime. In order to accomplish this, members often lived among the peasants and assisted them with their daily labour. In addition, the NLF often chose victims whose assassination would appeal to the peasants, while others were eliminated to reduce the government's ability to function in the countryside. George Carver, a CIA operative, described the impact of the Front's activities as a steadily growing 'pattern of politically motivated terror' which constituted a serious threat to South Vietnam's political stability.[15]

By 1960 the Diem regime faced a rapidly deteriorating security situation. The government controlled less than 50 per cent of the population of South

Vietnam. To make matters worse, in April a group of leading anti-communists issued the Caravelle Manifesto, a public critique of the government, and in November a failed coup resulted in nearly 400 deaths. As the NLF's campaign in the countryside gained momentum, Diem sought to regain the initiative. The United States, recognizing the severity of the situation, doubled down on its commitment. In November of 1961, the administration of John F. Kennedy issued National Security Action Memorandum (NSAM) 111 which called for 'a sharply increased joint effort' to defend the Republic of Vietnam (RVN) against communist aggression.[16]

Diem's challenges were threefold. He had to establish government authority in rural areas that in some cases had been under communist control since the First Indochina War. At the same time, he had to build a modern nation and stable government. And, he had to do both in such a way that he ensured the continued support of the United States, South Vietnam's key external backer which at the time was pushing him to implement far-reaching reforms. The question of how to use US aid without appearing to be a US puppet also weighed heavily on the president.

Announced in April of 1962, the Strategic Hamlet Program was the government's main effort for meeting the communist challenge. Of the programme, Diem said:

> This vast movement, born in the heat of war, is our preemptory reply to the Communist challenge. ... The strategic hamlet is also and primarily the point of impact of a political and social revolution which will serve as a foundation of our economic revolution.[17]

In what would today be referred to as a whole-of-government approach, the intent of the programme was to bring the full weight of the national government to bear at the village level in a collaborative effort to protect the peasantry and improve their overall quality of life.

The operational situation

At the operational level, the Strategic Hamlet Program pitted the Diem regime against the insurgents in the critically important rural areas of South Vietnam. Approximately 88 per cent of South Vietnam's population, estimated at 13,882,573 in 1960, lived in the countryside and most were engaged in agricultural pursuits.[18] There were vast regional variations in terms of administration, and organization. Traditionally, the village was the lowest level of political and administrative autonomy. The typical village had a village council, consisting of at least three officials, to handle administrative, security and financial matters. While the average village contained 4,447 individuals, the smallest reported 35 inhabitants and the largest 91,308.[19] Villages were typically subdivided into three to five semi-autonomous communities known as hamlets, which also displayed great variation in organization. On average, hamlets contained from 300 to 500 inhabitants with a single administrative official, the hamlet chief, though the largest hamlets contained 17,000 individuals.[20]

Despite regional variations, Bernard Fall, one of the leading experts on Indochina in the 1950s and early 1960s, observed that land tenure was by far the most important issue at the village level throughout South Vietnam. Two per cent of landowners, often absentee landlords, controlled 72 percent of the population held only 15 percent of the arable land. The majority of the population did not own the land they worked. He observed that the contest between the government and the NLF was at heart a battle of competing land reform programmes, and the side that came closest to meeting the peasants' needs was most likely to win.[21] The communist programme was relatively straightforward; they took land from the landlords and issued certificates of ownership to the peasants who actually worked the land. Any government programme that failed to adequately address land ownership would fail to secure the loyalty of the peasantry.

As described above, the communists had deep roots in the villages. The Diem regime had not completely ignored the countryside. Between 1954 and 1956, South Vietnam, with assistance from the United States, resettled approximately 605,000 refugees from the north in 319 villages in rural areas throughout the country as well as an additional 300,000 in urban areas. The post-Geneva programme gave the regime confidence in its ability to conduct resettlement on a massive scale.[22]

Furthermore, in 1959 the government began building agrovilles, the immediate precursor of the Strategic Hamlet Program. Agrovilles were intended to reduce communist access and protect local government officials by moving people from widely dispersed communities into concentrated centres of 300–500 families. The new villages, situated along lines of communication, made the people more accessible to government representatives. In this way the government could provide security and services while also controlling the population. The agrovilles were deeply unpopular. The peasants' old homes had been surrounded by gardens and trees with easy access to rice fields and family tombs. The new sites were often relatively barren and lacked easy access to the same. The government also required forced labour, a holdover from the colonial era and permitted easier access by landlords and tax collectors. Instances of soldiers committing rape, poor sanitation, and corrupt officials were also reported. By 1960, in response to negative reports, the regime slowed the programme and began searching for alternatives.[23]

Diem and Nhu cast a wide net in their effort to improve RVN efforts in the countryside. As reported by John B. O'Donnell, the US Operations Mission Provincial Representative for Kien Hoa Province from 1962 to 1964, the details were worked out by Vietnamese officials, including a number of former Viet Minh agents. In the process, they consulted the

Malayan and Philippine models, French practices in Algeria and Indochina, as well as previous Vietnamese schemes both nationalist and communist.[24] William C. Colby, the CIA Station Chief at the time, recalled Nhu reading extensively on counterinsurgency practices. Colby also kept Nhu informed of experimental efforts on the part of the CIA and US Special Operations Forces to help villages develop self-defence forces.[25] Historian Edward G. Miller noted the influence of French counterinsurgent Roger Trinquier who used the term 'strategic hamlets' to describe fortified Algerian villages.[26] In Miller's opinion, Trinquier's *La Guerre Moderne* (Modern Warfare) published in 1961, provided the blueprint for strategic hamlets.

What would differentiate the programme from previous models would be the improved quality of life in strategic hamlets. The goal was to use the power of attraction to make peasants participate voluntarily and enthusiastically. It is perhaps in this regard that the influence of former Viet Minh cadres and communist propaganda was most evident. Official government statements on the project made repeated references to revolution. Nhu, for example, said of the hamlets: 'The system of Strategic Hamlets is a revolutionary system. ... Strategic hamlets seek to assure the security of the people in order that the success of the political, social and military revolution might be assured by an enthusiastic movement of solidarity and self-sufficiency.' Furthermore, 'The achievement of a military, political, economic, and social revolution at the hamlet level is the present goal of the Government of the Republic of Viet Nam.'[27] The government's overall objective was to counter the communist revolutionary programme with its own revolutionary programme. The Diem regime believed the agroville concept was sound but implementation needed to be improved. The peasantry found it difficult to differentiate between the programmes.

Contrary to popular belief, the Strategic Hamlet Program was a South Vietnamese operation. At the time, and later, the programme was often credited to Sir Robert Thompson, formerly a staff officer during the Malayan Emergency and head of British Advisory Mission to Vietnam beginning in 1961. That year Thompson authored Delta Plan based in part on his earlier successes in Malaya as well as tours of the South Vietnamese countryside. Others credited US officials such as Roger Hilsman a former Office of Strategic Services operator in Asia during the Second World War who served as the State Department's Director of the Bureau of Intelligence and Research from 1961 to 1963, though Hilsman's own 'Strategic Concept for Vietnam', completed in early 1962, credited Thompson with the basic approach.[28]

In truth, Thompson's Delta Plan was only one influence among many. The similarity in goals – establishing security in rural areas followed by the delivery of government services – masked key differences between the Malayan model and the Strategic Hamlet Program, the most important being the role of resettlement. Nhu disliked the resettlement aspect of agrovilles because it bred resentment. Nhu believed that 'instead of herding people into "agricultural towns," the government needed to figure out how to reorganize and defend South Vietnam's existing villages and hamlets'.[29] Government statements on the topic were clear: 'The Strategic Hamlet Scheme calls for the building of defense works around existing villages.'[30] Local officials could resort to involuntary relocation in the implementation phase, but it was not the stated purpose of the programme.

In contrast, population resettlement was central to both Thompson's and Hilsman's plans. Thompson later recalled that for the RVN to be successful they would need to resettle at least 25 per cent of South Vietnam's population.[31] The worse the security situation the more Regroupement would be required. Similarly, Hilsman held that 'the creation of strategic villages in relatively secure areas involves the Regroupement of village hamlets into one compact, easily defended area'.[32] In essence, South Vietnam's allies advocated the resettlement of millions of peasants by a government that had no effective control over many of the areas in question. As evidenced by Nhu's statements above, the regime rejected this approach.

Phasing, scope and how much emphasis to place on population control were also contentious issues. In line with the 'ink blot' or 'oil spot' theory of counterinsurgency, the British favoured a methodical approach whereby the government started in secure areas and worked its way outwards from positions of strength. Government forces would not move on to the next hamlet until the preceding hamlet was secure. Thompson also argued that the regime should prioritize its efforts and begin with the Mekong Delta, economically the most important area of the country. For their part, the Americans favoured situating hamlets in key strategic locations such as near base areas or along vital lines of communication. Both the British and Americans agreed on population control in the form of censuses, identification cards and like measures. The Diem regime, on the other hand, wanted to build as many hamlets as possible throughout the country as quickly as possible. While the approach alarmed the British, the Americans were less concerned in light of their penchant for statistics and quantitative results. Furthermore, Saigon, at least in theory, preferred persuasion over control measures. The fences, moats and checkpoints were to keep the VC out, not inconvenience peasants.

There were also civil-military differences on the subject. Most senior Military Assistance Command, Vietnam (MACV) and ARVN officers wanted to minimize the ARVN's role in pacification in order to focus on conventional operations. Fearing a Korean War scenario, officers believed the primary threat to government survival was conventional North Vietnamese units invading from the north, not a home-grown insurgency. Thus, the ARVN's seven divisions were deployed to counter an invasion and trained to conduct large-scale combined arms operations. Military leaders also preferred to keep ARVN soldiers out of heavily populated areas so as to bring firepower advantages to bear while minimizing the chances of civilian casualties. Such views differed from civilian leaders and the handful of military advisers who believed insurgents at the village level should be the ARVN's primary target.[33] For the military, the priority of effort remained conventional operations.[34]

American civilian officials, on the other hand, tended to favour pacification programmes that stressed the political, economic and social aspects of the conflict. The perception of US vulnerability in the Third World with respect to its Cold War adversary was heightened by Nikita Khrushchev's famed 'Wars of National Liberation' speech delivered only two weeks prior to Kennedy's inauguration in January of 1961. The Soviet Premier highlighted recent successes achieved by the North Vietnamese and the Cubans, argued that such wars of national liberation were the wave of the future and pledged Soviet support for anti-colonial revolutionaries 'wholeheartedly and without reservations'.[35]

With nationalism, decolonization and what was often referred to as the 'revolution of rising expectations' spreading rapidly in the Third World, the Kennedy administration turned to the related concepts of modernization and counterinsurgency.[36] As outlined by Walt Rostow, an economist and special assistant to the president, modernization theory held that the United States could guide the processes of change sweeping the developing world and prevent communism from taking root.[37] The theory assumed that the United States, the most modern of nations, could channel revolutionary tendencies in 'traditional' societies and mould them in its own image through the measured application of US know-how and resources. According to its official policy statements, modernization held a special place in meeting the administration's overarching goal of regaining the initiative in 'the contest between communism and the Free World for primary influence over the direction and outcome of the development process'.[38]

Because communist insurgencies were active in many of the nations most in need of development, a key question emerged: How can a country modernize in the face of internal threats? The answer, counterinsurgency, paired modernization with the security initiatives required to protect it. As articulated by Secretary of State Dean Rusk, Americans had to do more than simply promote development through peaceful means; they also had to serve as the 'guardians of the development process'.[39]

Douglas Blaufarb, a CIA operations officer from 1950 to 1970, referred to Kennedy's first few months in office as 'the crucible for the policies that came to be called counterinsurgency'.[40] From the civilian perspective, the Strategic Hamlets represented a perfect example of the 'hearts and minds' approach to counterinsurgency, which he described as follows:

> An effective combination of measures of which security was a sine qua non, and that, in turn, was the product of coordinated intelligence and of local defense linked by good communications to paramilitary and military formations. Responsive government then could perform its necessary function of improving conditions of village life in ways that

answered felt needs. From this combination would come the commitment of the villagers to the cause of the government, for it would then be their own cause.

Such an approach was in sharp contrast to the views of the Army Chief of Staff, who in 1962 stated that the United States was in Vietnam to support military efforts that were primarily conventional in nature: 'It is fashionable in some quarters to say that the problems in Southeast Asia are primarily political and economic rather than military. I do not agree. The essence of the problem in Vietnam is military.'[41] Writing nearly two decades after the fact, two South Vietnamese officers acknowledged that the civilian assessment was more accurate. North Vietnam had likewise learned from the Korean War and had no intention of invading the South in the early 1960s. The real war was in the villages. It was Diem, not his American military advisers, who had correctly surmised the enemy's intentions.[42] Ultimately, the differences over the programme on the part of the civilians and the military as well as those between the Vietnamese and their foreign advisers were so great that Ngo Dinh Nhu described the situation as a 'clash of civilizations'.[43]

Despite differences of opinion there was enough overlap for all parties to conclude that they were moving in the same general direction. There was a shared vision of providing security assistance and civic action in the countryside but no common operational plan. In January of 1962, the Diem regime declared the Strategic Hamlet Program its top priority and its official pacification programme. Ongoing hamlet defence initiatives were subsumed under the programme. On 3 February 1962 Diem created the Inter-Ministerial Committee for Strategic Hamlets (IMCSH) comprised of the ministers of interior, civic action, education and rural affairs, as well as high ranking defence and law enforcement personnel. The president's brother, Counsellor Nhu, was the de facto head of the committee. Thus, the programme, at least conceptually, represented a whole-of-government approach that received attention at the highest levels of government.[44] Any and all ongoing pacification initiatives now fell under the programme and 1962 was declared the 'Year of the Strategic Hamlets'.[45]

The Strategic Hamlet Campaign

The government's goals were incredibly ambitious – the completion of 11,000 to 12,000 hamlets by 1964 that would protect the entirety of South Vietnam's rural population of roughly 13 million individuals.[46] That said, achieving these goals did not require resettling thirteen million people. Ideally, a hamlet could be secured and labelled 'strategic' without moving it. As mentioned above, Saigon tracked the number of completed strategic hamlets and the population living in them rather than the number of hamlets or peasants relocated. A common misconception at the time and up through the present was to look at the total number reported as living in strategic hamlets and conclude that they all had been resettled. More accurate estimates place the number relocated in the hundreds of thousands.[47]

The general plan for implementation called for the ARVN to move into an area and clear it of communist forces. The ARVN would then remain on site long enough to form local security forces and initiate civic action programmes. During this first phase, defences would be constructed in the form of moats, gates, barbed wire and bamboo fences, stockades and guard towers. The ARVN would also help to organize and train local militias, known as Self-Defense Corps (SDC), made up of hamlet residents and provide them with sufficient weapons and communications equipment. The SDC would be tied into a tiered security apparatus, with the Civil Guard operating at the district and province levels. The SDC was also expected to coordinate its actions with the local police. In theory, the various elements of the security apparatus would be integrated and mutually supporting down to the hamlet level.

According to the blueprint, once an area was cleared, Civic Action Teams took responsibility for providing services. The teams consisted of three elements, one focused on gathering intelligence and identifying VC agents, another for organizing labour and a third charged with political and propaganda activities. Economic efforts were focused on improving yields by introducing new varieties of crops, livestock and fertilizers, as well as improved methods for insect and rodent control. The two most commonly mentioned social programmes were the building of medical dispensaries and schools. The overall intent was to show the people that the Diem regime offered a better quality of life than the communists.[48] In order to provide security and deliver services, the Civic Action Teams, as well as administrators at the province, village and hamlet levels were authorized to relocate civilians. Here again, the quality of life in the new hamlet was supposed to be better than in existing hamlets. In addition, any civilians who had to move were to be compensated.

While the economic and social aspects were relatively straightforward, the political programme was not. The political cadres were expected to educate the people on their government and inspire them to actively support the regime. The regime's political philosophy, Vietnamese personalism, was a confusing and esoteric hodgepodge of Eastern and Western influences.[49] Political cadres, most of whom lacked a high school education and had only a few days of training, found it difficult to translate personalism into terms villagers could understand. At the hamlet level, democracy was understood to be elections for Hamlet Chiefs and participation in deliberations on hamlet matters.

For its part, the United States provided the financial and material backing for the programme. In many cases, young, idealistic US Agency for International Development (AID) officers were assigned to distribute aid in such a way as to advance the programme. As Rufus Phillips recalled, guidelines published in 1963 stressed the importance of helping peasants realize their dreams of a better life and making strategic hamlets something villagers were willing to risk their lives for.[50] Accordingly, in early 1962 US AID created the special office for Rural Affairs (Counter-Insurgency) within the US Operations Mission (USOM)/Saigon, to serve as the action unit in support of the Strategic Hamlet Program. US AID representatives were assigned at the national and province level to coordinate activities between the Vietnamese government and US military and civilian entities. Agents were expected to work with province chiefs to draft comprehensive provincial rehabilitation plans with estimates of resources needed for the hamlet programme. An initial US$10,000,000 was made available to get the programme off the ground.[51]

Because implementation was a local matter, it is useful to examine illustrative examples to gain an appreciation for regional variations and commonalities. Operation Sunrise, considered the first strategic hamlet operation launched after the official announcement of the programme, began on 19 March 1962 in Binh Duong province, which bordered Saigon to the North. The area selected was a hotbed of insurgent activity and had been under communist control since 1945. At no point since had the government been able to administer the province at the village level and below. Pacification efforts in the area had predated the Strategic Hamlet Program but were subsumed under it from 1962 on. Interestingly, Thompson recommended starting in a more secure area while the Americans advocated for concentrating on Binh Duong because it was an enemy stronghold and important geographically, though the Americans also recommended focusing solely on Bing Duong.[52]

Despite Nhu's statements against resettlement, Diem authorized severe methods in the area due to its VC leanings. In Ben Tuong, the first hamlet constructed, more than 200 families, approximately 1,000 people total, were relocated over the course of several days in a haphazard manner. Follow-on operations were no better. A British military attaché regarded the 'regroupements' as 'extremely badly conducted … with little or no consideration being given to the people or their wants'.[53] Those villagers who could not be persuaded were moved by force, and in some cases their previous homes were burned by soldiers.

John Donnell and Gerald Hickey, two RAND consultants with extensive experience in Vietnam and who were personally supportive of the programme, were surprised by the level of resentment they encountered during an inspection of the province. In their official report, they wrote that the relocated families were 'very dissatisfied', particularly by the forced labour requirements. To make matters worse, forced labour requirements took farmers away from own fields. One farmer termed the loss in income a personal 'defeat'. It is worth noting that unpaid, forced labour, also known as corvée labour, was a practice long associated with the French. In addition, payments promised to relocated families were not made.[54] Other complaints included high rents and taxes, the distance of hamlets from rice fields and the conscription of local youth. As a result of peasant dissatisfaction, the VC moved freely throughout the area.

Donnell and Hickey concluded: 'In the present war, the Vietnamese peasant is likely to support the side that has control of the area in which he lives, and he is more favourably disposed to the side which offers him the possibility of a better life.'[55] The report ended, however, by observing: 'In the Operation Sunrise region, in particular, farmers were unwilling to express enthusiasm for the program and appeared to harbour strong doubts that the sacrifices of labour and materials imposed on them could yield any commensurate satisfaction.'[56]

The operation also bogged down due to security challenges. The ARVN could not move on to new areas without leaving others unsecure. There were relatively few men of fighting age in the hamlets. Many had already joined the VC or the ARVN, others fled, leaving many communities without the manpower to defend themselves. For its part, the ARVN did not want to be tied down in the countryside. Over time, the ARVN and provincial security forces slowly pulled back into the larger towns and cities or were redeployed to protect key infrastructure. The government only controlled those areas where it had forces; the hamlet militia never reached the required degree of military effectiveness.[57]

Initially, the programme made it harder for the VC to operate. Insurgents had difficulties accessing the population, particularly in those areas with high concentrations of government forces. They also had to reorganize themselves to adjust to the increased government presence and new settlement patterns. These advantages for the government, however, were fleeting. According to an Australian military observer, there was no real improvement in the security situation once you looked 'below the smooth and artificial surface'.[58] In time, it becomes obvious that local officials could not meet either goal – security or services.

The shortcomings noted above did not bode well for the programme as a whole. In Binh Duong province, the government proved incapable of securing the loyalties of the rural population. Ben Tuong, the first strategic hamlet constructed, would be overrun by insurgents on 20 August 1963. As Krepinevich concluded, 'Operation SUNRISE was a microcosm of the Strategic Hamlets program, for the shortcomings of this first operation were extended and repeated again and again over the life of the program.'[59]

A slightly different situation pertained in Kien Hoa Province, located about 80 kilometres south of Saigon. John O'Donnell, a US AID Provincial Representative in Kien Hoa from December 1962 to August 1964 described the region as a top priority for both the NLF and the Diem regime due to its agricultural productivity. Under the Strategic Hamlet Program, the Diem regime hoped that efforts in Kien Hoa would serve as a model for the Mekong Delta. The insurgents, however, had deep roots in the region. Many Viet Minh cadre had gone underground in 1954.

Those who did go north retained close family ties to the region. As anti-communist repression increased in the late 1950s, many cadres returned while others went north for training in preparation for the resumption of hostilities. As the VC presence increased so too did attacks on government officials. By 1961, the VC goal was to push government forces out of the countryside and into the cities where it was expected that the government would collapse under its own weight. The government, on the other hand, sought to force the VC back to remote base areas where it would wither and die. To that end, Diem assigned a former Viet Minh officer, Major Tran Ngoc Chau, as province chief. Chau began with a careful study of the situation from May to October of 1962. He then secured funds for local development projects based on the expressed needs of the population. According to O'Donnell, Chau was effective because he empowered his subordinates to improve the quality of life for hamlet residents: 'The struggle was at the grass roots level, and it was the sine qua non of the Strategic Hamlet Program that the administration of the means to carry out the program be placed at the lowest practicable level.'[60] While Chau was successful in terms of securing the loyalties of villagers, Saigon considered his approach too slow and methodical, and he was criticized for not building hamlets quickly enough. In time, O'Donnell came to see that Chau was an outlier; far too few local officials were as committed or competent.

O'Donnell described a pattern of acceleration and overextension throughout the Mekong Delta: 'The intangibles involved in changing a person's mind, which was the primary aim of the Strategic Hamlet Program, were often sidetracked or lost in the rush to *get things done*.'[61] Many supposedly completed hamlets quickly collapsed in summer and fall of 1963. The programme had worked to a degree, but only when local officials such as Chau made a concerted and measured effort to respond to the needs of the population. According to O'Donnell, 'The Viet Cong in Kien Hoa Province, and in South Vietnam in general, were far ahead of their opponents in understanding the political and psychological nature of the struggle and exploiting the grievances and aspirations of the peasants.'[62]

Overextension was likewise evident in Long An province, also in the Mekong Delta region south of Saigon. Here, the communist apparatus was similarly firmly entrenched. Major Nguyen Viet Thanh, the province chief in Long An during the execution of the Strategic Hamlet Program arrived in the autumn of 1961. Initially, security was so bad he could not leave the province capital without taking fire. The insurgent political apparatus proved too strong to counter with the resources available. Thanh did not have enough troops or resources to arm, train and pay local forces to defend themselves. He would eventually resort to a 'massive relocation effort' but still could not eliminate the insurgency. In hindsight, such efforts were counterproductive. More relocations and more new hamlets only served to increase demands on limited resources.[63]

Corrupt and ineffective cadres also hindered execution. Mai Ngoc Duoc, a province chief from 1957 to 1961, remarked: 'The very best fertilizer for the communist apparatus is injustice and corruption. If a country can eliminate injustice and corruption – if it can clean out its government – then the communists cannot develop.'[64] This would prove a bridge too far. As Duoc explained to Jeffrey Race, whose book *War Comes to Long An* is regarded as one of best studies of insurgency at the local level: 'First and foremost, we must admit that the cadres were corrupt. If ten bags of cement were given out in Saigon, only one or two would actually be distributed.'[65] A village chief expressed similar sentiments in an interview with Race:

> During the Diem period the people here saw that the government was no good at all. That is why maybe 80 percent of them followed the VC. I was the village chief then, I just had to do what the government told me. If not, the secret police would have picked me up and tortured me to death. Thus, I was the very one who rigged the elections here.[66]

Thanh, the province chief mentioned above, was himself relieved in mid-1963 for refusing to rig an election. For their part, the communists eliminated effective local officials and protected the corrupt ones. They also targeted teachers and classified them as traitors for elimination. As the most politically astute and aware government officials, teachers were often the best able to explain any deficiencies in the communist programme.[67]

Unpopular government policies, notably the draft, also fuelled the insurgency and worked against the Strategic Hamlet Program. Conscription into the ARVN meant non-local service. Many young men joined the VC as protection against the draft. Taxes also bred resentment. Because the Strategic Hamlet Program provided government access to the people, many villagers came to associate the programme with conscription, taxes and rent, none of which were likely to inspire loyalty. But perhaps the biggest shortcoming when it came to government presence was 'talking a lot but not doing anything', according to one official.[68] The Viet Minh and later the VC had already divided the land better than the government could have. Land was the central issue and government programmes fell short compared to the communist programme. One captured communist document reported that peasants were willing to fight to the death to retain land given to them by the communists.[69]

Race concluded that the Strategic Hamlet Program failed to inspire loyalty because it reinforced existing political, social and economic arrangements that the majority of the population found unappealing. It was premised on self-defence but the peasants were not willing to fight for what the government was offering.[70] By the summer of 1963, the VC were undermining the programme throughout Long An by assassinating officials and attacking hamlets. The hamlet militias offered no resistance.[71]

As evidenced by the cases above as well as other local studies, several trends emerged in the execution phase that did not bode well for the Strategic Hamlet Program. The first was a tendency towards overextension and an overall lack of coordination. Rather than prioritize or take a measured approach the Diem regime implemented the programme throughout the entirety of the country simultaneously. Such a massive undertaking was difficult to resource and coordinate. Sir Robert Thompson reported in September of 1963 that nearly 5,500 hamlets had been constructed in the previous year. Thompson notes that in Malaya, it took 3 years to construct 500 villages, more than 8,000 in South Vietnam in less than 2 years.[72] His conclusion, one which he reported to Diem was 'that the strategic hamlet programme had now gone too fast, with a consequent dispersal of effort and a scattering of hamlets over too wide an area'.[73]

The second trend was the harsh manner in which resettlement took place. Two senior South Vietnamese officers recalled peasants being rounded up and moved against their will to new hamlets that lacked even the most rudimentary of support facilities. In their opinion, by foregoing voluntary participation, which they considered essential, government actions ensured that 'the strategic hamlet people found themselves living in a state of repressed feelings, suspicion and frustration'.[74] To make matters worse, government agents often lacked the resources to deliver on promises. According to many observers, it was not resettlement that angered people but rather the government's failure to live up to the promises made following resettlement – land, funds, security and so on. The premise of the programme was that quality of life would be better in strategic hamlets; the programme fell apart when this proved not to be the case. Media and propaganda likened the hamlets to 'concentration camps' at a time – less than two decades removed from the Second World War – when the Holocaust was much more vivid in the collective memory.[75]

Third, the government did not have enough committed and loyal cadres to execute the programme on the scale desired. As O'Donnell observed, 'The degree of progress in any given area depended to a great extent on the ability, honesty, and sincerity of the local officials.'[76]

Unfortunately for the government, the VC often killed competent or popular officials and left the inept and corrupt ones untouched. In O'Donnell's estimation, capable government representatives at the local level were the insurgents' 'number one enemy'.[77] Those who existed were often fighting an uphill battle. Major Chau recalled that communist cadres in his area of operations were viewed as direct representatives of Ho Chi Minh and seen as liberators as a result of the role they played in the defeat of the French. He and the other representatives of the Diem government were associated with colonialism and were viewed as oppressors.[78] The difficulty in finding loyal cadre was perhaps best evidenced by Colonel Pham Ngoc Thao, one of Counsellor Nhu's top aides and a senior player in the programme. After the war, the North Vietnamese made it known that

Thao had been a communist sleeper agent who had urged the acceleration of the programme in order to foster resentment and destabilize the regime.[79]

A fourth trend that hampered implementation was erroneous and overly optimistic reporting. From the outset, the measure of effectiveness within a given province or district was the total number of strategic hamlets within its borders. Local officials were incentivized to declare a hamlet 'strategic' as quickly as possible regardless of whether sufficient defences had been constructed or government services delivered. They were often punished or rewarded based on self-reported numbers which provided ample reason to exaggerate totals. It was also difficult to measure support for the government among the villagers, the Diem regime's ultimate objective. When questioned, the typical Vietnamese peasant often chose the path of least resistance and told their interlocutors what they thought the authorities would want to hear. Furthermore, available data could be interpreted differently. For example, as the number of hamlets increased there was a decrease in the number of VC attacks with less than 0.2 per cent being reported as overrun. The Joint Chiefs of Staff viewed this as an indication of success while Thompson concluded that the communists had either infiltrated the villages or did not consider them a threat.[80] Statistics on total hamlets constructed were also open to interpretation. The Diem regime celebrated the fact that nearly 8,000 hamlets were constructed by mid-1963 while the Americans considered it evidence of overextension. The lack of accurate data was yet another factor that hampered successful implementation of the programme.

A final factor, and perhaps the most important, was the effectiveness of the communist strategy that the Strategic Hamlet Program was attempting to counter. Although initially caught off guard, the communists recognized the effort as a threat to their freedom of movement and access to the population and took concrete steps to undermine the programme. The VC leadership outlined its response in a document released to local communist leaders in late 1962. Specific actions included encouraging military-aged males to leave the hamlets so that nobody would be available for the hamlet defence forces, a key tenet of the government's programme. Local communists were also encouraged to establish Viet Cong-controlled settlements just beyond the reach of government forces which offered a better alternative to the Strategic Hamlets, thereby enticing villagers to abandon government-controlled areas. Additionally, communist forces were encouraged to step up terrorist actions in major population centres to draw government security forces away from the countryside. Thus, while the Strategic Hamlets may have been an effective counter to communist efforts in 1961, the programme elicited a determined enemy response which the government was unable to meet.[81]

The enemy's capacity for adaptation was due mainly to the strength of its organization. In accordance with Maoist doctrine, the communists emphasized political organizing at the local level and had been doing so for nearly two decades in some areas. On this subject, Douglas Pike, a leading expert on communist strategy, wrote, 'The secret of success, since the enemy obviously can emulate technique, is superior organization to permit fuller mobilization. What is launched, in fact, is a war of competing organizational weapons. The rule becomes this: Victory will go to the side that becomes the best organized, stays the best organized, and most successfully disorganizes his opponent.'[82] Ultimately, it was the insurgents who did a better job. In most rural areas they were able to offer a fully developed alternative to RVN governance; an alternative that a critical mass of villagers considered to be better able to meet their needs.

Pike also noted the different conceptions of time held by the different parties to the conflict. In communist doctrine,

> The struggle is deliberately drawn out in time since that is the best way to enervate and dishearten the enemy. ... The objective is to gradually change the tide of the struggle and the balance of forces, increasing the tempo of the political struggle and the magnitude of the armed struggle, until it is possible to seek, fight, and win the final battle.[83]

All things considered, the communist approach was far more measured and thoughtful than the government programme, which attempted to build as many defended hamlets as quickly as possible.

The communist's strategic patience and level of commitment far exceeded that displayed by their South Vietnamese opponents. By comparison, the average South Vietnamese citizen did not view their government as something worth sacrificing for. One gets a sense of the level of commitment from the writings and statements of leading officials such as Ho Chi Minh, Vo Nguyen Giap and Pham Van Dong, who on numerous occasions expressed their willingness to fight for ten, twenty, even fifty years if necessary. Furthermore, research shows that a similar level of commitment was expressed by common soldiers and the civilian population as well.[84]

In light of the tenacity exhibited by the insurgency, it was imperative that the government ensures that villagers were adequately prepared to defend themselves. The Diem regime fell short in this area. According to the government's own reports, in April of 1963, of the 197,858 combatant youths responsible for defending the hamlets, only 60,496, less than a third, received any training, and of those, only 19,879 were actually armed.[85] The dearth of weapons was matched by shortages of other important supplies, notably barbed wire.

By comparison, a report signed by Roger Hilsman in December of 1962 noted that communist forces appeared to be getting stronger. While he thought the strategic hamlets had had some positive effects, 'the "national liberation war" has not abated nor has the Viet Cong been weakened'. In fact, they either controlled or had a degree of influence in 67 per cent of South Vietnam's villages.[86] The most visible expression of anti-Diem sentiment was the Buddhist crisis between May and November 1963, a period of political turmoil characterized by popular protests led by Buddhist monks followed by government repression. The crisis, along with the Strategic Hamlet Program, ended on 2 November 1963 when ARVN officers staged a coup d'etat and murdered Diem and Nhu in the back of an armoured car.

The political turmoil that preceded Diem's death, his murder and the series of coups and countercoups which followed were disastrous for the overall government programme in the countryside. Nguyen Cong Luan, a South Vietnamese officer involved in pacification, recalled that after the Diem regime collapsed, operatives in the field had no direction when it came to the hamlets; when he inquired he was told the leadership was still deliberating. In the meantime, the communists took advantage of the situation and many hamlets were destroyed or deserted. In Pleiku province, for example, ten of twenty-five hamlets were deserted. In Luan's opinion, abandonment of the programme was disastrous. Despite its shortcoming he considered it the government's best bid for long-term success and a lost opportunity.[87]

The military outcomes

Up through the summer of 1963, the Diem regime considered the programme a great success. On 7 July 1963, for example, President Diem reported that 8,150,187 peasants were then living in hamlets. Although there were significant discrepancies in the statistics. Diem's numbers were three million higher than those provided by his own Minister for the Interior. The Pentagon for its part reported numbers in excess of Diem's – 8.5 million people living in 7,205 strategic hamlets.[88] In the United States, Kennedy administration officials used the program as evidence that US efforts were bearing fruit and praised the program before House and Senate committees. For his part, President Kennedy cited the program as a reason for optimism in late 1962.[89]

Rosy statistics aside, following the coup it quickly became obvious to all that as a military campaign, the Strategic Hamlet Program was a complete failure. William Colby later recalled how the military junta that took over after Diem's murder likened the hamlets to concentration camps and replaced nearly all officials at the province, district and village levels; a process that was repeated when yet another group of officers overthrew the the first group only three months later. As Colby recalled, the communists took advantage of the instability to reassert their control in the countryside and destroy any support for the strategic hamlet concept among the rural population.[90] Journalist Stanley Karnow visited Long An in late 1963 and found the programme 'in shambles' with the defences destroyed and most of the peasants having returned to their original hamlets. Strategic hamlets that had been built the previous year looked like they 'had been hit by a hurricane'.[91]

One of the starkest testaments to the military failure of the Strategic Hamlet Program was National Security Action Memorandum 288. An attached memo from Secretary McNamara to President Johnson provided an assessment of the security situation in South Vietnam in early 1964. It describes a population that was apathetic and confused and security forces plagued by low morale and desertion. Of note, a memo written in March of 1964 concluded that the Viet Cong controlled 90 per cent of Binh Duong, Long An and Kien Hoa Provinces – areas that had received considerable government attention as outlined above.[92]

In a strictly military sense, the failure of the campaign can be attributed to a fundamental disagreement between civilian and military officials on the character of the war. According to Rufe Phillips whose views were representative of the civilian faction, the Strategic Hamlet Program's social and economic initiatives were frustrated by the heavy-handed approach of South Vietnamese military forces and their American advisers. He recounted the indiscriminate burning, shelling and bombing of villages as part of so-called search and destroy operations, a technique promoted by MACV.[93] Any goodwill engendered by the Strategic Hamlet Program often evaporated when military forces used excessive firepower. Despite Diem's orders and pronouncements, the military never accepted counterinsurgency, or a hearts and minds approach, as the main effort.

To truly appreciate why the campaign failed, however, one must look to the economic and political spheres. The programme was much more than a military campaign. It was intended to facilitate sweeping political, economic and social change. Military action was only intended to establish security in order to facilitate civic action. For the South Vietnamese nation-building project to succeed, the villagers had to view the Diem regime as legitimate and something worth fighting for. At a time when the communists prioritized the political aspects of the struggle, most observers found the political aspects and ideological underpinnings of the Strategic Hamlet Program confusing. Furthermore, the government failed to deliver on democratic reforms, the one aspect of its programme that was generally understood. In their post-mortem analyses, a number of mid-level officials, referred to democracy as the one thing that could have shifted the peasants' loyalties to the government.[94]

In the absence of any real change, villagers often regarded the Diem regime and its American backers as an extension of French colonialism; a logical conclusion considering the number of senior officials who had previously served in the colonial administration. Thus, the villagers were inclined to see policies emanating from Saigon as exploitative and repressive.[95] Under the auspices of Law 10/59, the government resorted to brutal tactics to maintain itself in power. The national police, the military and the Can Lao were employed to root out suspected insurgents and possible opposition leaders. While some targets were communists, others had simply made the mistake of expressing their displeasure with the regime or failed to express sufficient loyalty. By 1963, it was estimated that from 20,000 to 40,000 political detainees were being held in various government detention centres.[96] In addition, politically motivated murders were not uncommon. Public outrage at such incidents reached an unprecedented level by 1963 and ultimately contributed to Diem's downfall and the end of the Strategic Hamlet Program.

Additionally, the government's inability to address the central issue of land ownership hamstrung any chance for success in the countryside. Early and effective land reform was the best hope for the Diem regime and for South Vietnam writ large. In this regard, one of the most important shortcomings of the Strategic Hamlet Program was that while it moved peasants in some cases and disrupted settlement patterns, it did not provide peasants title to the land they worked. For example, in Long An Race calculated that 'less than 3 percent of an estimated 35,000 tenant families profited from the program in time for it to benefit the government'.[97] By comparison, the communists, in order to build political support, set aside calls for collectivization and redistributed land to the people who worked it. No element of the Strategic Hamlet Program inspired the loyalty of the peasantry to the degree that the communists' land distribution did.

Peasants also saw their rents and taxes increase once the areas they occupied were brought under government control. On the subject of rents and taxes, Race calculated that a family with six children farming two hectares in Long An in 1962 would pay 2400 per cent more under the government's system. All things considered, the average peasant got a far better deal economically under the communists.[98] By delivering on their promises of land ownership and lower taxes, the communists tied the peasantries self-interest to the success of their movement. Race concluded, 'In its overall impact, the revolutionary land program achieved a far broader distribution of land than did the government program.'[99]

No military campaign could solve the political and economic weaknesses and contradictions inherent in the government's programme in the countryside. Saigon's pacification efforts failed in large part because the government was never viewed as legitimate by the peasantry, the target population of the Strategic Hamlet Program. The peasants viewed the ruling elites as a corrupt and distant and never truly dissociated the Diem regime from its French colonial antecedent. When placed side by side, peasants found the insurgents' political and economic programmes more appealing. The communists pledged to reorder society and redistribute wealth and power downward while the actions of the Diem regime preserved the status quo and maintained a structure which villagers regarded as inadequate to their needs.

Conclusion

At best, the Strategic Hamlet Program was a comprehensive effort to fuse the military, economic, social and political spheres. It was fundamentally a Vietnamese programme designed and executed by Vietnamese leaders who were trying to adapt a counterinsurgency practice to local realities. Thus, it had a Vietnamese face, something that subsequent efforts lacked. It also targeted the enemy's centre of gravity – their political and economic organizations in the countryside. According to O'Donnell, the programme as conceived by the regime and executed in Kien Hoa Province 'came close to meeting the requirements for defeating a Communist war of national liberation. ... In areas where the basic problems of land, justice, and truly responsive government were handled well by the local officials, the people were willing to commit themselves to the government.'[100] Vien and Khuyen wrote, 'Regardless of what had been said about it, the strategic hamlet program remained a judicious national policy, a true antidote to Communist subversive and total warfare. Its chief merit lay in the fact that it had been comprehensively designed to improve the people's living standards through socio-economic development at the rice-roots level. It was a sound strategic concept.'[101]

Along these same lines, William Colby regarded the Strategic Hamlet Program as 'a genuinely Vietnamese initiative' which, despite its shortcomings, 'provided a basic strategy for the conduct of the war at the level of the enemy's attack, the rural communities, and it generated a major national and coordinated focus on its fulfilment'.[102] It was perhaps the only time during the war that Saigon seized the initiative and presented a true threat to the communists in the countryside. It was also the last time that counterinsurgency and pacification would take priority over conventional operations, and the last time that the South Vietnamese would be in the lead. It is worth considering what would have happened if the programme had been properly resourced, executed and supported by military.

Despite initial signs of success, the Strategic Hamlet Program ultimately failed. While promising in theory, implementation was problematic and uneven. The effort was hamstrung by a lack of skilled cadres capable of operating at the village level. South Vietnam also faced insurmountable structural weaknesses, particularly those transferred from the colonial system, in combination with a determined adversary. For the Strategic Hamlet Program to be effective would have required a complete restructuring of South Vietnamese society and economy. Although Counsellor Nhu recognized the need for just such a revolution, it could not be realized under the circumstances. Unlike its adversary, the Diem regime lacked both the political programme and committed cadres willing to suffer great hardships to execute it. In the end, the communist programme was simply more appealing to the average peasant.

It is difficult to determine with any accuracy how many peasants were forcibly relocated as a result of the programme. Probably a few hundred thousand of the approximately three million persons displaced by the war. And, unlike other persons displaced by the war, many of those who were moved under the auspices of the Strategic Hamlet Program returned to their original villages by 1964. As regards the deliberate removal of populations, involuntary resettlement, when it did occur, did more to hurt the Strategic Hamlet Program than help it. Forced relocations were, along with forced labour and taxes, one of the least popular aspects of the programme. Relocations garnered negative media attention, fuelled enemy propaganda and were one of the most oft-cited shortcomings of the programme mentioned by those who otherwise supported it. Even ARVN generals noted the 'concentration camp' feel of the hamlets. Relocations were acceptable practice but they were not effective militarily and ran counter to the overall political objective of building government support in rural areas.

The assumption on the part of counterinsurgency theorists such as Thompson and Hilsman, that resettlement would solve the problems presented by the insurgency, was incorrect. Resettlement ultimately aided the enemy by engendering resentment among the target population. In this case, resettlement as a tactic, much like indiscriminate bombing, alienated the very population the GVN was trying to win over. Counsellor Nhu, for all his faults, recognized the fundamental truth that people do not like to be moved against their will. The programme relocated people but never adequately addressed the underlying issue of land ownership. One could argue that the regime would have inspired far more loyalty had it left peasants where they were and granted them ownership of the land they worked.

The Strategic Hamlet Program was admirable in that it attempted to contest the insurgency in rural areas but ultimately could not match the strength of the enemy's programme. The Diem regime and its American advisers failed to offer a viable political and economic alternative to the communists. The failure of the programme had serious consequences for the United States. It was the centrepiece of the partnership and of US counterinsurgency efforts in the early 1960s. The deteriorating security situation following Diem's death would in time lead to the Americanization of the war, an effort which ultimately ended in failure with the reunification of the country under communist control in 1975.

Notes

1 Pamphlet, 'Viet Nam's Strategic Hamlets', February 1963, Saigon, Directorate General of Information, front matter.
2 Estimates of the number of villages and hamlets found in Lloyd W. Woodruff, *Local Administration in Viet-Nam: The Number of Local Units*

(Michigan State University Advisory Group, National Institute of Administration, Republic of Viet-Nam, Saigon, 1 November 1960), 2–5.
3 Keyes Beech, 'Strategic Hamlet Plan A Key to Viet Victory: Twofold Objective', *Washington Post*, 9 February 1963.
4 United States Department of Defense, *The Pentagon Papers*, Senator Gravel Edition, Volume 1 (Boston, MA: Beacon Press, 1971), 7–9 and William A. Williams et al. (eds.), *America in Vietnam: A Documentary History* (New York: Anchor Books, 1985), 33–6.
5 David L. Anderson, *Trapped by Success: The Eisenhower Administration and Vietnam, 1953–1961* (New York: Columbia University Press, 1991), 23.
6 'Agreement on the Cessation of Hostilities in Vietnam', 20 July 1954. Available at: https://www.mtholyoke.edu/acad/intrel/genevacc.htm (accessed 15 October 2015).
7 'Origins of the Insurgency in South Vietnam, 1954–1960', *The Pentagon Papers*, Vol. 1, 242–314.
8 Law 10/59, found in *Vietnam and America: A Documented History*, ed. Marvin E. Gettlemen, et al. (New York: Grove Press, 1995), 156.
9 Ibid.
10 Pierre Asselin, *Hanoi's Road to the Vietnam War, 1954–1965* (Berkeley: University of California Press, 2013), 43.
11 Ibid., 61.
12 Francis Fitzgerald, *Fire in the Lake: The Vietnamese and the Americans in Vietnam* (Boston, MA: Little, Brown and Company, 1972), 147–9.
13 *Program of the National Liberation Front*, Available at: https://web.archive.org/web/20100626065021/http://vietnam.vassar.edu/docnlf.html (accessed 25 July 2018).
14 *Pentagon Papers*, Vol. 1, 327.
15 Ibid., Vol. 1, 335.
16 Papers of John F. Kennedy. Presidential Papers. National Security Files. Meetings and Memoranda. National Security Action Memoranda [NSAM]: NSAM 111, First Phase of Vietnam Program. JFKNSF-332-013. John F. Kennedy Presidential Library and Museum [JFKL].
17 Pamphlet, 'Viet Nam's Strategic Hamlets'.
18 Woodruff, *Local Administration in Viet-Nam*, 5.
19 Ibid., 30–2.
20 Ibid., 42.
21 Bernard Fall, *The Two Vietnams: A Political and Military Analysis* (New York: Praeger, 1967), 308–10.
22 Jessica Elkind, '"The Virgin Mary Is Going South": Refugee Resettlement in South Vietnam, 1954–1956', *Diplomatic History*, Vol. 38, No. 5 (November 2014), 1003.
23 Joseph J. Zasloff, *Rural Resettlement in Vietnam: An Agroville in Development* (Washington, DC: Department of State, 1963), 1–24. *Pentagon Papers*, Volume 2, 133–4.

24 John O'Donnell, 'The Strategic Hamlet Program in Kien Hoa Province, South Vietnam: A Case Study of Counter-Insurgency', reprinted in Peter Kunstadter (ed.), *Southeast Asian Tribes, Minorities, and Nations* (Princeton, NJ: Princeton University Press, 1966), 710.

25 William Colby, *Lost Victory: A Firsthand Account of America's Sixteen-Year Involvement in Vietnam* (Chicago, IL: Contemporary Books, 1989), 94.

26 Edward G. Miller, *Misalliance: Ngo Dinh Diem, the United States, and the Fate of South Vietnam* (Boston, MA: Harvard University Press, 2013), 233.

27 Pamphlet, 'Viet Nam's Strategic Hamlets', 5 and 13.

28 Peter Busch, 'Killing the "Vietcong": The British Advisory Mission and the Strategic Hamlet Programme', *Journal of Strategic Studies*, Vol. 25, No. 1 (2002), 135–62. For Thompson's Delta Plan see *Foreign Relations of the United States, 1961–1963*, Volume II, Vietnam 1962, eds. David M. Baehler and Charles S. Sampson (Washington, DC: Government Printing Office, 1990), Document 51.

29 Miller, *Misalliance*, 232.

30 Pamphlet, 'Viet Nam's Strategic Hamlets', 4.

31 Sir Robert Thompson, *Defeating Communist Insurgency: The Lessons of Malaya and Vietnam* (New York: Praeger, 1966), 122.

32 For Hilsman's Strategic Concept for Vietnam see *Foreign Relations of the United States, 1961–1963*, Volume II, Vietnam 1962, eds. David M. Baehler and Charles S. Sampson (Washington, DC: Government Printing Office, 1990), Document 42.

33 Andrew Krepenivich, *The Army and Vietnam* (Baltimore, MD: Johns Hopkins University Press, 1988), 67.

34 Ibid., 69; General Cao Van Vien and Lt. General Dong Van Khuyen, *Reflections on the Vietnam War (Indochina Monographs), Vietnamese Conflict, 1961–1975* (Washington, DC: U.S. Army Center for Military History, 1980), 10.

35 Nikita Khrushchev, 'Address by Premier Khrushchev on January 6, 1961', *Two Communist Manifestos* (Washington, DC: The Washington Center of Foreign Policy Research, 1961), 52–66.

36 U. Alexis Johnson, 'Internal Defense and the Foreign Service', *Foreign Service Journal* (July, 1962), 21.

37 W. W. Rostow, 'Guerrilla Warfare in Underdeveloped Areas', speech reprinted in T. N. Greene (ed.), *The Guerrilla and How to Fight Him: Selections from the Marine Corps Gazette* (New York: Praeger, 1962), 56. See also W. W. Rostow, *The Stages of Economic Growth: A Non-Communist Manifesto* (Cambridge: Cambridge University Press, 1960), *passim*.

38 'U.S. Overseas Internal Defense Policy', 24 August 1962, Meetings and Memoranda, box 319, "Special Group CI," JFKL.

39 Dean Rusk, 'Problems of Development and Internal Defense', 11 June 1961. Speech delivered at the opening of the Foreign Service Institute's "Country Team" Seminar. Reprinted in *Foreign Service Journal* (July, 1962), 6.

40 Douglas S. Blaufarb, *The Counterinsurgency Era: U.S. Doctrine and Performance, 1950 to the Present* (New York: The Free Press, 1977), 52.
41 Quoted in David E. Kaiser, *American Tragedy: Kennedy, Johnson, and the Origins of the Vietnam War* (Cambridge, MA: Belknap Press of Harvard University Press, 2000), 165.
42 Vien and Khuyen, *Reflections on the Vietnam War (Indochina Monographs), Vietnamese Conflict, 1961–1975*, 17
43 Miller, *Misalliance*, 17.
44 *Pentagon Papers*, Volume 2, 144–5.
45 Eric M. Bergerud, *The Dynamics of Defeat: The Vietnam War In Hau Nghia Province* (Boulder, CO: Westview Press, 1993), 36.
46 Milton E. Osborne, *Strategic Hamlets in South Vietnam: A Survey and a Comparison* (Ithaca, NY: Department of Asian Studies, Cornell University, 1965), 32.
47 See page 3, note 4.
48 Pamphlet, 'Viet Nam's Strategic Hamlets', 11.
49 John C. Donnell, 'Personalism in Vietnam', in *Problems of Freedom: South Vietnam since Independence*, ed. Wesley R. Fishel (New York: The Free Press of Glencoe, Inc., 1961), 29 and Ministry of Information, *The Constitution of the Republic of Vietnam* (Saigon: The Secretariat of State for Information, 1956), 8.
50 Rufe Phillips, 'Before We Lost in South Vietnam', in *Prelude to Tragedy: Vietnam, 1960–1965* ed. Harvey Neese and John O'Donnell (Annapolis: Naval Institute Press, 2001), 32.
51 O'Donnell, 'The Strategic Hamlet Program in Kien Hoa Province, South Vietnam', 708–14.
52 Philip E. Catton, *Diem's Final Failure: Prelude to America's War in Vietnam* (Lawrence: University Press of Kansas, 2002), 171.
53 Ibid., 172–3, 175.
54 John C. Donnell and Gerald C Hickey, *The Vietnamese 'Strategic Hamlets': A Preliminary Report* (Santa Monica, CA: RAND, 1962), 11. Gerald C. Hickey, *Window on a War: An Anthropologist in the Vietnam Conflict* (Lubbock: Texas Tech University Press, 2002), 93.
55 Donnell and Hickey, *The Vietnamese 'Strategic Hamlets'*, 11.
56 Ibid., 16.
57 Catton, *Diem's Final Failure*, 182.
58 Ibid., 169.
59 Krepenivich, *The Army and Vietnam*, 68.
60 O'Donnell, 'The Strategic Hamlet Program in Kien Hoa Province, South Vietnam', 715.
61 Ibid., 719–20.
62 Ibid., 739.

63 Ibid., 722; Jeffrey Race, *War Comes to Long An: Revolutionary Conflict in a Vietnamese Province* (Oakland, CA: University of California Press, 2010), 133.
64 Race, 61.
65 Ibid., 61.
66 Ibid., 67.
67 Ibid., 83, 133.
68 Ibid., 70.
69 Ibid., 92.
70 Ibid., 192.
71 O'Donnell, 'The Strategic Hamlet Program in Kien Hoa Province, South Vietnam', 722.
72 Thompson, *Defeating Communist Insurgency*, 141.
73 Ibid., 138.
74 Van Vien and Khuyen, *Reflections on the Vietnam War (Indochina Monographs), Vietnamese Conflict, 1961–1975*, 20–1.
75 Fitzgerald, *Fire in the Lake*, 125.
76 O'Donnell, 'The Strategic Hamlet Program in Kien Hoa Province, South Vietnam', 732.
77 Ibid., 734.
78 Tran Ngoc Chau with Tom Sturdevant, 'My Story', in *Prelude to Tragedy: Vietnam, 1960–1965*, ed. Harvey Neese and John O'Donnell (Annapolis, MD: Naval Institute Press, 2001), 191.
79 Stanley Karnow, *Vietnam: A History* (New York: Penguin, 1997), 274.
80 *Pentagon Papers*, Volume II, 153–5.
81 "The Destruction of the Enemy's Strategic Hamlet Program," Vietnam Center and Archive. 2120208021 01 November 1962. Box 02, Folder 08. Douglas Pike Collection: Unit 01 – Assessment and Strategy. The Vietnam Center and Archive, Texas Tech University. https://www.vietnam.ttu.edu/reports/images.php?img=/images/212/2120208021.pdf and https://www.vietnam.ttu.edu/reports/images.php?img=/images/212/2120207002.pdf (accessed 1 September 2018).
82 Douglas Pike, *PAVN: People's Army of Vietnam* (Novato, CA: Presidio Press, 1986), 247–8.
83 Ibid., 247.
84 John E. Mueller, 'The Search for the "Breaking Point" in Vietnam: The Statistics of a Deadly Quarrel', *International Studies Quarterly*, Vol. 24, No. 4 (December 1980), 512–14.
85 Osborne, *Strategic Hamlets in South Vietnam*, 38.
86 Roger Hilsman, 'The Situation and Short-Term Prospects in South Vietnam', 3 December 1962, reprinted in *The Pentagon Papers*, Vol. 2, 690–716.
87 Nguyen Cong Luan, *Nationalist in the Vietnam Wars* (Bloomington: Indiana University Press, 2012), 240.
88 Osborne, *Strategic Hamlets in South Vietnam*, 35–7.

89 Ibid., 42–3.
90 Colby, *Lost Victory*, 167.
91 Karnow, *Vietnam: A History*, 339.
92 Memorandum for the President by Robert McNamara, 'South Vietnam', March 16, 1964, *The Pentagon Papers*, Gravel Edition, Vol. 3, 496–9.
93 Phillips, 'Before We Lost in South Vietnam', 40–1.
94 Cong Luan, *Nationalist in the Vietnam Wars*, 218. See also Chau with Sturdevant, 'My Story', 205.
95 Chau, 189.
96 'The Queen Bee', *Time*, 9 August 1963.
97 Race, 60.
98 Ibid., 95–6, and 167.
99 Ibid., 166.
100 O'Donnell, 'The Strategic Hamlet Program in Kien Hoa Province, South Vietnam', 736–8.
101 Vien and Khuyen, *Reflections on the Vietnam War (Indochina Monographs), Vietnamese Conflict, 1961-1975*, 20.
102 Colby, *Lost Victory*, 102.

12

Resettlement in the Portuguese Colonial Wars:

Africa, 1961–75

Dr Kalev I. Sepp

It is the organic essence of the Portuguese nation to carry out the historic function of colonizing overseas dominions and civilizing the indigenous populations therein contained.
Colonial Act of 1930[1]

Introduction

Portugal was first among the European nations to establish colonies in Africa in the mid-fifteenth century and the last to withdraw in 1975. From their inception, these colonial holdings provided their exports to fund further Portuguese imperial expansion around the world and maintain Portugal's prestige and economic viability. The Portuguese claimed that, in turn, they imported their European culture to help 'civilize' Portuguese Guinea, Angola and Mozambique. Yet in 1961, after almost 500 years of colonial rule, not a single university existed for a Portuguese African population of approximately 12,000,000.[2] Further indication of the resentment of the *indigenas* (black native-born inhabitants) towards Portuguese rule was the record of military expeditions sent from Lisbon to deal with local rebellions that colonial forces could not suppress – seven to Angola alone, in 1820, 1836, 1860, 1873, 1902, 1914 and 1930.[3]

Colonial origins

In 1933, Portuguese Prime Minister Antonio de Oliveira Salazar (who was to remain in power until 1968) wrote the policy of 'Racial Assimilation' into the new constitution, and in 1951 the colonies were given the status of 'overseas provinces' with seats in the National Assembly in Lisbon.[4] These actions were deceptive. Slavery, abolished in 1878, had actually been replaced by a system of low-wage 'contract labour' that was equally repressive and actually became more extensive as the demand for export crops grew.[5] Salazar's 1933 constitution, rather than eliminating societal classes, actually created new ones. In order to attain the citizenship category of *assimilado* (assimilated African), gain the right to vote and unrestricted travel and be exempt from the pass card and 'contract labour' systems, it was necessary to meet very stringent requirements. These included the ability to speak Portuguese, have income from a job and be over eighteen years of age and of 'good character'.[6] This was almost impossible for the majority of *indigenas*, and favoured only a few *mesticos* (half-castes); by 1961, only 1 per cent of all *indigenas* had gained *assimilado* status.[7] At any rate, the *noa indigenas* (non-native white Europeans) and to a lesser extent the *mesticos* still enjoyed special privileges well above those of the *assimilados*.

Exacerbating this social stratification of 'haves' and 'have-nots' was the tide of nationalism that swept across Africa as the Second World War ended, as France, Spain, Belgium, the Netherlands and Great Britain began to let go of their far-flung colonial possessions. The Philippines, India, Burma and Malaysia gained independence in the late 1940s; Guinea (formerly French Guinea), Ghana, Tunisia, Libya, Morocco and Sudan in the 1950s and in 1960 alone, sixteen former African colonies and territories became sovereign nations. Notably, directly on Angolas' eastern border, the Belgian Congo emerged as the free state of Zaire.[8]

These events had a serious impact in Portugal's 'overseas provinces'. Native independence movements and 'freedom parties' formed in the late 1950s, and shortly armed revolt began in Angola in 1961, followed by Portuguese Guinea in 1963 and Mozambique in 1964. Rather than following the lead of the other former imperial powers in Europe, Portugal sought to retain her colonial possessions for reasons of imagined international prestige and economic necessity.[9]

The three insurgencies

On 15 March 1961, a revolt on the northern Angolan coffee plantations left several hundred *colonos* (white farmers) and some 7,000 *indigenas* dead at the hands of Bakongo rebels attacking out of the Congo (formerly Congo-Brazzaville).[10] Insurgent Mbundu and Luandan *assimilados* in

Angola formed the *Movimento Popular de Libertacao de Angola* (Popular Movement for the Liberation of Angola, or MPLA); the northern Bakongos were the 'mass base' of the rebel *Frente Nacional de Libertacao de Angola* (National Front for the Liberation of Angola, or FNLA). In 1964, Jonas Savimbi broke with FNLA's chief, Holden Roberto, to lead the *Uniao Nacional para a Independencia Total de Angola* (National Union for Total Angolan Independence, or UNITA), supported by the eastern Angolan Chokwes and southern Angolan Orimbundus.[11]

During a violent 1959 strike in Bissau, Portuguese Guinea, Portuguese police shot and killed fifty *indigenas*, which led to full-scale guerrilla war in January 1963. The *Partido Africano da Independencia da Guine e Cabo Verde* (African Party for the Independence of Guinea and Cabo Verde, or PAIGC), drawing their rank-and-file personnel primarily from the Balante tribe, launched raids from sanctuaries in the neighbouring Republic of Guinea, and later from Senegal.[12] The Mandinkas and Moslem Fulas continued to support the Portuguese colonial government.

In northern Mozambique, a coalition of tribal groups, including the Makonde and Nyanja, formed in 1962. The *Frente de Liberta cao de Mocambique* (Mozambique Liberation Front, or FRELIMO) based itself initially in Tanzania and began raids from there on 25 September 1964, later extending their network of bases into Zambia.[13] The Portuguese were able to count on the Moslem Macuas to help counter the insurgents.[14]

Portuguese reaction was strong, but not decisive. The metropolitan army had not fought a general conflict since the First World War. Its garrison at the Portuguese colony of Goa had been quickly captured on 18 December 1961 by the Indian Army, following Prime Minster Salazar's refusal to recognize Indian sovereignty there. There were only 9,000 regular army soldiers scattered throughout the African territories. Three years later, that number reached 130,000, and by the early 1970s, 90 per cent of Portugal's armed forces, principally conscripts, were in combat on the African continent.[15]

To her North Atlantic Treaty Organization (NATO) allies, the Portuguese government rationalized that they were actively fighting part of the global battle to contain expansionist communism, as the rebel groups had strong Soviet Russian and Chinese ties. Further, airfields and port on the Cape Verde Islands off Portuguese Guinea supported NATO's control of the Atlantic sea lanes.[16] In any event, NATO – particularly the United States, France and Great Britain – actively aided Portugal's African colonial wars. The United States provided training for some 2,000 Portuguese military personnel by the wars' end, and the British and French gave the benefit of their experiences in counterinsurgent warfare in Malaya and Algeria, respectively.[17] For their part, FRELIMO and MPLA guerrillas trained at first in newly independent Algeria, and later Bulgaria, Czechoslovakia and the Soviet Union. Later, the People's Republic of China, Cuba, Guinea and Nigeria provided significant aid to the rebel forces.[18]

Counterinsurgency and resettlement

The Portuguese counterinsurgency campaign in all three colonies reflected study of recent guerrilla wars, and incorporated tactics such as small-unit patrolling, large-unit 'sweeps', psychological warfare and programmes like the 'Africanization' of military units, including the creation of several all-*indigenas* formations. They also employed extensive civil-military projects, called 'social operations', notably clinic- and school-building, well-digging and mass inoculations. Engineers emphasized road-building to create a transportation infrastructure, given the vast size of the colonies: Mozambique is as large as the state of California, and Angola is twice the size of the state of Texas.

As the colonial wars began, Portuguese military governors almost immediately instituted a system of camps to relocate or resettle portions of the native population to facilitate counterinsurgency operations. Resettlements had been attempted on a very small scale before the revolt, starting in Mozambique in 1951, to develop unpopulated areas to improve the economy and relieve overcrowding elsewhere.[19] The first of these wartime efforts was implemented in Angola, where hard fighting first broke out. The new Portuguese governor general there, Lieutenant Colonel Silvino Silverio Marques, authorized a pilot programme in May 1962 called *reordenamento rural* (literally, rural rearrangement) to resettle refugees returning from Zaire after fleeing the 1961 massacres. The army was ordered to build 150 new villages, each complete with a civic centre, school, clinic and store, while the refugees would be permitted to construct their new homes in their customary native fashion.[20]

As the wars widened, the Portuguese came to see population resettlement as essential to establishment of population control, in order to isolate the insurgents from their base of support. They also anticipated stimulation of economic and social development, to counter-balance the deleterious effects of population flight from traditional agricultural areas.[21] But not all senior Portuguese government officials agreed that resettlement was a good idea. Several argued that resettlement undermined social and psychological stability, and that military needs would override popular sentiment to remain on hereditary lands. Further, if the peoples being resettled had already aligned themselves with the insurgents, any relocation would be dangerously counterproductive.[22]

A comprehensive continental strategy agreed on among the three Portuguese provincial commanders might have enhanced their efforts and conserved scarce resources. Although such a unified plan never appeared, certain common elements and aspects of population relocation emerged in the three colonies. The general Portuguese objective of population resettlement was to secure control over the rural *indigenas*, separate them from the guerrillas and thereby deny the guerrillas food, shelter and intelligence.

To those ends, the Portuguese expected the *aldeamentos* to (1) enable administration of their counterinsurgency socio-economic programmes; (2) protect the resettled peoples from rebel terror and influence and (3) propagate pro-government psychological operations messages.[23]

The Portuguese utilized three basic types of resettlement camps: the *reordenamento rural*, basically a refugee camp, located outside conflictive areas; the *aldeamento* (literally, division into villages), roughly equivalent to the Malayan 'New Village' or Vietnamese 'Strategic Hamlet', deliberately situated inside combat zones; and the *colonato* (literally, small colony) for metropolitan Portuguese settlers, located in designated areas to deter guerrilla encroachment. The *colonatos do militares desmobilizados* (settlements for former servicemen) was a variant of the *colonato*.[24]

In Angola, these various projects resettled over 1 million Angolan *indigenas* – 20 per cent of the colony's population – into 2,836 *aldeamentos* across the country, in 13 years of war. The programme was often administered poorly, with arbitrary, unconsidered decisions, such as Angolan commander in chief Air Force general Joao de Almeida Viana's mandate to 'reorganize' the population of central Angola, where there had been no combat or guerrilla activity. As a result, the offended Ovimbundus, who were once neutral, gave support to the UNITA rebels.[25]

In Portuguese Guinea, the arrival of the charismatic and effective General Antonio de Spinola in 1968 brought resettlement operations in the form of *aldeamentos* to the forefront. During re-consolidation of his forces, he closed a member of previously established camps beyond the range of adequate military support, which prompted PAIGC claims that the withdrawal proved his 'fortified hamlet' system was failing.[26] Despite the risks and expense, Spinola halted the closures just to counter the PAIGC propaganda.[27] Spinola used the *aldeamentos* as the basis for an intensive civic-action effort – his 'hearts and minds' campaign – that clearly alarmed and worried the PAIGC leadership.[28] Amilcar Cabral, the PAIGC Secretary-General and chief, railed at his subordinates: 'Some three days ago three schools were opened in Bissora. Spinola was there ... in the midst of our people ... a grenade would kill Spinola or would stop him from calmly walking about.'[29] Before the war ended, 150,000 *indigenas*, fully 30 per cent of the total population of Portuguese Guinea had been resettled.[30]

Interdiction of FRELIMO guerrillas operating from bases in Tanzania and Zambia was the dominant factor in situating *aldeamentos* in northern Mozambique. The revolts in Angola and Portuguese Guinea had given the Portuguese colonial leadership the forewarning necessary to prepare contingency campaigns, which were quickly implemented when the revolt broke out in 1964. Despite sufficient time for preparation, inadequate planning resulted in poor placement of many of the 980 *aldeamentos* eventually constructed, and without the amenities necessary to support the relocated populace. In 1969, the dynamic and optimistic General Kaulza de Arriaga took command in Mozambique and initiated a massive 'social-promotion' programme to improve living and working conditions in the resettlement camps. He committed half of the 60,000 soldiers under his command to attendant construction projects, especially road-building.[31] Along with the other elements of Arriaga's overall counterinsurgency campaign, 969,396 Africans, comprising 15 per cent of Mozambique's population, were finally resettled into 953 *aldeamentos*.[32]

A variation on government-directed population relocation efforts was the colonato, modelled on the paramilitary Israeli kibbutz. It aimed at establishing European Portuguese, both civilians and ex-servicemen, in selected areas to preclude possible expansion of guerrilla influence. Despite inducements such as free passage, farm implements and land (sometimes appropriated from the *indigenas*), there were few volunteers from Portugal. Those who came, complained the official Mozambique Provincial Settlement Board in 1970, "lack any training or instruction ... [and] are difficult if not impossible prospects for good citizens". The argument was made that scarce funds were wasted on importing these unproductive and unskilled "colonizers," and would be better spent on training unskilled natives, who were "already there."[33] Ex-soldiers were difficult to attract because most wanted to return home to Portugal at the end of their tour of duty, where better opportunities for education and profitable employment existed. Also, the long-established Portuguese colonos were unsupportive and sometimes resentful of the intrusive military plan.[34]

Outcomes

The reactions of the indigenous African population to the resettlement projects variously offered and imposed on them were mixed. Some tribes feared guerrilla terrorism and found a measure of security in the 'fortified hamlets', where they were often organized into militias to provide their own defence. Others, like the semi-nomadic southern Angolan Ovambos and Herreros, found their traditional lifestyle and culture disrupted by camp life.[35] Most camps lacked the full range of facilities needed to make them attractive to the *indigenas*. Moreover, the intent of isolating the guerrillas from the population and their support was never realized. The rebels infiltrated and organized operative cells inside camps, and by one estimate, these agents smuggled out one-third of all food grown in *aldeamentos* in Mozambique to supply FRELIMO guerrillas.[36] A British observer of the Mozambican Civil War, Colonel Ronald Waring, made a pointed critique:

> On occasions, the new villages were badly sited in quite unsuitable places. ... Sometimes there was a degree of cooperation between villages and guerrilla bands ... where protected villages bought off enemy attacks by handing over food and even weapons rather than fight to defend a

village perimeter. [At times] there was hostility to the enforced relocation of a village. ... African villagers preferred to stay on their ancestral lands rather than move to new villages, even when, thereby, they would have a much greater degree of protection.[37]

These flaws in camp administration and security were exacerbated by a lack of high-level focus and direction. The senior Portuguese planners and executors of the resettlement schemes never resolved their argument over the central intent of the effort. The authorities remained divided throughout the war, unable to resolve whether population displacement was primarily done for population control, or for internal development. This was a major concern since most exports from the Portuguese colonies had declined, impacting on Lisbon's financial ability to support the war.[38]

Despite these weaknesses in the resettlement programmes, the African guerrillas were clearly hampered in their efforts by the *aldeamento*s. A Portuguese army situation report from Mozambique observed, 'The enemy effort recently had been concentrated on impeding the grouping of further people into protected villages.'[39] The South African vice-counsel in the Angolan capital of Luanda evaluated the long-term accomplishment of the resettlement programme:

> The *aldeamento* policy frustrated the enemy's attempts to set up consolidated base areas in the guerrilla-contaminated zones. By these means, Portugal succeeded in disrupting the prescribed revolutionary pattern of gradual expansion and regained the strategic initiative. After 1972 there were no 'liberated' or revolutionary-controlled areas within Angola. At the most there were areas of influence.[40]

As a counter-measure, the Angolan rebels set up their own 'protected villages', called *kimbos*, to grow much-needed food. These failed, as they were easy targets for aerial attack.[41] The worth of the *aldeamentos* can also be assessed by the reaction of the FRELIMO guerrillas, who propagandized the resettlements as 'concentration camps', and regularly bombarded them with mortars and rockets.[42] It is a fair assessment that the *aldeamentos* contributed to the achievement of military stalemate, forestalling a guerrilla victory.

Nonetheless, the *aldeamentos* did not cause defeat of the insurgent combatant forces. Military historian John P. Cann suggests the most important result of the resettlement programmes in Angola, Mozambique and Portuguese Guinea was the generation of time. As the combined civil-military counterinsurgency efforts checked the guerrillas, there was time for Lisbon to bring the *indigenas* into active political participation in their own countries. The goal could have been to build the basis for national political autonomy at the grassroots level, and so obviate the insurgents' manifesto of winning independence by violent revolution. But this was the missing strategic component of the resettlement plan, and as long as the Portuguese home government sought to keep a colonial empire in Africa, the *aldeamento* policy would ultimately make no difference in the outcome of the insurgencies.[43]

Conclusion

In the end, the enormous drain on metropolitan Portuguese material, financial and human resources forced the issue not in Africa, but in Portugal itself.[44] After thirteen years of fighting an exhausting guerrilla war, with no promise of a victory in Africa, the clandestine 'Captains' Movement' that became the *Movimento das Forcas Armadas* (Armed Forces Movement, or MFA) launched a military coup in Lisbon. On 25 April 1974, known soon as the 'Day of the Red Carnations', the civilian Portuguese government was ousted. The newly established junta quickly ended the conflicts in the 'overseas provinces', withdrew the Portuguese armed forces from Africa, and immediately reduced the size of the army by 80 per cent. Within two years, Guinea-Bissau (formerly Portuguese Guinea), Angola and Mozambique were independent nations, and the junta stepped down to reinstall democratic civilian rule.

Much as the Korean conflict had overshadowed the concurrent US-supported counterinsurgency successfully fought in the Philippines, so did America's preoccupation with its war in Vietnam mask the lessons of the Portuguese Colonial Wars, where Lisbon's military forces had never suffered a significant defeat on the battlefield, yet failed to win any of their three wars. Those African wars revealed the potential for population resettlement in counterinsurgency to be absolutely critical to the prosecution of a conflict, yet still remain wholly dependent for success on the statement of a clear and viable strategic objective. For any government contemplating directed resettlement of peoples to overcome an insurgent movement, this is the first lesson of Portugal's African wars.

Notes

1 Peter Karibe Mendy, 'Portugal's Civilizing Mission in Colonial Guinea-Bissau: Rhetoric and Reality', *The International Journal of African Historical Studies*, Vol. 36, No. 1, Special Issue: Colonial Encounters between Africa and Portugal (2003), 35–58 (50).

2 Antonio Henrique de Oliveira Marques, *History of Portugal* (New York: Columbia University Press, 1976), 256; Thomas H. Henriksen, 'Lessons from Portugal's Counter-insurgency Operations in Africa', *Journal of the Royal United Services Institute for Defence Studies* (June 1978), 33.

3   Douglas L. Wheeler, 'The Portuguese Army in Angola', *The Journal of Modern African Studies*, Vol. VII, No. 3 (1969), 428.
4   Ian F. W. Beckett, 'Portuguese Africa', in *War in Peace*, eds. Ashley Brown and Sam Elder (London: Orbis Publishing, 1981), 152.
5   Ibid.
6   Donald J. Alberts, 'Armed Struggle in Angola', in *Insurgency in the Modern World*, eds. Bard E. O'Neill, William R. Heaton, and Donald J. Alberts (Boulder, CO: Westview Press, 1980), 237.
7   Beckett, 'Portuguese Africa', 152.
8   Regine Van Chi-Bonnardel (ed.), *The Atlas of Africa* (New York: The Free Press, 1973), 52.
9   Portugal's then-Overseas Minister Adriano Moreira provides the rationale for his government's position in his *Portugal's Stand in Africa* (New York: University Publishers, 1962).
10 Beckett, 'Portuguese Africa', 153.
11 Ian F. W. Beckett, 'The Portuguese Army: The Campaign in Mozambique, 1964-1974', in *Armed Forces & Modern Counter-Insurgency*, eds. Ian F. W. Beckett and John Pimlott (New York: St. Martin's Press, 1985), 138; and Beckett, 'Portuguese Africa', 153.
12 Thomas H. Henriksen, 'Portugal in Africa: Comparative Notes on Counterinsurgency', *Orbis* Vol. XXI, No. 2 (Summer 1977), 396–7.
13 Ibid., 397.
14 Beckett, 'Campaign in Mozambique', 139.
15 Eugene K. Keefe, *Area Handbook for Portugal* (Washington, DC: U.S. Government Printing Office, 1985), 56.
16 Beckett, 'Campaign in Mozambique', 141.
17 Allen Isaacman and Barbara Isaacman, *Mozambique: From Colonialism to Revolution, 1900-1982* (Boulder, CO: Westview Press, 1983), 104–5. The authors make the extraordinary and unevidenced claim on page 104 that 'the United States provided ... B-52's [strategic heavy bombers]' to Portugal, although not specifying for what purpose or where they might have been used.
18 Beckett, 'Campaign in Mozambique', 140. In 1973, the Soviets delivered SA-7 manportable anti-aircraft missiles to the rebels in the Portuguese African colonies. While not decisive, the missiles diminished already-limited Portuguese air mobility and aerial fire support. Comparison to later US anti-aircraft weapons aid to mujahideen insurgents fighting the Soviets in Afghanistan is direct. See also Jeremy Black, *Insurgency and Counterinsurgency: A Global History* (Lanham, MD: Rowman & Littlefield, 2016), 167.
19 Brendan F. Jundanian, 'Resettlement Programs: Counterinsurgency in Mozambique', *Comparative Politics*, Vol. VI, No. 4 (July 1974), 520–2.
20 Wheeler, 'Portuguese Army in Angola', 433–4. The refugees built their new dwellings in accordance with local customs and design, with the sole government-mandated addition of corrugated tin roofs. In the event, these were covered with palm leaves, and many families built an adjacent house

without the tin roofing. John P. Cann, *Counterinsurgency in Africa: The Portuguese Way of War, 1961-1974* (Westport, CT: Greenwood Press, 1997), 154.

21 Bender, 'Limits of Counterinsurgency', 336–7.
22 Cann, *Counterinsurgency in Africa*, 155.
23 Ibid.
24 Jundanian, 'Resettlement Programs', 520. Portuguese Jesuit missionaries colonizing Brazil in the sixteenth century originated *aldeamentos* to bring nomadic natives under the influence of the Catholic Church. The Jesuits also meant to create local economies, and raise indigenous militias to defend the new villages against hostiles and criminals. The Portuguese colonial government took over control of the *aldeamentos* from the Church in 1758, and the concept of government-directed resettlement was validated. See also Cann, *Counterinsurgency in Africa*, 1.
25 Bender, 'Limits of Counterinsurgency', 338.
26 The Portuguese armed forces, in contrast to the US military, did not enjoy the advantages of numerous transport helicopters and abundant close air support aircraft. Reaction forces marched on foot, or moved in trucks. Their fire support was generally artillery of the Second World War vintage.
27 Al J. Venter, *Portugal's Guerrilla War: The Campaign for Africa* (Capetown: Citadel Press, 1973), 146.
28 As one example of Spinola's efforts, to increase the rice crop for resettlement villages in Guinea's coastal lowlands, Portuguese agronomists worked for years, successfully, to create saltwater-resistant rice seed. John P. Cann, interview with Gen. Pedro Alexandre Gomes Cardoso, 29 March 1995, Lisbon; cited in Cann, *Counterinsurgency in Africa*, 157.
29 Amilcar Cabral, 'Revolutionary War in Africa', in *The Guerrilla Reader: A Historical Anthology*, ed. Walter Laquer (Philadelphia: Temple University Press, 1977), 241.
30 Henriksen, 'Lessons', 33.
31 Beckett, 'Campaign in Mozambique', 142, 156. Asphalting roads had the additional benefit of making the emplacement of FRELIMO anti-vehicular mines without detection almost impossible. Road tarring became a major project in Guinea and Angola, as well.
32 Henriksen, 'Comparative Notes', 402, and Cann, *Counterinsurgency in Africa*, 156.
33 Jundanian, 'Resettlement Programs', 528–9.
34 Wheeler, 'Portuguese Army in Angola', 435–6.
35 Beckett, 'Campaign in Mozambique', 147.
36 Ibid.
37 Ronald Waring, Duke of Valderano, interview with John P. Cann, 17 November 1995, London, UK.; quoted in Cann, *Counterinsurgency in Africa*, 156–7.

38 The solitary economic bright spot was Angola, where coffee production (the leading crop) actually increased slightly during the war, despite the demographic turbulence. This was not enough to offset the overall decline in exportable goods production and attendant loss of revenue among the three Portuguese colonies. Bender, 'Limits of Counterinsurgency', 33.
39 Isaacman and Isaacman, 'Mozambique', 101.
40 Quoted in Willem S. van der Waals, *Portugal's War in Angola 1961-1974* (Rivonia, SA: Ashanti Publishing, 1993), 232.
41 Beckett, 'Portuguese Africa', 154.
42 Thomas H. Henriksen, *Revolution and Counterrevolution: Mozambique's War of Independence, 1964-1974* (London: Greenwood Press, 1978), 162.
43 Cann, *Counterinsurgency in Africa*, 159.
44 By 1974, 13,000 metropolitan Portuguese had been killed in Africa, and Portugal was spending a crushing 45 per cent of her national budget on her military. Beckett, 'Portuguese Africa', 153; and Al J. Venter, *Africa at War* (Greenwich, CT: Devin-Adair, 1974), 75.

Conclusions:

Relocation in counterinsurgency warfare

Dr Edward J. Erickson

> *The choice of explanation determines the nature of the problem's resolution.*
> LTGEN PAUL VAN RIPER, USMC (Ret)
> Quantico, Virginia, 5 August 2011

Introduction

Lieutenant General Paul Van Riper, US Marine Corps (Retired) is the Kim T. Adamson Chair of Insurgency and Terrorism at the Marine Corps University in Quantico, Virginia. I am fortunate to have the opportunity to know General Van Riper, and it is impossible for me to express how much I have learned from listening to him over an extended period. The epigraph above remains in my mind the singularly most memorable and most useful quote that I heard the general expound. He linked the quote to a discussion of how policy evolves and why policy development is often flawed. The general asserted that decision-makers, over and over, fit their solutions to match their perceptions of the problem. Van Riper maintained that often their perceptions were far removed from the reality on the ground. I believe his thesis is valid and I think that General Van Riper's ideas about decision making are especially applicable to the general problem of counterinsurgency.

Our contributors have examined twelve cases of a relocation-based approach to the problem of waging counterinsurgency campaigns (inclusive of counter-indigenous, counter-guerrilla and counter-fifth column campaigns) in modern warfare. In order to bring this book to a coherent conclusion I want to examine some themes which have emerged in this book about forcible relocation in wartime.

The explanation

In every case the decision-makers represented the people who were to be forcibly relocated as a threat to security in wartime. This is known from the actual historical record left behind by the decision-makers themselves. However, the extent to which they were an *actual* threat or whether they were the victims of a constructed case against them is, in some cases, hotly argued today. In some cases one might condemn the sincerity of the decision-makers, especially in the cases of the Russians in 1915 and the Americans in 1942. Those particular relocation decisions are surely the weakest, and the decision-makers relied on racially prejudiced notions and 'what if' thinking rather than actual acts of rebellion or sabotage. It is important to consider in those two cases that the Russian Jews were not sent into confinement but rather distributed well out of the war zone and Japanese-Americans were confined in camps which were well supplied and well managed. This might be considered as evidence that these two groups were not really considered as actual enemies of the state but were relocated for reasons other than they were an actual threat.

Included in the decision-makers' explanation, in the other cases examined in this study, was the idea of the impossibility of assigning individual accountability. Not all Acadians, Navajo, Cubans, Boers, Ottoman-Armenians, ethnically Chinese Malays, South Vietnamese villagers, Algerians or colonial Portuguese Africans were in rebellion or actively opposing the government. Perhaps not even a majority were even in sympathy with the insurgent groups; however, the decision-makers advanced the explanation that it was impossible to separate the innocent from the guilty. This underlying premise explains the way that the decision-makers resolved the problem. Added into this dilemma of individual 'identifiability' was the problem of how to deal structurally with insurgents and guerrillas. It must not be forgotten that until the mid-twentieth century no army in the world had any kind of doctrinal solution to what would come to be known as counterinsurgency. Thinking about how to structure an anti-rebel campaign was left entirely to commanders who had nothing except their own experiences and a few odd histories to fall back on for guidance on fighting or containing an insurgency.

Ends, ways and means

It is a truism that resources determine policy, and resourcing a counterinsurgency effort was never far removed from decision making. Compounding this were competing global or national demands for scarce resources, which varied from case to case but was, in every case, significant. The British in 1755, the Ottomans and Russians in 1915 and the Americans in 1942 were engaged in global large-scale conventional wars. Similarly, we can also argue that South Vietnam was a country engaged in a national war of survival. The Americans on the frontier and later in the Philippines had tiny regular forces forcing them into hard choices. In the era of decolonization the Spanish, British, French and Portuguese faced both declining resources and eroding national will in trying to wage extended and expensive counterinsurgency campaigns. In all cases we should note that the allocation of resources was a factor affecting operations and decision making.

In all cases the ratio of government forces to vast spaces and large populations figured heavily into decision making as well. How many soldiers does it take to win a counterinsurgency campaign? How many soldiers does it take to guard key infrastructure or to protect a vulnerable population? How long does it take? The short answer is that it takes a lot of men, a lot of money and an extended window of time to achieve success in counterinsurgency. In terms of the number of soldiers required, contemporary American doctrine uses a yardstick ratio, 'Most density recommendations fall within a range of 20 to 25 counterinsurgents for every 1,000 residents in an AO [area of operations].'[1] Of course this depends on such matters as the nature of insurgents, the cooperation of the population, spatial characteristics, and so on. British forces in Northern Ireland and Malaya peaked at 20 soldiers per 1,000 inhabitants, while the French in Algeria peaked at 60 soldiers per 1,000 inhabitants.[2] A recent study of modern counterinsurgencies presents these ratios: in Kenya the British deployed 9.3 men per 1,000 inhabitants, in Algeria in 1958 France deployed 46.3 men per 1,000 inhabitants, while in Angola in 1968 the Portuguese deployed 12.3 men per 1,000 inhabitants.[3] Using these figures as yardsticks, it is obvious why France and Britain were more successful than the Portuguese. Our contributors were not asked to compute force ratios in their case studies but the reader will note that in many cases the force ratio disadvantaged the government.

Likewise the temporal element loomed large for many of the decision-makers. British commanders in Malaya and American commanders in the Philippines, for example, laboured under policy constraints which demanded fast resolution to the problem. Likewise, the pressures of large-scale conventional war pushed the Ottomans and the Russians to deal with the problem of a potentially unfriendly population within their own empires in a rapid manner. I have previously written that forcible relocation as an approach to counterinsurgency is a 'Strategy of Poverty'.[4] The phrase strategy of poverty has come to mean 'doing more with less'. In its purest form, it imposes resource constraints on what might be done. Such a policy is not the optimum or the ideal, but it dictates what can or might be accomplished with the means at hand. In all cases the decision-makers never seemed to have quite enough soldiers to suppress the insurgency with regular forces. Thus, by weakening the interface between the population and the insurgents through forcible relocation, the insurgency itself weakened in turn. In this way decision-makers hoped that relocation would prove to be a more efficient approach than reinforcing the military with larger numbers of soldiers.

Decision-making

We can make a case that all of the decision-makers in this study were military professionals with large amounts of practical experience in waging war. More importantly every one of the principal decision-makers had experiences in irregular warfare or in actual counterinsurgency operations. The Americans had much experience fighting against hostile Native Americans, and both the British and French had plenty of experience fighting on the frontiers and quelling rebellions in their far-flung global empires. The Ottomans and the Russians put down dozens of rebellions by their subject peoples. Even the Portuguese were accomplished in subduing rebels. But, with that said, there was little formal professional military thought devoted to developing doctrines regarding the tactics and approaches to counterinsurgency until the mid-twentieth century.

In the nineteenth century the French probably put the most thought into the problem, notably with Thomas-Robert Bugeaud's theories of punitive *razzias* (raids) in Algeria and Joseph Gallieni's ideas of progressive occupation. The British caught up somewhat with C. E. Callwell's *Small Wars, Their Principles and Practice* in 1896, which was based on the Northwest Frontier experience and updated in 1906 using the experience of the Boer War. More ideas came to the fore in the mid-1920s from French general Hubert Lyautey, who developed the 'centres of attraction' and 'oil spot' theories. However, the first real attempt to formally define a doctrinal approach to the problem of fighting an insurrection came in 1940 when the US Marine Corps published the *Small Wars Manual*.[5] The Marines asserted that the solution to insurrection could not be simply military, but must necessarily include complementary diplomatic, economic, humanitarian and governmental activities as well. This was a conceptual breakthrough and continues to frame modern counterinsurgency theory.

The above ideas are important because, until the 1960s, commanders had little formal training about how to combat insurgents or guerrillas except their own hard won experiences. As mentioned in our chapter on

Malaya, British Generals Sir Harold Briggs and Sir Gerald Templer brought a 'hearts and minds' approach to the problem in the 1950s. In the early 1960s, French thinker and soldier David Galula advanced similar non-kinetic ideas in his *Counterinsurgency Warfare: Theory and Practice*, while French soldier Roger Trinquier advocated a countervailing hard power approach in *Modern Warfare, A French View of Counterinsurgency*. All of these ideas affected the American and South Vietnamese approach in the Second Indochina War.

When evaluating the decisions in this study, it is important to keep in mind that the counterinsurgency specialists and SMEs (subject matter experts) of today did not exist in any form until the mid-1960s. Moreover, until the early days of the twentieth century professionally trained and organized military staffs, as we know that term today, simply did not exist either. Even as the United States entered the Vietnam War its military reached out to Sir Robert Thompson, a British civil servant during the Malayan Emergency (who was considered the foremost expert in counterinsurgency), for recommendations on defeating the Viet Cong. Finally we should recognize that unlike modern military staff processes around the world (which include 'military decision making' and 'decision support templates') standardized operating procedures to assist commanders in decision making were non-existent until the early to mid-twentieth century.

Operational decision making in almost all cases until the 1960s was 'point-to-point' and cumulative rather than strategic or functionally long range. In addition to the absence of doctrine this was often caused by a lack of information, incomplete situational awareness or a lack of cultural awareness. As the reader has learned from a close read of this study the tactics and outcomes were often adjusted 'mid-stride' based on unfolding events and the availability of resources. While not excusing the decisions in these cases we must appreciate how commanders struggled in the absence of such aids as firm intelligence, doctrine, training, military staffs and specialized expertise.

War crimes

It may strike modern Americans that their ancestors figure so prominently in this narrative. Indeed there were always 'bill-payers' for the Manifest Destiny proclaimed by Americans in the early days of the republic. The contributors might remind readers that no country stands blameless during the course of human events in assuming responsibility for what are now termed war crimes and atrocities. However, as this study demonstrates, none of the nations described endorsed or legalized criminal activity or atrocity as national or military policy. While there were numerous instances (in many of our cases) of crimes against groups and individuals, these were localized and, in the main, were an unintended consequence of forcible relocation.

As a part of our narrative, criminality is reflected in the actions of individuals. Unfortunately, the opportunity for crimes against relocated persons was always present and manifested itself on a frequent basis. Sometimes the levels of violence inflicted on groups of relocated peoples approached what appear as what we call today crimes against humanity, mass murder and genocide.

Criminality did not always go unpunished and, in a number of cases, there was wide spread public concern and outcry over the treatment of the relocated peoples, particularly in Cuba, the Philippines, the Boer Republics, the United States and Algeria. In many places the perpetrators were tried and imprisoned or executed for their crimes. This was true of the Ottoman Empire and its Ottoman-Armenians. The nuanced point here is to get past modern-day indictments and judgements about whether it is historically appropriate to retrofit modern mores and definitions on governments or individuals who lived in the past. In several cases the actual decisions for relocation originated at the operational level but were then ratified at national level as policy like the one occurred in the United States in 1942. In other cases the relocation decisions originated and remained at the operational level. The extent to which these decision-makers were culpable in criminality is hotly contested today. In rendering judgements about these events we have tried to balance intentions versus outcomes.

Stolen economics and opportunity

In many of the cases, economic advantages and opportunity existed when an entire population was removed from the national or regional economy. In a number of cases other groups took immediate advantage of the window of opportunity which presented itself by seizing property, businesses and other assets. Indeed it is even part of the contemporary narrative, in some cases, that the targeted population was removed intentionally so that another group could take their property and their means of living. This is especially true of contemporary narratives regarding the Acadians, Native Americans, Ottoman-Armenians and Japanese-Americans. While these narratives have some merit, these outcomes were never the primary reason for the relocations, which were rather the result of military decision-making made in the exigencies of war.

The relocations in this book were military campaigns designed to achieve control of the population and weaken groups threatening security. Sometimes these cases are presented as population engineering executed for nefarious purposes. Objectively it is certainly true that in many instances the decision-makers were predisposed to thinking about the targeted population in bigoted and racially discriminatory terms. How much this actually affected the decisions to move people is far more subjective and a continuing source of debate among both scholars and the general public.

Unexpected outcomes

As the great military theorist Carl von Clausewitz noted in his magnum opus *On War*, outcomes are always uncertain in wartime. Even when a nation succeeds in gaining victory on terms it deemed favourable, there have always been and always will be unintended consequences. For example, Roman military victories created a great empire which then rotted from within largely due to the very security gained by conquest. Great Britain won two world wars on terms decided by that country and its allies, but the human and financial costs of the war destroyed the economic and military strength of the empire thereby encouraging subject peoples to revolt. The United States 'won' the 2001 war in Afghanistan and the 2003 war against Iraq, but it remains to this day mired in the 'Long War' in that region.

The forcible removal of targeted populations always led to a loss of life and a loss of property. In some cases, such as the Navajo, it led to the near extinction of a culture and a way of life. Colonial New Englanders, for example, saw economic opportunities in Acadia and the removal of French colonists led to the foundation of an entirely new culture. For the Ottoman-Armenians it led to a regional policy which left them desperately vulnerable to mass murder en route to camps as well as leading to the destruction of a thousand-year-old Eastern Anatolian homeland. Japanese-Americans returned home to find their homes and businesses appropriated by their neighbours.

In no cases were the relocated populations sent to destinations where the decision-makers intended them to die. Yet, in every case, except that of the Japanese-Americans, the destinations became to some extent 'death camps'. This was largely due to primitive and unfavourable sanitary conditions which left the relocated people vulnerable to disease. Frequently adequate food was not available causing malnutrition and starvation. This situation changed dramatically as medical knowledge and practices advanced in the mid-twentieth century. Nevertheless the mortality rate of relocated populations always exceeded the norms had they been left in place. We might characterize this as 'crimes of omission' rather than 'crimes of commission' since the decision-makers often failed to render adequate logistical and medical support for the relocated groups. This was certainly the case for the Navajo, the Cubans, the Filipinos, the Boers and the Ottoman-Armenians – and it is fair to say that the decision-makers should have known better.

In some cases, as C. E. Callwell had pointed out in the 1906 edition of *Small Wars*, relocation and punitive measures against civilians could easily become counterproductive to ending an insurrection. Callwell noted the enmity and hatred which accrued as a result of being forcibly removed from one's homeland sometimes created stronger anti-government sentiment than had existed previously. This certainly proved true in the case of the Boers, the Ottoman-Armenians, the Algerians and the Vietnamese. Oddly, in the case of the Japanese-Americans, relocation seemed to encourage increased expressions of patriotism as Japanese-Americans found ways to prove their loyalty to the United States.

The post-modern form

The world has not seen a counterinsurgency campaign waged using an operational-level relocation of people in the last half century and we might ask ourselves why? While the world has seen a number of large-scale counterinsurgency campaigns – for example, the Iraqis against their own Kurds, the *Intifada* on the West Bank, the Americans in Iraq and Afghanistan, the Sri Lanka Civil War, and in various places in Latin and South America – it has not seen a relocation campaign since the 1970s. We might make several observations about the absence of relocation campaigns which might lead to some conclusions that the form itself has changed.

The main point of forcible relocation has always been the control of the population in question. In the age of industrialization it was difficult to individualize responsibility and culpability and yet, reciprocally, it was fairly easy to relocate large masses of people. In the post-industrial age it has become easier to localize and individualize responsibility or culpability. Control of a hostile or potentially hostile population has become easier today because of (1) various forms of collective observation such as satellites, drones and CCTV street-corner cameras, (2) various forms of collecting information about individuals and groups including IT, computerized data and social media, (3) various forms of physically isolating component parts of the group such as walls, barriers and checkpoints and (4) various forms of socially isolating individuals and groups through cyber operations such as disinformation, hacking and trolling. In effect, we might conclude that relocation at the macro-level has been made obsolete because technological achievements have made individual and group identification possible at the micro-level. And, as a corollary, technological advances have enabled the counterinsurgent to deal effectively with leaving the population in situ rather than moving them en masse. Moreover, contemporary counterinsurgency tactics go well beyond the physical realm and include isolation via electronic, informational and social means as well.

Consider the form itself, then, in restated terms. What is known today as 'demographic engineering' and 'social engineering', such as the removal of Kurds from Kirkuk and Marsh Arabs from the Shatt al Arab marshes by Saddam Hussein in the 1980s, are recent forms of population control. Hussein literally changed the ethnic demographics by removing and relocating dissident groups and replacing them in situ with loyal Sunni Iraqis. By effectively recasting the demographic Saddam achieved de facto control of the population in a locally defined area. In another application the Americans achieved almost complete control of the population of Baghdad in 2007–8 by erecting a T-Wall barrier system throughout the city and its suburbs.[6] The Americans discovered that by controlling movement they were able to control the population. In effect they cut Baghdad into manageable sectors within which they and their Iraqi allies were able to crush an insurgency. The most well-known example of this was the subjection of Sadr City. The Israelis have walled off the Palestinians in the West Bank thereby achieving increased levels of security for the Jewish parts of Israel's population. Is it fair to state that today, functionally, an effects-based approach[7] to population control can be more efficiently delivered through measures other than relocation?

Finis

In modern times forcible relocation in counterinsurgency warfare was not just a localized phenomenon; rather it was a global phenomenon. It reared its ugly head on a global scale in many locations including the Americas, Europe, Africa and Asia. The cases in this book are not the only cases but they are the largest and the most well known in modern times. Relocation has served as an operational approach in counterinsurgency, counter-indigenous, counter-guerrilla and counter-fifth column situations in which the government sought to increase security by weakening or eliminating a threat. Functionally, the targeted population as a group was always easily identifiable ethnically, linguistically, culturally or racially, and this served to make it possible to identify large masses of people for relocation. However, the short-term effectiveness of forcible relocation in solving a wartime security problem has always been overshadowed by the long-term unforeseen negative consequences. Lastly, the authors of *A Global History of Relocation in Counterinsurgency Warfare* have expanded the Sepp thesis (see the Introduction) into a more comprehensive examination of this phenomenon. Lastly, we remind our readers that this book is a broad survey and not a definitive work. There is still much work to be done on the subject, and we hope our efforts generate further inquiry into the study of forcible relocation in counterinsurgency warfare.

Notes

1 US Army, *Field Manual 3-24, Counterinsurgency* (Washington: Headquarters Department of the Army, 2006), 1–13.
2 Steven M. Goode, 'A Historical Basis for Force Requirements in Counterinsurgency,' *Parameters*, Winter 2009–10, 46.
3 Ibid., 51.
4 Edward J. Erickson, *Ottomans and Armenians, A Study in Counterinsurgency* (New York: Palgrave Macmillan, 2013), 182–183.

5 US Marine Corps, NAVMC 2890, *Small Wars Manual* (Hqs USMC: 1940, republished as FMFRP 12-15, Quantico, Marine Corps Combat Development Command, 1990).

6 For the best recent summary of the barrier system in Baghdad see John Spencer, 'Stealing the Enemy's Urban Advantage, The Battle for Sadr City', Modern War Institute, USMA at West Point, 31 January 2019. https://mwi.usma.edu/stealing-enemys-urban-advantage-battle-sadr-city/?utm_source=Sailthru&utm_medium=email&utm_campaign=ebb%2001.02.2019&utm_term=Editorial%20-%20Military%20-%20Early%20Bird%20Brief accessed 1 February 2019.

7 'No definition of Effects Based Operations has yet been agreed on, but the following suffices for our present purposes: Effects-based operations are operations conceived and planned in a systems framework that considers the full range of direct, indirect, and cascading effects, which may – with different degrees of probability – be achieved by the application of military, diplomatic, psychological, and economic instruments.' Paul K. Davis, *Effects-Based Operations: A Grand Challenge for the Analytical Community* (Santa Monica: RAND, 2001), 7.

APPENDIX: RELOCATION STATISTICS

Conflict	Number of Relocated Persons	Percentage of the Target Population Relocated	Type of Confinement	Deaths
Acadian Rebellion	7,000	Over 50[1]	Permanent Exile	Unknown
Navajo Removal	9,000	85–90	Reservation	c. 1,500
Cuban Insurgency	500,000	Over 80	*Reconcentración*	155–170,000
Philippine Insurrection	600,000	Over 60	Zones of Protection	234,000
Second Anglo-Boer War	115,000 (w) 115,000 (b)	50[2]	Concentration Camps	26,000 (w) 16,000 (b)
WWI Armenian Removal	Over 500,000[3]	Over 99	Relocation Camps	c. 250,000[4]
WWI Jewish Removal	1–3,000,000[5]	Over 90	Interior Cities & Towns	Unknown
WWII Japanese-American Internment	120,000	Over 99	Internment Camps	Very few
Malayan Emergency	225,000+	Over 99	New Villages	c. 3,000
Kenyan Emergency	1,000,000	Over 80	Villagization	Unknown
Algerian Insurgency	2,350,000[6]	Over 30	Regroupement Centres	Over 45,000[7]

(Continued)

Conflict	Number of Relocated Persons	Percentage of the Target Population Relocated	Type of Confinement	Deaths
Second Indochina War	400,000	About 5[8]	Strategic Hamlets	Unknown
Portuguese Decolonization	1,000,000+[9] 150,000[10] 970,000[11] 2,120,000	Over 20 30 15	Aldeamentos	Unknown

Notes

1. This figure does not reflect the 2,000–3,000 Acadians previously removed from Acadia.
2. This figure does not reflect Boers living in cities and towns. The percentage removed of the rural population likely exceeded 95 per cent.
3. This figure reflects the number of relocated Ottoman-Armenians from the six Eastern Anatolian provinces and key cities on the lines of communications identified by the Ministry of the Interior's relocation directive of 31 May 1915.
4. This is a reasonable estimate of the death toll of Ottoman-Armenian population of the six Anatolian provinces and key cities who were relocated in 1915. The estimated 1915 death toll does not include the two subsequent periods of increased Ottoman-Armenian deaths (1918–22) or those who died in Russia.
5. No reliable figures exist for the total number or Russian Jews who were relocated. At least one million but, perhaps, as many as three million were forcibly evacuated. Within the Pale itself, a figure of 90 per cent relocated is not unlikely.
6. An additional 1,175,000 Algerians were relocated into existing Muslim villages. The combined total of some 3.5 million Algerians represented about 30 per cent of the total Algerian Muslim population.
7. Dorothee M. Kellou, *A Microhistory of the Forced Resettlement of the Algerian Muslim Population during the Algerian War of Independence (1954-1962): Mansourah, Kabylia*, MA Thesis, Georgetown University, 2012, 82.
8. The official RVN/USG figure of 8,000,000–10,000,000 living in Strategic Hamlets includes those who never moved but lived in villages designated as Strategic Hamlets. About 400,000 and 5 per cent of the country's population represents the scholarly consensus on the actual number moved.
9. Portuguese Angola.
10. Portuguese Guinea.
11. Mozambique.

INDEX

Abdelkader 211
Abenaki tribe 22
Acadia 1–3, 9
  origins of the name 21
Acadian expulsion 9, 17–38
  Acadian rebellion 22, 26–9
  outcomes 33–5
  relocation decisions 30
  who benefitted 32–3
Aguinaldo, Emilio 84–6, 91
Alekseyev, General Mikhail 151
Alexander II, Czar 145–6
Alexander III, Czar 146
Algerian Insurrection 11, 209–24, 232
  Centres de Regroupment 209, 215–20
  Code de l'Indigénat 211
  Constantine Plan 219
  effect of the Second World War 212
  French acquisition 210–11
  French Army 213–18
  French settlers (colons/pied-noir) 210–12
  Front de Libération nationale (FLN) 209, 213–18, 220–1
  Inspection Générale de Regroupment de Populations 217, 219
  legislation 211–12
  Morice Line 217–18
  numbers of relocated Algerians 218
  Quadrillage 209, 214–20
  relocation decisions 214–17
  restriction of population 216–17
  Thousand Villages project 219
  Touissant Rouge 214
  zones (operational/interdicted/forbidden) 217

American Civil War 48–9, 84
Anarchist movement 147
Apache tribes (Mescalero and Mogollon) 48–50, 53–4
Armenakan. See Ramkavar
Armenian genocide 115–16, 119
Armenian relocation. See Ottoman-Armenian relocation
Armenian Revolutionary Federation (ARF/Dashnaks) 117–22, 147
  plans to cut railways 122
  rebellions in 1896 and 1904 117
  revolt in Van 121
Arriaga, General Kaulza de 259
Azarian, Manuk 127

Baden-Powell, Colonel Robert 104
Balangiga Massacre 86–7
Barboncito 50, 52
Barsamian, Dikran 127
Bates, Brigadier General John 89
Beech, Keyes 226
Bell, Brigadier General J. Franklin 83, 87, 90–1
Bendetsen, Colonel Karl R. 167–70
Berezovsky-Godinsky, Antuan 118
Biddle, Attorney General Francis 168
'Black Week' 105–6
Blanco, General Ramon 70, 76, 78
Blaufarb, Douglas 234
Boekel, Lieutenant Colonel William E. 173
Boers (Boer republics)
  discovery of gold 101
  origins 98
  relationship with Germany 101–2
Boer War 10, 95–114
  conditions in camps 109–11
  human and property costs 99–100
  relocation decisions 107–11

INDEX

role of jingoism 98–100, 103
scope of removal 107–9
Boşgezenyan, Artin 127
Bosque Redondo Reservation 42, 50–3
Botha, General Louis 98, 104–7
Briggs, General Sir Harold 187–9, 197–201, 271
Briggs Plan 11–12, 187–9, 194–200, 203, 216
British army 97–8, 100, 102–3
  casualties 100
  conventional Boer War battles 103–6
  Malaya 194
  'rings' (cliques) 102, 106
British resistance leaders in Malaya 191
Bugeaud, General Thomas-Robert 270
Buller, General Sir Redvers 102, 104–6
Bureau of Indian Affairs 45
Burke, Edmund 33
Bury My Heart at Wounded Knee (book) 53

Callwell, General Charles E. (C.E.) 270, 273
campaign definition 8
Campbell-Bannerman, Sir Henry 95, 111
Campos, General Arsenio Martínez 63–7, 72, 77
Canadian relocations of Japanese-Canadians 172
Canby, Colonel Edward 48–9, 51
Cánovas, Prime Minister Antonio del Castillo 65–70
Carleton, Brigadier General James 42, 49–54
Carson, Kit 49–51
Carver, George 229
Cemal, Governor and Minister of Marine 127
Central Intelligence Agency (CIA) 229, 232, 234
Cevdet, Governor 121
Chafee, Major General Adna 86–7

Chapman, SOE Major Frederick S. 191
Charles X, King 209–10
Cherokee 'Trail of Tears' 12, 39
Chin Peng 192, 203
Clark, General Mark 170, 177
Clausewitz, Carl von 95–7, 111, 188, 273
Colby, William C. 232, 244, 246
Colley, Major General George 101
  at Battle of Majuba Hill 101
Committee of Union and Progress (CUP/ Young Turks) 118–20, 125, 127
concentration camp 109
  origin of term 109
Cope, Jean-Baptiste 28
Cornwallis, Captain-General Edward 27–8
counterinsurgency definition 7
Cronje, General Andries 104–6
Cuban Insurrection 9, 59–78
  consequences of relocation 76–7
  Cuban Liberation Army (CLA) 63, 65, 68–9, 74–5, 77
  Cuban Revolutionary Party (PRC) 62, 69, 74–6
  failure of relocation 70–6
  political parties 60–1
  reconcentration 59, 69–73
  relocation decisions 66
  role of disease 71–2
  Ten Years War 60–1

DeGaulle, President Charles 219
Delouvrier, Paul 219
Devel, Pierre 210
Devers, General Jacob 177
DeWet, General Christian 108
Dewey, Commodore George 84
  at Battle of Manila Bay 84
DeWitt, General John L. 162–78
  character of 166
  final report of 175
Diem, President. *See* Ngo Dinh Diem
Dien Bien Phu 228
Dodge, Henry 47–8
Drum, General Hugh 162, 177

Eisenhower, Milton S. 172
Ellis, MP John 109
Emmons, Major General Delos 173–4
ends-ways-means 269–70
Enver, Minister of War 123
   opinions on removal of Armenians 123
Erskine, General Sir George 12
Erwin von Scheubner-Richter, Max 121
Evangeline: A Tale of Acadie (poem) 1, 35

Fall, Bernard 231
Federal Bureau of Investigation 161, 167
fifth column definition and origin 161
Fort Beauséjour 19, 28–30
Fort Defiance 47–8
Fourth Geneva Convention 6
French, Major General John 104
French and Indian War 25
French Navy 122

Gallieni, General Joseph 70
Galula, David 209, 271
García, Calixo 69–70, 77
Gatacre, Lieutenant General Sir William 104
Geneva Accords 228, 231
Gillion, Major General Allen W. 167, 169–70
Gómez, Máximo 62–6, 69–70, 72, 74, 78
Goremykin, Chairman Ivan 151
Got, Mikhail 147
grand strategy 101
'Great Upheaval' 19
Greek Civil War 13
Gurney, Commissioner Sir Henry 194
Gwynn, Sir Charles 188

Hell Gate Treaty of 1855 89
Hemingway, Ernest 161
Herero relocation 12
Hilsman, Roger 232, 243, 248
HMS Doris 122
Hobhouse, Emily 110

Ho Chi Minh 227–8, 243
Holocaust 12
Hoover, Director J. Edgar 161
Hopson, Peregine Thomas 28
Hukbalahap Rebellion 13
Husayn Dey 209–10

Indian Removal Act of 1830 39

Jackson, President Andrew 44
Jackson, Associate Justice Robert 157
Jameson Raid 100, 102
Japanese-American internment 10–11, 157–83
   American military planning 159, 162–3, 166–7
   DeWitt's accusations 175
   economic effects 171
   effect of Pearl harbor attack 164
   Executive Order 9066 170, 172
   fifth column 160–3, 166–7
   Korematsu vs. US 157, 175
   numbers of aliens 163
   relocation decisions 166–71
   Roberts Report 168, 173
   vulnerability of the west coast 165, 167, 169
Joubert, Commandant-General Piet 104

Karnow, Stanley 244
Kearny, General Stephen 41–3, 48
Kendrick, Major Henry L. 47
Kennedy, President John F. 230, 234, 244
Kenyan Emergency 12–13
Khatissian, Alexander 120
Khrushchev, Premier Nikita 234
Kikuyu tribe 12–13
Kipling, Rudyard 83–4, 97
Kitchener, Field Marshal Sir Hubert H. 99–100, 102, 106–11
Knox, Secretary Frank 174
Kruger, President Paul 101, 103–4, 107

Lacoste, Governor Robert 216
Laguna Negre Treaty of 1855 46
Lai Teck 192, 203

Larkin, Captain Frank   122
Lawrence, Colonel Charles   19–21
Lawrence, Governor   25–6, 29–35
Lawton, Major General Henry W.   85
LeLoutre, Louis Joseph   27–8, 30
Lieber Code (General Orders 100)   85–6, 90
Lippman, Walter   169
Lloyd-George, MP (later Prime Minister) David   108
Longfellow, Henry Wadsworth   1
'Long Walk of the Navajo'   39–57
Lovewell, Captain John   22

MacArthur, General Douglas   88
MacArthur, Major General Arthur   85–6
McCloy, John   170, 173–4
Maceo, Antonio   62–3, 68–9
Mackenzie, Colonel Colin   108
McKinley, President William   84, 88, 91
McNamara, Secretary Robert   245
Mai Ngoc Duoc, Province Chief   240
Malayan Emergency   11, 185–207, 216, 232
  Briggs Plan   11–12, 187–9, 194–200, 203, 216
  British Army   194
  consequences   200
  costs   203
  declaration of emergency   195
  demographics   189
  effect of Chinese Communist Revolution   189–90
  initial failures   196–7
  Malayan Communist Party (MCP)   186–93, 195–8, 200, 203
  Malayan National Liberation Army (MNLA)   193
  Malayan People's Anti-Japanese Army (MPAJA)   187, 191–2
  Malayan Races Liberation Army (MRLA)   192–5
  Malayan Security Service (MSS)   193
  Malayan Special Branches Criminal Investigation Department (CID)   193
  MCP leadership   192
  Minh Yuen (People's Organization/ Mass Organization)   192, 194
  New Villages   194, 196–202, 216, 241
  relocation decision   198–9
  resistance to Japanese occupation   191
  terrorism   193
Manuelito   50–2
Manukian, Aram   121
Mao Zedong   190, 229
Marques, Lieutenant Colonel Silvino Silverio   258
Marshall, General George C.   163, 166–7, 170, 174, 177
Martí, Jose   62–3
Mau Mau rebellion. *See* Kenyan Emergency
Maxwell, Brigadier John   108
Medel, William   45
Meriwether, David   46
Merritt, Major General Wesley   84
Methuen, Lieutenant General Lord Paul   104–5
Mexican War   44
Mi'kmaq tribe   17, 19–23, 27–8, 30–1
Milner, High Commissioner Alfred   102, 108
Monckton, Lieutenant Colonel Robert   30
Musa Dagh   122

Namaqua relocation   12
Natanson, Andreyevich   147
Navajo relocation   39–57
  Bosque Redondo Reservation   42, 50–3
  Bureau of Indian Affairs   45–6
  decisions to relocate   49–51
  evolution of a vocabulary   48–50
  as guerrilla fighters   45
  Long Walk   50–1
  relocation   9, 39–57
  relocation decisions   49–51
  treaties with   46
Ndebele kingdom (tribe)   100
New Villages. *See* Malayan Emergency
Nicholas I, Czar   145

Nicholas II, Czar   145
Nihilist movement   147
Nikolai, Grand Duke   150
Ngo Dinh Diem, President (Diem regime)   225–6, 228–33, 235, 237–8, 241, 243–5
  death of   244
Ngo Dinh Nhu, Counsellor   226, 231–3, 235, 237, 241, 244, 247–8
  death of   244
Nguyen Viet Thanh, Major   239
Nubar, Boghos   119, 122

oath of allegiance   29
O'Donnell, John B.   231, 238–9, 241, 246
Office of Naval Intelligence (ONI)   161–2
Otis, Major General Elwell S.   84–5
Ottoman-Armenian relocation   10, 115–40
  Armenian links to Russia   117–20
  Armenian reforms   118
  arrests on 24 April 1915   124
  desertion of soldiers   120–1
  estimates of human costs   128–9
  exemption from relocation   126–7
  falsified documents   125
  impact of Gallipoli campaign   122
  location of camps   127
  military outcomes   128–9
  necessity for self defence   119
  number of insurgents   123
  punishment of perpetrators   127
  relocation decisions   123–6
  removal of other Christian minorities   125–6
  revolt at Van   121–3

The Pale   10, 141–5
  origin of the term   145
Parlange, General Gaston   216
Pasdermadjian, Garegin   120
Peace of Aix-la-Chapelle   25
Peace of Utrecht (Treaty of Utrecht)   19, 23–5, 29, 35
Peace of Zanjón   63

Percival, Lieutenant General Arthur E.   191
Permanent Indian Frontier   44
Philippine Insurrection   9, 83–93
  absence of troche   88
  Balangiga Massacre   86–7
  consequences of relocation   88–9
  human cost   88
  martial law declared   85
  relocation decisions   87
  US Army courts-martial   88
  'water cure'   88
  Zones of Protection   87, 89–91
Phillips, Governor Richard   27
Phips, Lieutenant-Governor Spencer   29, 33–4
Pike, Douglas   243
Polk, President James   44–5
Portuguese colonial wars   11, 255–65
  African Party for the Independence of Guinea and Cabo Verde (PAIGC)   257, 259
  aldeamentos   259–62
  Angola   256
  Armed Forces Movement (MFA)   262
  decolonization   256
  Mozambique   256
  Mozambique Liberation Front (FRELIMO)   257, 260
  National Front for the Liberation of Angola (FNLA)   257
  National Union for the Liberation of Angola (UNITA)   257, 259
  North Atlantic Treaty Organization (NATO)   257
  numbers relocated   258–9
  outcomes   260–1
  Popular Movement for the Liberation of Angola (MPLA)   257
  Portuguese Army   257, 262
  Portuguese Guinea   256
  racial assimilation and laws   256
  relocation decisions   258–60
post-modern form   274–5

Quadrillage 11
Quisling 161

Radkevich, General Nikolai 152
Rahman, Tunku Abdul 203
Ramkavar (Hunchaks) 116, 118–19, 122
   rebellions in 1862, 1878 and 1895–96 122
   rebellions in 1894–96 117
RAND consultants 237–8
ratios of counterinsurgents to insurgents 269
reconcentration. *See* Cuban Insurrection
relocation decisions
   Acadia 30
   Algeria 214–17
   Boer War 107–11
   Cuba 66
   Japanese-Americans 166–71
   Japanese-Canadians 172
   Kenya 12
   Malaya 198–9
   Navajo 49–51
   Ottoman-Armenians 123–6
   Philippines 87
   Portuguese colonial wars 258–60
   Russian Jews 149–51
   Vietnam 232–5
relocation definition 6
relocation statistics (Appendix) 277–8
Ramkavar 117
replacement of populations 28, 274
   German Protestants in Acadia 28
Rhodes, Cecil 100, 102
Roberto, Holden 257
Roberts, Chief Justice Owen J. 168
   Roberts Report 168, 173
Roberts, Field Marshal Lord Frederick S. 98, 102, 106–11
Robinson, Sir Thomas 30
Roosevelt, President Franklin 161, 167, 170–2, 176
Roosevelt, President Theodore 88
Rostow, Special Assistant Walter 234

Rubanovich, Illya 147
Rusk, Secretary Dean 234
Russian-Jewish relocation 10, 141–56
   anti-Semitism and repression 145–7
   expulsion from Spain 143
   laws effecting Jews 145–6, 150–1
   military situation 147–9
   numbers of Jews in 1648 and 1750 144
   numbers relocated 151–2
   origin of the Pale of Settlement 145
   origins of the Jews 143
   partitioning of Poland 144
   pogroms 146–7
   relocation decisions 149–51
   revolutionary movements 147
   Russification 146
   Social Revolutionary Party 147

Sait Halim, Grand Vizir 125
Salan, General Raoul 216
Salazar, Prime Minister Antonio de Oliveria 256
Scott, MP C. P. 109
Seminole tribe 39
Sepp Thesis (Sepp, Kelev I.) 3–4
Seropian, Archbishop Mushegh 118
Sherman, General William T. 53
Shimoun, Nestorian Patriarch Mar 126
Shirley, Governor William 19, 25–6, 30–3
Short, General Major Walter C. 164, 166, 173–4
Smith, Brigadier General Jacob 83, 87–8
   nickname 'Howling Jake' 87
Smuts, Jan 100, 103
Social Revolutionary Party 147
Spain
   conquest of American southwest 41
   consequences 76–8
   Cuban Insurrection 59–68
   governmental ministries 65–6, 71
   logistics 70–5, 78

Special Organization (SO)   127
Spinola, General Antonio de   259
Sri Lankan Civil War   13
stability operations   90–1
Steyn, Marthinus   103
Stillwell, Major General Joseph   165
Stimson, Secretary Henry L.   168, 170, 173–4
Strategic Hamlets   11, 225–53
strategy definition   7

Taft, Governor William H.   86
Talat, Minister of the Interior   123–5
  relocation order of 27 May 1915   124
Templer, General Sir Gerald   194, 199, 202, 271
Thompson, Sir Robert   232–3, 237, 241–2, 248, 271
Tran Ngoc Chau, Major   239
Trinquier, Lieutenant Colonel Roger   232, 271
trocha   63–72, 88, 109

United States Agency for International Development (USAID)   236–8
United States Army   48–50, 84–7, 162–6, 175–7, 235, 242
  courts-martial   88
  diversions of troops   162
  Military Assistance Command Vietnam (MACV)   233
Unites States Army units
  I Corps   163
  III Corps   165
  IX Corps   165
  3rd Infantry Division   165
  7th Infantry Division   165
  35th Infantry Division   165
  40th Infantry Division   165
  41st Infantry Division   165
  44th Regimental Combat Team   176–7
  9th US Infantry Regiment   86
United States Marine Corps   87, 270
  Small Wars Manual   270

Van Riper, Lieutenant General Paul   267
Varandian, Mikael   122
Vetch, Samuel   27
Vietnam   225–53
  anti-communist laws   228, 245
  arming hamlets   243
  Army of the Republic of Vietnam (ARVN)   229, 233–6, 238, 240, 244, 248
  Central Intelligence Agency (CIA)   229, 232, 234
  Civic Action Teams   236
  coups   230, 244
  Delta Plan   232
  demographics   230–1
  military outcomes   244–6
  National Liberation Front (NLF)   225–6, 229
  numbers relocated   226, 231, 233
  partitioning   227
  relocation decisions   232–5
  Strategic Hamlet Program   225–48
  Viet Cong (VC)   225, 234, 238–40, 242, 244
  Viet Minh   227–9, 231–2, 238, 240
  villages as centers of gravity   226, 231
Villagization   13
Vo Nguyen Giap, General   243
Vramian, Arshak   119, 121

Waller, Major Littleton   87–8
war crimes   271–2
Waring, Colonel Ronald   260
War of Austrian Succession   25, 27
War of Spanish Succession (Queen Anne's War)   23
War Relocation Authority (WRA)   172, 174, 177
Weyler y Nicolau, General Valerano   9, 66–78, 88, 109
  campaign plan   66
  relief of   70
White, Lieutenant General Sir George   104

Wilmot, Montague 35
Winslow, Lieutenant-Colonel
    John 17, 31
Wolseley, Field Marshal Lord
    Garnet 102–3

Yanushkevich, General Nikolai
    150

Zones of Protection 87, 89–91
Zulu tribe 100

www.ingramcontent.com/pod-product-compliance
Lightning Source LLC
Chambersburg PA
CBHW052213300426
44115CB00011B/1673